Low-Carbon Green Growth in Asia

Policies and Practices

A Joint Study of the Asian Development Bank and the Asian Development Bank Institute

ADB

ADBInstitute

Printed in Hong Kong, China

ISBN 978-4-89974-037-3

Cataloging-In-Publication Data

Low-Carbon Green Growth in Asia: Policies and Practices
1 Climate Change
2 Green Growth
3 Low-Carbon Technology
4 Regional Cooperation
I Asian Development Bank
II Asian Development Bank Institute

Asian Development Bank
6 ADB Avenue, Mandaluyong City
1550 Metro Manila, Philippines
Tel +63 2 632 4444
Fax +63 2 636 2444
www.adb.org

Asian Development Bank Institute
Kasumigaseki Building 8F
3-2-5 Kasumigaseki, Chiyoda-ku
Tokyo 100-6008
Japan
Tel +813 3593 5500
adbipubs@adbi.org
www.adbi.org

This publication can be downloaded free of charge from www.adbi.org/publications.books/

Acknowledgements

This joint ADB and ADBI study was conceptualized and guided by a steering committee consisting of ADB Heads of Department co-chaired by Masahiro Kawai (Dean and CEO, ADBI) and Bindu Lohani (Vice-President for Knowledge Management and Sustainable Development, ADB). The steering committee members included heads of ADB's operational and knowledge departments; Iwan J. Azis, Seethapathy Chander, Philip C. Erquiaga, Klaus Gerhaeusser, Juan Miranda, Changyong Rhee, Kazu Sakai, Kunio Senga, Vinod Thomas, Robert F. Wihtol, and Xianbin Yao.

A high-level advisory committee provided technical advice and valuable comments at various stages of the study. The advisory committee chaired by Rajendra K. Pachauri (The Energy and Resources Institute) consisted of Zhou Dadi (the Energy Research Institute), Hironori Hamanaka (Institute of Global Environmental Strategies), Huguette Labelle (Transparency International), Hoesung Lee (Korea University), Jeffrey D. Sachs (Columbia University), Emil Salim (Advisory Council to the President of Indonesia), and Klaus Toepfer (Institute for Advanced Sustainability Studies).

This study was managed and implemented by an ADB–ADBI working group comprising Jorn Brömmelhörster, Biswanath Bhattacharya, Jesus Felipe, Rana Hasan, Abid M. Hussain, Hoe Yun Jeong, Robert S. Lockhart, Teruhisa Oi, Stephen J. Pollard, Ancha Srinivasan, Suphachol Suphachalasai, Pradeep J. Tharakan, and Emma M. Veve who reviewed background papers and draft chapters. Jun Tian of the Regional Sustainable Development Department (RSDD) was the focal point at ADB. Venkatchalam Anbumozhi of ADBI served as the project task manager. Senior ADB managers especially Bindu Lohani and Xianbin Yao provided the leadership in guiding the directions of the study and drafting the introduction and conclusion chapters.

Several ADB and ADBI managers provided oversight and technical comments at various stages of the study: Jae-Ha Park, Woochong Um, Mario Lamberte, Worapot Manupipatpong, Ganeshan Wignaraja, Yuqing Xing and Nessim Ahmed. Comments and valuable inputs were also provided by Preety Bhandari, Hans Carlsson, Robert Guild, Sujata Gupta, Minquan Liu, Cinzia Losenno, David McCcauley, Cyn-Young Park, Michael Rattinger, and Carey Yeager.

Alex Bowen (London School of Economics) served as the principal consultant for the book. Fiona Harvey (The Guardian) was the language editor. Stéphane Harrison and Joe Fox (William Joseph) are the designers. ADBI's Robert Davis, Alastair Dingwall, Kurt Hanson, Stefan Wesiak, and Oonagh Duffy coordinated the production. ADB's Jose Antonio Tan III, Jason Rush, and Harumi Kodama provided valuable contributions to the reviewing process. The following ADBI research associates and staff provided inputs and assisted with administrative matters: Dharish David, Joana Portugal, Jiyoung Song, Diana Alwis, Yuko Ichikawa, and Chiho Hasegawa.

The book benefited from several background papers prepared by scholars from regional think tanks. The contributors include Jae Eun Ahn (Global Green Growth Institute), Jusen Asuka (Institute for Global Environmental Strategies), Qwanruedee Chotichanathawewong (Thailand Environment Institute), Rita Roy Choudhury (Asia Business Council), Tilak K. Doshi (National University of Singapore), Toru Hashimoto (City of Yokohama), Takashi Hongo (Japan Bank for International Cooperation), Stephen Howes (Australian National University), Tae Yong Jung (Global Green Growth Institute), Mikiko Kainuma (National Institute for Environmental Studies), Kaliappa Kalirajan (Australian National University), Sang In Kang (Korea Environment Institute), Jootae Kim (APEC Green Finance, Dankook University), Sivanappan Kumar (Asian Institute of Technology), Ritu Mathur (The Energy and Resources Institute), Brahmanand Mohanty (French Environment and Energy Management Agency), Jihwan Park (Global Green Growth Institute), Arianto A. Patunru (Institute for Economic and Social Research), Krishnamurthy Ramanathan (Asian and Pacific Centre for Transfer of Technology), Shiv Someshwar (Columbia University), Tomonori Sudo (Japan International Cooperation Agency), Pham Khanh Toan (Institute of Energy), Gamini Wijesekere (Australian National University), Heinrich-Wilhelm Wyes (The Regional Environmental Centre for Central Asia), Paul Wyrwoll (Australian National University), and Zhu Yuezhong (Energy Research Institute). Ruth Kattumuri (London School of Economics) and Gamini Wijesekere (Australian National University) also contributed to Chapters 4 and 5, respectively.

Five workshops were held during the study in Beijing, Jakarta, New Delhi, Seoul, and Tokyo, which contributed to an exchange of views among policy makers, scholars, and private sector experts on the background papers and draft chapters that make up the book. The workshop in Beijing was conducted jointly with the Energy Research Institute (ERI), the workshop in New Delhi with The Energy and Resources Institute (TERI), the workshop in Indonesia with Institute for Economic and Social Research (LPEM), and the policy conference in Seoul with the Global Green Growth Institute (GGGI) and the Climate and Development Knowledge Network (CDKN).

Grateful thanks are given to the following for permission to reproduce figures in the book: Sustainable Europe Research Institute (Figure 1.2 in Chapter 1), United Nations University Press (Figure 1.3 in Chapter 2), Ministry of the Environment, Japan (Figure 2.7 in Chapter 2), Asia Business Council (Figure 2.10 in Chapter 2), National Institute for Environmental Studies (Table 2.3 in Chapter 2), Nippon Keidanren (Table 2.4 in Chapter 2), Presidential Committee on Green Growth, Republic of Korea (Box 2.2 in Chapter 2), International Energy Agency (Figure 3.3 in Chapter 3), Organisation for Economic Co-operation and Development (Figure 4.11 in Chapter 4), United Nations Environment Programme (Table 4.3), and International Labour Organization (Table 4.4 in Chapter 4).

Contents

List of Boxes, Figures, and Tables

Tables

Foreword

Asia is at crossroads. While the region is experiencing much faster economic growth and poverty reduction than the world average, together with other world regions it is consuming more energy and natural resources than our planet's regenerative capacity can provide. With each passing day, Asia's carbon emissions grow, as does its vulnerability to climate risks. The poor are the most vulnerable to these disruptions, lacking options to adapt to changing climatic conditions.

Asia is beginning to heed the message that it must move onto a low-carbon green growth path. Many emerging economies are adopting a development model based on competitive green industries and green technologies. The People's Republic of China, for example, has become the world's top installer of wind turbines and solar thermal systems. India is expanding biofuels, solar, and other forms of low-carbon energy through the use of renewable energy certificates. Meanwhile, Indonesia is active in enhancement of forest carbon stocks through conservation and other countries have established targets on cutting carbon emissions.

The experiences of these and other countries can be scaled up, replicated, and adapted to conditions in other countries across Asia and the Pacific region. Taken together, we have ample reason to be positive, confident, and courageous. This ADB-ADBI study, Climate Change and Green Asia, sheds light on the experiences and lessons of Asian economies. In the study, the low-carbon green growth policies and practices of Asian countries are reviewed and assessed, and policy gaps and new opportunities for low-carbon green growth are identified. With input from policymakers and 15 prominent regional think tanks, the study will help to forge a regional perspective on low-carbon green growth challenges, options, and issues.

In light of accelerating environmental degradation and the growing threat of climate change, ambitious policies at the national level and a shift from the business as usual mindset are needed. In this regard, this study proposes three key points of action.

First, there is a need for clear long-term policy frameworks that put a price on carbon and other environmental externalities while phasing out subsidies to carbon and resource intensive sectors. This will send the right market signals and help speed the development and uptake of low-carbon and resource-efficient technologies.

Second, stronger regional cooperation is needed to effectively share knowledge and promote South-South policy dialogue, and to coordinate action leading to the creation of regional public goods such as regional carbon markets, joint R&D efforts, and technology cooperation.

And third, investment must be scaled up. Mobilization of the private sector, including through public–private partnerships, is crucial to the financing of low-carbon green growth initiatives. As the multilateral bank of the Asia and Pacific region, ADB is helping its developing member countries to access and scale up financing to create inclusive and sustainable growth. In less than a decade, ADB's annual clean energy investment increased nearly eightfold, from $226 million in 2003 to $1.9 billion in 2012. Through its various funding windows and technical assistance facilities, ADB also provides support to low-carbon projects in a range of other sectors, including transport, waste management, and agriculture.

Asia's adoption of a low-carbon green growth path is more than a climate response. It deals squarely with the triple bottom line of achieving favorable economic, environmental, and social outcomes through policies for inclusive and sustainable growth. I hope this book will give encouragement to practitioners in the region who are considering and evaluating concrete policy options and serve as a valuable resource for those seeking a comprehensive overview of low-carbon, green growth initiatives in Asia and the Pacific region and of the options going forward.

Haruhiko Kuroda
President
Asian Development Bank
31 January 2013

Abbreviations and Acronyms

ADB	Asian Development Bank
ADBI	Asian Development Bank Institute
APEC	Asia-Pacific Economic Cooperation
ASEAN	Association of Southeast Asian Nations
BIMSTEC	Bangladesh, India, Myanmar, Sri Lanka and Thailand Economic Cooperation
BOCM	bilateral offset credit mechanism
CAREC	Central Asia Regional Economic Cooperation
CCS	carbon capture and storage
CDM	Clean Development Mechanism
CER	certified emission reduction
CNG	compressed natural gas
CO_2	carbon dioxide
COP	Conference of the Parties
CP3	Climate Public Private Partnership
DFID	Department for International Development of the United Kingdom
EU	European Union
ETS	Emission Trading Scheme
FAO	Food and Agriculture Organization of the United Nations
FDI	foreign direct investment
FICCI	Federation of Indian Chambers of Commerce and Industry
FIT	feed-in tariff
FTA	free trade agreement
GDP	gross domestic product
GEF	Global Environment Facility
GGGI	Global Green Growth Institute
GHG	greenhouse gas
GMS	Greater Mekong Subregion
GNP	gross national product
GRT	generation rights trading
IEA	International Energy Agency
ILO	International Labour Organization
IPCC	Intergovernmental Panel on Climate Change
IPR	intellectual property rights
JBIC	Japan Bank for International Cooperation
LCGS	low-carbon goods and services
LPG	liquefied petroleum gas
MDG	Millennium Development Goal
MRV	measurement, reporting, and verification
MSMEs	micro, small, and medium-sized enterprises
NAMA	nationally appropriate mitigation action
N_2O	nitrous oxide
ODA	official development assistance
OECD	Organisation for Economic Co-operation and Development
PAT	perform, achieve and trade
PPP	public-private partnership
PRC	People's Republic of China
PV	photovoltaic
R&D	research and development
REC	renewable energy certificate
REDD	reducing emissions from deforestation and degradation
RPS	renewable portfolio standard
SAARC	South Asian Association for Regional Cooperation
SMEs	small and medium-sized enterprises
TERI	The Energy and Resources Institute
TRIPS	trade-related aspects of intellectual property rights
UK	United Kingdom
UN	United Nations
UNCOMTRADE	United Nations Commodity Trade Statistics
UNCTAD	United Nations Conference on Trade and Development
UNDP	United Nations Development Programme
UNEP	United Nations Environment Programme
UNESCAP	United Nations Economic and Social Commission for Asia and the Pacific
UNFCCC	United Nations Framework Convention on Climate Change
US	United States
WHO	World Health Organization
WIR	World Investment Reports
WITS	World Integrated Trade Solution
WTO	World Trade Organization

Executive Summary

Robust economic growth is lifting millions of people out of poverty in Asia, but is also driving resource and energy consumption to unsustainable levels. Climate change exacerbates the challenges of growth and development. The developing economies of Asia are highly vulnerable to changing climate. A warming of 2°C would lead to losses in high-income countries and a global loss of about 1% to 2% of gross domestic product (GDP), but Asia's middle- and low-income countries could lose as much as 6% of GDP. Climate change is harming many economies in the region, diverting resources from development programs, and making it more difficult for people to escape poverty.

Asia accounts for about 40% of global greenhouse gas (GHG) emissions and this share will rise to almost 50% by 2030 in a business-as-usual scenario. Yet some 650 million people in Asia lack access to clean fuels for cooking and heating, and millions more lack electricity. However, developing countries cannot simply follow the carbon intensive development path taken by industrialized countries. It is estimated that, by 2050, 67% of the people in Asia will live in cities. This increasing urbanization will require a massive expansion in transportation infrastructure, urban development, energy production, and agricultural output. This is a forceful reminder that finding low-carbon solutions for Asia is neither a luxury problem nor a climate problem. It is foremost a reality that will require a new development paradigm.

Low-carbon green growth is an avenue toward development that decouples economic growth from carbon emissions, pollution, and resource use, and promotes growth through the creation of new environment-friendly products, industries, and business models that also improve quality of life. Thus, low-carbon green growth entails: (i) using less energy, improving the efficiency with which resources are used, and moving to low-carbon energy sources, (ii) protecting and promoting the sustainable use of natural resources such as forests and peat lands, (iii) designing and disseminating low-carbon technologies and business models to reinvigorate local economies, and (iv) implementing policies and incentives that discourage carbon intensive practices.

How close are the emerging economies of Asia to turning their aspirations for a new development paradigm into a reality? What policies, institutions, and financial factors accelerate or inhibit a shift to resource-efficient green growth? What is the potential for the private sector, technology, financing, and regional cooperation to become drivers for future economic growth? This book aims to answer these questions by reviewing the low-carbon policy initiatives taken by Asian countries at the national, sectoral, and local levels, while assessing the achievements, identifying the gaps, and examining new opportunities for low-carbon green growth. The goal of this study is to share the experiences and lessons of several Asian countries with other developing nations and make recommendations for actions by the countries in the region, while deepening the actions of leading economies. This book is based on the recognition that benefits from low-carbon green growth are an imperative, not a luxury, for developing Asia. Asia must also find an answer to the mounting international competition for resources—energy, raw materials, water, and fertile agricultural land—that will dominate the coming decades.

Changing Perspectives, Converging Policies, and Transformation Strategies

On the move toward low-carbon green growth, a great deal is happening in Asia. Compared to the economies of other regions, Asia has the highest rate of policy innovations and commitments to low-carbon economic development. Many countries of the region have incorporated low-carbon growth components in their national development plans to attain a better balance between the environment, the economy, and social welfare. Heavily dependent on imported resources and energy, the emerging economies of Asia have been pursuing a new, low-carbon development paradigm that is improving industrial competitiveness and serving burgeoning green technology markets. The People's Republic of China, India, and Indonesia, for example, are becoming market leaders in a variety of low-carbon technologies such as wind turbines, solar cells, electric vehicles, and biofuels, among others.

Given the great potential of renewable energy sources and energy efficiency in most Asian countries, feed-in tariffs (FITs) and renewable energy portfolio standards could serve to attract

National Level Sector Specific Policy Actions for Accelerating Low-Carbon Green Growth

Energy

Seek cost-effective, market-based solutions for the uptake of existing technologies

- Invest in reducing the cost of existing low-carbon technologies such as solar, wind, and bio-energy.
- Continue to focus on lowering energy intensity and improving carbon productivity by changing the energy mix away from an over-reliance on fossil fuels.
- Gradually remove fossil fuel subsidies, introduce true energy pricing, and promote mechanisms such as FITs and renewable portfolio standards (RPS)
- Progressively amend laws in order to scale up renewable energy in a competitive market dominated by fossil fuels

Energy Efficiency

Improve energy efficiency through a combination of regulations and market-based instruments

- Launch top-runner programs for industrial technologies and electrical appliances
- Expand energy saving labeling programs and begin to test carbon labeling programs
- Develop a focused and well-packaged regulatory system for small and medium-sized enterprises (SMEs) that integrates efficiency standards and targets by assisting with compliance mechanisms, including providing funds and matching grants with goals
- Develop sectoral guidelines and training to achieve energy efficiency standards

Transport

Develop new regulations, policies, and financing mechanisms to alter current fleet growth patterns

- Introduce new performance-based targets and incentive systems, such as tax exemption for low-carbon vehicles for the transport sector
- Progressively improve the fuel efficiency and pollution standards for passenger cars and light-duty vehicles
- Introduce retail sales of biofuels such as ethanol in urban and rural markets
- Develop a consistent framework for integrating externalities such as local air pollution and use to promote efficient and seamless multimodal transport systems

investment and promote a national energy transition. Other policy innovations in industry, transportation, and urban sectors are also making low-carbon technologies affordable for many middle- and low-income countries. Asia's policy experiences and aspirations in tackling climate change through multi-sectoral, multi-level approaches show that there are co-benefits from these approaches in the short term, as well as the medium to long term. The table below summarizes actions some countries are taking that could be rolled out across the region.

Asia's experiences across different sectors show that technological innovation for increased resource efficiency is a catalyst for change. To encourage this change, governments should reduce the cost of technologies, support R&D, and improve education to generate low-carbon green growth. To conquer the cost barrier of new technologies, several Asian governments and industries have cooperated successfully in generating a mutually reinforcing cycle of market expansion and cost reduction. This has not only resulted in large-scale deployment of low-carbon technologies but also has provided the

Agriculture & Forestry

Identify and implement the immediate actions needed to restore carbon sinks

- Introduce new market-based incentives for restoring degraded forests and providing rural employment
- Increase inspection capacity and tighten penalties for illegal logging
- Scale up pilot schemes for enhancing carbon stock such as land sequestration and reduction of water and fertilizer use
- Extend awareness of market-based instruments to isolated communities and poor farmers

Urban Sector Measures

Scale up coordinated policies for land use planning, urban infrastructure, and finance

- Change regulations and standards in buildings that lead to the inefficient use of energy and materials.
- Pilot market-based mechanisms such as carbon pricing and cap and trade to encourage the efficient use of public resources
- Encourage and provide advice on low-carbon lifestyle choices and mentoring programs for neighborhoods
- Remove barriers to mass transit networks, improving inter-modality of transport and urban freight solutions, etc.

Industry & Trade

Create competitive markets focused on high value added, low-carbon products and services

- Integrate low-carbon targets and objectives into central and local level industrial policy
- Link industrial promotion incentives and private sector innovations to carbon performance
- Reduce the tariff rate for low-carbon environmental goods and services and strengthen intellectual property regimes
- Provide information and training on existing and emerging technologies, management practices, and related green business opportunities available internationally

Fiscal

Identify and implement immediate actions needed to introduce market-based instruments

- Pilot budgetary reforms with gradual increase in energy taxes or carbon pricing
- Introduce performance-based tax incentive systems for achieving sectoral emission targets
- Explore innovative financing instruments and accelerate research and development (R&D) support for future industries
- Improve efficiency, transparency, and accountability in the financial sector by including rating programs and/or carbon credit schemes with measurement, reporting and verification (MRV) requirements.

means for other countries to overcome cost barriers. A strong partnership between the public and private sector ensures an effective flow of financial resources to firms and households that reinforces the long-term implementation of programs organized around market-based incentives. Most of the finance required will be for investment in new or improved infrastructure. This means these public finance mechanism must facilitate investment in productive capital with a long life span where costs can be amortized over the life of the assets. The key therefore will be to link public finance mechanisms to sources of private finance suitable for low-carbon infrastructure investment. The private sector is also partnering with governments to implement governance circles, ensuring appropriate monitoring and reporting activities. Low-carbon development thus requires a contribution not just from environmental policy, but also from finance, trade, science, technology, governance, and other policy areas.

The analysis also shows that developing Asia needs to worry not only about the effects of climate change, but also whether they are locking themselves into a high-carbon future. Emerging Asia is growing faster than other regions of the world. The infrastructure resulting from the high growth era and development introduces an element of inertia that locks in carbon footprints for many years. Power plants and factories have lifetimes of 15 to 40 years, while road, rail, and power distribution networks can last 40 to 75 years, or more. Decisions on land use and urban planning have effects that can last more than a century. Hence, opportunities to shift from high- to low-carbon infrastructure must be seized sooner rather than later. Delaying action by a decade could increase the cost of mitigation two to five times.

Going Green as an Inclusive Growth Strategy

The outlook for developing Asia's carbon emission growth is substantial in absolute terms. Many inefficiencies drive today's high-carbon intensity. High-carbon energy consumption could be cut 45% by changing lifestyle choices and improving energy efficiency in factories, buildings, transportation, agriculture, and electricity generation. Such climate-smart development initiatives would trigger investments in new technologies and create green jobs. These green jobs could employ as much as 1% to 2% of Asia's workforce. This figure could be even higher in poorer countries because of the greater need to improve the environment and adopt more sustainable infrastructure, as well as the greater scope for increasing employment in forestry and agriculture.

If countries are to achieve major benefits from green jobs, active labor market policies will be required, not least to cushion the potential impact of green growth policies on employment in high-polluting and resource-intensive sectors. Macroeconomic policies must stimulate demand while ensuring that debt-financed spending supports economic activities with high social returns.

Inclusive growth remains the foremost goal for emerging Asia. Many of the great benefits of low-carbon green growth are rarely quantified. Providing access to clean energy will vastly improve people's education, employment, and quality of life—in particular, cleaner, more affordable energy for cooking will reduce the toil of women and the devastating health effects of indoor air pollution among the 600 million people in developing Asia. Lower emissions from transport will improve air quality and lead to health benefits in urban areas. Large populations in developing countries depend on climate-sensitive sectors such as agriculture, forestry, and animal husbandry: the natural resources that underpin these, such as soil, water, grazing land, biodiversity, and forests, are subject to degradation as a result of the changing climate and their exploitation for short-term benefits. There are several measures, such as low-till agriculture, afforestation, and community forest management that simultaneously reduce degradation, sustain the livelihoods of the rural poor, cut emissions, and increase forest carbon stocks.

Financing from developed countries will be key as it is also in the global community's interest for developing Asia to cut emissions. From the perspective of equity and historical responsibility, developed countries should show leadership and share responsibility in filling the significant financing gap. This must be done in addition to official development assistance, if growth and development are not to suffer.

Effectively engaging the private sector is crucial to filling the financing gap for mitigation. The pricing of carbon through taxes or implementation of emissions trading schemes can provide strong incentives to improve efficiency as market participants seek the lowest cost abatement options wherever they occur. Setting a price on carbon will also influence the consumption and investment decisions of billions of households and firms that are consuming subsidized high-carbon fuels. As many low-carbon projects have a long payback time, governments can play a catalytic role by setting up guarantee mechanisms, risk sharing schemes, and low-carbon funds; and changing tax policies and subsidies to mitigate private investment risks.

Regional Cooperation for Seizing the Opportunities

Scientists argue that delaying climate change mitigation by 10 years would likely make it impossible to keep global warming from exceeding 2°C. The carbon dioxide emitted today will remain in the atmosphere for a century and temperatures will continue to rise for a few centuries after GHG emissions in the atmosphere have stabilized. Therefore, today's decisions will determine tomorrow's options. Action to limit global warming to 2°C by the end of this century will be feasible only if all countries play their part in mitigation.

The international climate financing architecture currently delivers an estimated $171 billion annually to projects in developing countries, from sources including development finance institutions ($70 billion), project developers ($65 billion), corporate actors ($13 billion), and commercial financial banks ($12 billion). The private sector share of climate finance in developing countries is around 57%. However, investment of more than $6 trillion will be needed in the region by 2030 in the energy sector alone. Filling the financing gap will require all the tools at our disposal, spanning efficiency gains, reform and integration of carbon markets, and the creation of innovative financing instruments. The Clean Development Mechanism (CDM), among other carbon market mechanisms, can be termed a success but it is still very uncertain whether it can deliver the required financial resources to developing countries due to oversupply and low demand caused by international and national policies and financial and economic crises. As agreed at the Copenhagen Climate Change Conference in 2009, long-term funding to support climate action in developing countries should reach $100 billion annually by 2020 through various sources. Therefore, climate finance must be scaled up significantly through all possible ways and means.

But carbon pricing alone will not generate the needed flows of technology across borders. Developing Asia and other advanced economies should work together to embrace the challenge of diffusing low-carbon products, services, and innovations. Liberalization of trade and reduced tariff rates for low-carbon green products and services would accelerate technology transfer, and developing Asia would benefit too from the knowledge created by emissions reduction activities in advanced economies such as Japan, the Republic of Korea, and Singapore.

Cooperative action in this region would be in the political interest of all governments for the following three reasons. First, a more direct, region-wide push on energy efficiency, technology, investment, and deforestation is essential to add credibility to the voluntary pledges and national targets without losing economic competiveness. Second, given the scale of investment required and the deterioration of public finances in many countries, cooperation, consultation, and coordination among governments in this region can leverage private sector capital. Third, because it will take time to agree on the details to implement a global climate deal, it is important to advance with concrete actions to provide the international community with experience and lessons for increased financial and technical assistance to developing Asia.

Developing Asia is expected to be at the center of the global agenda on low-carbon green growth. Asia has much at stake in the fight against climate change as the region is the world's most populous and has had high economic growth with a rising share of global GHG emissions, and Asia's subregion are among the most vulnerable to looming climate risks. Nowhere are production, resource consumption, and emissions growing faster than in developing Asia.

Action on the following 10 key issues is crucial to achieving low-carbon green growth in Asia.

Regional Level Actions for Accelerating Low-Carbon Green Growth in Asia

Regional Carbon Market

- Promote the linkage of national carbon trade schemes, which will require the creation of a regional public–private policy dialogue and framework to prepare the ground for the linkage of carbon trade schemes including transparent agreements and rules (for instance, MRV systems) and institutional arrangements.
- Encourage investment in cross-border low-carbon energy infrastructure and transport projects

Regional Energy Partnership

- Promote a regional partnership on renewable energy, setting national renewable energy targets and favorable feed-in tariffs (FITs) and renewable portfolio standards (RPSs).
- Promote the partnership to work toward a set of applicable national efficiency standards developed and applied to a limited but critical range of energy-intensive industrial and consumer goods, and buildings. Governments may also develop energy efficiency labeling for electrical appliances, consumer products, and industrial manufacturing processes, building on work under way according to a mutually agreed timetable.

Private Sector Participation

- Implement an effective capacity development program at regional or subregional level to help create an enabling policy and legal environment to attract private sector participation International development institutions, national governments, and financial institutions should use risk-mitigating products (e.g., political risk guarantees, credit risk guarantees) to encourage private sector investment in low-carbon infrastructure development.

- Promote a regional public–private portfolio of several large-scale integrated smart city and smart grid demonstration projects across different regulatory regimes.

Technology Transfer

- Establish a network of regional low-carbon innovation centers modeled on the Consultative Group on International Agricultural Research, to help developing countries accelerate the uptake of low-carbon technology. Regional development institutions such as ADB may play a leading role in promoting climate technology transfer and diffusion, helping countries learn from each other.
- Forge a free-trade agreement within Asia for high-impact green and low-carbon technologies and services.

Finance

- Encourage the phasing out of pervasive fossil fuel subsidies, using a regionally coordinated approach. This should be done as a prelude to introducing fiscal reforms that encompass a range of pricing and taxation instruments, including taxes on fossil fuels and other resources.
- Set up a regional platform to encourage REDD+ (reduced emissions from deforestation and degradation) projects. This platform should be hosted by key forest nations of the region and involve the international community, regional financial institutions, civil society, and the private sector.

What the Book is About

Measuring Mitigation Efforts by Asia

This book reviews greenhouse gas (GHG) emissions in cumulative and absolute terms, and the voluntary targets and efforts taken by the emerging economies of Asia to tackle climate change. This study recognizes that low-carbon green growth is an imperative, not an option for Asia, the world's most populous and rapidly growing region. The theoretical aspects of low-carbon green growth and the issue of adapting to climate change are not the focus of the study.

Capturing Asian Perspectives

Emerging Asia is different from the developed advanced economies as it is experiencing rapid growth rates that need to be decoupled from energy use and emissions, reaping co-benefits in areas such as health. These countries have only recently witnessed an increase in manufacturing and their per capita levels of material consumption remain low. Asia is diverse, with a large and growing population that has given way to consumption-oriented and new lifestyles, environmental degradation, and declining forest cover. However, social inclusion is the top priority for emerging Asia. This book captures the Asian perspectives on the trade-offs, equity issues, and interdependence in working together.

Policy Relevance

This study suggests actionable, solution-oriented policy recommendations in the medium and long term to meet national and sectoral targets, and a strategic framework to implement low-carbon green growth policies and reap benefits from regional cooperation and working collectively.

Participatory

This study was done in cooperation with 23 think tanks, with researchers from those institutes contributing the background papers and chapters. Inputs from policy makers, private sector representatives, and international organizations were received at a technical workshop and stakeholder meetings and policy dialogues held in Tokyo, Beijing, New Delhi, Jakarta, Seoul, and Manila.

Added Value

This book is built on the ongoing projects of ADB and ADBI and the knowledge that exists in regional thinks tanks. This study served as a knowledge-sharing platform for ongoing works and to facilitate countries' low-carbon green growth policies and implementation.

A Readers Guide to Navigating the Chapters

Chapter 1

Why is Low-Carbon Green Growth imperative for Asia?

Asia's challenges:
- Future growth is needed for poverty alleviation
- Climate change—if not halted will undermine growth and lock in high-carbon footprints
- Decoupling is possible with the right technological change, market incentives, and collective action

Low-carbon green growth as an integrated approach can be attractive in the short run, too:
- Environmental co-benefits
- Economic co-benefits
- Social benefits

Chapter 2

Why the changing perspectives and what is the scale of the challenge?

- Externalities of Asia's economic renaissance
- Implications of globally agreed 2°C ceiling for emerging Asia
- MDGs related to environment and energy
- NAMAs as national objectives and size of the investment needed

- Converging Asian perspectives on tackling climate change
- Evolving frameworks for low-carbon green growth
- Monitoring systems to track the results of policies and public investments

Chapter 3

What are the successful transformation strategies, policies, and practices?

- Country strategies for reducing emissions in key sectors such as energy supply, energy efficiency, transport, waste management, agriculture land use
- Evidence on the technological, regulatory, fiscal, and market-oriented policies that have been successfully implemented at national, sectoral, and subnational levels
- Critical evaluation of the actions, achievements, organizational structure, public-private partnerships, and budgetary reforms

Lessons for scaling up and widening low-carbon green growth transformation

Chapter 4

How to make LCGG more inclusive?

The policy conditions under which low-carbon green growth can help deliver development objectives beyond the environmental ones—turning co-benefits into primary objectives along climate change mitigation
- Social inclusivity and equity
- Expansion of demand
- Green jobs
- Innovation
- Energy security

Chapter 5

How to seize new opportunities?

Public goods need collective action. More direct coordinated actions are essential to seize opportunities across borders and bring economic competitiveness to countries.
Regional cooperation is critical to accelerate LCGG
- Knowledge sharing and policy networking
- Free trade in environmental goods and services
- Joint research and innovation
- Joint mobilization of finance

Chapter 6

Conclusion: Low-Carbon Green Growth in Asia: Policies and Practices

- Much of Asia is taking policy actions to tackle climate change and accelerate green growth—which are measurable, comparable, and replicable
- Introducing policies to support low-carbon green growth need not be a costly undertaking if instruments are designed to address the poverty reduction agenda and private sector mobilization
- Countries can use a combination of policy matrix and checklist of indicators to assess the quality and capability of their existing framework and to identify specific areas that can be strengthened through regional cooperation

Chapter 1
Putting Sustainable Development and Climate Change Policies into Practice

Chapter 1
Putting Sustainable Development and Climate Change Policies in Practice

1.1 Introduction

The pursuit of economic growth has been the single most important policy goal of emerging Asian countries in the recent past. Asia's economic output surged tenfold between 1980 and 2009. With an annual average gross domestic product (GDP) growth rate of more than 7% since 2000 the world share of developing Asia's trade doubled from 13% in 1990 to 26% in 2008 (United Nations [UN] 2009). In 2010, the Asian share of global output was 28%, against less than 12% in 1990. If it continues to follow the recent trajectory, the Asian GDP per capita income in purchasing power parity terms of $6,700 in 2010 will rise significantly to $40,800 in 2050 (Kohli, Sharma, and Sood 2011). More countries are looking for strategies to reach the status of developed economies, to facilitate the changes in patterns of growth, production, and consumption that have historically taken place as income levels have changed.

The extraordinary ramping up of economic activities since the 1970s has no historical precedent. Nevertheless, this fast-paced economic growth has been accompanied by high rates of material and energy consumption. Resource extraction[1] for economic use increased from 9 billion tons in 1985 to 13 billion tons of resources in 1995, and reached almost 18 billion tons in 2005 (Giljum et al. 2010). The growth of resource extraction in Asia has been much faster than the global average. The share of the emerging Asian countries—including the People's Republic of China (PRC), India, and the Association of Southeast Asian Nations (ASEAN)—in global resource extraction increased notably, from 22% in 1985 to 31% in 2005. The composition of extracted resources also changed considerably over this period. While in 1985, renewable resources such as biomass accounted for almost half of all extraction, this share diminished to 36% in 2005, as extraction of nonrenewable resources increased at a much higher pace. This growing share of nonrenewable resources is one characteristic of the ongoing process of industrialization, which has accelerated significantly in many Asian countries since the beginning of the 1990s (Weisz et al. 2006). The region consumed 20% of world energy in 2000, but the share rose to about 27% by 2007 (Asian Development Bank [ADB] 2011). This poses a serious challenge to the sustainability of growth considering the finite resource base, the impacts of climate change, and the fragile ecology on which emerging Asia depends for economic expansion. Within the context of attaining sustainable development, natural resources and ecosystem services provided by the environment are essential to support economic growth, social well-being, and human development.

To sustain these growth rates, and achieve the Asian Century by 2050,[2] developing Asia has to deal with serious challenges, such as large-scale poverty eradication and reducing socioeconomic inequality. During the last decades of development since 1992, income inequalities as revealed by the Gini coefficient have been increasing. In Asia, more than 50% of the population lives on less than $2.50 a day, and has limited access to basic services.

—

1 In general, four major types of resources are considered: (i) agriculture, forestry and fishery, and biomass products (including textiles and wood products such as paper); (ii) fossil energy carriers (coal, oil, gas, peat) used for energetic and non-energetic purposes (including chemicals based on fossil materials); (iii) minerals (industrial and construction minerals) and mineral products (such as glass or natural fertilizers); and (iv) metal ores and metal products (including, for example, machinery).

2 The Asian Century scenario extends Asia's past success into the future, putting it on the cusp of a historic transformation. In this scenario, Asia's GDP increases from $17 trillion on 2010 to $174 trillion in 2050, or half of global GDP, similar to share of its global population. It would have no poor countries (those with average per-capita GDP of less than $1,000), compared with eight in 2012.

Figure 1.1

Energy and Human Development

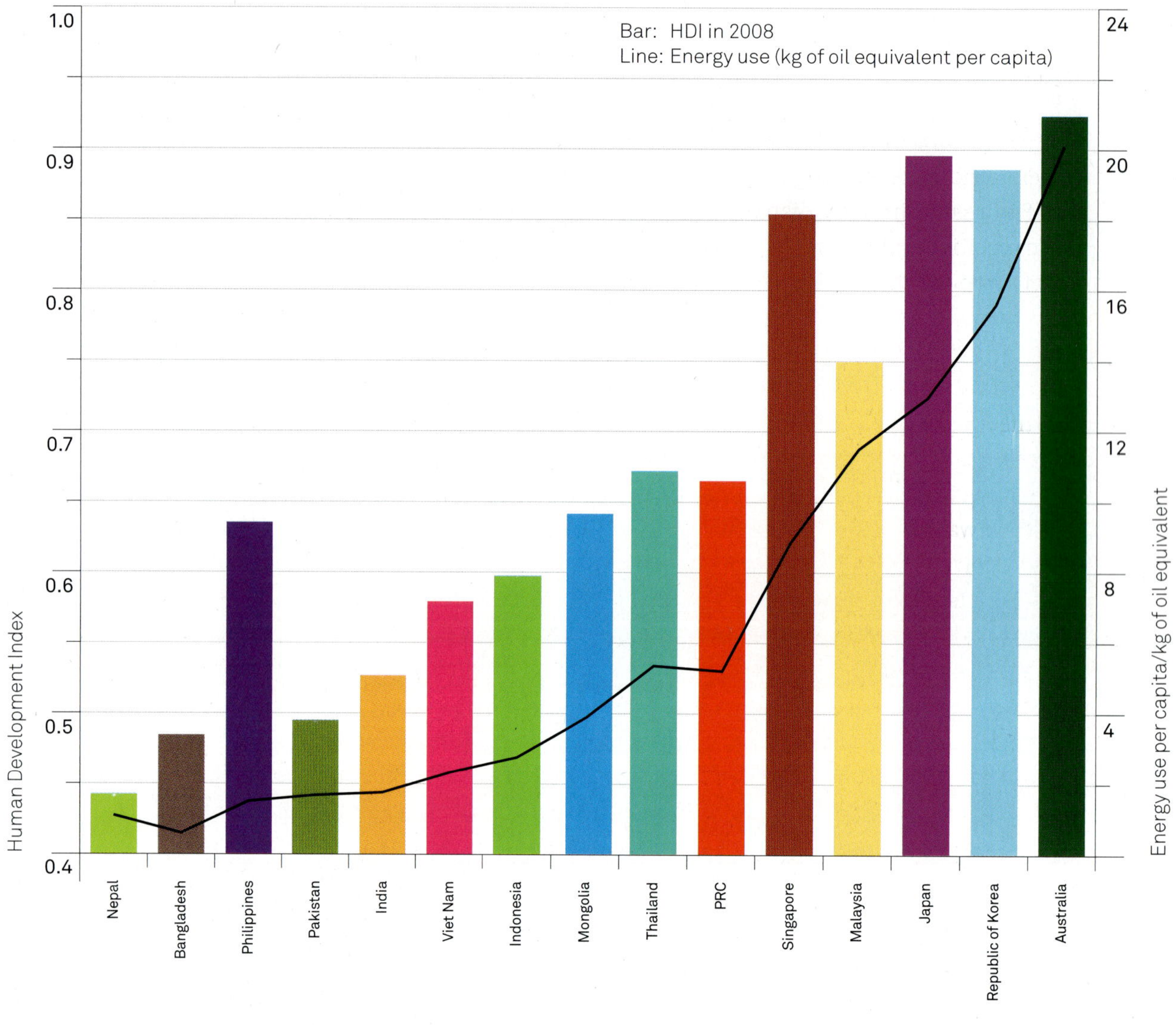

Sources: World Development Indicators (2011).
http://data.worldbank.org/data-catalog/world-development-indicators
(accessed December 2012). Human Development Report (2011).
http://hdr.undp.org/en/statistics/ (accessed December 2012).

Currently, 650 million people across Asia are conservatively estimated to be without access to electricity. The number of people unable to cook with modern fuels and lacking minimum lighting to read or carry out other household activities will grow as the population increases. Variations in modern energy consumption across countries explain the wide differences in human development among developing and developed countries (Figure 1.1). Similarly, disparities in economic capacities and natural as well as social capital have created different levels of development in Asian countries.

Despite all the past achievements and periods of short-term prosperity, economists within and outside of the region agree that in the long run, this type of development, without due regard to social inclusiveness and environmental protection, is not sustainable (Kawai and Lee 2010; Stiglitz 2011; Salim 2011; Sachs and Someshwar 2012). Most disturbing is the fact that past development models have disrupted the equilibrium of ecological systems to the extent that biological diversity has been eroded, nature's life support systems have been adversely affected, and climate change is increasing.

1.2 The Concept and Imperativeness of Low-Carbon Green Growth

1.2.1 Climate Change, Development, and Poverty Reduction

Climate change epitomizes the developmental challenges in a still highly unequal but increasingly globalized world. The evidence for climate change is overwhelming and has been confirmed by successive international studies (ADB 2009a; Stern 2007; UNFCCC 2007). They indicate warming of 2°C would lead to minimal losses in high-income countries and a global GDP loss of about 1% (Stern 2007), but could result in a 6% permanent reduction in annual per-capita income in Asia (ADB 2009). The losses would be primarily driven by increased variability and more frequent and intense extreme weather events (UNFCC 2007). The poor populations of emerging Asia are likely to suffer disproportionately. Most of the warming trend observed since industrialization is due to increases in anthropogenic greenhouse gas (GHG) emissions, particularly carbon dioxide (CO_2), caused by activities such as fossil fuel burning and land use changes. The Intergovernmental Panel on Climate Change (IPCC) in its First Assessment report stated the need to reduce current GHG emissions by 60%–80% if concentrations are to be kept at the 1990 level (IPCC 1990). The most recent Fourth Assessment Report of the IPCC found stronger links between human-induced emissions and increased global average temperatures and climate change (IPCC 1995; 2000a; 2007a).

The Stern Review (2007) confirmed that not only is the cost of taking action now far smaller than the cost of inaction, but that even when the most aggressive action to address climate change is taken, it would have an almost imperceptible impact on the 150% growth in the global economy predicted by 2050. Burning fossil fuels is the main source of GHG emissions. Many Asian countries are reliant on significant imports of fossil fuels to meet their energy needs. A dependency on imports for energy resources means energy supplies and prices are vulnerable to uncontrollable events or political developments in the exporting countries.

Addressing climate change, social inequality, the depletion of resources, and energy security will be a central development challenge for emerging Asia. The question arises to what extent climate policies can help alter energy and resource consumption and increase resource productivity—in other words, to what extent can emerging Asia's climate policies contribute to the achievement of multiple development co-benefits.[3] Figure 1.2 correlates material consumption and energy-related CO_2 emissions in 14 Asian countries for 2009. The trend line illustrates a high correlation between these indicators, implying that countries with high absolute levels of resource consumption and economic growth are also those with high CO_2 emissions.

According to projections of global GHG emissions in standard reference scenarios, continued business-as-usual development of the global economy, driven by an emerging Asia and a world population that in 2012 has reached 7 billion, will lead to a probable doubling of global emissions by 2030 (IPCC 2007), most of which will be emitted by Asian developing countries (ADB 2009b). As GHGs continue to accumulate in the atmosphere, CO_2 atmospheric concentration could reach 500 parts per million (ppm).

As a result, the world's mean temperature by 2100 could increase from 3.0°C to 4.8°C above 1980–2000 levels under a high emissions scenario (ADB 2009a). On the basis of comprehensive modeling, and as published in the scientific literature, some scenarios estimate global average temperature increases of up to 6.4°C by the end of this century. Net economic losses could result in many countries at all magnitudes of warming (IPCC 2007). The poor in developing countries, especially in South and Southeast Asia, are estimated to be those most vulnerable to the changes and their associated impacts.

—

3 The co-benefits approach to climate change means integrated efforts to address climate change concerns, while meeting development needs in developing countries. The co-benefits approach helps developing countries increase their ownership while engaging in efforts to address climate change, by introducing measures to achieve tangible development benefits. It is also considered to be a practical approach for developed countries to cooperate with developing countries, where economic and social development is a priority at the national and local levels.There are also local air pollution benefits from pursuing greenhouse gases emissions mitigation policies, which lower the net costs of emission reductions and thereby may strengthen the incentives to participate in a global climate change mitigation agreement.

Figure 1.2

CO_2 Emission and Resource Consumption in Asia, 2009

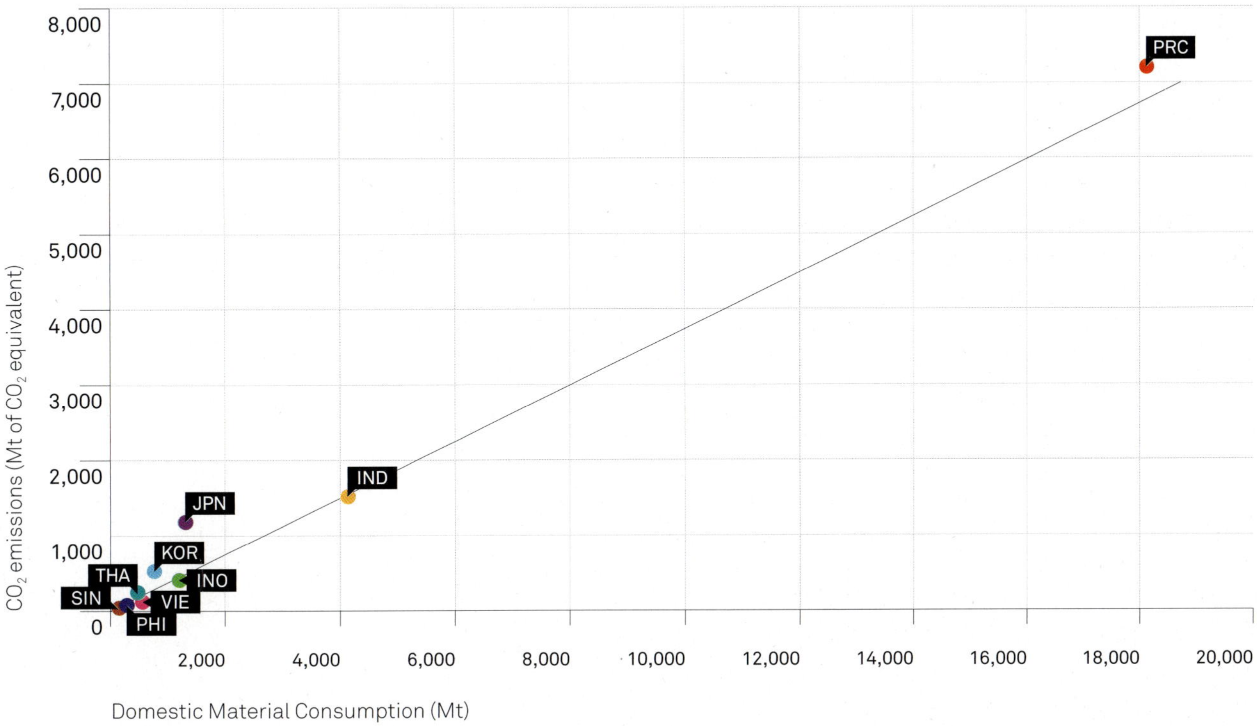

Source: World Resource Institute Climate Analysis Indicators Tool (CAIT) Version 9.0 by the World Resource Institute (2012) and Sustainable Europe Research.

Notes:
- IND: India
- INO: Indonesia
- JPN: Japan
- KOR: Republic of Korea
- PHI: Philippines
- PRC: People's Republic of China
- SIN: Singapore
- THA: Thailand
- VIE: Viet Nam

Figure 1.3

Climate Change, Poverty, and Development Nexus

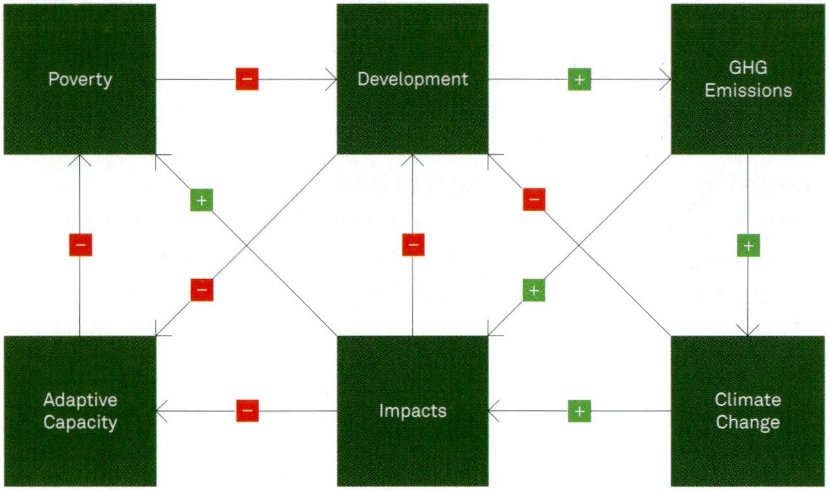

Source: Kameyama et al. (2008).

Climate change is identified as a serious challenge for poverty reduction efforts in developing countries, particularly because these countries have limited capacity to cope with current climate variability and extremes, not to mention future climate change (Figure 1.3). Indeed, poverty and environmental needs exacerbate the adverse consequences of climate change. Therefore, the development and climate change communities can bring their perspectives together for environmentally sustainable and socially inclusive economic growth and low-carbon, climate-resilient development through integrated approaches (IPCC 2007). Aggregate annual losses for Asia would be 2.6%–8.1% of GDP in 2100 (ADB 2009a). At the same time, development will lead to emissions of GHGs that will eventually contribute to climate change.

1.2.2
Global Actions for Mitigating Climate Change

The new understanding of the link between human-induced emissions of GHGs and climate change spurred the agreement called the United Nations Framework Convention on Climate Change (UNFCCC) in 1992, followed by the adoption of the Kyoto Protocol at the Third Conference of the Parties to the Treaty (COP 3) in 1997. The Kyoto Protocol, which entered into force in 2005, governs the quantitative emission reduction commitments of industrialized countries that became signatories to the protocol. While the IPCC reports imply a need for CO_2 reductions of 60%–80% from developed countries by 2050 (IPCC 2007), the Kyoto Protocol required only a reduction of 5.2% on average from 1990 levels for the 2008–2012 period. Developing countries, because of their developmental needs, are not required to commit to quantitative emission reduction objectives until 2012 under the protocol.

However, to be more effective, future mitigation efforts would need to achieve deeper reductions covering a higher share of global emissions, which will become more difficult with time.

If nothing is done, global emissions will continue to increase as a result of demographic change, social and economic development, and the current rate of technological change. Between 1970 and 2004, global GHG emissions caused by human activities increased by 70% since pre-industrial times (IPCC 2007) and CO_2 emissions from the use of fossil fuels have been growing at 1.9% per year (IPCC 2007). Under certain scenarios, the International Energy Agency (IEA) found that non-OECD countries could be responsible for almost 90% of growth in energy demand and account for nearly three-quarters of global CO_2 emissions in 2050 compared with 2007 (IEA 2010a).

The significant risks of an increase in global average temperature of more than 2°C above pre-industrial levels are well-documented and represent threats, especially for the poor and vulnerable countries of Asia (ADB 2009a; Zhai and Zhuang 2012; Cline 1992). Governments agreed at the 15th session of the Conference of the Parties (COP 15) in Copenhagen on the need to stabilize the global temperature increase at 2°C above pre-industrial levels to limit the impacts of climate change. The "best estimate" assumption shows that the most stringent scenarios, which could limit global mean temperature increases to 2.0°C–2.4°C above pre-industrial levels, require emissions to peak within 10 years from 2007 (IPCC 2007). Eleven of the 12 years from 1995 to 2006 rank among the warmest years in the instrumental record of global surface temperature, measured since 1850. Global average surface temperatures increased by about 0.74°C over the 100 years from 1906 to 2005 (IPCC 2007). The global average temperature increase can be limited to 2.0°C–2.4°C if we are able to stabilize the global concentration of CO_2, the principal anthropogenic GHG, at 445–490ppm. In 2005, atmospheric CO_2 concentrations had increased by almost 100 ppm above pre-industrial levels, reaching 379 ppm (IPCC 2007). The numerous mitigation measures that have been undertaken by many parties to the UNFCCC are inadequate for revising overall GHG emissions trends to the extent needed.

During the UNFCCC conferences in Copenhagen in 2009 and Cancun in 2010, several developing countries submitted nationally appropriate mitigation actions (NAMAs), which describe domestic emission mitigation activities (Table 1.1) carried out with and without international support, and which are subject to domestic measurement, reporting and verification (MRV), reported through national communications.

At the UNFCCC Durban COP 17 in 2011, governments agreed to draw up a new deal with legal force to be signed by all countries, to be prepared by 2015 and take effect in 2020. The Durban Platform for Action (Box 1.1) noted with grave concern the significant gap between countries' mitigation pledges for 2020 and the likely chance of holding the increase in global temperature to 1.5°C–2.0°C above pre-industrial levels. Big differences exist in the commitments of various Asian countries, based primarily on the structure of their energy economies. Indeed, primary energy requirements and the resulting emissions depend on factors such as the level of industrialization, economic structure, energy mix, level of motorization, and the type and availability of domestic energy resources.

Table 1.1

Voluntary Pledges made in Copenhagen through Nationally Appropriate Mitigation Actions

Country	Mitigation actions
Bhutan	Ensuring that emissions do not exceed country's sequestration capacity
PRC	Reduction of GHG emissions per unit of GDP by 40%–45% below 2005 levels by 2020
	Increase of share from non-fossil fuels to supply 15% of primary energy consumption by 2020
	Increase of forest cover by 40 million hectares by 2020
	Increase of forest stock volume by 1.3 billion cubic meters above 2005 levels by 2020
India	Reduction of GHG emissions per unit of GDP by 20%–25% below 2005 levels by 2020
	Increase of the fraction of electricity derived from wind, solar, and small hydro to 20% in 2020 (from the current level of 8%)
	Adoption of building energy codes by 2012
	Adoption of fuel efficiency standards by 2011
	Increase of forest cover to sequester 10% of annual emissions in India's forests
Indonesia	Reduction of emissions to 26% below business-as-usual levels by 2020 achieved through: • Sustainable peatland management • Reduction in the rate of deforestation and land degradation • Improvement of carbon sequestration • Promotion of energy efficiency, and alternative and renewable energy sources • Reduction in solid and liquid waste • Low-carbon transport
Japan	Economy-wide reduction of GHG emissions by 25% below 1990 levels by 2020 based on the premise of the establishment of a fair and effective international framework in which all major economies participate
Republic of Korea	Reduction of emissions to 30% below projected levels by 2020, which equates to approximately 4% below 2005 levels
Malaysia	Reduction of GHG emission intensity by 40% below 2005 levels by 2020
Maldives	Achieve carbon neutrality as a country by 2020
Mongolia	A series of actions including increase of photovoltaic (PV), solar, and wind utilization, and improvement of energy efficiency
Singapore	Reduction of GHG emissions to 16% below projected levels by 2020, contingent on a legally-binding global agreement
Thailand	Reduction of energy intensity measured by energy per GDP to 1:1
	Increase to share of renewable energies to 20% by 2022
Viet Nam	Reduce energy consumption by 5%–8% by 2015
	Increase contribution of renewable energy sources to over 5% in 2020, and 11% in 2050

Source: UNFCCC (2011).

Box 1.1

Durban Platform, Rio+20 Summit, and Doha Climate Gateway

At Durban in December 2011, delegates agreed to a compact, two-page document that sets out a motivation and process for reaching a new agreement on emissions reduction by 2015, to be implemented by 2020. It achieves one small step by asserting that the outcome will be "applicable to all parties." The Cancun agreement of 2010 allows countries to state their domestic emissions reduction commitments publicly and allows those commitments to be reviewed by the international community. At Durban, delegates agreed new procedures for measurement, reporting and verification (MRV) for voluntary commitments, and for international consultation to increase confidence in progress toward the fulfillment of these pledges.

The Durban platform contains three important elements. First, it notes with grave concern the significant gap between countries' mitigation pledges in terms of global reduction of GHG emissions by 2020 and the likely chance of holding the increase in global temperature to 1.5°C–2.0°C above pre-industrial levels. This statement reinforces the scientific agreement that a target of 1.5°C or 2.0°C warming would result in far less significant impacts from climate change than a higher global temperature increase. Second, the platform asserts that countries should "launch a process to develop a protocol, another legal instrument or an agreed outcome with legal force under the UNFCCC applicable to all parties." Third, it states that this agreement should be prepared by 2015 and that any resulting reductions should begin by 2020. The 2015 deadline is relatively short by international negotiation standards, increasing the pressure to conclude a deal in the near future.

The 2012 United Nations Conference on Sustainable Development, also known as Rio+20, took place 20 years after the landmark summit in Rio de Janeiro in 1992. A key theme that dominated the deliberations was the concept of a green economy. At a time when the economic and financial crises make the headlines, world leaders agreed to push forward a green economy to achieve sustainable development and poverty eradication, based on the principle of common but differentiated responsibility and low-carbon development. The outcome document "The Future we want" urges countries to measure human well-being and sustainability with a broad set of tools, rather than a narrow metric such as gross domestic product (GDP). It reemphasizes the fulfillment of official development assistance (ODA) commitments, including the commitments by developed countries to achieve the target of 0.7% of gross national product for ODA to developing countries by 2015, as well as a target of 0.15%–0.20% of gross national product for ODA to least developed countries. It is important for the rapidly growing nations of Asia to capitalize on the opportunities available for low-carbon green growth and to invest heavily in human capital to encourage citizens and industries toward sustainable consumption and production practices.

The Doha Climate Change Conference that concluded on 8 December 2012 has resulted in decisions (clubbed together as "Doha Climate Gateway") aimed at advancing the implementation of the United Nations Framework Convention on Climate Change (UNFCCC) and its Kyoto Protocol (KP). The Doha Conference has succeeded in carrying out amendments to the KP making the second commitment period of emission reduction by KP parties effective immediately beginning 1 January 2013. Although the emission reduction obligations undertaken by the Annex I parties are not as ambitious as required by science, the KP parties have agreed to implement the targets over an 8 year period (2013–2020), thus providing a degree of certainty to the carbon markets. It has been agreed that the KP parties will revisit their targets in 2014 with a view to increasing their ambition; this will be unconditional and will have no linkage with the work of the Durban Platform. At Doha, the work of the Durban Platform set up for devising the post-2020 arrangements progressed satisfactorily. In a significant and positive advance, it has been agreed that the work of the Durban Platform will be based on the principles of the Convention. As announced by the UN Secretary General, the decision recognizes the possibility of holding a meeting of heads of governments and states in 2015 to finalize the Agreement.

Source: ADB–ADBI study team.

1.2.3
Sustainable Development Dilemmas of Emerging Asia

As a consequence of rapid carbon-intensive growth, the region is becoming the fastest growing emitter of GHG emissions. Recent estimates suggest that Asia accounts for 27% of the world's energy related CO_2 emissions and the share is likely to increase to 44% by 2030 (Figure 1.4). The region is predicted to experience a steady rise in urban population (Kohli, Sharma, and Sood 2011); a sharp increase in energy use (Institute of Energy Economics, Japan 2011); a surge in the size of the vehicle fleet; and an increase in the output of carbon-intensive industries (Schipper, Fabian, and Leather 2009). The future of global economic growth depends on the prospects and performance of emerging Asian countries. While the general trend suggests major economies of the region, such as the PRC and India, have become and will continue to be major sources of emissions, per capita emissions continue to be lower than those of industrialized countries.

An inventory of GHG emissions (Table 1.2) for major countries across Asia indicates a pressing need for significant emission reductions within a short time frame. To have a greater chance of achieving lower stabilization levels, an emissions peak and then decline would have to occur quickly, and greater emissions reductions by 2050 would be required (IPCC 2007).

The implications of global warming help to set the frame for policy making aimed at GHG emissions reductions. While modeling future temperature increase is sensitive to key assumptions about economic growth and policy interventions, it is worth noting that paleoclimatic information supports the interpretation that the warmth of the last half century is unusual at least in the previous 1,300 years. The last time the polar regions were significantly warmer for an exceeded period (about 125,000 years ago), reductions in polar ice volume led to a sea level rise of 4–6 meters (IPCC 2007).

Geographically, North America, Asia, and the Middle East have driven the rise in emissions since 1972. Developed countries (UNFCCC Annex 1 countries) hold a 20% share in world population but account for 46% of global GHG emissions. In contrast, the 80% of the world population living in developing countries accounts for 4% of GHG emissions. While some studies argue that even if the majority of emissions are the responsibility of only a few nations, all countries must share the commitments to reduce them for reasons of fairness and equity, others argue that countries have differentiated historical responsibility (IPCC 2007). Since 1800, economic growth has enabled Europe and the United States (US) to reduce hunger, poverty, and hardship. Hopefully, over the coming decades, Asia will do the same. Energy has a particularly critical role in development. Access to energy is critical for the provision of basic services such as lighting and cooking; it improves education, increases productivity, enhances competitiveness, and promotes economic growth. Reliable, affordable, and available energy is crucial for economic development, and national development strategies consider this. While some development activities exacerbate vulnerability to climate change, efforts to cope with the impacts of climate change and attempts to promote sustainable development share common goals.

Figure 1.4

Regional Emissions, 2009 and 2035

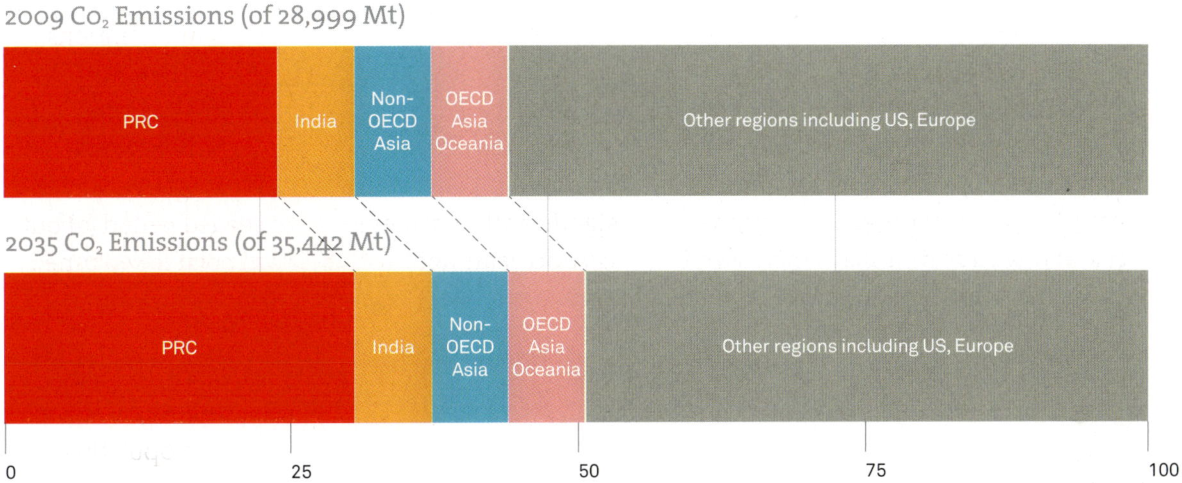

Mt=million tons.
Source: IEA (2009).

Table 1.2

Current and Projected Emission Trends of Asia

Country/Region	CO_2 emissions		CO_2 emissions per capita		Emissions intensity	Electricity consumption per capita	Total energy demand	
Year (unit)	2009	2035 (Mt)	2009	2035 (t/capita)	2009 (tCO_2/GDP)	(kWh/capita)	2009 (Mtoe)	2035
PRC	6,877	10,253	5.14	7.39	0.6	2,648	2,271	3,835
India	1,548	3,535	1.37	2.34	0.35	597	669	1,464
Indonesia	376	...	1.64	...	0.4	609	198	...
Thailand	227	...	3.36	...	0.41	2,073	107	...
Viet Nam	114	...	1.31	...	0.38	904	59	...
Non-OECD Asia (excluding India, PRC)	1,565	2,899	1.49	2.11	...	...	784	1,472
Japan	1,088	918	8.58	...	0.32	7,833	472	478
Australia	395	...	17.87	...	0.56	11,038	130	...
Republic of Korea	515	...	10.57	...	0.45	8,980	...	...
OECD Asia Oceania	2,021	1,655	9.96	8.15	...	...	850	912
World	28,999	35,442	4.29	4.14	0.45	2,730	12,271	16,748

Notes: All emissions figures are for energy-related emissions only.
Mtoe: million tons of oil equivalent. kWh: kilowatt-hour.
Projections are for the "New Policies Scenario" from the IEA's World Energy Outlook 2011.

Source: Howes and Wyrwoll (2012).

Climate change also raises issues of equity because of the large differences in emissions, present and past, among countries and their widely differing vulnerability to the effects of climate change. Further, mitigation programs that aim to serve societies at the global scale may require a development in global governance that would require a participative approach with the involvement of emerging economies. From the development point of view, carbon emissions are to be treated as the utilization of the global common space available in the global atmospheric commons, and should not be seen only in terms of environmental damage they can cause. This implies that developing countries in Asia are simultaneously facing the challenging tasks of reducing significant climate change risks and other major environmental disruptions, and of lessening global inequalities, as Figure 1.5 shows. This is also a challenge derived from the principle of common but differentiated responsibility. It implies, as stated by the UN, that the active participation of developing countries is now required and such participation can occur only if it allows economic growth and development to proceed in a rapid and sustainable manner" (UN-DESA 2009). The differentiated part of responsibilities implies that absolute emission reductions should come from developed economies, while the decoupling of economic growth and emissions is a viable strategy for developing Asia, where per capita emissions continue to be lower and growth will bring poverty alleviation. Figure 1.5 illustrates the challenge that confronts emerging Asian economies today. However, there is reason for optimism.

Based on the economic performance of Asia since 1970, these economies have successfully made the transition from least developed to fast growing ones, showing that such a transition is possible under favorable circumstances and policies.

Figure 1.5

Developmental Dilemma of the Emerging Asian Economies

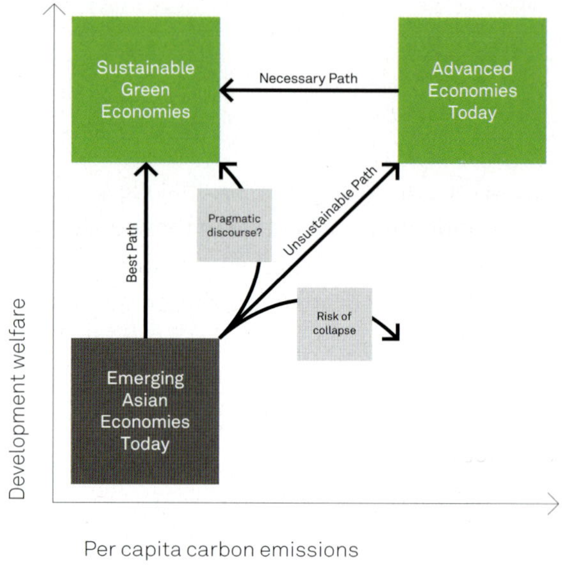

Source: ADB–ADBI study team.

Within Asia, experience from the industrialized economies of Japan, the Republic of Korea, and Singapore suggests that development efforts that facilitate environmentally sustainable growth and poverty alleviation are possible. Such a development path needs to be increasingly based on low-carbon energy to tackle climate change. Development along such a path can be labeled low-carbon green growth when it is a reflection of a more general concern to avoid environmental degradation and resource depletion.

1.2.4
Defining Low-Carbon Green Growth

Since the 2008 financial crisis, the concepts of low-carbon development, the green economy, and a global green new deal have increasingly come to the fore in the global policy debate (United Nations Environment Programme [UNEP] 2011;

Barbier 2010; World Bank 2011). There is no universal definition of the concept of low-carbon green growth, but the term underscores the economic dimensions of sustainable growth with a focus on the interaction between emission reductions and the economy. UNEP (2011) emphasizes the crucial point that economic growth and environmental stewardship can be complementary strategies, countering the still strongly influential view that significant trade-offs exist between these objectives. UNEP (2011) has defined the green economy as a development pattern that not only improves human well-being and lessens inequality but also reduces environmental risks and addresses ecological scarcities—a growth paradigm pattern that is low-carbon, resource-efficient, and socially inclusive.

Low-carbon green growth thus entails (i) using less energy, improving the efficiency with which resources are used, and switching to low-carbon energy resources; (ii) protecting and promoting natural resources such as forests and peatlands; (iii) designing and disseminating low-carbon technologies and business models to reinvigorate local economies; and (iv) implementing policies and incentives that discourage carbon-intensive practices. It presents the emerging economies of Asia with a unique opportunity to invest in change. Many analysts (Kawai and Lee 2010; Stiglitz 2010; Frankel 2009) believe that the sooner countries take advantage of low-carbon green growth, the better it will be for their long-term development prospects.

This provides an opportunity to sweep away the short-term development thinking that has plagued the past several decades and replace it with paths toward development that flourish within ecological limits. The challenge is to create the enabling policy architectures, both at the domestic and international levels, under which this is possible.

1.3 Impacts and Co-benefits of Low-Carbon Green Growth

The concept and practice of low-carbon green growth is consistent with the broader concept of sustainable development. The concept encompasses three pillars of development—economic, social, and environmental—and a focus on intergenerational equity. It abandons the conventional linear economic model of development, with its overemphasis on material wealth, to explore different aspects of growth that emphasize co-benefits apart from wealth creation, including the enhancement of social cohesion and the preservation of ecological equilibrium. Moving to a low-carbon green growth paradigm will benefit developing Asia in at least three major ways: environmental co-benefits, economic benefits, and social co-benefits.

1.3.1 Environmental Co-Benefits

Many low-carbon interventions have important co-benefits, including human health benefits, from measures that reduce air pollution, waste, and other pollutants. Environmental co-benefits include lower particulate pollution and the conservation of forests. This helps poor people directly and should not be treated as a superfluity. Providing clean energy can produce major improvements in public health, in particular cutting exposure to high levels of indoor air pollution, which currently account for an annual mortality of 0.6 million in Asia. Household coal use in countries such as the PRC and India poses health risks, especially in many areas where highly polluting toxin-containing coal is used.

Historically, poor households have moved to the use of cleaner fuels as economic development occurred but this process alone would not suffice to reduce the health risk substantially in the long term. Low-carbon green growth has the potential co-benefit of a cleaner environment for poor populations. Similarly, the substantial effect of urban air pollution and traffic congestion on the health of the urban poor is largely due to fossil fuel combustion, accounting for an annual mortality of about 0.3 million at the global level (World Bank 2005). The burden of outdoor pollution in rural areas, which is not well measured but affects an even larger population, would increase this toll even further. With urbanization and vehicle fleets growing at historically unprecedented rates in Asia, the total health burden on the poor could be relieved by implementing low-carbon development policies.

1.3.2 Economic Co-Benefits

Numerous no-regret low-carbon interventions—such as creating the infrastructure necessary to increase energy efficiency and investments in renewable energy that have positive economic rates of return even without taking into account the carbon savings—can contribute significantly to economic development in emerging Asia. The economic benefits could be from three sources. First is the creation of extra aggregate demand through such measures as stimulus packages, in economies that have suffered an adverse shock as a result of the global economic slowdown. This is not such a big advantage for the PRC and India, because they were less affected than Europe and the US, but along with other Asian countries involved in international trade they will benefit from increased investment spending on the transition to low-carbon economies as long as they have low-productivity labor (e.g., in rural areas) that could be more productive in the new green sectors of the economy. Second, countries can benefit even in the short run from correcting some of the market failures that hold back the transition to a green economy and restrain productivity. Examples include improving incentives to import cutting-edge technologies and adapting them to local circumstances; and enhancing endowments, introducing smart electricity grids, encouraging low-carbon public transport, managing forests better, and introducing low-till agriculture. Third, low-carbon green growth requires international collective action in emissions reductions and the transfer of technologies, knowledge, and finance to the poorer Asian countries for assistance with mitigation and adaptation. This can come from the public and private sectors through carbon markets, the Clean Development Mechanism (CDM), the Green Climate Fund, and other routes. The current high emitters outside Asia are likely to be the main source of these financial flows, and emerging economies of Asia can reap these strategic benefits for their competitive advantage. The immediate economic co-benefit is energy supply security, reduction in price volatility, and savings in foreign exchange. Distribution of oil, gas, coal, and other energy resources is uneven globally. Trade in oil contributes much of the import bills of Asian countries. The rapid increase in oil prices and the prospects of peak oil (the point when the rate of oil production is expected to enter terminal decline after the maximum rate of petroleum extraction is reached) have renewed interest in energy security. Low-carbon green growth would help emerging Asia to move toward long-term energy independence.

Evidence exists that the impacts of policies for mitigating climate change include growth and reduction of income inequality; employment and the availability of green jobs in renewable energy, buildings and construction, transportation, industry, and forestry; and positive effects on government fiscal budgets and competitiveness within a globalizing market (IPCC 2007). The current global market for environmental goods and services is about $1,370 billion and is projected to grow to $2,740 billion by 2030. The strongest growth seems to be not in the traditional environment sector, but in low-carbon technologies and renewable energy technologies and services (Eco Canada 2010; Asia Business Council 2009). About 2.3 million people are employed in the renewable energy sector globally (Wyden 2010). Greening buildings could create 10 million jobs globally (Sharp 2009). Increasing forest cover for its carbon sink services could create another million jobs.

1.3.3 Social Co-Benefits

Coping with climate change entails collective action on a global and local scale. When individuals make consumer choices, they shape the markets and the potential to cut emissions. In the context of collective choices about how to deal with climate change, two types of behavior are especially relevant for emerging economies. The first is energy efficiency—the substitution of more energy-efficient appliances, motor vehicles, or other devices for less energy-efficient ones. The second is the curtailment of energy use, such as using public transport or a bicycle to commute rather than driving, and living in small sustainable communities rather than in urban sprawls. In both cases, the aim of such policies is to create incentives for individuals to choose lifestyles that are low-carbon. Among sectors and industries, there are leaders and laggards. Similarly, among individuals and societies, there are those who are oppressed, isolated, and not well informed of opportunities. By informing such groups of opportunities arising through climate policy making, and thereby enabling individuals to take action themselves, innovative approaches to reduce GHG emissions through behavioral changes are more likely to be achieved rapidly and democratically. Developing the capacity for collective action to be supportive of growth and job creation, of the poor and of the environment, also promotes equity and freedom (Arts 2009; Murshed 2009; Salim 2011). In emerging Asia, millions of people are involved in recycling, often under dangerous and dirty conditions. Converting these jobs to be cleaner and safer could help to make green growth inclusive. Poor communities, particularly women, need to be involved in decisions regarding local energy infrastructure and land management, and given a voice about nonmarket objectives such as low-carbon consumption choices. This will help promote equity and fairness in other respects, such as empowering women and marginalized groups like waste-pickers and the rural landless poor.

Thus, the transition to low-carbon green growth offers developing Asia many co-benefits such as healthier and more productive citizens; cleaner neighborhoods; and more competitive agricultural, industrial, and service sectors, capable of sustaining the region's high growth rate over the long term. Given the synergies between poverty alleviation and low-carbon green development, there are "triple dividends" (economic growth, environmental preservation, social equity) in resources allocated for development purposes.

1.4 Macroeconomic Dimensions and the Feasibility of Low-Carbon Green Growth

Low-carbon green growth is more than just environmental in scope. Based on the economic performance of Asia since 1970, Asia's 49 economies could be grouped into three categories: (i) high-income developed economies such as Brunei Darussalam, Japan,and Singapore; (ii) fast growing converging economies such as the PRC, India, and Indonesia; and (iii) slow or modest growth aspiring economies such as the Philippines and Sri Lanka. The fast growing converging economies of the PRC, India, Indonesia, Viet Nam, and Thailand produce 52% of regional GDP and comprise 77% of Asia's population. It is useful to use them as proxies for Asian countries and explore a set of macroeconomic and associated policy issues, as discussed below.

1.4.1 Low-Carbon Green Growth as a Process of Structural Change

Conventionally, growth analysis looks only at the dynamics of macroeconomic aggregates such as GDP, investment, labor force, and productivity—and ignores the fact that growth usually comes with changes in production structures such as variations in sectoral contributions to GDP, employment, investment, and patterns of specialization in the context of global markets. The assumption is that these transformations are just a consequence of economic growth. The alternative structuralist view of low-carbon green growth suggests instead that these changes are not mere by-products of development, but are actually among the prime movers, thereby defining low-carbon development as the capacity of an economy to generate new dynamic activities. New activities can overtake the old ones in a process of creative destruction (Ocampo 2005; Schumpeter 1962). This structuralist view carries with it major policy implications. Assuming that the production structure must change for growth and development to proceed, a conscious choice of policies that will drive the transformation of the system toward new dynamic activities will have to be taken and will play an essential role for long-term economic growth.

Fulfilling the potential of low-carbon green growth requires a technological revolution and major changes in production and consumption patterns (Sachs and Someshwar 2012). This technological revolution is likely to differ from previous processes of this sort in at least three major ways. First, policy making will play a more central role than in past industrial revolutions. Second, given the level of integration of Asian economies today and the fact that such a revolution would address major global challenges, international institutions will play a fundamental role in coordinating regional cooperation. This includes environmental agreements, trade regulations, and the establishment of financing facilities that developing countries are likely to require.

The process of creative destruction can have distributive impacts, across the region and within countries (Salim 2011). The essential issues are which segment of the population benefits from technological change and generating new economic activities and demand, and who will be negatively affected by the activities for which there will be reduced demand. Issues associated with the cost of low-carbon technologies, and the capacity to both generate and absorb technology and intellectual property rights are crucial. This process requires mechanisms to disseminate technology, such as green agricultural methods, energy-saving technologies for small and medium-sized manufacturing firms, and mechanisms to disseminate knowledge to households and construction firms about better building practices, to just mention a few.

Fundamentally, the speed required to put this low-carbon technological revolution in place and to guarantee that its benefits are shared equitably requires a much larger role for policy action than has been typical in recent decades. It will involve a judicious mix of regulation, taxes, and subsidies; and both market and nonmarket measures. For this reason, an investment-based strategy is essential to manage the transition to a low-carbon green economy in developing Asia. The two keys to such a strategy are public investment and industrial as well as trade policies, aiming at encouraging in both cases a strong private sector response. The trade policies should include a strong technology policy, with a focus on the adaptation and dissemination of low-carbon green technologies; the treatment of green firms as infant socially responsible industries that require support, such as time-bound subsidies and/or protection; and government procurement policies that mainstream emission reduction targets. The investment policies should include triggering public sector investments that support these industrial policy efforts and build the necessary infrastructure, both hard and soft, as well as access targets for basic energy and other services for the poor.

Pervasive subsidies for fossil fuels also present a challenge to low-carbon green growth. In 2009, subsidies for consumption of fossil fuels reached at least $312 billion (IEA 2010b) at the global level. This is a formidable sum spent in furtherance of emissions. It is estimated that the complete removal of consumption subsidies would lower demand and cut energy-related CO_2 emissions by 6% by 2020. They are also a formidable obstacle to the uptake of renewable energy and the implementation of energy efficiency measures. While most consumption subsidies do not involve actual cash outlay, they do involve opportunity cost. The sums involved are staggering—for example, Indonesia's direct subsidy payment in 2007 was close to 25% of its budget (Patnuru 2012), which cannot be directed toward important social developmental goals. Fossil fuel subsidies are often defended as pro-poor, particularly in countries with high levels of energy poverty, such as India. However, analysis indicates that only 15% of consumption subsidies actually reach the poor: the rest is consumed by the middle class, which owns automobiles and air conditioners. Reforming fossil fuel subsidies will enhance the uptake of low-carbon technologies.

1.4.2
Strategies and Technologies for Stabilizing Greenhouse Gas Emissions

One way of illustrating potential solutions to the major challenge of stabilizing and then reducing emissions of GHGs and promoting green growth is to identify so-called stabilization wedges, where a wedge is 1 gigaton of CO_2 equivalent per year of emissions savings, achieved by a single strategy. Socolow and Pacala (2004) propounded the idea of stabilization wedges, harnessing seven different ways of cutting emissions using available technology (Figure 1.6). Their goal was to draw a road map for reducing CO_2 emissions that is realistic, effective, scientifically robust, and politically feasible. Each of the strategies they identified could prevent a total of 25 billion tons of emissions by 2056.

Princeton University's Carbon Mitigation Initiative wedges consist of 15 different wedge strategies that are broadly grouped into (i) energy efficiency (four strategies), (ii) decarbonization of power (five strategies), (iii) decarbonization of fuel (four strategies), and (iv) forest and agricultural soils (two strategies). Table 1.3 illustrates sectoral strategies and wedges.

Figure 1.6
Emission Wedges

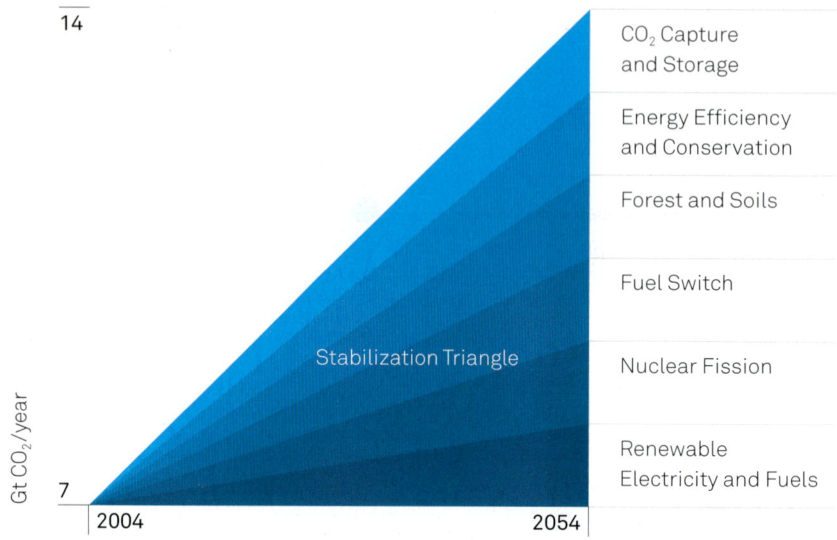

Gt=gigatons.
Source: Derived from Socolow and Pacala (2004); ADB–ADBI study team.

Implementing wedges of appropriate magnitude will put the global economy on track for the stabilization of GHG emissions concentrations at less than double pre-industrial levels. Although there are uncertainties, this approach indicates the likely magnitude of change required and the available mix of sector specific policy options. The advantage of this approach is that policy makers can compare the feasibility of applying each wedge and decide on the number and type of wedges that should be implemented in their countries.

Low-carbon development challenges cannot be met by just applying carbon-efficient technologies in niche markets and leaving others unchanged (Sachs and Someshwar 2012). What is required is the development and deployment of beneficial technologies, across the whole spectrum of sectors. Key mitigation technologies and practices projected to be commercialized before 2030 include:

1 Carbon capture and storage
2 Advanced nuclear power
3 Renewable energy
4 Second-generation biofuels
5 Advanced electric and hybrid vehicles
6 Integrated design of commercial vehicles
7 Land-use strategies
8 Non-CO_2 GHG emission reductions.

Many studies have analyzed these technologies[4] to identify mitigation strategies. Other studies suggest it is economically feasible to halt, and possibly reverse, the growth in emissions with currently available technologies in a cost-effective way (World Bank 2009c). This has already been happening in some Asian countries like the PRC, India, and Indonesia.

4 The 17 technologies distinguished as low carbon by the IEA are, carbon capture and storage, nuclear power plants, onshore and offshore wind energy, biomass integrated gasification combined cycle, photovoltaic systems, concentrating solar power, coal integrated gasification combined cycle, coal ultra-supercritical steam cycles, energy efficiency in buildings and appliances, heat pumps, solar space and water heating, energy efficiency in transport, second generation biofuels, electric and plug-in vehicles, hydrogen fuel cell vehicles, fuel transformation, and industrial motor systems.

Table 1.3

Sectoral Strategies and Wedges Relative to 14 Gt of CO_2 Equivalent per Year

Category	Technology	Electricity	Fuel	Heat	Sink
Efficiency	Efficient vehicles		●		
	Reduced use of vehicles		●		
	Efficient buildings	●	●	●	
	Efficient baseload coal plants	●			
Decarbonization of power	Gas baseload power for coal baseload power	●			
	Capture CO_2 at baseload power plant	●			
	Nuclear power for coal power	●			
	Wind power for coal power	●			
	Photovoltaic power for coal power	●			
Decarbonization of fuel	Capture CO_2 at H_2 plant		●		
	Capture CO_2 at coal-to-synfuels plant		●		
	Wind H_2 in fuel-cell car for gasoline in hybrid car		●		
	Biomass fuel for fossil fuel		●		
Forests and agricultural soils	Reduced deforestation, plus reforestation, afforestation, and new plantations				●
	Conservation tillage				●

Gt=gigatons.
Source: Carbon Mitigation Initiative, Princeton University.

Furthermore, technology innovation should be understood in its broadest sense, encompassing any technology that cuts emissions, preserves the local environment, and increases resource efficiency. Emerging Asia has good reason to implement ideas from scratch as many of its factories, infrastructures, and buildings are yet to be built; and the market potential for deploying innovative technological systems is high. Infrastructure built today will remain for 20–50 years, and by implementing low-carbon green technology now Asia can avoid being locked in to high-carbon infrastructure for decades to come. Moreover, it has a chance to be a front-runner in low-carbon green innovation, to become the most energy- and resource-efficient region in the world. In so doing, it can strengthen its global competitive position. If implemented effectively, innovations for low-carbon technologies and green services will become a key driver of growth, competitiveness, and employment for emerging Asia.

Current policy debates on low-carbon green growth are oversimplified, largely overlooking the innovation factor. Technologies to mitigate climate change are treated as given or as emerging spontaneously, and can be transferred for free from where they are first introduced, ignoring the fact that tomorrow's portfolio of available technologies depends to a large degree on what policy choices are taken today. There is a danger in subsidizing the use of relatively inefficient technologies and postponing action to later years in the hope that new technologies will be freely transferred. Such approaches would lock in outmoded, high-carbon technologies in emerging Asia. To foster the development and deployment of currently available technologies, developing Asia has to strengthen its national innovation systems (Ramanathan 2012).

The institutions in advanced economies like Japan, the Republic of Korea, the US, and Germany will determine the speed of development and diffusion of the most advanced technologies. Firms from those countries are the main holders of intellectual property rights. According to optimistic assessments, however, there is enough competition within and across technologies to guarantee that developing Asia should be able to obtain licenses on reasonable terms (Barton 2007; Lee, Iliev, and Preston 2009). Mechanisms for transferring technologies to emerging Asian countries will be crucial to ensure they have a range of appropriate low-cost options at their disposal. A few developing countries of Asia, notably the PRC and India, hold a minority but growing proportion of patents, particularly in solar photovoltaic (PV) and wind technologies. Ethanol and biodiesel industries exist in several developing countries (e.g., Indonesia, Malaysia, Pakistan, and Thailand), indicating that this sector has low barriers to entry.

In any case, as most Asian developing countries will be second movers, there is a need to generate global institutional arrangements that create incentives to increase international cooperation and collaboration on research and development (R&D) in all areas relevant to low-carbon green growth and to accelerate the transfer and diffusion of those technologies. These should include a large component of open innovation systems and publically financed innovations. The model of the green revolution and the network of research institutions linked under the Consultative Group on International Agricultural Research could be replicated.

Table 1.4

World Market for Environmental Goods and Services Average Annual Rate of Growth, 2004–2010: High and Low Growth Estimates

	GDP Growth	Environmental Expenditures		Environmental Imports (import region)	
		High	Low	High	Low
Europe	2.5	5.4	2.1	6.5	3.0
North America	3.3	9.9	6.3	11.5	8.0
Asia	4.8	8.3	6.0	12.2	9.7
Rest of world	3.8	9.0	7.0	10.7	8.7
World as a whole	3.5	7.7	4.7	9.4	6.4

Source: German Institute for Economic Research (DIW Berlin 2009).

1.4.3 Trade and Investment Cooperation for Low-Carbon Green Growth

The nature of the inter-sectoral linkages also plays a critical role in disseminating new technologies. In this regard, liberalization of trade and investment rules will facilitate access to green technologies and services. One obvious way that trade policy might help in greening economies is by lowering tariff and non-tariff barriers to low-carbon goods such as wind turbines and efficient light bulbs, and services such as energy auditing and financing. The World Trade Organization (WTO) Doha Round has a mandate to liberalize trade in so-called environmental goods and services, though environmental goods in particular have yet to be definitively defined in those talks (WTO 2001; Cosbey 2010; Jha 2008; Stillwell 2007). Environmental goods and services offer tangible environmental benefits to importers (Table 1.4), particularly in developing countries where access to distributed renewable energy can be a key plank in addressing poverty, and where many governments are beginning to grapple in earnest with urban environmental issues such as air pollution (Steenblik 2006).

The German Institute for Economic Research (DIW Berlin 2009) estimates that the global market for low-carbon environmental goods and services will grow to $1.2 trillion–$1.9 trillion by 2020. Sharp (2009) reaches a far higher estimate even of the current market, using a rigorous bottom–up compilation of the sector, estimating its size in 2007–2008 to be $6 trillion, and noting major growth in the area of low-carbon goods and services and renewables.

This should be reflected in low barriers for developing countries' import and exports of PV cells, wind turbines, and biomass fuels, the biofuel being the area where more developing countries are active but where protectionism is high. Furthermore, aside from avoiding border carbon adjustments, which would operate in practice as an additional import tariff, any GHG emission targets set should be consumption- rather production-based, to avoid discriminating against production in developing Asia.

Much of this low-carbon technology market could also be pushed by regulatory demands in Asia's trading partners. The European Union (EU) Biofuels Directive, for example, mandates a 10% minimum share of transport fuels to be sustainably derived biofuels by 2020 (European Commission 2008).

That mandate is estimated to raise the demand for imports of biofuels to the EU market significantly, with imports of 9 megatons (Mt) by 2020 of bioethanol and 1.6 Mt of biodiesel, mainly from Asia (Banse and Grethe 2008).

A number of developing Asian firms have already gained significant market share in the low-carbon technology market. The PRC in 2009 exported over $10 billion worth of solar panels and cells, more than twice as much as the second biggest exporter and almost 80 times the value exported only 10 years earlier, when it was not even among the top five world exporters (UN Commodity Trade Statistics Database, 2011). India's Suzlon Energy is now a global power in supplying wind turbines, with a 6.4% share of the global market (BTM Consult 2009). PRC companies now rank in the top 10 for market share in wind power as well, though they are almost exclusively focused on meeting domestic demand (BTM Consult 2009). The sizable domestic markets of both the PRC and India have been springboards for export success, driven as in the European countries by ambitious domestic targets for renewable energy generation.

The question is whether these are special cases of trade and investment, since the PRC and India in many ways are not representative of other developing countries. Does their success have any relevance for the rest of Asia, in particular for the slow or modest growth aspiring countries? Low-carbon green goods and services are a heterogeneous group, and not all have the same demanding character. For example, Steenblik (2006) argues that biofuels, solar thermal, and geothermal energy are all less complex technologies in which less developed countries have either resources or existing expertise, or good chances of developing competitive export streams. The most relevant lesson from both the PRC and India is the importance of concerted support by governments in the drive to succeed in low-carbon green development, though the characteristics of that success will vary from country to country. Many countries in Asia use a judicious mix of government support and domestic targets to stimulate their respective green sectors.

There will probably be more economic opportunities for developing Asia as the new international climate change regime takes shape. At the Doha climate change conference in December 2012, the Kyoto Protocol, as the only existing and binding agreement under which developed countries commit to cutting GHGs, was amended so that a second commitment period would begin from 1 January 2013. The length of the second commitment period is 8 years (up to 31 December 2020). Countries that are taking on further commitments under the Kyoto Protocol have agreed to review these commitments at the latest by 2014, with a view to increasing their respective levels of ambition with regard to further cuts. However, backers of the Kyoto Protocol will dwindle from 2013 to a group including Australia, Norway, Switzerland, Ukraine, and the EU. Together, they will account for less than 15% of global GHG emissions. Mechanisms may also exist for sizable transfer payments to cover reduced emissions from deforestation and forest degradation (UN-REDD) and to reward NAMAs. It remains to be seen how broad a scope there will be for any of these mechanisms, and what levels of funding, but it is worth noting that NAMAs and REDD are essentially transfer payments to governments for taking certain low-carbon policy actions. The CDM, by creating incentives for private sector actions, may suffer less from that shortcoming, but is likely to be limited in scope because it operates on a project-by-project basis and since underlying demand from the EU's Emissions Trading System will probably be limited.

Other barriers to increased trade opportunities in low-carbon products and services, particularly for developing countries, are the different product energy performance standards, testing procedures, and labeling requirements for various export markets. Harmonizing these standards at a high level would be a huge boon for small and medium-sized enterprises (SMEs) in particular, for whom meeting different requirements in every country of export is very difficult. Harmonization could have enormous benefits in quickly disseminating energy-efficient low-carbon products at a lower cost.

1.4.4 Critical Role of Public–Private Partnerships in Low-Carbon Green Growth

Besides investments, the switch to low-carbon development requires large and interconnected actions across sectors such as energy, transport, agriculture, and urban development; and increased involvement of the private sector. Much of the resource extraction and depletion of resources in Asia has been the result of corporate activities (ABCSD 2005). Hence, low-carbon green growth policy should target private sector actors and should include measures such as subsidies and access to credit for producers to switch to low-carbon practices, as well as trade and technology policies to support the new entrepreneurial activities. Private sector companies have to operate in an intensely competitive environment, with imperatives to minimize costs and maximize profits in a short-term critical horizon. Governments have to establish frameworks for regulation, incentives, and disincentives, so that corporate practices are aligned to low-carbon green growth objectives.

The Stern Report (2007) called the climate change crisis the greatest market failure the world has ever seen. Thus, public–private partnerships (PPPs) are important.

Despite welcome progress in the UNFCCC hosted negotiations on climate change, a transfer of public funds likely will not be sufficient to meet the costs of moving to a low-emission growth path. Nor, in the short run at least, will the finance available from carbon markets or international offsets. This means that public finance mechanisms to leverage private finance on the scale required must be rapidly developed.

Most of the finance required will be for investment in new or improved infrastructure. This means public finance mechanisms must facilitate investment in productive capital with a long life span where costs can be amortized over the life of assets. The key therefore will be to link these public finance mechanisms to sources of private finance suitable for infrastructure development—sources of finance that can offer patient equity and long-term debt, giving time for cash flows from domestic and international sources to meet current capital costs.

Some institutions that manage institutional private capital such as pension funds, sovereign wealth funds, insurance companies, and endowments are currently less capital-constrained than many governments. If the terms and conditions of the public finance mechanisms are right, some of this private institutional capital could be mobilized on a large scale to help meet low carbon investment needs in developing economies. This sort of PPP Mode is evident in renewable energy sector projects, which could be replicated for other sectoral actions.

While some private institutional investment can be mobilized through public finance mechanisms for individual low carbon transport projects, dimensionally larger capital can be mobilized by establishing investment funds. To get equity investment to scale, multilateral and bilateral development finance institutions should scale up their support for low-carbon focused funds and develop risk mitigation and other products that support investments of such funds. This will attract institutional co-investment on a much larger scale.

There is also an increasing trend of creating market-based mechanisms such as emissions trading schemes and relying on markets, whereby companies can emit beyond their assigned limit by buying emissions certificates from other companies.

Besides their regulatory function, governments have also an important role in strategic policy making to reorient private sector activities onto a low-carbon development pathway. This includes both market and non-market measures, which may be different for each sector.

The Cost of Managing the Transition

There is a wide range of estimates of the macroeconomic costs of the very large shift in GHG emissions patterns that will be required to achieve atmospheric stabilization at 450–550 ppm. UNEP's recent Green Economy Report (UNEP 2011) estimates the investment needs for the green economy to be $1.05 trillion–$2.59 trillion per year (about 1.6%–4.0% of estimated world GDP in 2011). It then builds its scenarios for the impact of these investments on the basis of a figure of $1.3 trillion (2% of world GDP). Close to three-fifths of this sum would be invested in energy efficiency—particularly in buildings, industry, and transport—and in renewables; the remainder would be invested in agriculture, waste management, and forestry. The resources allocated to energy—slightly over 1% of global GDP—are broadly consistent with the Stern Review estimates of mitigation costs for emissions of 450 ppm CO_2 by 2050, and similar estimates by Oppenheim and Beinhocker (2009). The UN Department of Economic and Social Affairs (2009) estimated that the annual additional cost of mitigation strategies for the world would range from $400 billion to $1,200 billion and over $200 billion to almost $1,000 billion for developing countries, to limit CO_2 concentrations to 450 ppm. The World Bank (2012b) estimated that in developing countries mitigation would cost $140 billion–$175 billion over the next 20 years, with associated financing needs of $265 billion–$565 billion. A more comprehensive study by ADB (2009a), which included the cost of adapting to climate change in Southeast Asia, has far higher estimates (5.5%–6.2% of GDP). Over half of the estimated needs will come from developing Asia, particularly for energy. Compared with these needs, those of adaptation are much smaller: 0.04%–0.15% of world GDP in 2030, according to estimates by the UNFCCC (2010).

In this context, the commitment at COP 15 to mobilize $100 billion a year by 2020 through the Green Climate Fund to address the needs of developing countries looks encouraging, though at the low end of estimates of how much is needed, whereas the target of $30 billion as "fast start" financing to be delivered in 2010–2012 is clearly low. According to the Report of the Secretary-General's High-Level Advisory Group on Climate Change Financing (UN 2010), the $100 billion a year target is challenging but feasible, using a wide variety of sources of finance, but largely carbon taxes: (i) $30 billion from allocating 10% of carbon taxes raised in developed countries for transfers to developing countries, assuming a carbon price of $20–$25 per ton of CO_2 by 2020; (ii) $10 billion from carbon pricing on international transportation (aviation and shipping); (iii) $10 billion from redeployment of fossil fuel subsidies and some form of financial transaction tax; (iv) $10 billion in additional capital for multilateral development banks, which can generate $40 billion in gross financing with a $11 billion grant equivalent; (v) direct budget contributions; and (vi) $100 billion–$200 billion a year in gross private capital flows, generated by the above carbon price, or an estimated $10 billion–$20 billion as net flows. The fund could also generate $30 billion–$50 billion in carbon market flows, but there was debate as to whether these contributions should count to the $100 billion objective as they are really a substitute for the domestic mitigation commitments that firms have to meet in industrial countries.

For major emerging economies of Asia, incremental costs of mitigation are projected to rise from 0.8% to 1.4% in 2030, which is less when climate change induced losses are take into consideration under business-as-usual scenarios (Table 1.5). According to the IEA, total investments from 2005 to 2030 from producers and consumers can be reduced by $560 billion in relation to a business-as-usual case, but these savings result from consumers spending $2.4 trillion more in using more energy-efficient technologies while reducing energy supply investment by $3 trillion (IEA 2010b). Significant up-front investments may be needed. This creates a strong case for establishing a subsidy on energy-saving building standards and appliances financed by a tax on energy consumption.

The argument for an ecological tax reform, with a shift in the burden of taxation from economic goods (e.g., incomes) to public bads (e.g., emissions), has been broadly accepted, but progress is yet to be made implementing such reforms. An important aspect of tax shifting programs implemented in several European countries is the principle of revenue neutrality, meaning the increase in the tax revenues generated by eco-taxes is offset by a reduction in other taxes or charges. Changing the tax structure in Asia to achieve the financing needs of the low-carbon transition is also feasible.

A number of market-based approaches are possible, including economy-wide cap-and-trade systems (Ward 2008). Each approach creates a carbon price within the economy, either explicitly through an allowance price or implicitly through the incremental cost of policy requirements (OECD 2010). On the one hand, stronger use of economic instruments such as a carbon tax at both regional and national level could create the market dynamics that bring about more radical technological shifts, as with the EU Emissions Trading System. On the other hand, low-carbon investments in Asia could lead to substantial job creation. Using eco-taxes on material and energy inputs could help to reduce labor taxes, leading to increased employment (International Labour Organization 2009). Well-designed carbon tax policies and green labor policies can contribute to realizing the "double dividend" of emissions reductions and economic growth. Lessons learned from European experiences, and bilateral and multilateral official development assistance (ODA) activities on integrated adaptation and mitigation financing, will be important in supporting national and regional level financing mechanisms for low-carbon development.

Financing low-carbon development through the private sector is also feasible for Asia, which could achieve the targets without significant loss of economic growth and public spending. The CDM has provided valuable experience in mobilizing capital for investments in low-emission technologies in developing countries. However, it is unlikely to be a complete answer. As commercial investments are driven by risk and return, the level and directions of investments are determined by both long-term financial viability and the degree of regulatory certainty. At present, weak regulatory frameworks and the absence of positive incentives limit the flow of private capital from institutional investors to low-carbon green investment options. Judging by the success of infrastructure funds for energy and transport projects, tax incentives to climate change fund related bonds could also be feasible.

Table 1.5

Cost of Achieving 450 Parts per Million CO_2 by 2050

	Billion tons /year						Cumulative Investment		Cumulative low-carbon Investment	Incremental Investment	
Country/Region	1990	2007	2020 (ref)	2020 (450 ppm)	2030 (ref)	2030 (450 ppm)	2010–20 ($billion)	2020–30	2010–30 ($billion)	2020 (as % of GDP)	2030
● World	20.9	28.8	34.5	30.7	40.2	26.4	2,400	8,100	6,600	0.5	1.1
● PRC	2.2	6.1	9.6	8.4	11.6	7.1	400	1,700	1,500	0.8	1.5
● US	4.8	5.7	5.5	4.7	5.5	3.2	520	1,500	1,100	0.5	1.0
● EU	4.0	3.9	3.6	3.1	3.5	2.3	500	1,100	1,300	0.3	0.6
● Russian Fed.	2.2	1.6	1.7	1.6	1.9	1.3	18	180	220	0.3	1.0
● India	0.6	1.3	2.2	1.9	3.4	2.2	100	500	550	0.9	1.4
● Others [a]	3.5	5.0	6.7	6.1	9.1	6.4	400	1,500	1,450	0.6	1.2

Russian Fed. = Russian Federation.

Notes: Emissions are energy-related; ref.; reference/business-as-usual; Renewables (incl. hydro, wind), nuclear and CCS.
[a] Other Developing Countries: including India but excluding the PRC, Brazil, South Africa, and the Middle East.

Source: World Energy Outlook (2009).

A sound institutional and regulatory framework, including a predictable long-term price on emissions, would be an important driver guiding capital market formation and overcoming premium costs.

This has major implication for the design of financing facilities to support developing Asia's efforts to build a low-carbon green economy. Priority should be given to financing programs that are in line with national priorities, capacities, and efforts. Another area may be mechanisms that facilitate the leveraging of domestic financing to overcome the short-term capital mobilization by private sector. One possible way would be to use the capitalization of multilateral development banks to expand considerably their bond issuance and lending in the domestic currencies of the developing countries, and to support domestic financial development in these countries, particularly the efforts of domestic development banks.

1.5 Measuring Asia's Progress in Tackling Climate Change and Accelerating Green Growth

1.5.1 Overview of this Book

This book is based on the hypothesis that low-carbon green growth is an imperative, feasible, and attractive option for developing Asia. In a region heavily dependent on imported resources and energy, the emerging economies of Asia are already embarking on the application of a new development paradigm that brings competitiveness to its industries and serves the growing green technology markets. How close are the fast growing emerging economies of Asia to turning their aspirations of low-carbon growth into a reality? What national and sectoral experiences currently exist? What policies and institutional and financial factors currently accelerate a shift toward resource-efficient green growth? What is the potential for technology diffusion, financing, and regional cooperation to become drivers for future economic growth? The book aims to answer these questions, reviewing the low-carbon green policy initiatives taken by Asian countries at national, sectoral, and local level; and assessing the achievements made while identifying the gaps and examining new opportunities for low-carbon green growth. Building on this through analysis, the book presents key conclusions and recommendations for policy makers in the region.

What makes this book so interesting and worthwhile for policy makers? First and foremost, the book takes a practical approach to low-carbon green growth, as applicable to emerging Asia. It aims to include contributions that address the practical implications of emission reduction policies from an Asian perspective and the various ways to incorporate the concept in day-to-day policy making. Chapter 2 discusses low-carbon green growth as integral to an inclusive and sustainable development agenda. By providing a framework that will help governments to track the results of their policies and public investments, it develops a set of testable propositions to be assessed in the following chapters. This is particularly important for the countries that are in the early stages of low-carbon green growth, and currently designing national, subnational, and sector level actions.

Second, this book assesses, at an Asia regional level and with considerable depth, a wide range of current policies relevant for climate stabilization. Chapter 3 carries out an empirical analysis of the countrywide actions to reduce GHG emissions, focusing on key economic sectors such as energy supply, energy efficiency, transport, waste management, and agricultural land use. This is crucial, as these sectors will determine the overall trend in emissions reductions and whether reducing climate impacts can be achieved while increasing people's well-being. Many of the models of policy reforms and sectoral case studies exemplified in this chapter are potentially of global importance as they are replicable and scalable. This section also includes a critical evaluation of the organizational structure, pledges and mandates, budgets, human resources, and technical skills that are essential for implementing such measures. As emerging economies are adopting the new low-carbon development paradigm, it becomes necessary to consider the policy lessons and public–private partnership models designed and implemented in the advanced economies of Asia. This is also covered in Chapter 3.

Figure 1.7

Analytical Methods and Structure of the Book

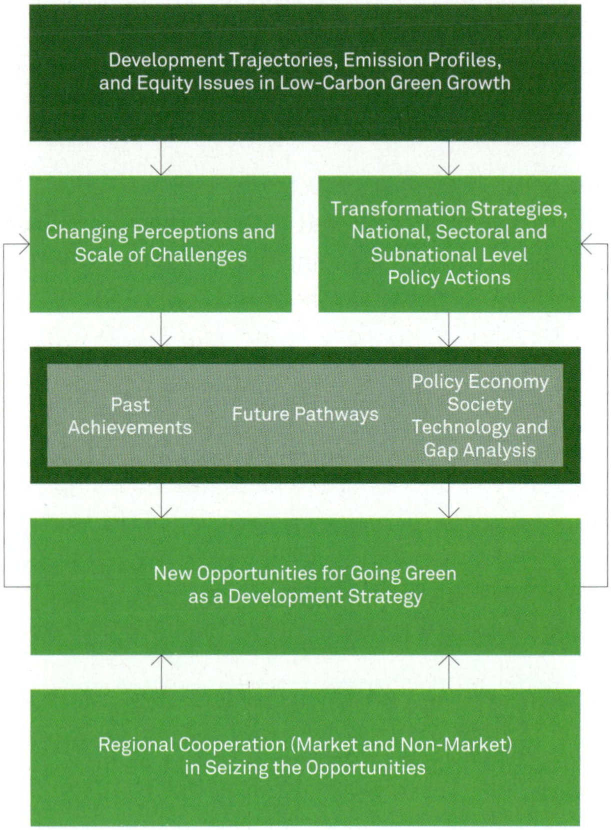

Source: ADB–ADBI study team.

Chapter 4 of the book presents the most challenging aspects of incorporating a low-carbon development process in Asia, employing a socioeconomic perspective. It compares the lessons learned from the business-as-usual development scenario and tries to debunk several myths and misconceptions related to the social impacts of low-carbon green development, providing practical guidance to policy makers on what policy interventions will unlock the potential of co-benefits and productive employment. It integrates low-carbon choices into broad development strategies and focuses on empirical analysis of the impacts and implications of low-carbon choices on employment and social inclusion. In doing so, it gives some guidance about the plausibility of recent pledges made by Asian governments to reduce GHG emissions while maintaining high levels of economic growth and employment. This chapter further analyzes how innovation systems are to be developed and strengthened for technology and institutional development to promote synergies of low-carbon, green, and inclusive measures.

The fifth chapter focuses on how to seize opportunities that lie across national boundaries—both market-based opportunities such as trade and investment flows in low-carbon green products and services, and nonmarket opportunities for regional collective action (joint research, finance mobilization, policy networking, and knowledge sharing). It emphasizes the need for a system of MRV as a policy management tool for understanding the impact of these strategies. The strategies must be embedded comprehensively in the economic policies, regulations, and new investment programs of any country. They cannot be an afterthought or a half-baked effort, and must go hand in hand with the national development strategy.

The sixth chapter summarizes the key policy messages, distilling lessons and insights from what has been done to date and what could be done in the future, including picking the "low-hanging fruits"—the easiest options for decarbonization—over the next 10 years, especially highlighting those recommended in Chapters 3, 4, and 5. It also identifies further areas for policy studies.

1.5.2
Asia's efforts toward Low-Carbon Green Growth

This book collects contributions on low-carbon green growth in its more operative and applied sense. The task for Asia and the goal of the book is to disseminate the actions of some Asian countries to other developing nations, by learning and sharing their experiences and lessons. Figure 1.7 illustrates the analytical framework used and the structure of the book.

Many countries have taken steps to reduce carbon intensity by adopting technology-based and fiscal policies (Figure 1.8). The PRC's 2010 renewable energy law is one of the exemplary efforts. Managed by the State Council, it promotes the establishment of performance standards for the power sector, creating a renewable energy market for wind, solar, hydro, biomass, and geothermal energy. New related industries are promoted, with banks offering preferential loans with interest subsidies to energy efficiency projects. The PRC leads the world in renewable energy investment, India ranks 10th globally in clean energy investment, and Indonesia had the 4th largest growth in this area from 2005 to 2010. Whether for export or to meet domestic expansion, growth in the renewable energy sector presents an important stimulus for domestic manufacturing and economic growth more generally. India's mandatory energy efficiency trading scheme of perform, achieve and trade (PAT), covering eight sectors for 54% of India's industrial energy consumption, is replicable in other countries (Hongo 2012). Capital subsidies, sales incentives, and reimbursement of fees for solar thermal projects as well as automatic approval for foreign direct investments are part of India's rural clean energy development program. Policies being taken across countries in Asia and the Pacific, which are being used to promote low-carbon energy transition, are shown in Table 1.6.

As a large country with huge tracts of carbon-absorbing forests, Indonesia is making efforts to cut carbon emissions by 26% from business as usual by 2020. This is creating employment opportunities in isolated regions. While the scope for REDD as a new global strategy is still being defined, Indonesia and the Philippines are undertaking actions in the forest sector without any internationally binding obligation driving them. Forest-based mitigation policies are being achieved in three ways: (i) through the maintenance of existing forests, (ii) through the restoration of lost carbon stocks from degraded or cleared forest, (iii) and through the creation of new forest areas. Malaysia, too, has implemented policies to shift the economy structurally from polluting energy-intensive industries. Thailand is the first country among the emerging economies to develop carbon labels; these help its economy move toward low-carbon consumption patterns without retarding economic growth.

Capitalizing on the latecomer advantage, countries like Viet Nam are taking initiatives in areas such as public transport, green buildings, adoption of energy saving equipment, and switching to natural gas and smart power plants. To strike a balance between short-term economic needs and the long-term environmental imperative, the emerging Asian economies have begun to put in place policy frameworks for financial and regulatory incentives and to build institutional capabilities for low-carbon green growth in the long term. Japan, the Republic of Korea, and Singapore's success in following green sectoral policies owes much to their planning capabilities—capacities that have evolved under PPPs, which were able to take a long-term perspective. These policy experiences are replicable and can be scaled up.

Table 1.6

Policies that Promote Low-Carbon Energy Transitions in Selected Countries of Asia

	Feed-in Tariff	Renewable Portfolio Standards	Capital subsidies, grants, rebates	Tax credits	Tax reduction	Tradable renewable energy certificates	Public investment loans, or refinancing	Public compe-titive bidding
Australia	[a]	●	●			●	●	
PRC	●	●	●	●	●		●	●
India	[a]	[a]	●	●	●	●	●	
Indonesia	●			●	●			
Japan	●	●	●	●		●	●	
Republic of Korea	●		●	●	●		●	
Malaysia							●	
Philippines	●	●	●	●	●		●	●
Thailand	●				●		●	

[a] Policies have not been implemented at national level.

Source: Adapted from REN21 (2011).

Figure 1.8

CO_2 Intensity of Gross Domestic Product

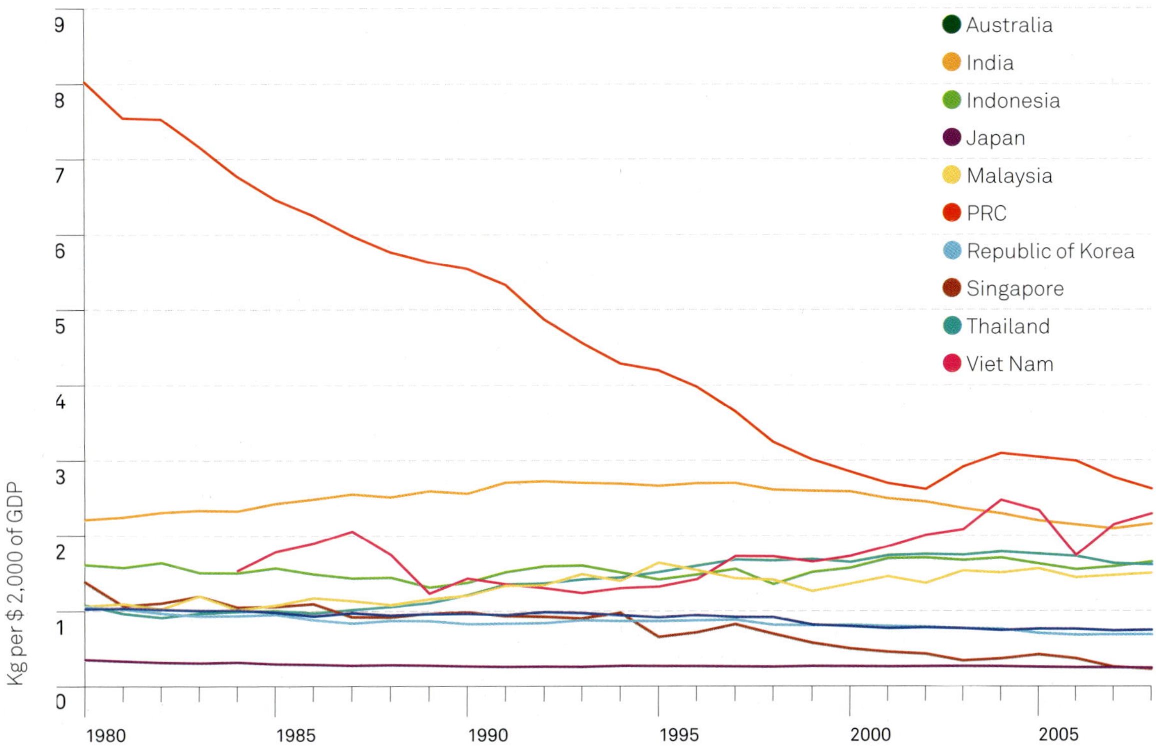

Source: World Development Indicators (2012).
http://data.worldbank.org/data-catalog/world-development-indicators
(accessed December 2012).

[redacted]

1.6 Challenges of Low-Carbon Green Growth in the Context of Social Inclusion and Regional Cooperation

Figure 1.9

Socio-Economy of Low-Carbon Green Intervention

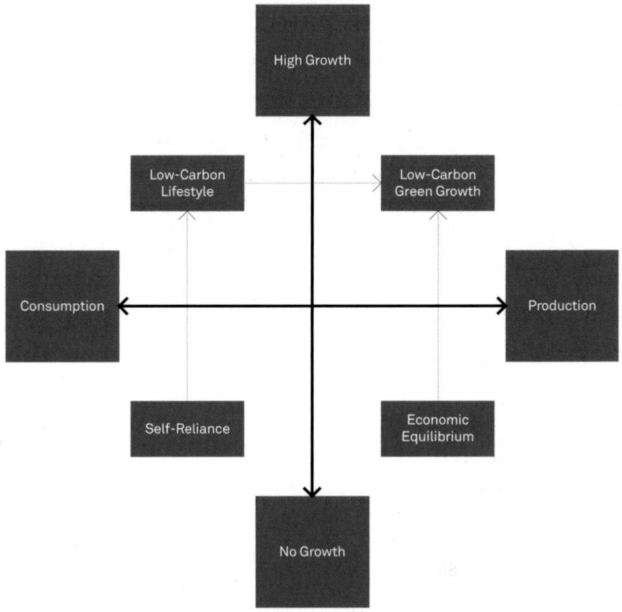

Source: ADB–ADBI study team.

It is becoming clear that fast growing converging economies such as the PRC, India, and Indonesia, along with their counterparts in Latin America and Africa, will drive the future of global economic growth. Estimates by the Asia 2050 study (Kohli, Sharma, and Sood 2011) indicate that about half or more of the purchasing power of the global economy will stem from developing countries. The current developmental landscape of emerging Asia suggests that two trends are at work in driving the patterns of growth. On the one hand, as countries get richer, there is demand for a greater variety of goods, many of which may be produced domestically; so there is a force toward sectoral diversification. On the other hand, countries only become richer if they specialize in what they do best, based on their comparative advantage and competitiveness. Low-carbon green growth can be thought of in terms of changes in production such as changes in supply or economic growth and consumption such as demand, consumption patterns or lifestyles. Figure 1.9 give four contrasting interpretations , resulting from where policy makers place themselves on two different dimensions of response: their approach to growth; and their focus on production or consumption-related policy measures.

The first two types of growth, green growth and lifestyle, assume that economic growth is compatible with significant reductions in carbon emissions. The latter two, self-reliance and economic equilibrium, assume it is not. Green growth and equilibrium economy approaches both put emphasis on reducing carbon emissions through technological changes (from inefficient to more efficient, from polluting to less polluting) or structural changes taking place in the economy. For example, in the PRC, many inefficient old coal-fired power plants are being replaced with more efficient, less polluting new plants; and in India, the service economy has been rapidly growing over recent years, while the share of agriculture value added has declined.

The green lifestyle and self-reliance approaches focus on reducing demand through lifestyle and behavioral changes as well as through sectoral and technological changes. Using public transport instead of travelling by car, switching to green electricity instead of fossil fuel powered electricity and buying local products instead of imported products. This suggests that new strategies that favor specialization must be adapted at some point by Asia's developing countries, if they are to grow their economies and avoid lock in.

While much policy attention has been given to making production patterns and systems less carbon-intensive, less focus has been placed on changing consumption patterns, which often drive the pace of production and greatly influence the composition of goods and services produced. In addition, the poor, in urban and rural areas, still do not have access to basics, so an improvement in the pattern of income distribution is required if low-carbon development objectives are fully met at national, subnational, and sector levels. Regulations and tax policies play a key role in addressing the failure of market prices to reflect real environmental values. However, this should be done in a manner that does not penalize the poor, especially when the products and services concerned are essentials.

For a long time, the debate on sustainable development policy has focused on the cost-effectiveness of potential measures and policies. This is particularly true when low-carbon policies are framed in terms of short-term policy targets, as policy makers are primarily interested in the current impact of policies on their economies while benefits will occur in the long term and thus fall beyond the current policy horizon. The issue of financing low-carbon green growth is not restricted to ODA or the transfer of funds through channels such as the Green Climate Fund, but also to mobilizing private sector resources. It is also linked to other issues in the global economy that greatly influence the amount and volatility of the flow of financial resources to developing Asia. These issues include external debt, trade terms, commodity and fossil fuel prices, volatility of private funds, and reforms of the international monetary and financial system.

Asia's current policy experiences and aspirations for tackling climate change through multi-sectoral, multi-level approaches demonstrate that benefits can occur in the short term, too. Capacity limitations critically restrict the degree to which countries can take action. There is a need to strengthen capacity at local level, and strengthen the coordination and sharing of knowledge on mitigation policies. Through this approach, Asian countries can help the global community to achieve its climate change targets.

Obstacles to the design and implementation of emissions reduction policies in Asia include the lack of a coherent regional strategy for the diffusion of proven technologies across the region, difficulties in obtaining international financing for innovative technologies, and building effective monitoring systems. Asia's experiences in designing and executing low-carbon policies also suggest policy guidelines suitable for other emerging economies around the world. Current economic structures should be adapted to place greater emphasis on increasing the productivity of all resources, above all energy resources, by investing heavily in new technologies, human capital, and local wisdom. Not all will be clear winners; some sectors will feel the pain of transition, and countries that specialize in those sectors will be challenged accordingly. Low-carbon green growth policies must be linked with sector level adjustments, labor force development, and establishing social safety nets. These structures could generate a certain level of welfare and income.

Indeed, even the policies to address these challenges are entirely new; many are in wide use, though not yet wide enough.

There is a heightened urgency for regional cooperation, and a stronger argument for immediate new policy actions to avoid countries being locked in to high-carbon infrastructure that could be built in the next few years but will be around for decades (Figure 1.9). Given the urgency of the multiple crises facing us—climate change, economic slowdown, and increasing inequality—

it is in our common interest that low-carbon green development be widely achieved. It is urgent, for example, for emerging Asia to become an incubator for globally competitive firms and adopters of new technologies. It is also urgent that there be lower barriers to trade in low-carbon goods and services, even if that means liberalizing trade in co-benefit technologies. It is also urgent that new targets and standards be used fairly but effectively. This book finds that regional cooperation is an important driver for structural change that will ensure all countries grow and change in ways that have benefits both nationally and globally.

Chapter 2

The Asian Renaissance and Low-Carbon Green Growth: Changing Perceptions and the Scale of the Challenges

Chapter 2

The Asian Renaissance and Low-Carbon Green Growth: Changing Perceptions and the Scale of the Challenges

2.1
Asian Renaissance and Economic Growth

Emerging and developing economies of Asia are facing challenges quite different from those of advanced economies. Kohli, Sharma, and Sood (2011) suggest that with over half of the world's population residing in Asia and the Pacific, it is in the region's interest to implement early and aggressive action on climate change—socially, economically, and politically. Contrary to some political opinion, Asia does not need to tackle climate change because the West is asking, but because it is in its own interest to do so. This chapter discusses the evolving and converging perspectives on low-carbon green growth as integral to inclusive and sustainable development in Asia.

2.1.1
Unfolding of Renaissance

The economic landscape of Asia has transformed since the 1960s. The eradication of mass poverty was the overarching objective of economic development that drove policy makers in most developing countries of Asia when they achieved political independence in the 1940s. Most of the countries in the region have achieved sustained rapid economic growth, some countries at about 10% a year since the 1980s. In the emerging economies of Asia, this economic growth lifted as many as 500 million people out of poverty. Asia and the Pacific as a whole achieved an increase in gross domestic product (GDP) of 75% from 1992 to 2010. The number of people in absolute poverty[1] dropped from 46% in 1990 to 27% in 2005 and is heading toward 15% by 2015. Life expectancy has leapt ahead, from an average age of 40 to just over 70 over the last 50 years, as health has improved and some killer diseases such as tuberculosis have been brought under control (World Bank 2009). Modern machinery has replaced manual labor in agriculture in most of the countries. Individuals are richer, and the demand for consumer durable goods is growing.

Many factors effected this change: openness to foreign trade, a rising flow of foreign direct investment, steady growth in world markets, a sharp decline in transport costs, increased intra-regional trade, and the spread of information and communication technology (Srinavasan 2000; Azis 2001; Kawai and Wignaraja 2011). In many countries, the spark came in the form of sectoral reforms, accelerated absorption of technology and knowledge, and pragmatic market polices implemented gradually (Sachs 2011). During the recent global financial crisis, Asia's continued growth was a significant stabilizing force that partly counterbalanced the impact on global economic activity of the downturn in the advanced economies of Europe and the United States (US).

Under business-as-usual conditions, by 2030, the emerging economies of the Association of Southeast Asian Nations (ASEAN), India, and the People's Republic of China (PRC) are poised to quadruple their economic output and emerge decisively from a history of poverty. Asian Development Bank (ADB) projections suggest that by 2030, the region will increase its share to nearly 40% of world gross domestic product (GDP) in purchasing power parity terms (Table 2.1). The region's rise will be led by the giant economies of the PRC and India, but the projections suggest that other Asian economies, benefiting increasingly from a unified market and production base, will also participate in this rapid progress.

—

1 A level of poverty at which the minimum standard of living – e.g., nutrition, health, and shelter cannot be met. People in that condition earn less than $2 a day (World Bank 2012).

Table 2.1

Projections of Gross Domestic Product Growth of Asian Economies, 2030 (at 2010 constant prices)

Country/Region	2010 Population (million)	2010 GDP ($ billion)	2010 World share (%)	2010 GDP/capita ($)	2030 Population (million)	2030 GDP ($ billion)	2030 World share (%)	2030 GDP/capita ($)	GDP growth 2010–2030 (%)
ASEAN	592	1,852	2.98	3,127	704	5,587	4.31	7,936	5.52
Brunei Darussalam	0.4	11	0.02	26,771	0.5	22	0.02	42,610	3.67
Cambodia	14	11	0.02	795	17	55	0.04	3,152	7.91
Indonesia	240	707	1.14	2,946	280	2,116	1.63	7,566	5.48
Lao PDR	6	7	0.01	1,177	8	34	0.03	4,386	7.70
Malaysia	28	238	0.38	8,373	37	695	0.54	18,642	5.36
Myanmar	48	45	0.07	946	54	260	0.20	4,791	8.73
Philippines	93	200	0.32	2,140	126	765	0.59	6,058	6.72
Singapore	5	209	0.34	41,044	6	365	0.28	61,097	2.80
Thailand	69	319	0.51	4,608	73	823	0.64	11,220	4.74
Viet Nam	88	106	0.17	1,211	101	452	0.35	4,449	7.23
PRC	1,341	5,927	9.54	4,418	1,393	24,477	18.89	17,571	7.09
India	1,225	1,727	2.78	1,410	1,523	7,706	5.95	5,058	7.48
Japan	127	5,459	8.79	43,141	120	6,755	5.21	56,189	1.07
Republic of Korea	48	1,014	1.63	21,055	50	1,976	1.52	39,247	3.33
Taipei,China	23	430	0.69	18,683	23	886	0.68	38,579	3.62
Rest of Asia	503	929	1.50	1,846	653	3,350	2.59	5,128	6.41
US	310	14,587	23.48	46,996	362	22,981	17.74	63,539	2.27
Europe	498	16,194	26.07	32,492	514	24,239	18.71	47,178	2.02
LAC	537	4,514	7.27	8,404	640	11,025	8.51	17,238	4.47
MENA	323	2,140	3.44	6,628	414	5,416	4.18	13,080	4.64
Sub-Saharan Africa	741	1,005	1.62	1,355	1,151	3,519	2.72	3,058	6.27
Rest of the World	372	6,346	10.22	17,071	386	11,631	8.98	30,161	3.03
World	6,641	62,124	100	9,355	7,933	129,547	100	16,331	3.67

ASEAN: Association of Southeast Asian Nations;
Europe: member countries of the European Union (except Slovenia where data is not available);
Lao PDR: Lao People's Democratic Republic;
LAC: Latin America and Caribbean;
MENA: Middle East and North Africa.
Notes: GDP and GDP/capita in 2010 constant prices.

Sources: Economic Research Department (ERD); ADB (2011);
World Development Indicators Online database;
World Economic Outlook database (April 2012);
UN World Population Prospects: The 2010 Revision.

2.1.2 Limits to Growth

Economic growth is an important dimension of and means to human development. If current levels of economic growth continue, by 2030 extreme poverty in the region could be eliminated, driving down the number of people spending less than $1.25 per day (in 2005 purchasing power parity prices) from about 600 million to just tens of millions. By 2030, the middle classes of developing Asian economies—defined as people with expenditures of $2–$20 per day—would grow from an estimated 2.1 billion people in 2012 to over 2.5 billion. Most dramatically, the number of people now considered modestly affluent—those who spend more than $20 per day—would grow from about 50 million to over 1 billion.

To be sustainable in the long term, growth must be accompanied by the conservation of ecosystem services and greater social coherence. These are necessary conditions for the Asian renaissance to be transformed into an Asian century (Salim 2012). This is because past economic achievement was not well distributed; it was accompanied by an increase in inequality, both among countries and within them. Inequality widened in 11 of the 25 economies with comparable data, including the three most populous countries and drivers of the region's rapid growth—the PRC, India, and Indonesia. From the early 1990s to the late 2000s, the Gini coefficient, a common measure of inequality, worsened from 32 to 43 in the PRC, from 33 to 37 in India, and from 29 to 39 in Indonesia. Treating developing Asia as a single unit, its Gini coefficient rose from 39 to 46 during that period. As a result, about 300 million people are without basic sanitation and electricity services, about 26 million children are undernourished, and 67 million people lack access to primary school —while the population is still growing (Figure 2.1).

The vast majority of Asian populations can share the future gains of economic growth provided that governments act to make growth inclusive. The steps required will stimulate growth: connecting lagging areas to centers of prosperity; providing health, education, and energy services to develop skills and improve productivity; and creating safety nets to make people more secure. In doing so, governments will also build essential political support for growth-oriented policies.

Figure 2.1

Access to Basic Needs in 2010

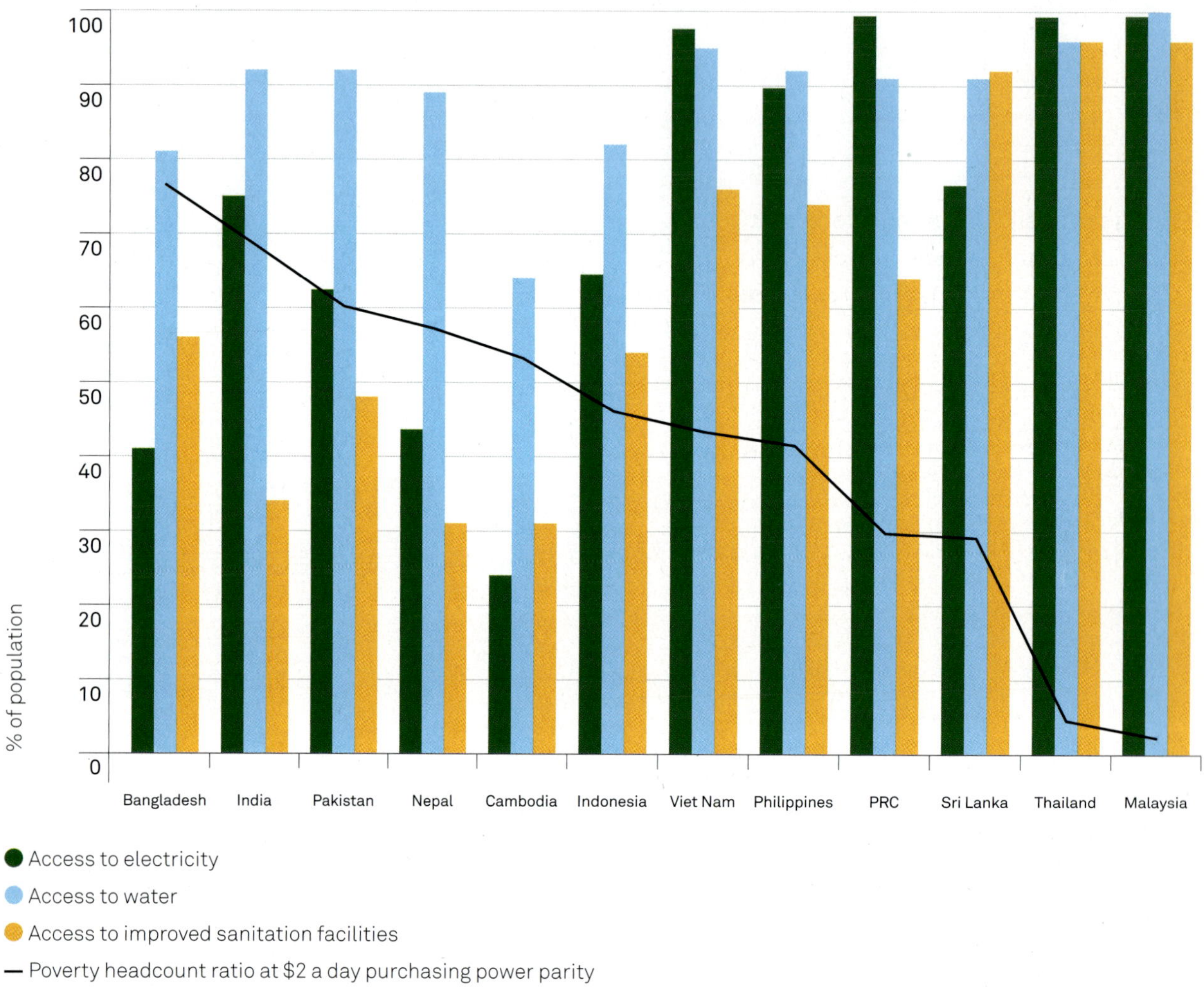

Sources:
Derived from World Energy Outlook (2011); World Development Indicators (2011). http://data.worldbank.org/data-catalog/world-development-indicators (accessed December 2012); UNDP: ADB–ADBI study team.

2.2
From Growth to Green Growth

2.2.1
Externalities of Asian Economic Renaissance

Asia's economic renaissance is placing considerable stress on its ecosystems—land, air, and water—and the availability of natural resources. Development economists have for years been concerned that unsustainable levels of consumption and degradation of natural resources have accompanied economic growth in the region. Additionally, the global climate crisis is one of the most daunting crises precipitated by past economic growth (fuelled by fossil fuels) and will be aggravated by future growth, if it too is reliant on fossil fuels. Studies show that Asia and the Pacific is already being affected by climate change—including increasing temperatures and precipitation, sea level changes, and extreme weather events—and recent climate events in the region have been drastic. Asia will be one of the regions most affected by climate change. The cost of climate change to major Asian countries each year could be equivalent to a loss of 6.7% of combined GDP by 2100, more than twice the world average (ADB 2009a). Therefore addressing climate change is a pressing need for Asia, and a matter of self-interest. Because of rapid economic expansion, both Asia's total annual and per capita emissions are increasing at a high rate (Figure 2.2). Today, four of the 10 countries in the world with the highest carbon dioxide (CO_2) emissions from fossil-fuel use are located in Asia: the PRC (first), India (fourth), Japan (fifth), and the Republic of Korea (seventh). These rankings do not include the CO_2 emissions from the burning of firewood and other biomass,

Figure 2.2
Unfolding of Renaissance – CO_2 Emissions and Gross Domestic Product

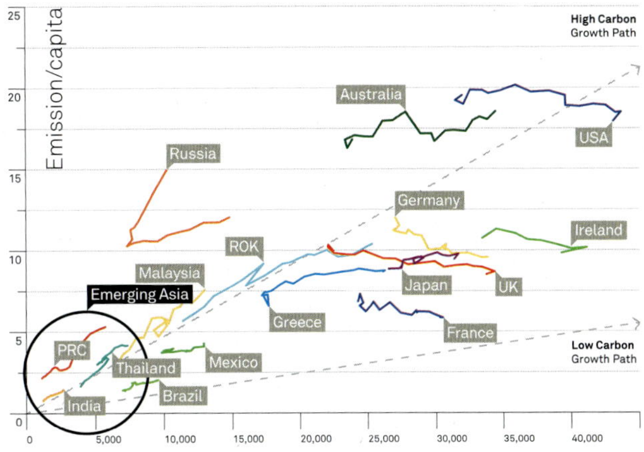

Sources: World Development Indicators (2012). http://data.worldbank.org/data-catalog/world-development-indicators (accessed December 2012); ADB–ADBI study team.

which are large sources of energy in many Asian countries. Further, changes in land use, particularly as forests are exploited for agriculture and urban development, represent significant contributors to CO_2 emissions in many of the larger Asian countries such as Indonesia and the Philippines.

Energy is needed for growth. At present, carbon intensity is closely correlated to energy intensity. Asia's total primary energy demand as well as CO_2 emissions are likely to continue to increase significantly until 2030 (Figure 2.3). The PRC will lead with a near fivefold increase in primary energy demand, from 872 megatons of oil equivalent (Mtoe) in 1990 to 4,320 Mtoe in 2030 and a rise of about six times in CO_2 emissions from 2,244 megatons (MT) in 1990 to 13,290 MT in 2030. India's primary energy demand will increase almost fourfold from 318 Mtoe in 1990 to 1,204 Mtoe in 2030 and CO_2 emissions are also likely to increase by almost five times from 589 Mt in 1990 to 2,856 MT in 2030.

One of the factors behind Asia's economic growth has been that carbon-intensive manufacturing has moved from other countries to Asia, where it is cheaper. This has delivered a huge economic benefit for Asian economies but it has contributed to the large increases in emissions.

This trend will continue and emissions are also likely to increase, though at a lower rate in ASEAN than those of the PRC and India (Table 2.2).

The assumptions made in Matsuoka et al. (2012) are that countries will be able to achieve the reduction targets by 2020 in accordance with their target submissions to the United Nations Framework Convention on Climate Change (UNFCCC) following the Copenhagen Accord (Table 2.3). After 2020, it is assumed that the countries aim to reduce their emissions by the amount of emissions allocated according to globally agreed allocation schemes that will halve global emissions by 2050.

Considering per capita emissions ratios among the Asian countries, Japan and the Republic of Korea are expected to make the most reductions. They are followed by Malaysia, the PRC, and Thailand. These are very severe reduction requirements for emerging Asian countries as well as developed countries in the region like Japan and the Republic of Korea.

What can be done to combine the need for growth in Asia with emission reduction objectives? This can be achieved with growth that is efficient in its use of energy and natural resources, green in that it minimizes emissions, inclusive in that it brings co-benefits to society, and resilient in that it avoids locking economies into unsustainable patterns of high-carbon growth.

2.2.2
Low-Carbon Green Growth

Sustainable development is economic growth that meets the needs of the present without compromising the ability of future generations to meet their own needs. Sustainable development requires countries to make simultaneous progress in their economy, environment, and society. Through sustainable development, people will be able to live in an inclusive and equal, protected and stable, economically advancing society while the environment on which all our wealth depends would be protected and well-maintained.

A new global development paradigm is imperative—before it is too late to turn things around, and generate opportunities out of our current challenges and crises. If we invest today in high-carbon infrastructure—energy generation, transport systems, or industrial manufacturing plants—we will put a low-carbon future in reach within a few years, because this infrastructure will continue to be used for decades. Thus, the investments of the next few years are crucial. The next section focuses on how low-carbon green growth offers a way out of this high-carbon, unsustainable future.

According to the Global Green Growth Institute (GGGI), "green growth is the new revolutionary development paradigm that sustains economic growth while at the same time ensuring climatic and environmental sustainability. It focuses on addressing the root causes of these challenges while ensuring the creation of the necessary channels for resource distribution and access to basic commodities for the impoverished. Under this new paradigm, new ideas, transformational innovations and state-of-the-art technology will become the major drivers for growth."

Figure 2.3

Key Indicators of Carbon Emissions in Asia and the Pacific, 1980–2008

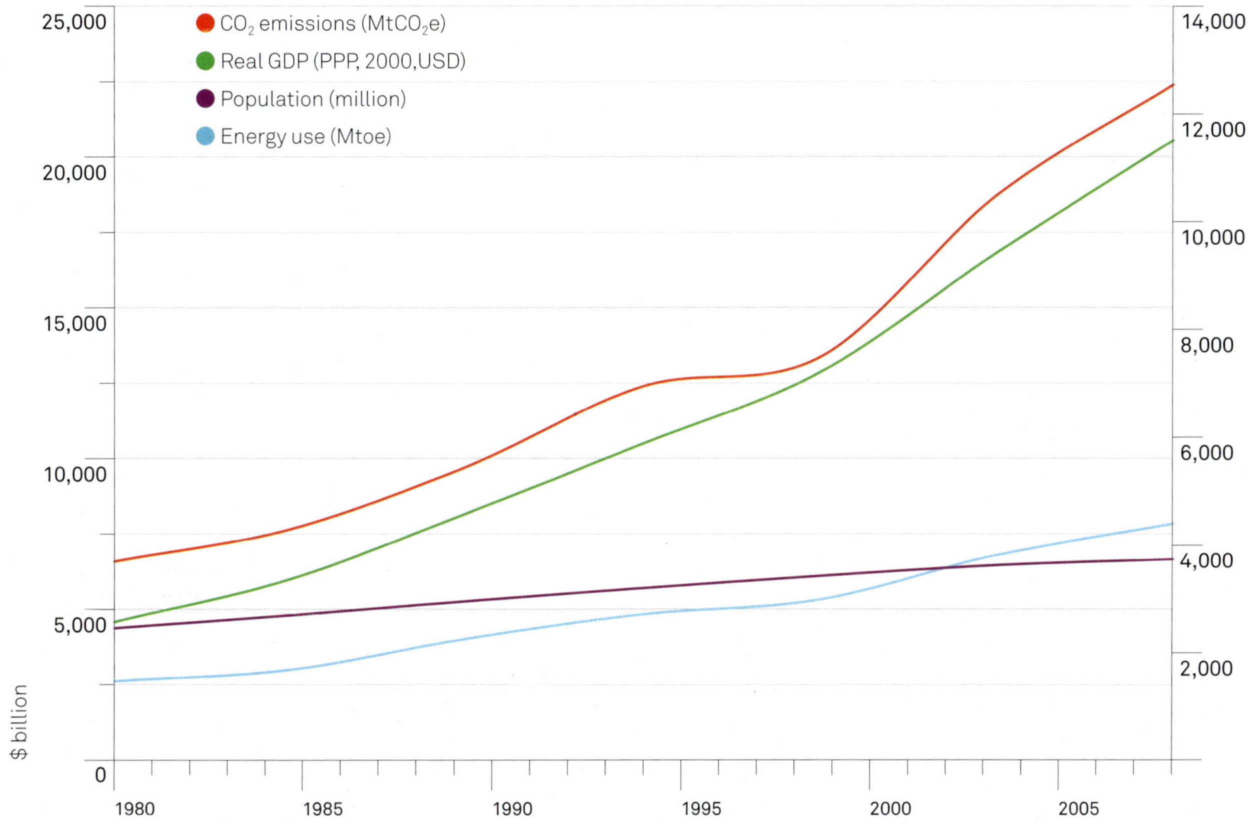

Notes: Applied countries include Australia; Bangladesh; Bhutan; Brunei Darussalam; Cambodia; Hong Kong, China; India; Indonesia; Japan; Kazakhstan; Lao PDR; Malaysia; Mongolia; Myanmar; Nepal; New Zealand; Pakistan; Papua New Guinea; Philippines; People's Republic of China (PRC); Republic of Korea; Singapore; Sri Lanka; Tajikistan; Thailand; Uzbekistan; and Viet Nam.

Sources: Climate Analysis Indicators Tool (CAIT) Version 9.0 by the World Resource Institute, 2011 (accessed March 2012) and World Development Indicators (WDI) & Global Development Funds (GDF) by the World Bank, April 2012 (accessed April 2012).

Table 2.2

Past and Projected Energy Demand (Reference Scenario) and CO_2 Emissions

	Primary energy demand (Mtoe)			CO_2 emissions (Mt CO_2 eq.)		
	1990	2007	2030	1990	2007	2030
ASEAN	243	513	988	361	1,013	2,079
PRC	872	1,970	4,320	2,244	6,071	13,290
India	318	595	1,204	589	1,327	2,856

Sources: 1990 and 2007 data from Fan (2011), 2030 data from ADBI study.

Table 2.3

Required Greenhouse Gas Reduction Ratio Compared with 2005 Level

	World	Annex-I	Non-Annex	Asia[a]	PRC	India	Indonesia	Japan	Republic of Korea	Malaysia	Thailand	Viet Nam
pCAP Burden share scheme — per capita emissions will be the same after 2050	58	83	42	42	68	-51	15	83	85	67	61	12
pGDP Burden share scheme — per capita GDP will be the same after 2050	58	46–58	57–65	58–63	59–61	41–53	67	18–43	49–57	57–60	54–65	60–74
pCUM Burden share scheme — Cumulative country emissions from 2020 to 2050 divided by country population remains the same	58	95	34	43	97	-100	49	94	99	93	85	32

pCAP=per capital emissions.
pGDP=per capita GDP.
pCUM=cumulative country emissions.

Notes: Minus is an increase of allowable emission compared with 2005.
Values of Indonesia and Malaysia are excluding emission/sink of land use and land cover (LULC) sectors.
Ranges of pGDP are corresponding with ranges of GDP projections in references.
[a] Excluding Japan.

Source: Matsuoka et al. (2012); ADB–ADBI study team.

Low-carbon green growth requires, among other things, state-of-the-art green technology for the development and improvement of alternative energies, energy efficiency, natural asset management, and waste management; infrastructure to enable and support green industries and other green activities; capital mobilization for green technology, infrastructure, and other activities; policy, legal, economic, and social institutions to support the above activities; and social awareness to enable and participate in these activities. To achieve these requirements, a country needs comprehensive and coherent government policies and effective institutions.

The conventional growth paradigm has been based on fossil fuels as its energy source and has been sustained by labor- and capital-intensive production. It has been measured by GDP or gross national product (GNP)—more products and services, at any environmental cost—while ecological services have been neglected. So, a reliance on high-carbon energy sources and sole focus on the consumption of goods and services have been accompanied by a lack of attention to other important aspects of human life, such as the environment and social development and welfare. The economic system on which that growth has been built for the past 50 years has recently shown its extraordinary vulnerability to economic shocks and crises.

Green growth adds environmental value to growth, by addressing the shortfalls of the conventional high-carbon development paradigm. Green growth is designed to diversify energy sources, particularly through renewable and cleaner energies, and increased efficiency in energy use. However, green growth extends beyond energy, to construction and green improvements for existing buildings; development of green infrastructure for transportation, information and communication networks, electricity, water, and other supplies, among others; environmental protection and recycling and waste management businesses; and other green businesses including environmental health, green management consulting, green legal services, and green engineering. Green growth plans often encompass the improvement of natural assets such as land, air and water, resource management, and biodiversity.

While the details of this new conception of growth are still being developed, there is a consensus—that economic growth and climatic and environmental sustainability are not merely compatible objectives, but can be made mutually reinforcing for the future of humankind. Implemented correctly, green growth can also be effective in achieving poverty reduction; inclusive economic growth; and social development and protection, such as the provision of education, access to basic needs and health services, and ensuring equality across sectors and societies.

2.2.3 Composition and Trends of Decoupling in Asia and the Pacific

Low-carbon green growth opportunities enable a country to continue its path of economic growth, while maintaining harmony between the economy and the environment—promoting economic growth while reducing emissions, minimizing waste, and encouraging the more efficient use of natural resources.

In Figure 2.4, all factors are normalized to 1 at 2000, as the base year. The analysis shows that economies in Asia and the Pacific have been progressing and their population has been increasing. It also suggests that energy intensity has been improved since 2000, as has carbon intensity.

Figures 2.5, 2.6, 2.7, and 2.8 show how some economies have decoupled emissions growth from economic growth during the 1990–2000.

Figure 2.4

Decomposition of CO_2 Emissions in Asia and the Pacific, 1980–2008

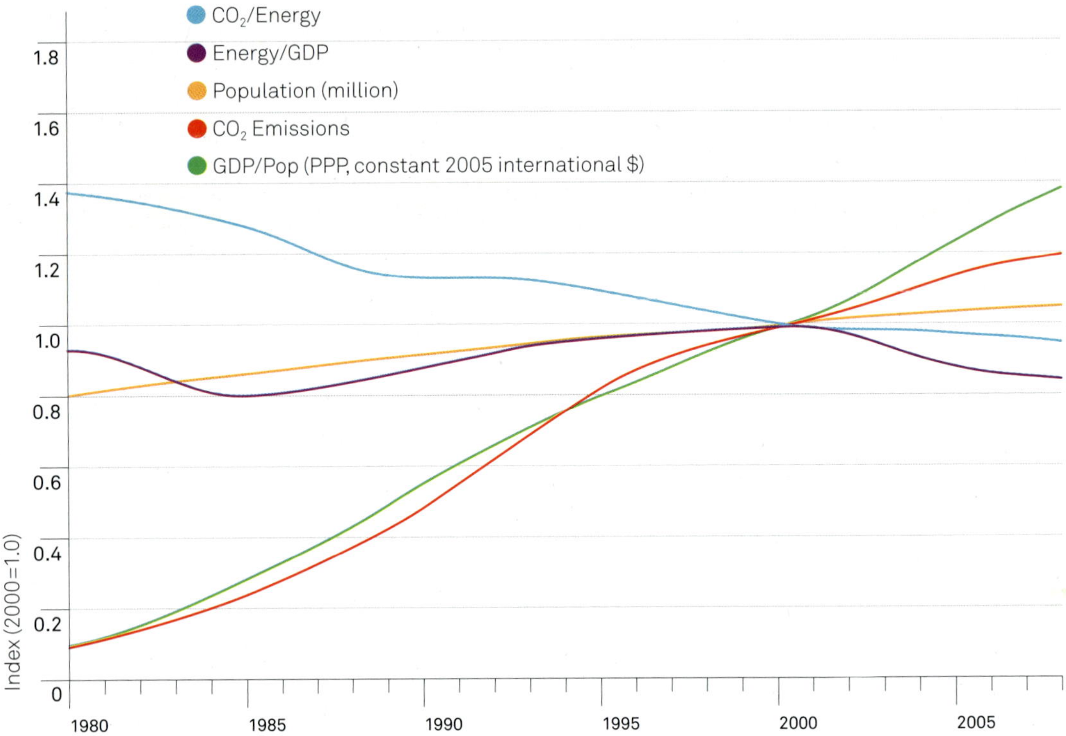

Notes: Applied countries include Australia; Bangladesh; Bhutan; Brunei Darussalam; Cambodia; Hong Kong, China; India; Indonesia; Japan; Kazakhstan; Lao PDR; Malaysia; Mongolia; Myanmar; Nepal; New Zealand; Pakistan; Papua New Guinea; Philippines; PRC; Republic of Korea; Singapore; Sri Lanka; Tajikistan; Thailand; Uzbekistan; and Viet Nam.

Sources: World Resource Institute Climate Analysis Indicators Tool (CAIT) Version 9.0 by the World Resource Institute, 2011(http://cait.wri.org [accessed March 2012]) and the World Bank's World Development Indicators and Global Development Funds, April 2012 (http://databank.worldbank.org/ddp/home.do [accessed April 2012]).

Table 2.4

Key Low-Carbon Technologies that have Widespread Practical Introduction and Expansion Phases

Electric vehicles	Hybrid and plug-in hybrid vehicles	Organic Electric Light		
Solar power generation	Stationary fuel cells	Heat pumps (including inverter control)	LED lighting	
Lithium ion batteries	Nickel hydrogen batteries	Energy-saving home appliances		
Green IT (energy-saving IT devices, environmental IT solutions)	Eco-housing			
Sodium sulfur (NaS) batteries	Cogeneration	Green logistics		
High-efficiency electric motors	High-efficiency boilers	High-efficiency industrial furnaces	High-efficiency reaction processes (membrane separation, catalysts, etc.)	
Geothermal power generation	Power generation from waste	Power generation using waste heat	High-efficiency production processes (process improvement)	Super coke oven
Nuclear power generation	High-efficiency thermal power generation (operation and maintenance, clean coal)	Use of biofuels		
Modal shift to railways (including bullet train)	Water-related technologies	Hydroelectric power generation (including micro hydroelectric power generation)		
Power transmission and distribution	Insurance supporting environment business, assistance and loans forintroduction of environmental facilities, etc.	Soil remediation		
Wind power generation	Waste recycling (simplification and speeding up of administrative procedures, etc.)			

Source: Nippon Keidanren (2010).

Figure 2.5

Production-based CO_2 Productivity, 1990–2000 Decoupling Trends

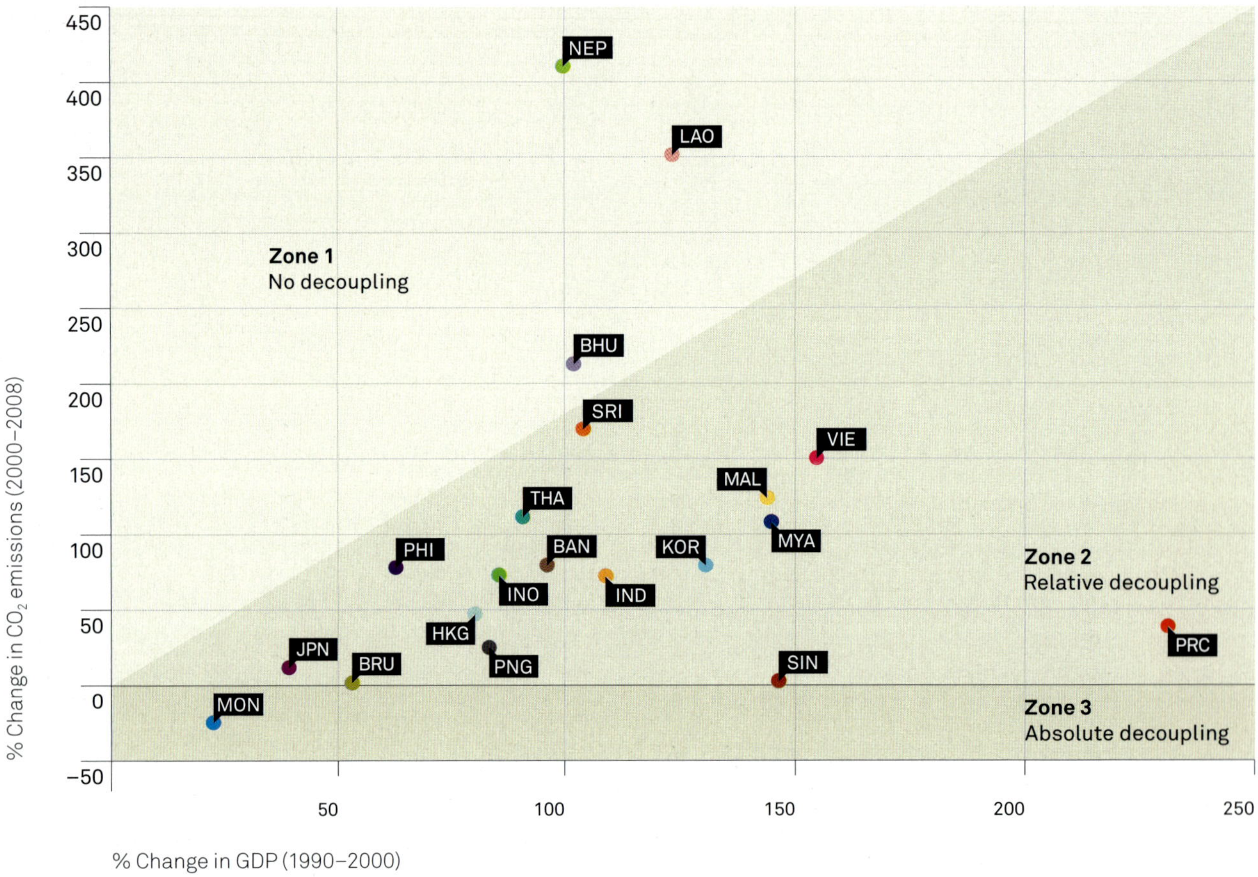

Source: Carbon Dioxide Information Analysis Center (2012). http://cdiac.ornl.gov (accessed December 2012).

Notes:

- BAN: Bangladesh
- BHU: Bhutan
- BRU: Brunei Darussalam
- CAM: Cambodia
- HKG: Hong Kong, China
- IND: India
- INO: Indonesia
- JPN: Japan
- KOR: Republic of Korea
- LAO: Lao PDR
- MAL: Malaysia
- MON: Mongolia
- MYA: Myanmar
- NEP: Nepal
- PHI: Philippines
- PNG: Papua New Guinea
- PRC: People's Republic of China
- SIN: Singapore
- SRI: Sri Lanka
- THA: Thailand
- VIE: Viet Nam

Figure 2.6

Production-based CO_2 Productivity, 2000–2008
Decoupling Trends

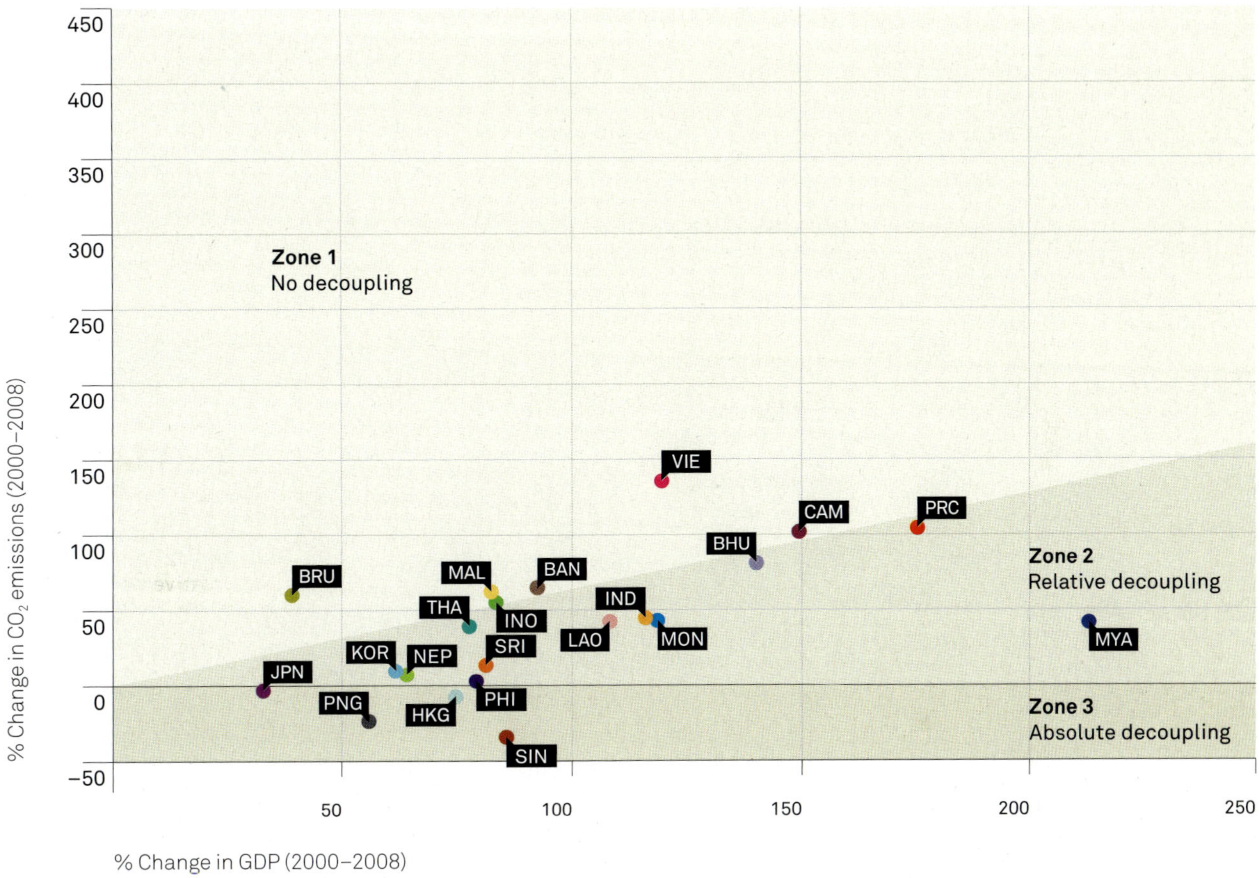

Source: Carbon Dioxide Information Analysis Center (2012).
http://cdiac.ornl.gov (accessed December 2012).

Figure 2.7

Demand-based CO_2 Productivity, 1990–2000 Decoupling Trends

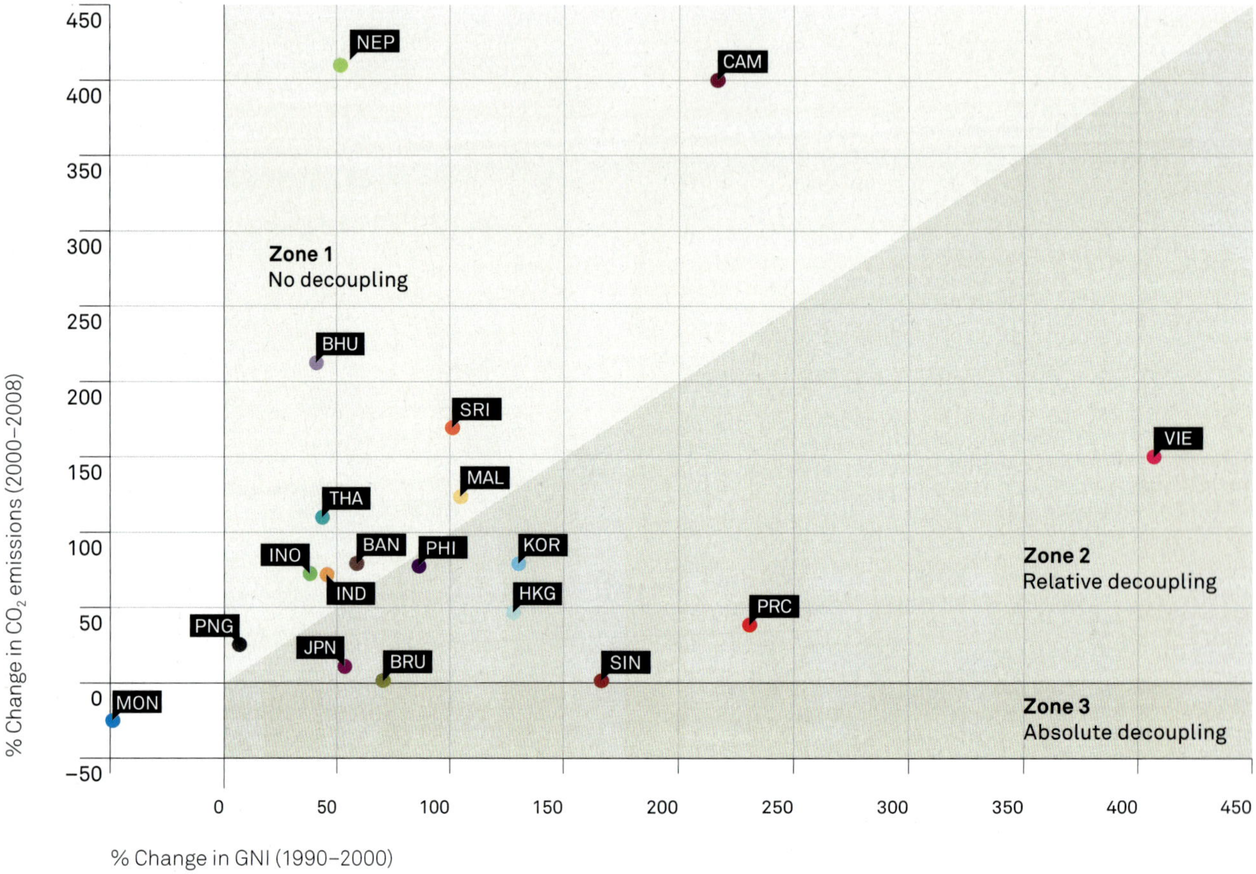

GNI=gross national income.

Notes:

- BAN: Bangladesh
- BHU: Bhutan
- BRU: Brunei Darussalam
- CAM: Cambodia
- HKG: Hong Kong, China
- IND: India
- INO: Indonesia
- JPN: Japan
- KOR: Republic of Korea
- LAO: Lao PDR
- MAL: Malaysia
- MON: Mongolia
- MYA: Myanmar
- NEP: Nepal
- PHI: Philippines
- PNG: Papua New Guinea
- PRC: People's Republic of China
- SIN: Singapore
- SRI: Sri Lanka
- THA: Thailand
- VIE: Viet Nam

Source: Carbon Dioxide Information Analysis Center (2012). http://cdiac.ornl.gov (accessed December 2012).

Figure 2.8

Demand-based CO_2 Productivity, 2000–2008
Decoupling Trends

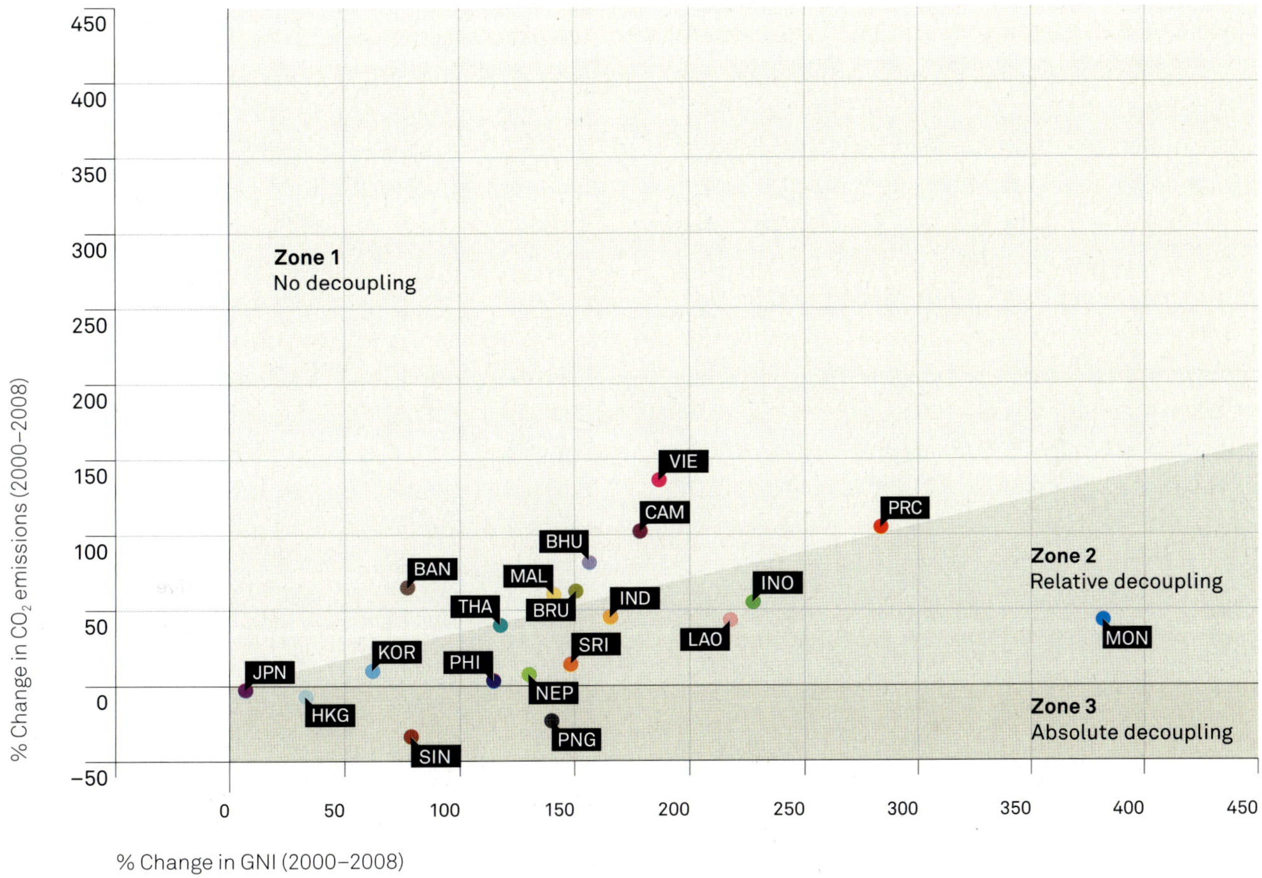

Source: Carbon Dioxide Information Analysis Center (2012). http://cdiac.ornl.gov (accessed December 2012).

Some important factors determining how far carbon emissions have been decoupled from economic growth are listed below.

1 **Economic structure**
Different economic sectors generate very different amounts of value added per ton of energy and resource input. Carbon and energy or material productivity in terms of value added per resource input is low in the primary resource extraction and processing sectors; this value improves with an increasing contribution of higher manufacturing industries and service sectors to GDP (Howes and Wyrwoll 2012).

2 **Resource endowment**
Countries that have limited endowments of raw materials such as coal tend to be more resource-efficient than countries with resource abundance. Relative resource scarcities support the implementation of policies to increase resource efficiency (Dittrich et al. 2010). In contrast, small and rich countries with large reserves and extraction of key resources with high global demand tend to have the highest per capita consumption and have less incentive to increase resource efficiency.

3 **International trade**
A factor closely related to emissions and resource endowments is international trade. Countries that import high shares of their raw materials and products have higher material productivities than countries that extract and process raw materials within their borders.

4 **Sectorial strategies and technology choices**
A low-carbon green growth strategy requires sector policy interventions that promote climate-friendly technologies, and thereby reduce carbon emissions despite rapidly growing demand. Developing and implementing such a program is affected by sector-specific economic policies (notably subsidies, tariff barriers, and industrial policies); institutions; consumer preferences; political economic considerations; and technological choices. Many commercially proven technological innovations already accelerate decoupling. Japan alone accounts for 37% of inventions in climate-smart technologies, particularly in the area of energy efficiency, transport, and electrical appliances. Table 2.4 illustrates such technologies. An Institute of Energy Economics, Japan study estimates that advanced technologies commercially used in Japan in three industries (steel, cement, and paper and pulp) and for three appliances (refrigerators, air-conditioners, and lighting)—if diffused globally—could save 1.5 billion tons of CO_2 emissions, an amount greater than Japan's annual GHG emissions (Hongo 2010).

5 Financing

The demand for funding to shift to a low-carbon growth path is enormous. The 2009 Copenhagen Accord stated that industrialized countries must mobilize $30 billion by 2012 and increase this to $100 billion a year in 2020 to support both cuts in emissions and measures to adapt to climate change in developing countries. The International Energy Agency (IEA) estimated that to achieve a 50% emissions reduction by 2050, an additional investment of $400 billion would be needed globally in 2020. Developing countries are required to make the $200 billion investment as additional investment: half of the funding is expected to come from industrialized countries but the remaining half will be procured in developing countries. Securing such large commitments of funding requires active participation from the financial markets, and the crucial question is how best public policies can be deployed to leverage private finance. A whole different policy framework needs to be established, by which the incubation and incremental costs of green technologies are supported through public finance, key pieces of legislation, analytical tools, and regional carbon markets. For projects that are only marginally profitable or not profitable at all, policies should provide a balancing factor aimed at leveling the field and compensating investors for taking risks. The type of financing instruments needed are presented in Table 2.5.

A summary of energy intensity and areas of potential mitigation and associated challenges is presented in Table 2.6.

Box 2.1

Japan's Low-Carbon Society Strategy

Japan is one of the most energy-efficient countries in the world, in manufacturing. Its energy intensity decreased 26% from 1980 to 2009. Nevertheless, Japan pledged to go further with its 2007 proposition of a low-carbon society, as a contribution to halving global emissions by 2050. Skea and Nishioka (2008) define a low-carbon society as one that should take actions that are compatible with the principles of sustainable development, ensuring that the development needs of all groups within the society are met and that an equitable contribution is made toward the global effort to stabilize the atmospheric concentration of carbon dioxide and other greenhouse gases at a level that will avoid dangerous climate change, through deep cuts in global emissions. A low-carbon society in the ultimate sense would be a society that emits greenhouse gases only to the extent that they can be absorbed by nature (a carbon-neutral society).

The principles for a low-carbon society are envisaged as (i) carbon minimization in all sectors, (ii) a simpler lifestyle that realizes richer quality of life, and (iii) coexistence with nature. The Low Carbon Society implementation strategy fosters energy conservation technologies and develops a benchmarking approach to monitor progress. In addition to promoting the most advanced technologies and business models across all sectors, including transport and housing, it created a mechanism that encouraged consumers to select products that incorporate low-carbon technology. Japan's Top Runner Program tests 21 types of appliances—to determine the most efficient model, and make the models' efficiency the new baseline. Smart communities are the newest initiative under the low-carbon society program. Four large-scale pilot projects, launched in 2010, maximize the use of renewable energy and rely on smart grids to reduce emissions.

Source: Matsuoka, Kainuma, Fujino, and Ehara (2012).

Table 2.5

Understanding Four Dimensions of Low-Carbon Green Finance

Type of financing instrument	Is there a financing gap?	Comments
Financing new types of services to promote low-carbon energy	Possible for short term	Initial support to develop and test business models for "bottom of pyramid" markets may be useful. In some infrastructure services, such as water and public transportation, market-oriented institutional reforms necessary for improving sector accountability.
Financial intermediation between demand and supply for green investments	Yes	Phasing out stimulus money and phasing in equity and loan funds requires major policy reforms.
Creating markets in spot and short-term futures instruments for green investments	Not yet available in developing Asia	SWAPs and derivatives, among others, to attract hedge funds and institutional investors.
Providing insurance services by pooling exposure to climate risks	Yes, needs to be filled by public financing (e.g., catastrophic bonds)	Develop parametric insurance instruments for weather and climate related risks to infrastructure.

Note: Bottom of pyramid is the largest, but poorest socioeconomic group; in global terms it is the 4 billion people who live on less than $2.0 per day.

Source: Turner (2010).

Table 2.6

Energy Intensity and Areas of Potential Mitigation

Sector	Relative energy intensity	Energy units MJ per $/output	CO_2 mitigation potential	Policy challenges
Subsistence farming	Low	3–6	High	Low available capital to invest in new technologies. Little financing available.
Industrial agriculture	High-large input	15–25	Medium to low	Yield dependent on application of fossil fuel derived fertilizers/pesticides, as well as biotech engineering.
Mining	High	20–40	Low	As resource quality declines, more material must be extracted at higher cost to achieve a constant level of output.
Small-scale manufacturing	High	7–12	Low	This small-scale sector (for example in textiles or manual food processing) is affected by technologies.
Industrial manufacturing	High	15–20	Low	Large embodied energy and capital investment required. Requires steady supply of electricity/energy for production.
Construction	High	15–20	Low	With large embodied energy content in building materials and high susceptibility to interest rate rises, this sector is at risk from rising resources cost.
Transportation	Moderate to high	8–15	Medium	Investment in electrification of transportation systems (e.g.,car, rail) requires large-scale energy-intensive infrastructure investments.
Services	Relatively low	2–6	High	In many cases requires goods and materials produced at low energy and labor costs.

Source: Institute for Integrated Economic Research (2011); ADB–ADBI study team.

Box 2.2

The Republic of Korea's Green Growth Agenda

In 2008, the President of the Republic of Korea, Lee Myung-bak, proclaimed low-carbon green growth as the Republic of Korea's new national vision for the next six decades.

The program highlights a shift from quantity-oriented, fossil fuel dependent economic growth to quality-oriented growth that relies on new and renewable energies. The following year, the Republic of Korea announced its goal to become the world's seventh largest green economic power by 2020 and the fifth largest by 2050.

To achieve these, the government established the Presidential Committee on Green Growth (PCGG) in 2009 to realize the new vision and coordinate green growth activities. The same year, the Republic of Korea announced 27 green technologies, finalized the Five-Year Plan for Green Growth, and announced its voluntary target of cutting greenhouse gases (GHGs) to 30% below business-as-usual levels by 2020. In 2010, the Republic of Korea enacted the Framework Act on low-carbon green growth, putting these aims into law.

Under the Five-Year Plan for Green Growth, the Republic of Korea will annually invest about 2% of its gross domestic product in the field of green growth, including climate change and energy, sustainable transportation, and developing green technologies.

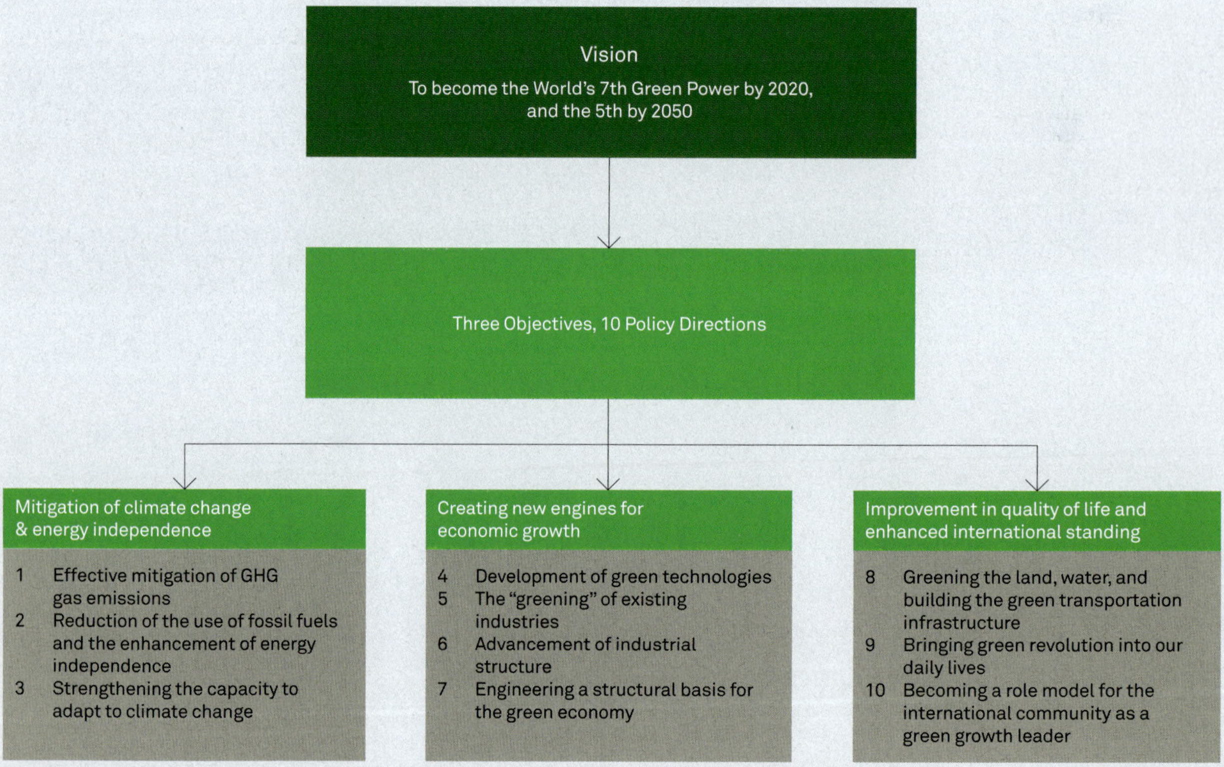

Source: Presidential Committee on Green Growth (2009).

Box 2.3

Green Growth in Indonesia

The National Strategy for Green Growth's three main strands:

1 **Mitigation of climate change and improvement of energy independence**
- Mitigation of GHG emissions
- Reduction in the use of fossil fuels and enhancement of energy independence
- Improvement of capacity to adapt to climate change

2 **Creation of new growth engines**
- Development of green technologies and the creation of new growth engines
- Greening of existing industries and nurturing of emerging green industries
- Advancement of industrial infrastructure
- Laying the institutional foundation for a green economy

3 **Improvement in quality of life and enhancement of international standing**
- Creation of a green homeland and green transportation system
- Bringing green revolution into daily life
- Becoming a role model for the international community as a green growth leader

Indonesia has committed to cut emissions by 26% by 2020; and lays great emphasis on ensuring sustainable economic growth, creating green jobs, and eradicating poverty.

Indonesia's legal framework on green growth includes the Law of the Republic of Indonesia on Environmental Protection and Management, 2009; the Renewable Energy Law, 2008; the Presidential Instruction on Energy and Water Efficiency, 2008; and the Presidential Regulation on National Energy Policy, 2006.

Indonesia's notable green growth efforts include the country's reducing emissions from deforestation and forest degradation (REDD+) strategy. REDD+ is a climate change mitigation strategy that aims to provide incentives for developing countries to reduce emissions through forestry conservation and the sustainable management of forests.

Indonesia is covered by more than 123 million hectares of forest area, accounting for about 60% of the land area. However, as the country with the highest deforestation rates in the world, sustainable management of forest resources is crucial to Indonesia. The government in 2011 announced plans to reduce its greenhouse gas emissions by 26% and to transition its forestry sector from a net carbon source to a net carbon sink through the national REDD+ strategy by 2020. To achieve this goal, Indonesia has set aside about 37.5 million hectares of its forests for REDD+ projects, involving various donor countries and international organizations.

Source: Bratasida (2011). Low carbon green growth and development policies in Indonesia; REDD+ data based on the United Nations Framework Convention on Climate Change (UNFCCC) Bali Action Plan. (http://unfccc.int/files/meetings/cop_13/application/pdf/cp_bali_action.pdf).

Table 2.7

Examples of Emissions Reduction Targets

	Emission Reduction Goal	National Development Plan	Formulation date
PRC	Reduce CO_2 emissions per unit of GDP by 40%–45% by 2020 compared to 2005	11th 5-Year Plan (2006–2010); 12th 5-Year Plan (2006–2010); National Climate Change Programme	March 2006 March 2010 June 2007
India	Reduce CO_2 emissions (except agriculture) per unit of GDP by 20%–25% by 2020	National Action Plan on Climate Change (NAPCC)	June 2008
Indonesia	Reduce GHG emissions by 26% by 2020	National Action Plan Addressing Climate Change; Climate Change in Indonesia National Development Planning; Mid-term Development Plan (RPJM 2010–2014)	December 2007 July 2008 May 2010
Republic of Korea	Reduce GHG emissions by 30% below business-as-usual by 2020	4th Comprehensive National Action Plan for Climate Change (2008–2012); 5-year National Action Plan for Green Growth; Basic Law on Low-Carbon and Green Growth	2008 July 2009 January 2010
Singapore	Reduce GHG emissions by 16% below business-as-usual by 2020	National Climate Change Strategy; Sustainable Singapore Blueprint	March 2008 July 2009
Marshall Islands	Reduce GHG emissions by 40% below 2009 level by 2020	National Energy Policy and Energy Action Plan; National Climate Change Framework Policy (NCCFP)	October 2009 November 2010

Source: Institute for Global Environmental Strategies (2011).

2.3
Evolution and Convergence of Asian Perceptions on Low-Carbon Green Growth

2.3.1
Convergence in Asian Perspectives on Tackling Climate Change

Countries are already making various efforts to cut their carbon emissions and pursue sustainable development, but there are also international efforts to enhance developing countries' actions on climate change. The role of Asian countries in global climate change has changed enormously since the Kyoto Protocol was signed in 1997, and they are playing a much more active role in UNFCCC Conference of the Parties (COP) meetings to address this important global issue.

As recently as the early 1990s, the perception in Asia was that the region was an "impactee" rather than an "impactor"—i.e., the region was likely to be affected by global climate change, but the duty to reduce future greenhouse impacts rested with the industrialized countries. This was reflected in the Kyoto Protocol, which did not place any limits on emissions from developing countries, while requiring industrialized countries to cut them by 5% from 1990 to 2012.

The UNFCCC obliges developed countries to take the lead but suggests developing countries should voluntarily take actions to cut emissions based on the principle of common but differentiated responsibility. Accordingly, Annex I countries submit emissions reduction goals, while Non-Annex I countries submit nationally appropriate mitigation actions (NAMAs) to the UNFCCC.

The UNFCCC defines NAMAs as "measurable, reportable and verifiable nationally appropriate mitigation commitments or actions, including quantified emission limitation and reduction objectives, by all developed country Parties, while ensuring the comparability of efforts among them, taking into account differences in their national circumstances" (UNFCCC 2010).

As of March 2011, 48 Non-Annex I countries—including countries in Asia and the Pacific such as the PRC, India, Indonesia, the Republic of Korea, and Singapore—had submitted their NAMAs (Table 2.7).

Table 2.8 lists key developments within the global climate regime and associated policy initiatives taken by emerging economies of Asia. These policy actions and NAMAs present proof that the importance of climate change mitigation actions has been increasing in all major economies of Asia. Although each country has different priorities in terms of the sectors and technologies needed to achieve the target, most Asian countries have now set their own target for GHG emissions or relevant indicators, including emissions intensity or energy efficiency.

The pledges made around the world do not add up to a big enough or early enough cut in global emissions. That means countries need to increase their ambitions to meet the emissions targets scientists say are necessary.

In 2011, the nearly 200 countries meeting under the UNFCCC in Durban, South Africa, agreed to write a new global treaty on climate change by 2015, to come into force from 2020. The framework conditions of the Durban Platform are illustrated in Figure 2.9.

Table 2.8

Converging Perspectives on Low-Carbon Green Growth

- ● Key Developments within the Global Climate Change Regime

Key Policy Initiatives and Low-Carbon Actions Taken by Emerging Asia

- IND: India
- INO: Indonesia
- PRC: PRC
- THA: Thailand
- VIE: Viet Nam

Source: ADB–ADBI study team

Notes:

COP:	Conference of Parties
CDM:	Clean Development Mechanism
CMP:	Conference of the Parties serving as the meeting of the Parties to the Kyoto Protocol
MDG:	Millennium Development Goal
EMC:	Energy Management Contract
ENCON:	Energy Conservation
ESCO:	Energy Service Company
PV:	Photovoltaic
IPCC:	Intergovernmental Panel on Climate Change
NAMA:	Nationally Appropriate Mitigation Action
PRC:	People's Republic of China
UNFCCC:	United Nations Framework Convention on Climate Change

1975

THA Enhancement and Conservation of National Environmental Quality Law (revised 1992)

1979

First World Climate Conference

1982

IND Environmental Information System

1985

PRC Law on Grasslands

VIE National Conservation Strategy

1986

IND Environmental Protection Act

1987

IND Renewable Energy Development Agency

1988

Toronto Conference

1989

Ottawa Conference, Tata Conference, and the Hague Conference and Declaration

Noordwijk Ministerial Conference and Cairo Compact

PRC Environmental Protection Law

1990

Bergen Conference, Second World Climate Conference, and IPCC released its First Assessment Report

THA Community Forest Bill (revised 2002)

1991

VIE Law on Environmental Protection and National Plan for Environment and Sustainable Development

Global Environment Facility

1992

Rio Declaration on Environment and Development (Earth Summit and Agenda 21) and UNFCCC signed

1992

THA Small Power Producer and Very Small Power Producer programs, Energy Conserv-ation and Promotion Act

VIE Law on Forest Protection and Development (revised 2004)

1993

THA ENCON Fund

VIE Law on Environmental Protection (revised 2005)

1994

UNFCCC enters into force, COP set up, and Barbados Declaration

THA Reforestation Program, Energy Conservation Promotion Fund, Mass Transit Development for Urban Areas (revised 2011)

1995

COP 1 Berlin

1996

COP 2 Geneva and IPCC Second Assessment Report

PRC Brightness Programme

THA Divide Energy by 2 Program

1997

COP 3 and Kyoto Protocol

IDN Environmental Protection and Management (revised 2009)

THA Enhancement and Conservation of National Environmental Quality (1997–2016)

1998

COP 4 Buenos Aires

1999

COP 5 Bonn

PRC Green for Grain Program (until 2006)

2000

COP 6 The Hague, operational rulebook for the Protocol, and UN Millennium Development Summit, and MDGs

IDN Carbon and Environmental Research and Training (until 2008)

PRC CDM capacity building projects (2000 onward)

THA 20-Year Vision and National Strategy on Scientific and Technology, Forestry Protection Program

2001

COP 6 Part 2 Bonn; COP 7 Marrakech, Morocco; protocol ready for implementation; IPCC Third Assessment Report

VIE Renewable Energy Action Plan

2002

Johannesburg Declaration on Sustainable Development

VIE National Action Plan on Reducing Vehicle Emissions

2003

IND National Urban Renewal Mission

IDN Emission Standard for Stationery Sources, Emission Standards for Vehicular Engines

PRC Circular Economy Legislations and Initiatives, Eco-cities, Law on Agriculture

2004

Buenos Aires, Argentina COP 10

VIE Second Rural Energy Project

2004

THA Strategic Plan for Ethanol Promotion (revised 2011), Strategic Plan for Renewable Energy Development

2005

Montreal, Canada COP 11 and CMP 1

IND National Electricity Policy

IDN National Energy Blue Print, National Energy Conservation Plan, 5-Year Forestry Strategic Plan

THA New Energy Strategic Plan, Strategic Plan on Biodiesel Promotion and Development, Energy Conservation Targets for Factories and Buildings

VIE Energy Efficiency Building Codes, National Strategic Program on Energy Savings and Effective Use

2006

Nairobi, Kenya COP 12 and CMP 2

IND National Energy Labeling Programme, Rural Electrification Policy, Energy Conservation Building Code, National Urban Transport Policy

IDN 20-Year National Biofuel Roadmap, Medium Scale Power Generation using Renewable Energy

PRC Green poverty alleviation project, Mid- and Long-term Development Plan for Science and Technology

2007

Bali, Indonesia COP 13 and CMP 3

2007

IND 11th Five Year Development Plan with specific objectives regarding climate change mitigation

IDN Energy Law, National Action Plan Addressing Climate Change, Supply and Utilization of Biofuels as Alternative Energy, National Mitigation Actions

PRC National Climate Change Program, Medium and Long Term Development Plan for Renewable Energy, Preferential Tax Policies for Renewable Energy, Special fund for renewable energy development, PRC's Science and Technology Program on Climate Change

THA Power Development Plan and Solid Waste Management Program, Alternative Energy Development Plan, Five-Year Scientific and Technological Strategic Plan (2007–2011)

2008

Poznan, Poland COP 14 and CMP 4

IDN Climate Variability and Climate Change Programs and Loan, National Carbon Accounting System, Forest Resources Information System

PRC Energy Conservation Law, Vehicle Fuel Economy Standards, Vehicle Excise Tax Rates, Law on Land Management

THA ESCO Fund

2008

IND National Action Plan on Climate Change, National Mission on Strategic Knowledge of Climate Change, City Development Plan, National Mission on Sustainable Habitat, National Mission for Sustainable Agriculture, National Mission for a Green India

2009

Copenhagen Accord, Denmark COP 15 and CMP 5

Voluntary pledges by developing countries through NAMAs

IND National Policy on Biofuels, Renewable Energy Tariff regulations, Forest Survey of India, Auto Fuel Policy, Indian Network for Climate Change Assessment

IDN Regulation on reduction of emissions from deforestation and forest degradation, Indonesia Climate Change Trust Fund

PRC Green Stimulus

THA Clean Technology Fund Investment Plan

2010

Cancun, Mexico COP 16 and CMP 6

IDN 15-Year Green Energy Plan, Indonesia's Green Investment Fund, One Billion Indonesian Trees

PRC 12th Five-Year Development Plan, Financial Incentives on Energy Management Contracts

2010

IND National Clean Energy Fund, State level Action Plans on Climate Change, Mandatory Energy Managers and Energy Audits, Energy Efficiency Financing Platform

VIE National Environment Protection Strategy

2011

Durban, South Africa COP 17 and CMP 7

PRC National Solar PV feed-in tariff, Top-10,000 Energy-Consuming Enterprises program

THA Reduce agricultural field burning

VIE Law on Energy Saving and Efficiency, National Strategic Program on Energy Savings and Effective Use, Action Plan on Response to Climate Change and roadmap to vehicle emission standards, and Scientific and Technological Program on Climate Change

2012

United Nations Conference on Sustainable Development (Rio+20)

Qatar COP 18 CMP 8

PRC Vehicle and Vessel Tax Law

THA 11th National Social and Economic Development Plan (2012–2016) emphasizes the importance of an efficient and sustainable economy to promote an inclusive society

Figure 2.9

Framework Concluded at the 17th Conference of the Parties in Durban

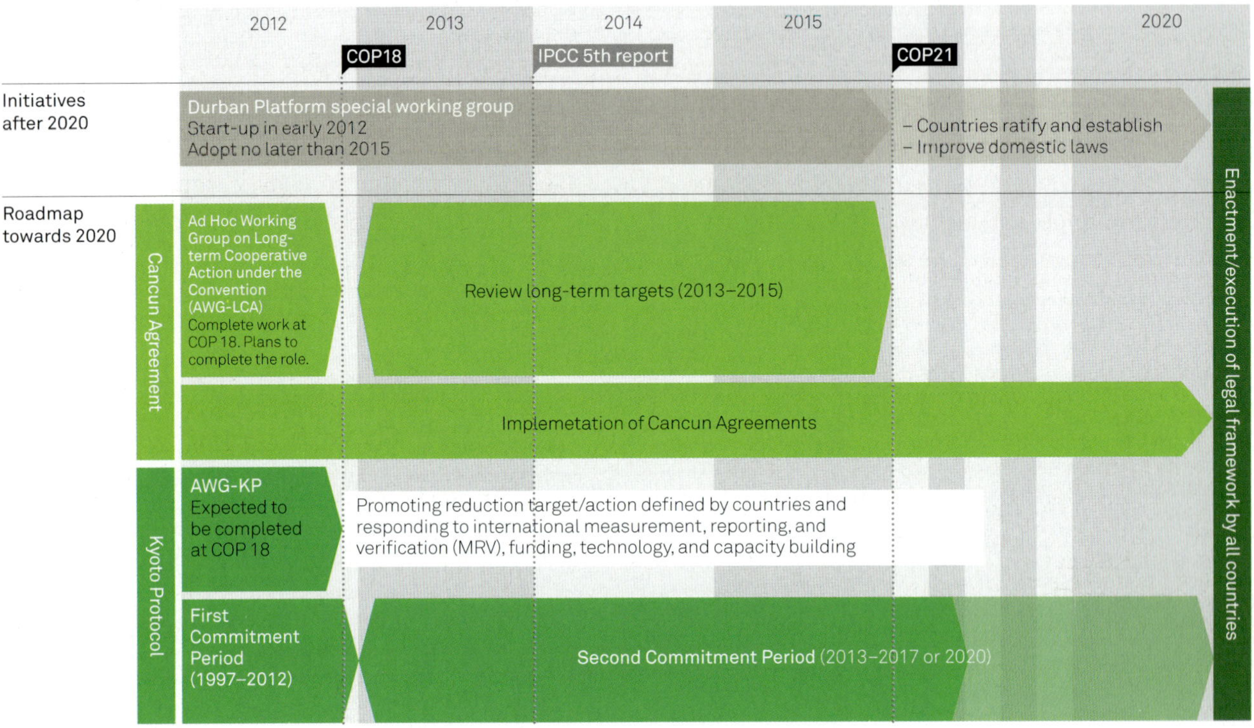

Source: Ministry of the Environment (2012). Japan; ADB–ADBI study team.

2.3.2
Evolving Frameworks for Low-Carbon Green Growth

Achieving the multiple benefits of reduced emissions is the objective of low-carbon green growth in most of the developing countries, as observed in NAMA pledges. This also indicates increasing recognition by Asian governments that the old-fashioned "grow first and clean up later" paradigm has no relevance when it comes to climate change, and arguably with any other environmental concern. The science of climate change is clear—carbon emissions once poured into the atmosphere stay there for a century. It will not be possible in future to remove from the atmosphere emissions that are put there today—only by reducing emissions now can countries avoid the perils of dangerous climate change. Acting early is critical when the choice of technology infrastructure can lock in a high-carbon lifestyle and infrastructure. This is particularly true in the case of energy, transport, and heavy industries, which will be built in most of the emerging economies in the next few decades.

Major Asian economies recognize that there is an urgent need for rapid growth and poverty alleviation, as well as a need to avoid irreversible and costly damages from climate change and other environmental degradation. Their efforts to foster low-carbon green growth must focus on what is required in the next 5–10 years to sustain robust growth, while avoiding locking in their economies to unsustainable patterns, preventing irreversible climate change, and reducing the potential for regret. This can be done with growth that is efficient in the use of natural resources, by decoupling growth from emissions and from environmental degradation. Low-carbon green growth policies can be considered an investment, particularly as the benefits of spending on climate change mitigation are likely to be received over a long period in the future.

Another factor making low-carbon green growth attractive to Asian economies is that it can increase conventionally measured GDP through the following four channels:

1. **Input effects**
   Increasing the quantity of physical capital, labor, and financial capital, which allows more economic production. A good example is giving clean energy to households to improve health and physical capital, including through better access to education.
2. **Efficiency effect**
   Increasing productivity by correcting market failures and enhancing the efficiency of resource use. Many firms and households fail to make cost-effective energy-saving and resource efficiency investments because of market failures and behavioral biases.
3. **Stimulus effect**
   Occurs during economic slowdown, when capacity utilization and employment are low. Green investments increase demand, potentially increasing employment.
4. **Innovation effect**
   Occurs through policy interventions that encourage green technologies, such as investments in research and development (R&D).

These form the basis for many Asian governments' recent stimulus programs, which have focused on supporting the development and deployment of low-carbon technologies.

Boxes 2.4–2.7 detail more low-carbon green growth efforts and practices.

Box 2.4

The Circular Economy in the People's Republic of China

Although the economic growth of the People's Republic of China (PRC) has been spectacular, averaging close to 9% per year for over the last 3 decades, the level of energy and materials used per unit of gross domestic product (GDP) has been much greater than that of other advanced economies. The high intensity levels have led to both economic and ecological costs that are unacceptable. So, the PRC has been setting ambitious goals for energy and resource efficiency, and the concept of a circular economy has become a mainstream development goal

The national leadership in the PRC has decided that continued development in the traditional linear manner, starting from resources extraction from nature on one end and ending in waste disposal at the other end, is no longer feasible. It is not only destructive in terms of emissions and pollution affecting climate change and nature, but it is also costly both to secure fresh resources all the time and lose resources in the form of waste. This is an understanding that the PRC now shares with the rest of the developed world, especially Japan and Germany, where efforts have been made to embed the concept into a regulatory framework (Triebswetter and Hitchens 2005; Moriguchi 2007).

The PRC has officially adopted the concept as a development goal, moving it from the domain of environmental policy to the sphere of economic and development policy.

Under the 11th Five-Year Plan, 2006–2010, the National People's Congress approved a 20% reduction of energy intensity by 2010 compared with the end of 2005, and this was raised from 40% to 45% by 2020, compared with 2005 levels, as a voluntary pledge at the Copenhagen climate change summit in 2009. In mid-2008, the National People's Congress passed the Law for the Promotion of the Circular Economy, which came into effect on 1 January 2009, promoting the circular economy as a national policy and providing a framework in which incentives and penalties can be put in place to encourage firms and municipalities to take eco-industrial initiatives and create networks of by-product exchanges.

To achieve these goals, the PRC has implemented a range of options, including closing down inefficient factories and power plants, and has been the first country to release nationally focused circular economy indicators. Chains of resource and energy utilization have been interconnected, for instance where wastes from one process can be captured and used as raw material for another. These indicators are valuable metrics for policy and decision makers and can help achieve circular economy outcomes. These efforts provide valuable information to developed and developing nations that are keen on implementing sustainable development policies and developing the necessary regulatory frameworks.

Source: Productivity Commission (2011).

Box 2.5

Snapshots of India's Low-Carbon Development Strategy

India's largest sources of emissions are from energy (67%) and agriculture (24%), with more than 50% of total energy demand met through coal, 6% from hydroelectric power plants, 1% by nuclear power plants, and less than 1% from renewables. India's greenhouse gas (GHG) emissions were estimated at 1.55 billion tons in 2000. Concerns over energy security and scarcity are a high priority for the government. The Prime Minister has a Council on Climate Change that recently launched a National Mission to Green India. He released India's first National Action Plan on Climate Change in 2008, outlining existing and future policies and programs.

The plan identifies eight core national missions running to 2017 and directs ministries to submit detailed implementation plans to the Prime Minister's Council on Climate Change. At the end of August 2009, India announced its intention to implement mitigation targets in the form of Perform, Achieve and Trade (PAT) targets for the most energy-intensive industries, as a contribution to international efforts to address climate change.

The country has invested heavily in recent years in renewable sources of energy, including wind, solar, biomass, and hydroelectricity. As of 2008, India's installed wind power generation capacity stood at 9,655 megawatts (MW), making it the fourth largest in the world. Through a variety of programs and policies, India is encouraging low-carbon energy generation, including the following:

- A strengthened policy framework and subsidies to reduce up-front costs to wind power investors
- Capital subsidies, sales incentives, and reimbursement of fees for solar thermal projects; and automatic approval for foreign direct investments[2]
- Accelerated deployment plans and incentives for hydro and nuclear energy
- Incentives for biomass power generation, biofuels for transport, and compact fluorescent lamps
- Retirement of inefficient coal power plants and plans for coalbed methane
- Programs to increase forest cover by 1% a year until 2012, and restore degraded forest

Source: The Energy Resources Institute (2012).

Box 2.6

Cambodia's Green Growth Road Map

Cambodia's Green Growth Roadmap provides an example of aligning all relevant ministries and stakeholders for green growth. The Ministry of Environment of Cambodia has developed the Green Growth Roadmap to integrate ideas and projects on green growth into national strategic development. This road map will create the basis for environmentally sound economic development through the promotion of sustainable infrastructure, green tax and budget reform, and monitoring eco-friendly indicators. The road map aims to align all relevant ministries, institutions, nongovernment organizations, and academia to cooperate in addressing challenges to sustainable development.

The national Green Growth Roadmap envisages a combination of objectives for economic growth and development, human well-being, and environmental quality, which will promote the improvement of Cambodian livelihoods. The Green Growth Roadmap will focus on access to clean water and sanitation, renewable energy, information and knowledge, means for better mobility, finance and investments, food security and non-chemical products, and sustainable land use.

Sources: Government of Cambodia, Ministry of Environment and UNESCAP (2010).

2 Solar water heating systems are required for some building types in New Delhi. In July 2009, India unveiled a $19 billion plan to produce 20,000 MW of solar power by 2020.

Box 2.7

Kazakhstan's Astana Green Bridge Initiative

Kazakhstan has been supporting the concept of green growth, pursuing a policy of transition to innovative and sustainable development. As a part of Kazakhstan 2030, a long-term strategy of development proclaimed by the President of Kazakhstan in 1997, Kazakhstan has a plan to reduce the energy intensity of gross domestic product (GDP) by 10% by 2015 and 25% by 2020. As part of the Copenhagen Accord, the country announced its commitments to reduce greenhouse gas emissions to 15% below its 1990 emission levels by 2020.

During the 6th Ministerial Conference on Environment and Development in Asia-Pacific in October 2010, the Government of Kazakhstan established the Astana Green Bridge Initiative to promote partnership between Europe and Asia and the Pacific in implementing green growth plans and programs. The five identified priority program areas and comprehensive actions are (i) eco-efficient use of natural resources and investment in ecosystem services, (ii) low-carbon development and adaptation to climate change, (iii) promotion of sustainable urban development, (iv) promotion of green business and green technology, and (v) promotion of sustainable lifestyles and improvement of quality life. The initiative has also indicated five strategic approaches: (i) catalyzing high-level, high-visibility policy dialogues on emerging and persistent issues; (ii) undertaking normative and analytical research on emerging and cutting-edge policy solutions and tools; (iii) building the capacity of policy makers to develop, adopt, and implement such policies while taking stock of best practices and methodologies and legislative and economic instruments; and (iv) developing mechanisms to attract green investments and innovative environmental management approaches.

Source: ADBI (2011).

Figure 2.10

Low-Carbon Green Growth

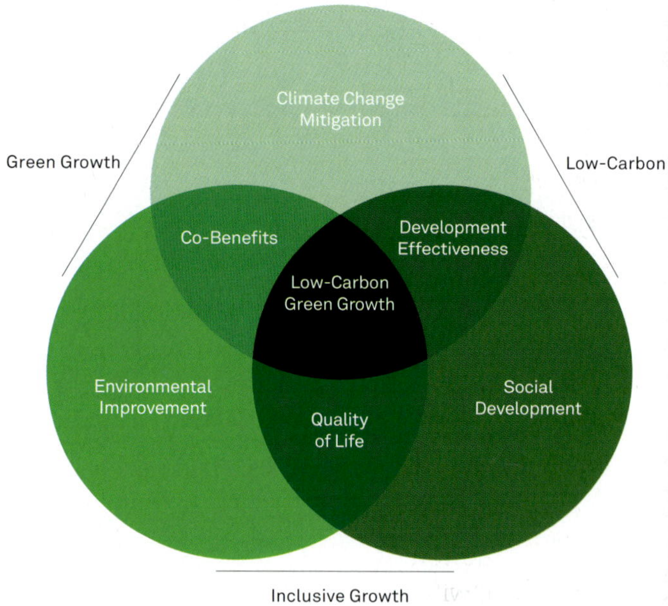

Source: ADB–ADBI study team.

These strategic frameworks are assisting these countries in shifting their development path to a low-carbon climate-resilient economy. Most of those frameworks have a long-term component that includes a strategic vision, and a short- and medium-term component that shows which actions will be undertaken to get on a low-carbon green growth pathway (Figure 2.10, above).

2.4 Emerging Policy Perspectives and Monitoring Frameworks

2.4.1 Policy Perspectives for Pursuing Low-Carbon Green Growth

To effectively pursue low-carbon green growth that is also inclusive, governments must provide a comprehensive and coherent policy package and commit funds for the long term. Markets by themselves will not deliver what is needed (because of externalities, public goods, and non-marketed goods and services). The government has to step in to give the right incentives and correct market failures, but without introducing policy failures and corruption. A low-carbon green growth policy package must be comprehensive—covering all sectors at all levels—and coherent across sectors and levels to be efficient and effective.
At the same time, the package should be tailored to each country, taking consideration of its social, environmental, economic, and cultural characteristics. Low-carbon green growth policies should complement or include social development policies. Table 2.9 shows the correlation between MDG and low-carbon-climate change mitigation measures.

What is also evident from this policy framework is that many of the policy instruments are country-specific. In countries such as Japan and the Republic of Korea, which lack abundant fossil fuel resources, the clear imperative for energy independence is clean energy; in others like the PRC, India, and Indonesia, focusing on energy security does not necessarily lead to clean energy unless specific policy instruments are introduced to promote low-carbon green growth.

The objective of creating new engines of economic growth also depends on the country's level of economic development and its specific comparative advantage. In the developing countries of Asia, the focus is likely to be more on tackling competing demands on limited energy resources, local externalities in the form of growing traffic congestion, and air and water pollution.
Citizens should be more knowledgeable about the consequences of their actions and be equipped with the ability to act in a low-carbon, green, and sustainable way. Local engagement—from local authorities to local nongovernment organizations, from the planning stage to the implementation stage—is an important factor for successful and effective low-carbon green growth. Local knowledge and participation are indispensable for green growth policy implementation. Everyone should participate to achieve the full potential of green growth.

Accordingly, a government should gather all ministries and agencies from all levels under the country's green growth umbrella and coordinate their actions. Government agencies must be empowered to plan, coordinate, and implement green growth.

Table 2.9

Millennium Development Goals and their Overlaps with Climate Change Issues

Millennium Development Goal	Mitigation
To halve, between 1990 and 2015, the proportion of the world's population whose income is below $1 a day.	Expanded access to energy services and, to some extent, agro-forestry, can lead to increased income for beneficiaries. Expanded access to energy services may lead to increased emissions.
To halve, between 1990 and 2015, the proportion of people who suffer from hunger.	Expanded access to energy services and agroforestry increases food productivity. Expanded access to energy services may lead to increased emissions.
To ensure that, by 2015, children everywhere will able to complete a full course of primary schooling.	Access to energy services allows for the development of more schools. Energy access allows children to have adequate lighting during the evening studying. Expanded access to energy services may lead to increased emissions.
To ensure that girls and boys have equal access to primary and secondary education, preferably by 2005, and to all levels of education no later than 2015.	Increased access to modern energy services allows women and children to have more time for education rather than gathering fuelwood. Access to modern energy services reduces exposure to high levels of indoor pollution caused by dirty energy systems.
To reduce by two-thirds, between 1990 and 2015, the mortality rate for children under the age of five.	Expanded access to energy services will allow better health services for children. Expanded access to energy services may lead to increased emissions.
To reduce by three-quarters, between 1990 and 2015, the rate of maternal mortality.	Expanded access to energy services will allow better health services for pregnant women. Expanded access to energy services may lead to increased emissions.
To reduce the prevalence of HIV/AIDS, malaria, and other major diseases.	Expanded access to energy services will allow better health services overall, including in rural areas, and better preventive measures. Expanded access to energy services may lead to increased emissions.
To stop the unsustainable exploitation of natural resources.	Mitigating climate change can reduce unsustainable exploitation of natural resources and increase access to renewable resources.

Source: ADB–ADBI study team.

2.4.2
Measuring the Progress of Low-Carbon Green Growth

Low-Carbon Green Growth Indicators

Part of defining, pursuing, and achieving low-carbon green growth is measuring its progress. Governments need guidance to monitor progress, review their past performance and the effectiveness of policies, identify better opportunities for public and private investments, and enhance the implementation of their policies. This point has been recognized both in work by the Organisation for Economic Co-operation and Development (OECD) and some development banks. The OECD has identified four clusters of indicators for monitoring progress toward green growth.

1. **Environmental and resource productivity:**
   To capture the need for efficient use of natural capital and capture aspects of production, which are rarely quantified in economic models and accounting frameworks.
2. **Economic and environmental assets:**
   To reflect that depleting the natural asset base (e.g., water resources, agricultural productivity, and biodiversity) presents a risk to growth, and that sustained growth requires the natural asset base to be maintained.
3. **Environmental quality of life:**
   Capturing the direct impact of the environment on people's lives, e.g., through access to water or biomass energy, or through the damaging effects of fossil fuel use.
4. **Economic opportunities and policy responses:**
   These can be used to discern the effectiveness of policy in delivering low-carbon green growth.

Not all the desired OECD indicators are measurable in Asia and an optimum set of low-carbon development indicators is being developed (Kumar et al. 2012). Figure 2.11 depicts an indicator framework used to assets the status of low-carbon green growth as applied to Asian countries. The two most important areas for defining indicators are the quantity and quality of growth.

For quality of growth, in addition to measuring economic output, such as GDP, it is important to measure the change in people's well-being. For the quality of growth, indicators are needed at the sector or even subsector level. One challenge is to keep the indicators to a manageable size. A highly selective but informative set of indicators for the quality of growth includes:

1. **Energy productivity:**
   Increasing GDP per unit of energy used is greener because it is a sign of increasing energy efficiency.
2. **Share of renewables:**
   Increasing the share of renewable energy.
3. **CO_2 emissions intensity per unit of GDP:**
   Increasing GDP per unit of carbon used is green as it is a sign of decoupling.
4. **Per capita CO_2 emissions:**
   Reducing per-capita emissions is sign of sustainable consumption and production.

Table 2.10 presents an informative set of such indicators for major Asian economies. One of the important functions provided by low-carbon green growth indicators is the ability to benchmark performance against international good practice. As Asia transforms, both benchmarks and NAMA targets will be useful in measuring progress toward low-carbon green growth. A good example of developing indicators on green jobs and industrial competitiveness can be seen with the work being done at the Asia Business Council (ABC 2009).

Figure 2.11

Indicators Framework

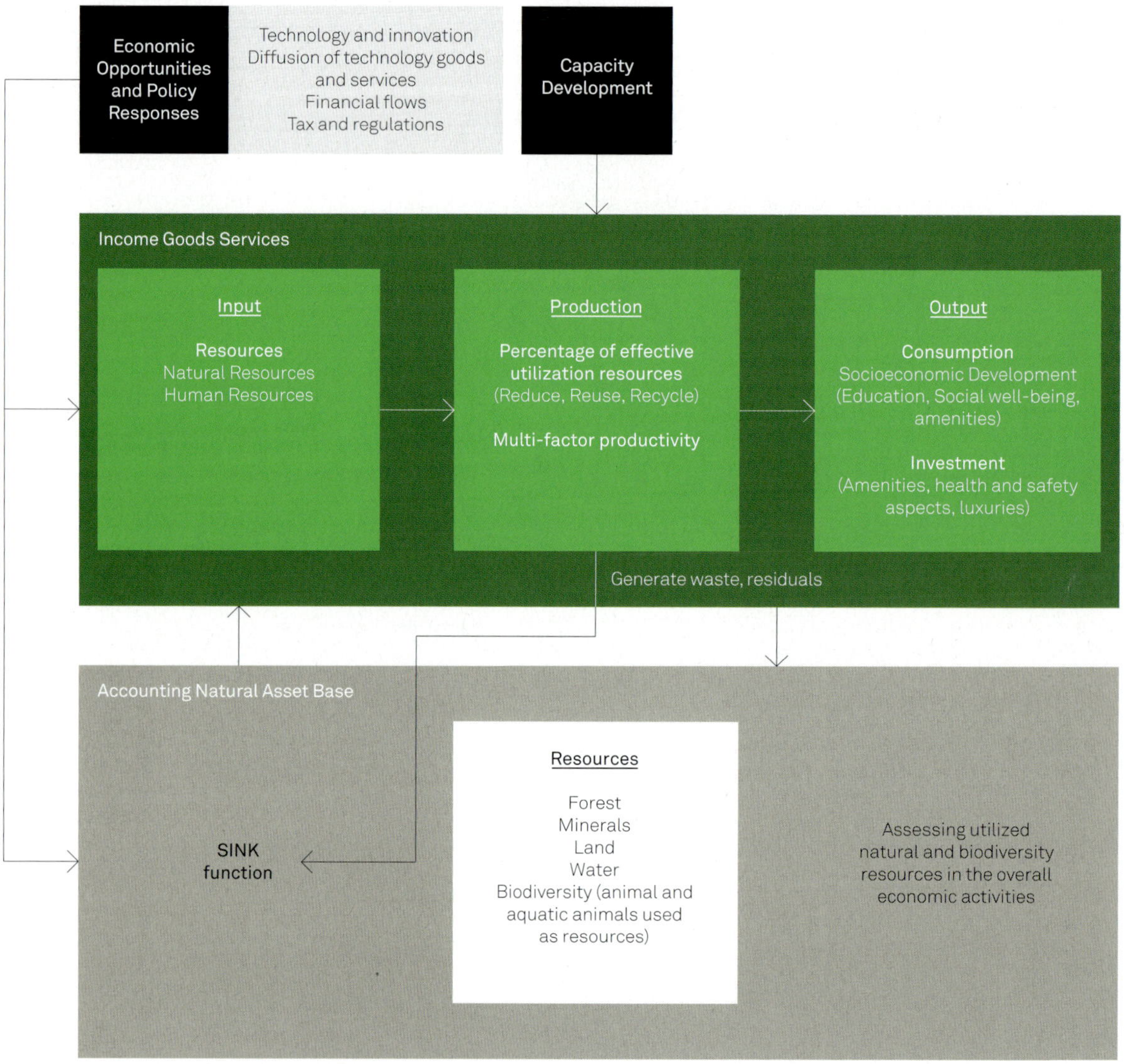

Sources: OECD (2011); Government of Japan, Ministry of the Environment (2012); Kumar et al. (2012); ADB–ADBI study team.

Table 2.10

Selected Indicators for Measuring Progress in Low-Carbon Green Growth

	Growth rate[1] 2010–2020	Growth rate[1] 2020–2030	Growth rate[1] 2010–2030	Quality of life[2] (ADB Index)	Quality of life[3] (UNDP HDI)	Energy productivity[4] (TPES per GDP 2008)	Share of fossil fuel[5] (TPES 2006)	Share of renewable[6] Energy (TPES 2000)	Carbon intensity[7] (MT CO_2* $ GDP)	Carbon emissions[8] (MT CO_2) per capita	Environ-mental health[9]
PRC	8.17	6.01	7.09	0.55	0.69	0.72	85.0	11.4	2.18	5.31	46.3
India	8.06	6.90	7.48	0.31	0.55	0.77	69.0	26.5	1.38	1.46	25.7
Indonesia	5.63	5.34	5.48	0.40	0.62	0.78	67.1	34.5	1.03	1.73	48.2
Japan	0.93	1.20	1.07	0.81	0.90	0.10	81.6	3.3	0.25	9.46	98.1
Republic of Korea	3.97	2.70	3.33	…	0.90	0.30	80.8	0.7	0.57	10.40	91.3
Cambodia	8.22	7.61	7.91	0.26	0.52	0.69	28.4	72.1	0.43	0.33	31.2
Lao PDR	8.46	6.93	7.70	0.27	0.52	…	…	…	0.29	0.25	…
Malaysia	5.41	5.31	5.36	0.64	0.76	0.49	95.2	5.5	1.06	7.57	85.3
Philippines	6.53	6.91	6.72	0.43	0.64	0.35	51.0	36.6	0.69	0.92	52.6
Singapore	3.54	2.05	2.80	0.85	0.87	0.13	99.9	0.6	1.01	6.67	100.0
Thailand	4.88	4.61	4.74	0.52	0.68	0.59	82.3	19.7	1.33	4.19	71.4
Viet Nam	7.95	6.50	7.23	0.48	0.59	1.09	49.7	28.8	1.52	1.50	51.6
US	2.26	2.28	2.27	0.80	0.91	0.19	85.7	5.6	0.42	17.96	94.5
EU	2.12	1.91	2.02	…	…	0.17	85.9	9.2	…	7.83	…

Notes: MT CO_2/1,000 year 2005.

Sources:
1 World Development Indicators Online database; World Economic Outlook database (April 2012).
2 Juzhong Zhuang and Yoko Nimi ADB Measuring Quality of Life in Asia (preliminary results) 2011 (equal weights are assigned to each dimension).
3 HDRD calculations based on data from UNDESA (2011), Barro and Lee (2010b). UNESCO Institute for Statistics (2011), World Bank (2011a), UNSD (2011) and IMF (2011).
4 OECD World Indicator TPES (Total primary energy supply), (accessed 7 Aug 2012).
5 World Bank 2010 – World Development Report (EU: 15 countries).
6 Renewables Information (2012 Edition), (EU value introduced from OECD Factbook 2011).
7 U.S. Energy Information Administration 2010.
8 World Bank – World Development Indicators (accessed 7 August 2012).
9 Yale University, Environmental Performance Index (EPI) 2012.

As is the case in advanced economies, low-carbon green growth indicators and future targets are works in progress in Asia. However, it is important to note that, even without fully developed indicators, economies in the region are moving forward as they must in implementing low-carbon green growth policies and practices.

Measurement, Reporting, and Verification Systems for Low-Carbon Green Growth

The concept of measurement, reporting, and verification (MRV) was introduced within the framework of the Bali Action Plan in 2007 under the UNFCCC. The plan foresees MRV of nationally appropriate mitigation commitments or actions for developed countries, MRV of NAMAs for developing countries, and MRV of financial and technical support for NAMAs.

Several different aims of any MRV provisions on GHG emissions and actions could be comprised in the regional MRV structure. These could include the following:

1. Generating a more timely and comprehensive picture of regional and national or sectoral GHG emissions trends, i.e., to assess if global action on GHG mitigation needs to be enhanced.
2. Collecting qualitative or quantitative information on what GHG mitigation actions different regions/countries are taking, i.e., to provide international recognition for these actions.
3. Quantifying the GHG impact of such actions, i.e., calculating the difference between performance and baseline.
4. Identifying promising areas for future GHG mitigation action in the regional scope.
5. Building trust, by providing information for an MRV system that will inform if the actual state of GHG mitigation actions reflects the actions/commitments that different countries have agreed to.
6. Allowing exchange of information about applied actions and their performance in GHG emission reduction regarding regional conditions.

While these options are not all mutually exclusive, they do differ, sometimes substantially. The design of any regional MRV system may therefore vary, depending on which of the above aims they are trying to fulfill. These aims are all potentially valid and agreement on which of them will be fulfilled by the MRV provisions will need to be reached during the negotiation process.

Early experiences in establishing independent MRV systems in the region have been encouraging (Box 2.8).

Box 2.8

Japan Bank for International Cooperation Measurement, Reporting, and Verification System

The Japan Bank for International Cooperation (JBIC) launched operations of the Global action for Reconciling Economic growth and ENvironmental preservation (GREEN) in April 2010. Using GREEN, JBIC aimed to support the efforts of developing countries through financing emission reduction projects and propagating advanced Japanese environmental technologies across the world, aiming to prevent global warming by using simple and practical quantification measures.

To assess the eligibility of the projects, JBIC required the measurement, reporting, and verification (MRV) of the greenhouse gas (GHG) emission reductions—so it developed the J-MRV. JBIC intends J-MRV to be a simple, practical, and internationally acceptable process, based on JBIC's operational experience with reference to international good practices on quantification of emission reductions. JBIC shall make the guidelines public and continue to improve them through lessons learned from implementing J-MRV as well as taking account of international discussions regarding quantification of emission reductions.

The J-MRV procedure is carried out at the project preparation stage or at the renovation or improvement of an existing facility, since not all eligible projects are determined at the time of financing decisions in credit lines or funds. JBIC calculates the expected emissions (projection), with reference to a feasibility study report provided by the borrower and/or the project proponent, and determines the baseline emissions applying J-MRV methodologies. The difference between the baseline emissions and the projection is defined as the planned emission reductions. Prior to making the financing decision, JBIC agrees with the borrower or the project proponent on a monitoring plan, and can retain outside experts for calculation of the planned emission reductions. The borrower or the project proponent then measures the project emissions according to the monitoring plan and reports them to JBIC starting on an annual basis.

Promoting the overseas business having the purpose of preseving the global environment, such as preventing global warming

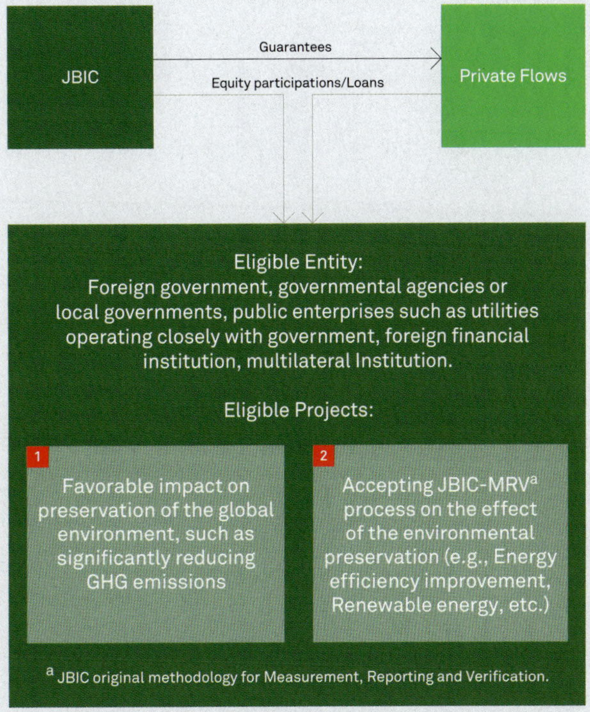

Source: Japan Bank for International Cooperation (2012) http://www.jbic.go.jp/en/about/environment/j-mrv/pdf/jmrv-guideline-en.pdf.

The process of carrying out MRV of mitigation actions can also vary. Thus, countries may need to agree on issues such as the following:

1 **Measurement:**
Countries could agree to guidelines, rules, and best practices to be followed when estimating the impacts of measures that mitigate GHG emissions. Agreement will also be needed on whether measurement and monitoring requirements should vary, e.g., according to type of action. Alternatively, country- and action-specific estimation methodologies and processes could be used.
2 **Reporting:**
Countries could agree to a common reporting format and common reporting guidelines outlining how actions are reported, such as which language, what units, what timing, where reports are collected, what should be reported, and when reporting should take place.
3 **Verification:**
Agreement will be needed on the type of verification body or bodies (national or international), what the verification process should look like, how results should be reported, and how to make any needed adjustments in reports on GHG mitigation. Agreement will also be needed on the consequences of problems raised at the verification stage.

Several challenges are associated with regional MRV systems. One of the biggest issues is the transparency and reliability of data. Another constraint is related to institutional capacity at the national level. Estimating a country's emissions will need some country-specific activity data (e.g., energy use). Obtaining the data, and country-specific factors, requires time and resources.

The resource cost of establishing a country's emissions inventory can vary widely, depending on the country and its economy. For example, developing India's GHG inventory for its initial national communication involved 150 entities (research centers, nongovernment organizations, industry organizations, and government institutions) and about 700 experts. Viet Nam has pointed out that a huge increase in human capacity is needed to address all of its obligations under the UNFCCC.

An analysis into NAMAs based on a case study from the PRC concluded that MRV systems might be credible where procedures are encoded in explicit rules that are transparently communicated, include provisions for quality control and quality assurance, and are based on institutional arrangements that provide accountability in ways appropriate to the national context. It was suggested that climate MRVs should be based on already existing MRVs, such as the ones from agriculture, to reduce the costs for both MRV readiness and implementation in the developing Asian countries (Wilkes et al. 2011).

This chapter began by explaining the relevance of low-carbon green growth against the background of the unfolding Asian economic renaissance, noting that the rising class of consumers in emerging Asia is adding significantly to emissions. However, many countries are acting to make sure their growth is low-carbon, hoping to attain a better balance between the environment, economy, and societal welfare. Low-carbon green growth strategies must be tailored to real developmental needs and political realities. The starting point is to classify the potential for low-carbon green growth policies together with the co-benefits they create. Low-carbon green growth policies can increase conventionally measured GDP through various means, but countries need an MRV framework to assess the progress and identify gaps, so that financing for the enormous changes ahead can made be made available from the market.

Chapter 3
Transformational Strategies, National and Subnational Level Actions: Progress and Findings

Chapter 3
Transformational Strategies, National and Subnational Level Actions: Progress and Findings

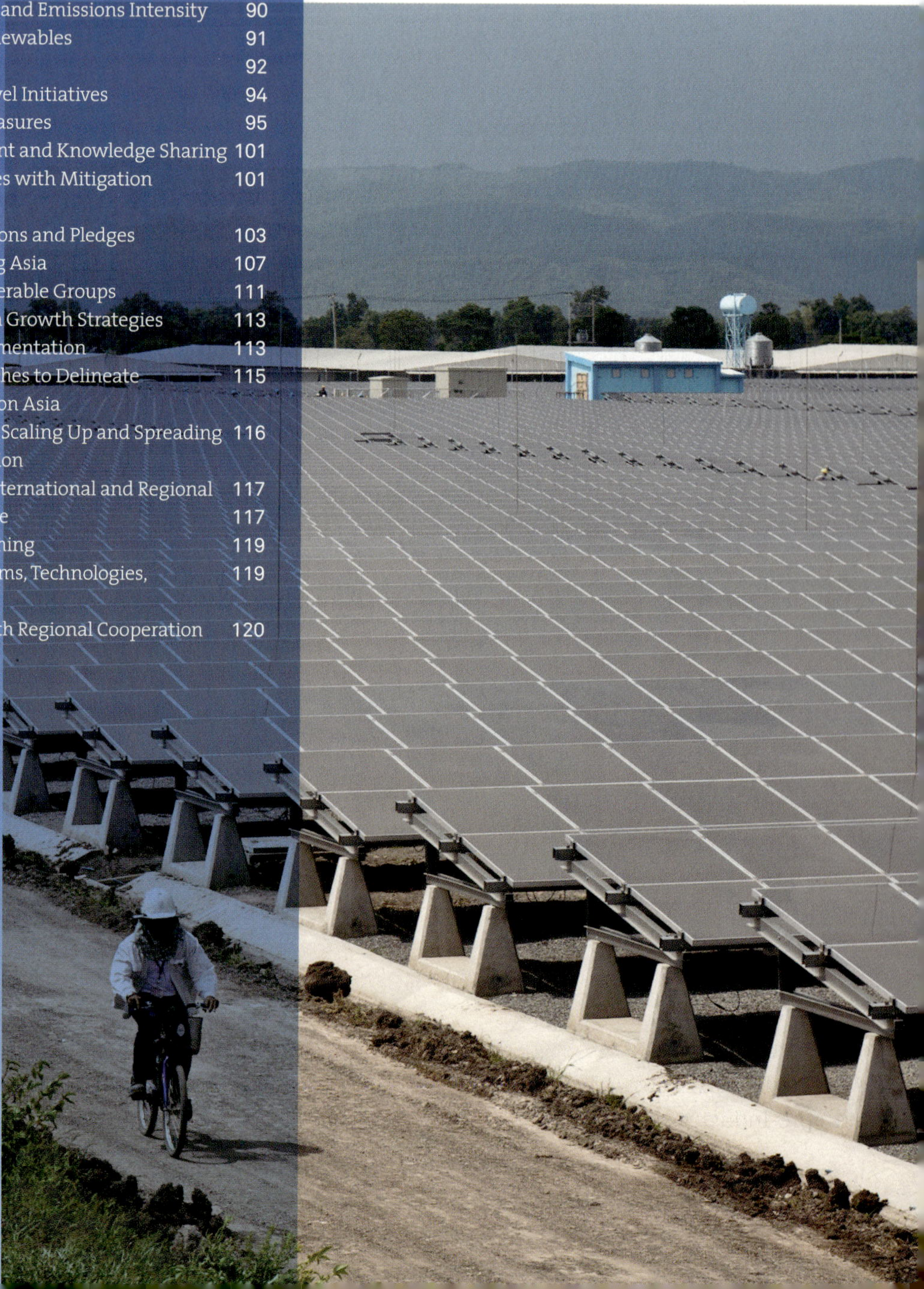

3.1
Changing Climate, Changing Economies

This chapter conducts an empirical examination of similarities and differences in policies and actions across developed and developing Asian countries. It seeks to examine whether current policies and plans in developing Asia are aligned with low-carbon pathways, and what were the main factors responsible for these countries undertaking these policies, plans, and initiatives. It reviews the strategies and actions undertaken by the major economies of developing Asia—the People's Republic of China (PRC), India, Indonesia, Thailand, and Viet Nam—comparing and contrasting these with initiatives in some of the developed countries such as Japan, the Republic of Korea, and Singapore. The analysis discusses the challenges that countries in developing Asia face in aligning their development paths with low-carbon trajectories. Success stories and initiatives that can provide lessons to the entire region, and could be scaled up or accelerated based on experiences across countries, sectors, or specific user groups are also highlighted. Opportunities for regional cooperation to move Asia toward a low-carbon green growth trajectory are discussed. While much has been achieved and significant efforts are being made across developing Asia, various analyses indicate that the current and planned efforts are not sufficient in terms of the scale of action that will be required globally, if greenhouse gas (GHG) emissions are to be limited to levels that would contain climate change within a 2°C rise, compared with pre-industrial levels.

Asia has been successful in multiple ways: examples of innovative applications of know-how in industrial units, frameworks or models for examining and changing behavior and consumption patterns, and the application of targeted policies and initiatives that have enabled efficiency improvements or influenced market dynamics toward alternative technologies.

Most of the large developing countries in Asia have exhibited a high rate of gross domestic product (GDP) growth during the last decade, despite the economic crisis. In keeping with their plans for achieving high growth and improving the levels of development, these countries have made efforts to accelerate the provision of energy, infrastructure, and services to their people; enhance industrial output; and improve governance and policy making. With further development, however, energy consumption in these countries could continue to increase rapidly unless major shifts in the patterns of production and consumption are effected.

In the PRC, the market reforms initiated in the 1970s and 1980s brought about structural changes and improved productivity, while increased government spending on research and development (R&D) provided a further impetus. Consequently, the country's energy demand has undergone unprecedented growth, with energy consumption more than doubling from 2001 to 2010 (Zhu 2012). Similarly, India's GDP has grown at about 8% since 2003/04 and the country plans to maintain this growth rate during 2012–2017. Thailand has moved from an agrarian to an industrial economy, and is forecast to grow at about 3%–5% a year from 2010 to 2030, according to the National Institute of Development Administration. In Viet Nam, the economy grew at about 7.5% per year from 2000 to 2009, but still lags in terms of development, and is characterized by low efficiencies and competitiveness, low productivity of labor, and low

Figure 3.1
Gross Domestic Product of Major Asian Economies, 2001–2011

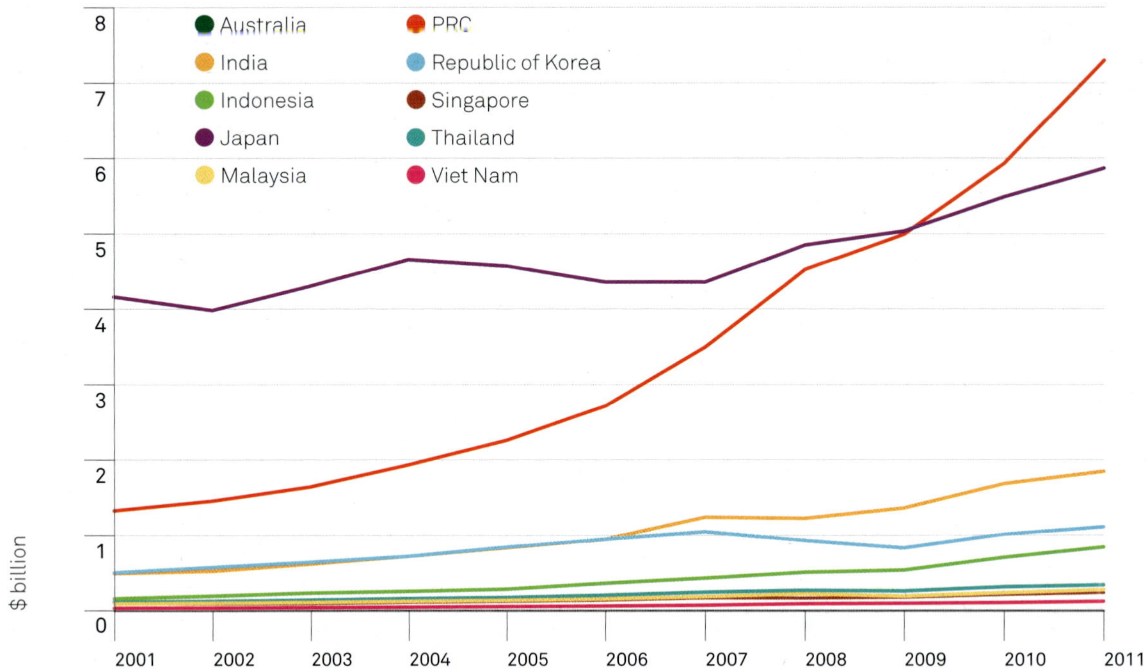

Source: World Development Indicators (2012). http://data.worldbank.org/data-catalog/world-development-indicators [accessed December 2012]; ADB–ADBI study team.

Figure 3.2

Energy Consumption in Major Asian Economies, 2001–2009

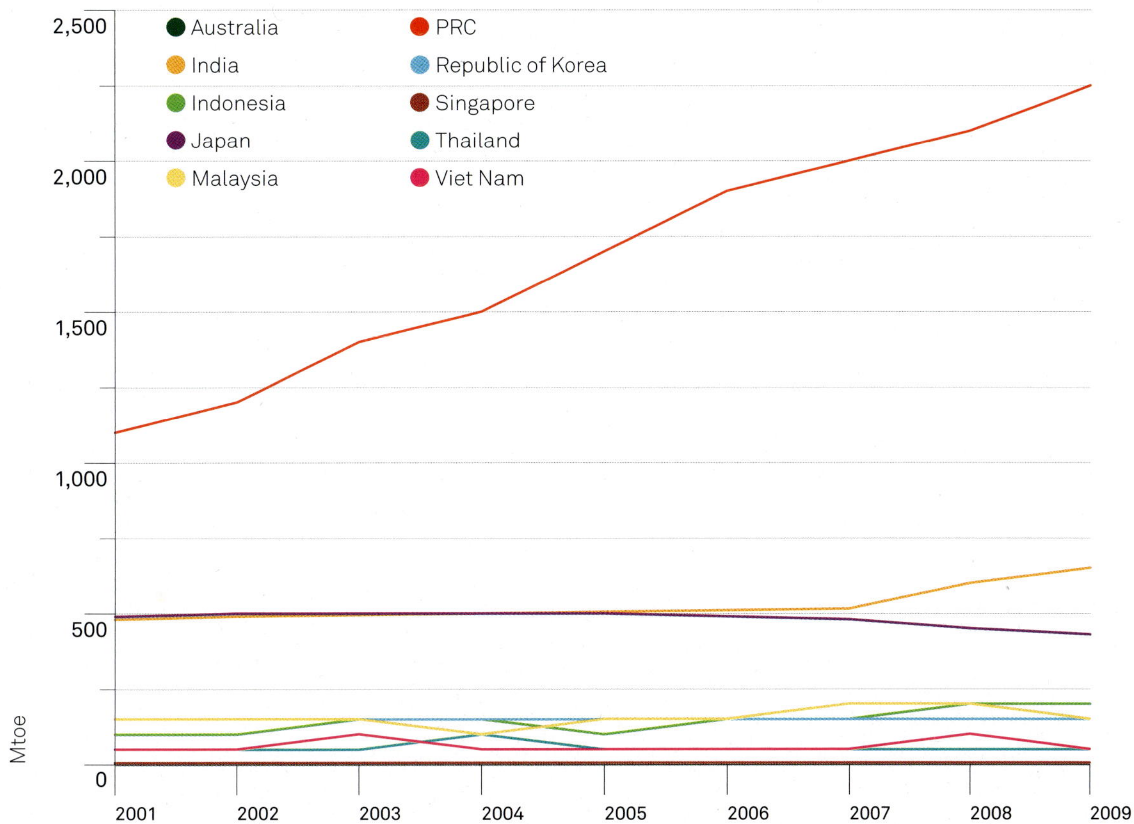

Source: World Development Indicators (2012). http://data.worldbank.org/data-catalog/world-development-indicators [accessed December 2012]; ADB–ADBI study team.

effectiveness of policies and strategies. Indonesia is already one of the biggest GHG emitters in the world, with 37% of the country's emissions attributed to actions in forests on non-peat soils, whether from deforestation, forest degradation, or forest fires. The country's emissions are expected to grow at 1.9% annually, and while the emissions from the power and the transport sector are small at present, they are increasing rapidly (Patunru 2012). A large share of Indonesia's population is employed in agriculture and the informal sector, making it more vulnerable to climate change. This makes it all the more important that poverty reduction and environmental protection strategies in the country be viewed synergistically.

The major developing economies in Asia have exhibited robust economic growth since 2001, as indicated in Figure 3.1. Figure 3.2 shows energy consumption that accompanied economic growth. However, despite the progress in social and economic development across developing Asia, much remains to be done to address the development challenge in these countries.

Large variations remain in the level of economic and social progress of different income groups, between rural and urban areas within a country, and among countries in the region. In the PRC, the per capita income in rural areas was only 30% that of urban areas and about 27 million people in the country are still below the poverty line (Zhu 2012). About 72% of India's population lived in rural areas in 2001, with significant variation in levels of energy use and access to fuel. About 293 million people in India did not have access to electricity and 772 million people continued to rely on biomass for cooking in 2010 (International Energy Agency [IEA] 2012a). Only about 30% of India's population uses liquefied petroleum gas (LPG) for cooking, with over 50% dependent on firewood and chips (National Sample Survey Organisation 2008, India). As for access to basic services such as primary education, sanitation, and health, the situation is far from satisfactory, and the country faces a huge challenge in providing the energy and infrastructure needed for better living conditions.

A comparison of basic indicators (Table 3.1) across each of the countries under study clearly shows a large gap in terms of unmet demands that need to be filled. Poverty alleviation, improvement in human well-being, and social equity are priority areas for countries such as India, Indonesia, the PRC, Thailand, and Viet Nam. Accordingly, countries in developing Asia find it all the more difficult to focus on options that could bring about emission reductions while seeking on the one hand to achieve higher levels of growth and on the other being faced with huge economic, infrastructural, policy, and institutional challenges.

3.2
Country-Level Pledges and Targets

Recent projections and scenarios from the IEA point to the need for large-scale transformations in energy use as well as production and consumption at different levels. Meanwhile, however, progress on global climate change negotiations under the UNFCCC has been slow and there is still a lack of agreement on a common goal.

With time running out rapidly, rather than watching and waiting, most Asian countries have been taking steps to ensure lower energy use and emissions in both per capita and aggregate terms. Even though developing countries are not currently under any legally binding obligation to reduce emissions, most countries in developing Asia have begun to include climate change considerations in their planning processes and have voluntarily articulated targets on GHGs. Further, independently of policies and plans from central governments, several state, city, and sector level initiatives have also begun, which clearly reflects the willingness of these countries to play a role in responding to climate change and exploiting opportunities where clear synergies exist between development and low-carbon pathways.

3.2.1
Voluntary Targets and Initiatives Addressing Emissions

In the lead-up to the United Nations Framework Convention on Climate Change summit in Copenhagen in 2009, the PRC for the first time articulated a specific target for curbing carbon emissions. Apart from the National Climate Change Program, the PRC's 12th Five Year Plan laid out a series of relevant targets to 2015. Additionally, the government aims to reduce nitrous oxide emissions by 10%, and install extra capacity of non-fossil fuel power generation (including 70 gigawatts (GW) wind, 15 GW solar, 120 GW hydropower, and 40 GW nuclear), among other quantitative targets.

India launched the National Action Plan on Climate Change in June 2008, with eight missions covering both mitigation and adaptation issues prior to its voluntary Copenhagen pledge of reducing emissions intensity by 20%–25% of 2005 levels by 2020. The Jawaharlal Nehru National Solar Mission is accorded the highest prominence, as reflected by the statement of the Prime Minister during the launch:

> Our vision is to make India's economic development energy-efficient. Over a period of time, we must pioneer a graduated shift from economic activity based on fossil fuels to one based on non-fossil fuels and from reliance on non-renewable and depleting sources of energy to renewable sources of energy. In this strategy, the sun occupies center stage, being literally the original source of all energy. We will pool our scientific, technical and managerial talents, with sufficient financial resources, to develop solar energy as a source of abundant energy to power our economy and to transform the lives of our people. Our successes in this endeavor will change the face of India. It would also enable India to help change the destinies of people around the world (GOI 2008: 1).

Table 3.1

Comparison of Basic Indicators across Countries

	PRC	India	Indonesia	Thailand
GDP/capita ($/person)	$7,535	$3,585	$4,428	$8,612
Population <$2/day	36%	75%	51%	27%
Access to energy and services	**48%** of the population continued to depend on solid fuels in 2007. **55%** had access to improved sanitation facilities.	**59%** of the population continued to depend on solid fuels in 2007. **31%** had access to sanitation facilities.	**52%** of the population had access to sanitation facilities in 2008.	**96%** of the population had access to sanitation facilities in 2008. Only **23%** of household waste was recycled in 2008.
Commercial energy consumption 2009	91.1%	75.3%	74%	80%
Per capita commercial energy in 2009 (toe/person)	1.48	0.43	0.62	1.18
Per capita CO_2 emissions in 2009 (t/capita)	5.14	1.37	1.64	3.36

Source: Derived from IEA (2011b): World Development Indicators (2012). http://data.worldbank.org/data-catalog/world-development-indicators accessed December 2012;CIA (2010); ADB–ADBI study team.

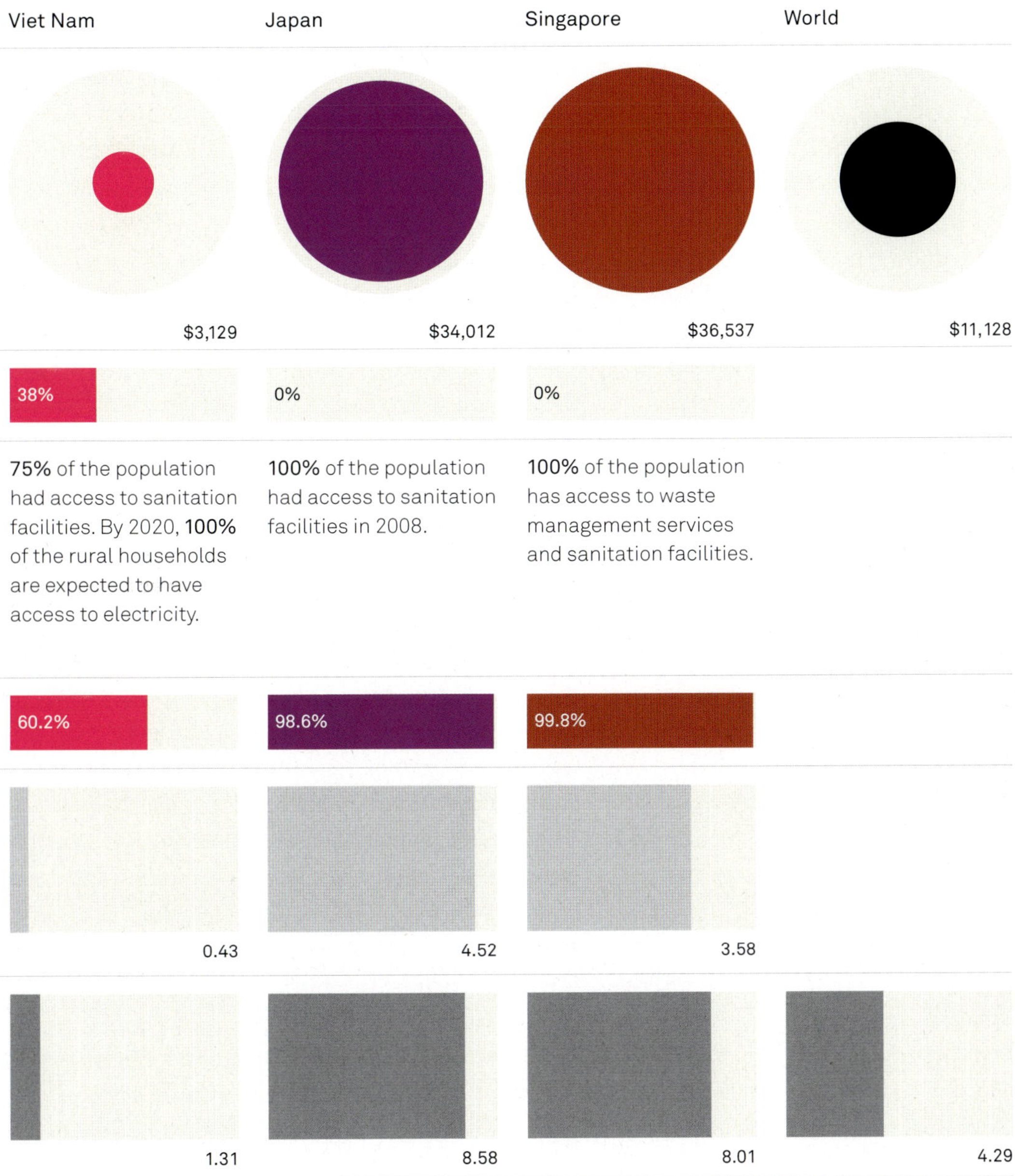
Viet Nam
Japan
Singapore
World
$3,129
$34,012
$36,537
$11,128
38%
0%
0%
75% of the population had access to sanitation facilities. By 2020, 100% of the rural households are expected to have access to electricity.
100% of the population had access to sanitation facilities in 2008.
100% of the population has access to waste management services and sanitation facilities.
60.2%
98.6%
99.8%
0.43
4.52
3.58
1.31
8.58
8.01
4.29

The Jawaharlal Nehru National Solar Mission aims at generating 20,000 megawatts (MW) of solar power by 2022 and working toward making India a global leader in solar energy deployment through the extension of electricity access. Other targets relating to this objective include 2 GW of off-grid solar plants, 20 million square meters of solar collectors to be installed, and 20 million solar lighting systems to be created and distributed in rural areas, saving about 1 billion liters of kerosene every year (about 8%–10% of the country's total annual kerosene consumption). India's 12th 5-Year Plan is also expected to align the planning process with these targets, and for the first time will include a specific chapter on climate change (Mathur 2012).

Indonesia has voluntarily pledged to reduce its emissions by 26% compared with business as usual by 2020, and up to 41% with international support. At present, land use and land-use change, particularly forestry and peatland, comprise 85% of national carbon emissions. Consequently, the government plans to achieve 87% of its emissions reductions for both higher and lower targets in these sectors. Indonesia, apart from articulating its National Action Plan Addressing Climate Change, has included climate change in national development planning and in its National Medium Term Development Plan, 2010–2014, which focuses on both mitigation and adaptation, supporting activities including the development of data, information and communication, the strengthening of institutional capacity, and science and technology development.

While Thailand has not specifically articulated a climate change response, its Energy Conservation Program and the 15-Year Renewable Energy Development Plan lay out energy saving and renewable energy development targets that clearly align with low-carbon pathways (Chotichanathawewong and Natapol 2012). According to these programs, 44% of the country's savings are intended to be found in the transport sector, followed by industry (37%) and buildings (17%). With a target of 5.6 GW of renewable energy, 3.7 GW is intended from biomass, 0.8 GW from wind, 0.5 GW from solar, 0.32 GW from hydropower, and 0.16 GW of methane from municipal waste. Viet Nam has developed the National Target Program to respond to Climate Change, which assigns ministries, sectors, provinces, and cities the task of developing and implementing plans to reduce carbon emissions, assess climate change impacts, identify responses, and integrate climate change concerns into strategies, programs, and plans. Viet Nam's laws and policies directed at energy efficiency, conservation, and renewable energy further align the development plans with a low-carbon path.

The Republic of Korea put forth the 4th Comprehensive National Action Plan for Climate Change (2008–2012), the 5-Year National Action Plan for Green Growth in July 2009, and the Basic Law on Low Carbon and Green Growth in January 2010. Singapore launched the National Climate Change Strategy in March 2008, and the implementation of the Sustainable Singapore Blueprint started in April 2009 (Doshi 2012).

In accordance with the Copenhagen Accord, Japan has a target to reduce GHG emissions by 25% compared to the 1990 level by 2020, on the premise that a fair and effective international framework in which all major economies participate is established and ambitious targets agreed by the major economies. In November 2009, Japan also announced that it would aim at an 80% reduction in its emissions by 2050 and support a target for halving global emissions by 2050 (Kainuma 2012). Table 3.2 summarizes the targets of the major Asian economies under study across four major indicators: emissions, renewable energy, energy efficiency, and deforestation. A few of the major Organisation for Economic Co-operation and Development (OECD) countries (Australia, Japan, and the Republic of Korea) are included for comparison. Across all countries under study, within the energy sector, energy efficiency and renewable energy are the two key options to address energy security and economic growth, as well as climate change (Howes and Wyrwoll 2012). Further, given the relatively low base of renewable energy installation and the challenges of higher up-front investment costs, the plans to reduce energy intensity and cut the share of fossil fuels in countries such as the PRC, India, Thailand, and the others in the table are fairly ambitious. Most of the countries also have targets for increased forest cover.

Table 3.2

Climate Change Mitigation Targets for Major Asian Economies

	PRC	India	Indonesia	Thailand
Emissions	Emissions intensity 2005–2020: 40%–45% 2010–2015: 17%	Emissions intensity 2005–2020: 20%–25%	Emissions below BAU By 2020: 26%–41%	Emissions below BAU By 2020: 30%
Renewable Energy Targets	8.3% in 2010 11.4% in 2015 15% in 2020	~4% in 2010 15% in 2020 20,000 MW solar by 2020	15% in 2025 (including nuclear)	20.3% in 2022
Energy Efficiency	Energy intensity 2010–2015: 16%	Energy savings 10,000 MW solar by 2020	Energy intensity 1% average pa 2005–2025 Electricity elasticity/GDP ▼ 1 2025	Energy intensity 2005–2015: 8% 2005–2020: 15% 2005–2030: 25%
Deforestation	Forest cover 20.36% in 2010 21.7% in 2015 +40m ha in 2005–2020	Forest cover +20m ha in 2010–2020	Forestry As net carbon sink by 2030	Forest cover 25% in 1998 37% in 2010 40%* in 2020

Source: Derived from UNFCCC (2011); Howes and Dobes (2012); Chotichanathanwewong and Natapol (2012); Mathur (2012); Patunru (2012); Toan (2012); Zhu (2012); ADB–ADBI study team.

* target introduced in 1991

1 All emissions targets by 2020 unless stated otherwise.
2 Emissions intensity refers to the volume of carbon emissions produced per unit of GDP.
3 Energy intensity refers to the volume of energy consumed per unit of GDP.
4 The absence of specific targets for particular issues does not indicate an absence of policy; rather, the absence of a stated national target. For example, the Government of the Republic of Korea is implementing a large number of policy actions relating to energy efficiency, but does not have a specific national target.

3.3 Policies and Measures with Implications for Emissions Reduction

While Japan continues to be seen as a leader in efficient use of energy and resources, other developed countries such as the Republic of Korea and Singapore have demonstrated commendable progress toward emissions reduction, and provide several examples across sectors and at different scales of moving successfully toward higher resource efficiencies. Empirical evidence indicates that in most countries in developing Asia, while climate change has not always been the main objective, policies and measures have been formulated and implemented at various levels and sectors, which have led to a decoupling of emissions intensity from the development trajectory. In India, for instance, while energy use in absolute terms is increasing, carbon dioxide (CO_2) emissions per unit of GDP (based on purchasing power parity) have decreased from 0.41 in 1990 to 0.35 in 2009—a 15.8% reduction (IEA 2010b).

3.3.1 Policies to Reduce Energy and Emissions Intensity

The plans and pledges across developing Asian countries are supported by policies and initiatives at the national as well as sectoral levels. Recognizing the unsustainable trajectory of soaring energy use and local environmental degradation, the PRC has set a number of targets relating to energy efficiency, renewable energy use, reduced industrial water use intensity, and afforestation in its 11th and 12th Five Year Plans. As a result of such policies, the country achieved a 19.1% reduction in energy intensity following the 11th Plan. The 12th Five Year Plan focuses more directly on reducing GHG emissions with targets to reduce nitrous oxide emissions by 10%, and install additional capacity of non-fossil fuel power generation (i.e., wind 70 GW, solar 15 GW, hydropower 120 GW, and nuclear 40 GW by 2015), among other quantitative targets (National Development and Reform Commission 2011).

The PRC's Energy Conservation Law came into effect in 1998 and was revised in 2007 to include an energy saving responsibility system, including energy saving assessment and review systems for fixed asset projects, the elimination of outdated high-energy consuming products, equipment and production technologies, energy efficiency labeling systems, and energy saving recognition and reward systems (Zhu 2012). The PRC initiated the energy efficiency labeling program in 2004, and now all refrigerators and air-conditioners have energy labels graded over five levels of efficiency. Most provincial governments have also developed their own energy saving target evaluation and assessment, with the results publicized periodically.

In November 2004, the National Development and Reform Commission promulgated Ten Key Energy-Saving Projects to achieve a 20% energy intensity reduction. As a result, during the 11th Five Year Plan, energy consumption decreased by 35% in copper refining and caustic soda production, and 28% in cement and crude processing, while the overall energy per unit production for coal-fired electricity generation, steel, and aluminum decreased by more than 10%.

Since the mid-1990s, the Government of India has instituted a series of targets and plans to promote energy efficiency, which have had co-benefits in emissions reductions. Apart from the National Action Plan on Climate Change, launched in 2008, several other policies and programs targeting energy conservation and efficiency improvements have been implemented, including the Energy Conservation Act in 2001, the Electricity Act in 2003, the Re-structured Accelerated Power Development and Reform Program, and the standards and labeling program.

With a large part of its population working in the agriculture and informal sectors, Indonesia's policy efforts toward poverty reduction and environmental protection have largely been geared toward improving agricultural productivity and providing alternative technologies and choices to people involved in agriculture (Patunru 2012). In its Law 32/2009 on Protection and Management of the Environment, Indonesia also states its commitment to base national economic development on environmental sustainability principles. While land use and land-use change comprise 85% of national carbon emissions, energy-based emissions are the largest source of emissions growth, and are projected to reach parity with land-based emissions by 2020. Accordingly, the government further formulated energy-specific targets and, in 2010, put forward a goal of tripling geothermal energy generation to 4 GW by 2015 and up to 9 GW by 2025. Thailand established its Energy Conservation Program in 1995, which is now a rolling plan revised each year. In Viet Nam, the National Strategy for Environmental Protection until 2010 and vision to 2020 aims to increase the rate of clean energy use to 5% of total annual energy consumption in 2010. The National Target Program on Efficient Use and Saving Energy aimed for a saving of 3%–5% of total national energy consumption from 2006 to 2010 and 5%–8% from 2011 to 2015.

3.3.2 Initiatives to Increase Renewables

Most of the countries in developing Asia have put in place measures to enhance the share of renewables in their energy mix. While this may have been driven primarily by the desire to enhance fuel diversification for energy security, this is increasingly being viewed as a catalyst for the creation of markets that could provide opportunities for employment, industrial growth, and increase in economic activity and trade.

The PRC, through the Renewable Energy Law and other policies and measures, has been able to increase the use of renewables massively. The 11th plan provided a major thrust to resource diversification and resulted in enhanced wind, hydro, and nuclear capacities. Asian rivers enable the continued operation of the most hydropower projects. Countries like the PRC, India, Indonesia, and Thailand have a long history of designing and implementing dam projects, where proven technology exists. The focus on hydropower from the perspective of climate change in the coming years must not be on building new dams, but on maximizing efficiency, responsible operation, and environmental performance. A significant number of large hydropower projects were approved for construction in 2010, the capacity of small hydro power in rural areas was stepped up, and the Ministry of Water Resources and the National Development and Reform Commission proceeded with the checking and rectification of 5,200 problematic hydro power stations and strengthened the construction and management of small hydro power stations. As a result, the installed capacity of hydropower exceeded 200 GW and the grid-connected operational capacity of wind power surpassed 30 GW. The 12th plan has for the first time put in place a target to increase the share of renewable energy in primary energy consumption from 8.3% to 11.4% by 2015, and aims for 15% non-fossil energy consumption by 2020.

The PRC has rapidly developed into an R&D and manufacturing base for wind power equipment and the 100 MW offshore wind power project along the Shanghai Donghai Bridge was put into operation as the first commercial project outside the European Union. A concession bidding process for the first round of 1 GW offshore wind power has been completed, marking the initiation of offshore wind in the PRC.

With the steady development of the solar photovoltaic (PV) market, the PV industry has seen continuous development in the PRC. Driven by the development of international as well as domestic markets, the price of solar generation has been decreasing, and in 2010 the newly increased installed capacity of generation units in the global PV market grew at about 120%, reaching above 17 GW. In September 2010, the Notice on Strengthening the Management of Golden Sun Project and Solar Photovoltaic Demonstration projects in building sector was issued. Through this, enterprises are to actively support grid connection on the demand side through demonstration projects. With regard to solar thermal applications, a subsidized program exists for rural families to purchase solar products, which has resulted in the installation of 168 million square meters of solar heaters, substituting about 22 million tons of fossil fuel (Zhu 2012).

Biomass energy has also enjoyed diversified development in the PRC. By 2010, the PRC had 6.7 GW of biomass-based generation capacity, including: bagasse power generation; straw and forestry-based power generation and urban waste; biogas; and landfill power. Renewable energy has been recognized as an important element in India's energy mix for over four decades, and the country has among the world's largest programs for renewables. Grid-connected renewable power contributed to about 19,974 MW of electricity in March 2011, accounting for about 10% of India's installed generation capacity. Having initiated its wind power program in the early 1980s, India had a capacity of 14,158 MW in 2011, with Tamil Nadu, Maharashtra, Gujarat, Karnataka, and Rajasthan among the leading states. The Jawaharlal Nehru National Solar Mission is the most prominent mission within India's National Action Plan on Climate Change. It is aimed at installing 20,000 MW of grid solar power and 2,000 MW off-grid capacity, including 20 million solar lighting systems and 20 million cubic meters of solar thermal collector area by 2022. Several measures and schemes have been initiated to ensure that the mission achieves its objective of helping to reach grid parity by 2022 and to set up an indigenous manufacturing capacity.

In Thailand, energy efficiency and renewable energy development have received an impetus, with the 15-Year Renewable Energy Development Plan, the 20-Year Energy Conservation Plan, and the Power Development Plan 2010.

The 15-Year Renewable Energy Development Plan includes ethanol, biodiesel, solar, wind, hydro, biomass, biogas, waste heat, and municipal waste; and focuses on implementation in terms of R&D, development and demonstration, human resource development, public relations, and management. With the successful implementation of the plan, a GHG reduction of about 42 million tons of CO_2 equivalent ($MtCO_2$ eq.) is expected by 2022 (Ministry of Energy 2011).

Viet Nam's National Strategy for Energy Development until 2020 and vision toward 2050 aims to develop energy quickly and sustainably in close association with the national socioeconomic development strategy, in parallel with diversifying energy sources and applying energy-saving technologies. Indonesia also plans for increased energy diversification, with emphasis on renewable energy and energy conservation.

3.3.3
Sectoral Initiatives

Countries have also put in place sector level development policies and initiatives that have clear environmental co-benefits, and have helped improve efficiencies and bring about emission reductions. Industry accounted for 70% of energy consumption in the PRC, so the government launched the 1,000 Energy Consuming Enterprises Program in April 2006 across nine key sectors. With the aim of changing to the best available technologies, this initiative is estimated to have saved 150 million tons of oil equivalent (mtoe) energy during the 11th plan period (2007–2012). Energy efficiency benchmarking was launched in the cement, steel, and chemical industries and became compulsory for key industries.

In the power and industry sectors, efforts have been made across most of the developing countries of Asia toward the research and diffusion of low-carbon technologies. These include ultra-super critical thermal power plant technology, dry quenching technology, low-temperature waste heat power generation, and regenerative combustion technology. Both the PRC and India, for instance, have made significant improvements in energy intensity in certain subsectors such as cement and steel with some plants already having state-of-the-art technology. Countries such as the PRC and India have also been eliminating small outdated and inefficient production capacities across the electricity, iron and steel, cement, glass, pulp making, and other sectors.

Many countries have also initiated measures to enhance energy conservation and integrate renewables in the housing and buildings sector. The 11th plan of the PRC had a target of more than 90% of new buildings to be constructed under mandatory standards for energy saving. Large public buildings integrated renewables into their construction planning, and energy conservation projects have been promoted in heating and air conditioning systems in hotels and commercial buildings. Similarly, in India, the Ministry of New and Renewable Energy has initiated several programs focusing on renewable energy sources in buildings. An Energy Conservation Building Code was launched in May 2007, which addresses the design of new large commercial buildings to optimize buildings' energy demand. All buildings with a built-up area above 20,000 square meters are appraised by the Ministry's Environmental Appraisal Committees and the State Environmental Appraisal Committees. In 2011, India put forward a Mission on Sustainable Habitat within its National Action Plan on Climate Change, of which green buildings are an important element. This plan also aims to develop a comprehensive approach to managing water, solid waste, and wastewater and to tap the potential for recycling, reuse, and energy creation in urban centers. Other initiatives, such as the Programme for Energy Recovery from Urban and Industrial Waste, aim to tap power generation potential from industrial waste.

The transportation sector has played a key role in the PRC development process, but has also put increasing pressure on oil imports and emissions. The Government of the PRC has supported rail development and accelerated the construction of passenger-dedicated lines and interurban railways, apart from improving the highway development and water transportation simultaneously. During the 11th plan, the Ministry of Transport launched eight major energy conservation projects in companies, test units for fuel conservation access and withdrawal, energy-efficient driving, test units for energy saving in transportation with dumping trailers, construction of a public travel traffic information service system, and construction of energy saving ports. Significant progress has been made in the diffusion of energy-efficient and new energy automobiles. In Thailand, policies exist on waste, especially in Bangkok and other large cities.

Sectoral actions and policies are not limited to energy, transportation, and waste, but are spread across sectors that are relevant from other socioeconomic dimensions in these countries. Many of the countries under study have made commitments to emission reduction policies in forestry. While a few of these commitments are aspirational targets to increase the land area under forests or to increase the forest stock, some countries have also put forward policies that use financial incentives and land-use regulations to increase forestry coverage and reduce emissions from land clearing. The National Mission for a Green India, under India's National Action Plan on Climate Change, aims to increase forest cover on 10 million hectares of land, and to increase CO_2 sequestration in forests by 50–60 Mt per year by 2020. While the Government of India has allocated funds to the Compensatory Afforestation Fund Management and Planning Authority to support programs for the conservation, regeneration, and management of existing forests and wildlife habitats, the path has not been detailed and it is still unclear how the commitments will be achieved. Similarly, the PRC has an aspirational target to increase forest cover by 40 million hectares and forest stock volume by 1.3 billion cubic meters by 2020 from the 2005 level, but the path to achieving this is still nebulous. Indonesia and the Philippines have taken actions that help to maintain existing forest cover, restore lost carbon stocks from degraded or cleared forests, and promote of afforestation in new forest areas to increase carbon sinks. The PRC and the Republic of Korea have also announced policies to reduce emissions from rice cultivation, although these have not been laid out in detail.

3.3.4
Subnational and Local Level Initiatives

Apart from national level pledges and policies, many countries in developing Asia—including the PRC, India, and Indonesia—have also embarked on subnational and local initiatives to enhance efficiency and reduce emissions. In the PRC, in 2010, the National Development and Reform Commission, the Ministry of Finance, and the Ministry of Agriculture awarded 108 cities the title of National Green Energy Demonstration County. Subsidies are provided for the construction of green energy demonstration cities to facilitate the development and use of renewable energy, and establish a service system for rural energy. In India, in 2008, the state of Himachal Pradesh introduced a voluntary green tax on vehicle users to create a fund for combating climate change—one of the first of its kind among Indian states. The state government also announced an environment plan in 2008. By 2020, the state plans to become carbon neutral. The state of Gujarat has similarly undertaken innovative measures to bring in sustainable and greener development by enhancing the exploitation of clean and efficient options. For example, a multi-benefit pilot project generating 1 MW electricity from solar panels atop the Narmada branch canal was set up jointly on an experimental basis by state-owned Sardar Sarovar Narmada Nigam and the Gujarat State Electricity Corporation. Solar panels have been fitted over a 750-meter stretch on the Sanand–Kadi Narmada branch canal to generate 1.6 million units of clean electricity annually. Besides producing clean energy without causing any pollution, the solar panels would spare a large amount of land otherwise required if the solar power project were land-based. It is estimated that the project could prevent the evaporation of about 9 million liters of water annually as the canal will remain covered.

Several Indian states have started articulating their state action plans in line with the missions specified in the National Action Plan on Climate Change. Recognizing the growing role of the transport sector in energy demand, the Government of India has started another scheme, the Jawaharlal Nehru National Urban Renewal Mission, providing support to city bodies to plan their transportation and infrastructure in the most efficient manner. Several state governments have come up with proposals for integrated urban transport that rely on the development of public or mass transit systems.

Japan has already undertaken initiatives to curb emissions, and has extensive experience that can be spread far and wide (Kainuma 2012). The Sustainable Shiga initiative, Low Carbon Kyoto, Carbon-Minus Tokyo, and the Clean Energy Demonstration Town: Kuzumaki Town are among the initiatives taken up by Japan at the local level. Box 3.1 provides an example of a local initiative.

Box 3.1

Environmental Model City and Eco-Future City in Japan

An Environmental Model City is a municipality designated by the Government of Japan as a model for making large cuts in greenhouse gas emissions and realizing a low-carbon society. These cities will provide the world with models for the low-carbon cities of the future, and lead the way to the realization of regional models in which low-carbon and sustainable development co-exists through the collective power of local communities.

From 11 April to 21 May 2008, the Environmental Model City received applications from 82 cities and 13 were certified. On 22 July 2008, six municipalities were designated: Obihiro, Shimokawa (Hokkaido), Yokohama (Kanagawa), Toyama (Toyama), Kitakyushu (Fukuoka), and Minamata (Kumamoto). In addition to these cities, seven municipalities were designated on 22 January 2009.

Based on the experiences of the Environmental Model City, the Government of Japan has developed a new concept named Eco-Future City, which aims to (i) create the world's top success stories for low-carbon city planning with technology, mechanisms and institutional arrangements, and services; and (ii) expand the experiences domestically and internationally.

Expanded use of renewable energy, energy management systems with smart grid technology, renewables, next-generation vehicles, and the restructuring and development of related industries, are concentrated strategically in selected regions of the Environmental Model City, and new laws will be developed for promoting and supporting the Eco-Future City. The plan is to promote partnerships between governments in Asian countries and extend the experience to other cities in Asia.

Source: Kainuma and Ashina (2012).

3.3.5
Fiscal and Regulatory Measures

Each of the five countries under study have implemented fiscal and regulatory measures directed at improving energy efficiency, changing consumption, and promoting specific technologies or fuels (Table 3.3). The driving force for most of these measures is the country's domestic concerns centering on energy security, development, equity, improving access to energy, and local environmental considerations. However, a few measures that have been introduced more recently are linked directly to climate change.

Feed-in Tariff

Feed-in tariffs have been successfully applied in several countries to promote renewable energy generation and work by providing a guaranteed tariff for prescribed technologies, long-term contracts, and a guarantee that the power generated will be purchased by grid companies at higher prices than energy from fossil fuels. Countries such as Japan, the Republic of Korea, Germany, and the United Kingdom (UK) have applied feed-in tariffs at the national level, while the PRC and India operate national and subnational level schemes. Not only does the type of renewable technology eligible for feed-in tariffs vary by country, but the feed-in tariff rates also vary between generation types. Generally, average feed-in tariffs are more than the average annual wholesale electricity price in each country. In the Republic of Korea, this is so only for solar PV, while feed-in tariffs for hydroelectricity, biomass, and biogas are below the average wholesale electricity price (Kang 2012). Setting feed-in tariff rates too low results in difficulties in stimulating investment and does not encourage renewable power generation.

Table 3.3

Comparison of the Current Application of Various Instruments in Each of the Study Countries

	Feed-in Tariffs	Renewable Energy Certificates	Trading markets for energy efficiency	Renewable quotas/ portfolio standards	Mandated biofuel blending	Fuel economy/ vehicle emissions standards	Capital subsidy, grants or rebates	Tax incentives	Public R&D institutions	Public invest-ment, loans or grants
PRC	W S B		●	●	●	●	●	●	●	●
India	W S B H	●	●	●	●	●	●	●	●	●
Indonesia	R				●	●	●	●	●	●
Thailand	W S B G A				●	●	●	●	●	●
Viet Nam						●	●	●	●	●

W Wind S Solar B Biomass H Small-Hydropower R Renewable (inc. geothermal) G Gas A Waste

Source: Howes and Wyrwoll (2012); ADB–ADBI study team.

Renewable Energy Certificates and other Market-Based Mechanisms

Several new market mechanisms have recently been initiated in Asian countries. Table 3.4 exemplifies those being implemented in the PRC, India, and the Republic of Korea. Renewable energy certificates create a market for utilities to meet mandated targets for renewable energy or renewable portfolio standards, a regulation that requires increased production of energy from resources such as wind, solar, biomass, and geothermal. Renewable energy generators are issued credits for the electricity they produce and these can be bought or traded by utilities to fulfill their portfolio obligations. The system encourages competition between renewable energy generators, leading to lower costs.

In India, several strategies have been planned to achieve energy savings, including the Perform, Achieve and Trade (PAT) energy certificate trading scheme, the Market Transformation for Energy Efficiency, the Energy Efficiency Financing Platform, and the Framework for Energy-Efficient Economic Development. The PAT scheme covers about 477 designated consumers across eight subsectors (thermal power, fertilizer, cement, pulp and paper, textiles, chloralkali, iron and steel, and aluminum). Each of the designated consumers is mandated to reduce their energy consumption by a specified percentage. According to the PAT scheme, the percentage reduction for a facility would depend on its current level of efficiency—with the most efficient facility in a sector having a lower percentage reduction requirement, and the less efficient a larger requirement. This should result in energy savings of about 5.5% by 2014/2015 compared with 2009/2010, amounting to a saving of 6.6 Mtoe by 2014/2015. For better cost-effectiveness, facilities that achieve savings in excess of their mandated reduction are issued Energy Savings Certificates that can be used by other facilities for compliance if they find it expensive to meet their own reduction target.

The PAT instrument is similar to the Generation Rights Trading (GRT) mechanism in the PRC, by which coal generators are assigned tradable quotas. Estimates indicate that in 2007, the use of Generation Rights Trading across 23 provinces involved a total transaction quantity of 54 terawatt-hours (TWh), saving 6.2 million tons of coal equivalent. The Republic of Korea has also initiated a Greenhouse Gas and Energy Target Management System to regulate GHG emissions from "controlled entities" in the industrial, building, waste, and agriculture sectors (Box 3.2).

Taxes and Pricing Policies

Taxation is used to encourage energy conservation and/or to subsidize alternative energy implicitly. For example, in the PRC, the consumption duty levied on small cars has been fixed at a lower rate than for large cars. Central and local governments in the PRC have also implemented a series of price, tax, and fund-raising policies favorable to energy saving and emission reduction in industry.

Rational and appropriate pricing is a key element that deserves special attention in low-carbon green growth. While reflecting external social costs and benefits is important, large numbers of people need to be supported by subsidies and affordable energy. However, it should be noted that the gains of subsidies are often reaped by the better-off. So, there is a need to adopt innovative models that address the requirements of the poor. Innovative and targeted subsidy mechanisms have been attempted in some countries. The lessons from India in technology innovation in solar lighting are expected to extend to Nepal, Bangladesh, Kenya, and other countries. Regional cooperation in Asia can provide a platform to share knowledge and disseminate the benefits of such models.

The PRC also proposes a new tiered pricing system for household electricity in the commercial and civil sectors, as part of its efforts to rationalize the use of energy. An energy quota system by which consumers would be rewarded if some quota remains unused, or be penalized if they over-consume, is to be implemented in public buildings. In most countries, market mechanisms are preferred to taxes on carbon.

Even countries like the Republic of Korea, which are extremely progressive with regard to policies and strategies directed at low-carbon growth, have so far not been able to implement a carbon tax (Kang 2012). However, carbon taxes could be designed to be revenue neutral and could accompany a reduction in income tax or corporate tax. Revenue raised from carbon taxes could also finance energy-efficient and carbon-saving technologies.

The idea of introducing Emissions Trading Schemes (ETSs) has been mooted in the PRC. However, in Japan and the Republic of Korea, which have announced they would introduce ETS, implementation has been delayed. Tokyo has put in place a unique cap-andtrade system for GHG emissions at city level (Box 3.3).

Box 3.2

Case Study of the Republic of Korea's Target Management System

The Republic of Korea adopted the Target Management System to regulate greenhouse gas emissions from industries. In this system, the government consults with major companies to set individual level reduction targets, which once agreed become mandatory. The government not only provides incentives to support the implementation of the agreed targets, but also imposes penalties against noncompliance. While factories emitting more than 25,000 tons of carbon dioxide equivalent (tCO_2) are currently subject to the Target Management System, this may be extended to factories emitting over 20,000 tCO_2 and then to 15,000 tCO_2.

The government also provides financial assistance, which increased threefold from $125 million to $360 million between 2010 and 2011. In addition, the government supports 50% of the cost of preparing a greenhouse gas inventory, and 90% for small and medium-sized enterprises. Loans and tax exemptions are provided to companies that install energy-efficient and low-carbon technologies, including renewable energy. To encourage an early market for green products that serves as a test bed for the product before its launch, and to enhance public confidence, the government has a mandatory eco-friendly product procurement scheme called Minimum Green Standard for public institutions.

Source: Kang (2012).

Table 3.4

Examples of New Market Mechanisms in Asia

PRC	India	Republic of Korea
Pilot testing of Emissions Trading in selected provinces and cities	Perform, Achieve and Trade (PAT) scheme	GHG and Energy Target Management System
Objective To study the feasibility of utilizing market mechanisms in helping achieve emission reduction objectives.	**Objective** To improve the energy efficiency in energy-intensive large industries and facilities through certification of energy savings which can be traded.	**Objective** To promote efficient achievement of the national goal (30% compared with business as usual in 2020) by appointing a GHG energy consuming business of a certain minimum specified scale.
Target sector and potential participants Sectors to be decided. Participating provinces include Guangdong, Liaoning, Hubei, Shanxi, and Yunnan. Cities include Tianjin, Chongqing, Shenzhen, Xiamen, Hangzhou, Nanchang, Guiyang, and Baoding.	**Target sector and potential participants** Large energy-intensive industries and facilities notified as developing countries in the following 8 sectors: thermal power, fertilizer, cement, pulp and paper, textiles, chloralkali, iron and steel, aluminum.	**Target sector and potential participants** About 500 energy users notified as "controlled entities" in industry, building, waste, and agriculture sectors. These account for about 60% of the total emissions.
Excerpt of scheme/project To be decided.	**Excerpt of scheme/project** Specific targets will be set for each developing country to reduce energy consumption to a certain level, according to their baseline levels, within 3 years. Developing countries shall comply with targeted level. Developing countries can buy energy saving certificates if targets are not met.	**Excerpt of scheme/project** Target was set based on base-year emissions, prospective growth rate, and negotiation between each controlled entity and a competent ministry. Controlled entities submit implementation plan. Controlled entities report mitigation performance and prepare statement for emissions and energy consumption. Fines will be levied if failure to meet targets.
Target year of implementation 2013 in Guangdong province	**Target year of implementation** First cycle of commitment period: 2011–2014	**Target year of implementation** 2012–2014
Expected outcome To be decided	**Expected outcome** Saving of about 10 Mt of oil equivalent by 2011–2014	**Expected outcome** Emission reduction of about an aggregate 1.4% from business as usual in 2012

Sources: ADB–ADBI study team, derived from IGES (2011); World Bank (2011); Energy Efficiency Services (2010); Korea Environment Corporation (2011); Virtual Center for Korea Environmental Technology Exchange (2012).

Box 3.3

Case Study of Tokyo's Emissions Trading System

Tokyo's Emissions Trading System (ETS) is the first city level cap-and-trade system on emissions. The target is to reduce CO_2 by 25% below 2000 levels by 2020. The ETS applies to the heaviest emitters, including factories, office buildings, administrative institutions, and commercial buildings. About 1,400 large-scale facilities, which account for about 20% of Tokyo's greenhouse gas (GHG) emissions, are included—most of Tokyo's skyscrapers fall under the scheme. To be included, facilities must have a total consumption of fuels, heating, and electricity of at least 1,500 kiloliters per year (crude oil equivalent).

These facilities are awarded a limited number of allowances (the cap) to produce emissions. Tenants are responsible for controlling their CO_2 emissions. Units that emit less than their quota can trade their unused allowances to other participants who exceed their cap. Allowances are allocated at the beginning of each compliance period. Their number is calculated as follows (first period): [Base year emissions – required reduction or "compliance factor" (6% for industrial buildings or 8% for rest of the buildings)] X compliance period (5 years).

The first compliance period, from 2010 to 2014, foresees a reduction of 6% of GHG emissions on average for 5 years; the second, from 2015 to 2019, aims at a reduction of 17% of emissions on average for 5 years.

The ETS started functioning in April 2010 and the first performance evaluation shall be made in 2015. For participants that do not meet their targets, the system foresees financial (fines) and moral ("shaming" system where names of defaulting institutions are released) sanctions. At present, the ETS covers only CO_2 but will be extended to other gases.

Source: TMG (2012).

Fiscal Budgetary Support

The private sector is often hesitant to take the first steps to invest in R&D in new areas and innovative technologies because of uncertainty regarding investments and the likelihood of early movers producing a public good that could be replicated at much lower costs by competitors. The government therefore has an important role to play in facilitating and providing for increased levels of public and private funds directed at measures that would support low-carbon green growth.

The total financial investment by the Government of the PRC on energy efficiency and pollutant reduction in the 11th plan was about CNY223 billion, of which 43% was on energy efficiency. Viet Nam has put forward the National Target Program to Respond to Climate Change with a budget of D1,965 billion for 2009–2015. Such budgetary allocations are an important step for countries, which already have constrained budgets.

The PRC has set up funds to support key energy saving technological transformation projects, building energy saving reconstruction demonstration projects and energy saving technology demonstration. Grants have been substituted by awards. Special funds have also been set up to provide transfer payments to economically underdeveloped regions to encourage them to eliminate outdated production capacity and address issues of personnel settlement, asset compensation, and land handling.

Governance and Regulation

Both the PRC and India have set up energy saving companies to assist efficiency with the support of the government. Some energy saving companies in the PRC are now playing a larger role as supervisory organizations to eliminate obstacles, accelerate energy conservation, and strengthen institutional agencies to assist in the enforcement of local energy conservation laws (Zhu 2012). Several nongovernment organizations involved in energy saving activities that have played a key role in decision making, project evaluation, public advocacy, education, and training. Apart from enhancing the reward and punishment system, improving technical standards, and increasing the cost of inefficient enterprises, governments in developing Asia also want to ensure social stability and skill development.

Table 3.5

Public Policy Mechanisms for Supporting Low-Carbon Innovations

Stage	1 Early research	2 Demonstration and commercialization	3 Market update
Key policy challenges	Increase the volume of early-stage research Improve the flow of funding to promising research Transfer academic research into commercial environment Do not write off promising technologies too early	Identify scalable, lab-proven technologies Provide soft credit where it is required to achieve target returns Establish clear performance standards Do not try to pick winners, but cull losers aggressively Develop a replicable blueprint for large-volume rollout Provide support to close cost gap with mature technologies Ensure availability of credit despite market and policy risk Ensure economic system can absorb new technologies and remain stable Support/create lead customers	Ensure energy diversity, if necessary provide long-term support for higher-cost technologies Protect public budgets Avoid locking in uncompetitive market structures Shift emphasis to "polluter pays" rather than maintaining subsidies indefinitely
Enabling policies			
Regulation		National/state/local procurement targets Feed-in tariffs Reverse auctions/requests for contract Renewable portfolio standards/green certificates/PET Renewable fuel standards	Top-runner requirements utility regulation
Finance Mechanisms for Innovation	Incubators National laboratories Prizes National/state-funded venture capital National/state-run venture capital R&D grants	Project grants	Technology transfer funds National/State/Local infrastructure funds
Credit Mechanisms		Venture loan guarantees Green bonds Loan guarantees Debt funds	Export trade credit Microfinance Sovereign/policy risk insurance National/state/local Energy Service Co. (ESCO) funds
Tax-based Policies	Capital gains tax waivers R&D tax credits	Innovation clusters Accelerated depreciation Investment tax credits Production tax credits	Carbon tax
Carbon Market Mechanisms		Measurement, reporting and verification (MRV)	Domestic cap and trade Project-based carbon credits National/Multilateral carbon funds

Source: ADB–ADBI study team.

3.3.6
Research and Development and Knowledge Sharing

Adequate and timely R&D in low-carbon fuels and green technologies can help countries stay in an advantageous position and reap the benefits of being early movers. Governments in all countries under study fund R&D in alternative efficient or clean energy technologies. Table 3.5 characterizes public policy mechanisms that support low carbon innovations.

The Government of the Republic of Korea established the Presidential Committee on Green Growth (PCGG) in January 2009 by a Presidential Decree that led to a strategy for the development and commercialization of 27 core green technologies (PCGG 2009). The Green Technology Network integrates the existing green technology information systems of eight public institutes and provides practical information on 27 core technologies (categorized into five thematic groups) in terms of basic technical information, industry and market analysis, policy actions, R&D progress, road map, etc.

The government has also set up a step-by-step investment plan and strategy for these 27 core green technologies based on current investment priorities, the level of technology progress, and prospects of commercialization. Simultaneously, the government has worked on expanding infrastructure to facilitate commercialization of developed technology. A comprehensive analysis was also made on the market potential and competitiveness of each of the 27 technologies, and tools and measures for commercialization of technologies were identified. Further, recognizing that one of the main challenges for the development of green technology is limited access to financial investment caused by high uncertainties and the long payback period of R&D, the government introduced the Green Certificate System. This acts as a supporting mechanism that allows individuals and business groups not only to obtain easier access to funds for green technology development, and provides tax breaks for green finance, but also incorporates tools and measures to help private enterprises throughout the business stages including public financing, R&D, marketing, commercialization, and distribution.

3.3.7
Aligning Plans and Policies with Mitigation Pledges and Targets

National governments have a key role to play in determining how fast countries are able to progress along their planned emissions reduction pathways. For example, in the Republic of Korea, by setting midterm targets, the government has been able to provide a strong and consistent signal to industries and consumers. Further, in July 2011, apart from the national level target of 30% reduction by 2020, the Government of the Republic of Korea announced sectoral reduction goals across six sectors. Recognizing that voluntary measures are unlikely to achieve the planned reductions, the Government of the Republic of Korea has put in place regulatory policy measures such as the target management system and provides for comprehensive institutionalization of national green growth through a detailed implementation program and strong political leadership. Table 3.6 presents a summary of the measures and initiatives being undertaken across the Asian countries. This indicates that efforts are undoubtedly being made at various levels and across all sectors in several ways.

Table 3.6

A Summary of Low-Carbon Green Growth Policies and Measures Practiced or Proposed by Emerging Economies in Asia

		PRC	India	Japan	Australia	Singapore	Republic of Korea	Indonesia	Thailand	Viet Nam
Energy supply	Advanced fossil generation technologies	●	●	●	●	●	●			
	Transition/distribution grid improvements	●	●					●		●
	Retiring old, inefficient plants	●								
	Feed-in tariff	●	●	●	●	●	●	●	●	
	Renewable portfolio standards	●	●	●	●					
	Subsidies, grants, rebates	●	●	●	●	●	●			
	Investment excise and other tax credits	●	●	●		●	●	●		
	Public investment and loans	●	●	●	●	●	●	●	●	
Energy demand	Efficiency labels	●	●	●	●	●	●	●	●	●
	Sales tax, energy tax, VAT reduction	●	●		●	●	●	●	●	●
Transport	Mass transit goals	●	●	●	●	●	●			
	Control of individual vehicle ownership					●				
	Vehicle fuel efficiency goals	●	●	●		●				●
	Vehicle emission standards	●	●	●	●	●	●	●	●	●
	Biofuel standards	●	●			●	●	●	●	
Agriculture	Fertilizer management	●	●	●	●		●	●		
	Crop carbon sequestration	●	●	●	●		●			
	Methane mitigation	●	●	●	●		●	●		
	Reduction of open-field burning	●	●	●				●	●	
	Afforestation/reforestation programs	●	●	●		●	●	●	●	
	REDD							●		●
R&D	Clean and/or energy efficiency programs	●	●	●	●	●	●		●	
	Carbon sink programs	●	●	●	●	●	●	●	●	
Financing	Climate funds			●	●			●		
Capacity building	Public awareness campaigns	●	●	●	●	●	●	●	●	●
	Institutional capacity	●	●	●	●	●	●			
	Human resources development	●	●	●	●	●	●	●	●	●
City-level measures	Demand-side energy management	●	●	●	●	●	●	●	●	●
	Net metering			●	●				●	
	Sustainable transport systems	●	●	●	●	●	●	●	●	
	Compact cities	●	●	●		●		●	●	●
	Low-carbon lifestyle	●	●	●	●	●	●	●		
	Shift of energy intensive industries	●	●	●	●	●	●	●		
	Use of market-based instruments	●		●	●					

Source: Adapted from REN21 (2011); USAID (2010), and country background papers from ADB–ADBI Climate Change and Green Asia Study.

3.4 Critical Evaluation of Actions and Pledges

Whatever the driving factors, significant efforts toward energy savings and the adoption of low-carbon fuels are being made, and economic growth and carbon emissions have begun to decouple. Carbon intensity in the PRC has decreased by 23% since 1990, while India's energy and emissions intensity has also declined consistently over the last two decades. Based on purchasing power parity (PPP), India's CO_2 emissions per unit of GDP fell from 0.41 in 1990 to 0.35 in 2009—a 15.8% decrease (IEA 2010b).

Converting the pledges to common metrics demonstrates that the PRC in particular is embarking on mitigation activity commensurate, in both outcome and relative cost, with that being planned in developed countries (Jotzo 2010; McKibbin, Morris, and Wilcoxen 2011). However, several studies have shown that the Copenhagen pledges by all countries will not be sufficient to avoid breaching what has become the international standard for dangerous climate change—2°C of warming—equivalent to atmospheric GHG concentration of 450 parts per million (ppm) CO_2 equivalent. Recent IEA projections of future global emissions indicate that, to move from the new policies to the 450 scenario, twice the level of effort is required compared with moving from the current policy to the new policy scenario (IEA 2011).

The IEA study also indicates that, in the new policies scenario, emerging Asia would account for about 46% of global emissions in 2035, and the combined share of emissions from the PRC and India would be 38%. Figure 3.3 shows the emissions profiles for the PRC and India according to the IEA scenarios. It is clear that an extremely large gap exists between what the 450 ppm pathway calls for and what is likely to be achieved by these countries (Howes and Wyrwoll 2012).

Low-carbon green growth needs to be transformational rather than incremental. The IEA scenario analysis indicates (Box 3.4) that even if today's developed economies reduce their emissions to zero by 2035, that would be insufficient to achieve 450 ppm—equivalent to a trajectory of annual emissions falling to 21.7 Gt of CO_2 equivalent (Figure 3.4). That means currently developing economies must also play a key role in emissions reduction. Scenarios developed by The Energy and Resources Institute (TERI) in India that show the implications for India of achieving 450 ppm indicate that (i) the country will need transformational changes and will need to consider retiring much of the fossil-based power generation capacity likely to be set up in the next few years, and (ii) new transport would need to rely almost completely on renewable electricity (TERI 2008).

Box 3.4

Modeling of Alternative Scenarios in *World Energy Outlook 2011*

The projections of emissions and other related variables used in this report originate in the *World Energy Outlook 2011* of the International Energy Agency (IEA). The IEA models three different scenarios from 2010 to 2035.

The current policies scenario envisages the world if policies enacted by mid-2011 continued in their present form without any additional policies. The generated emissions trajectory is consistent with long-term global warming of 6°C. The new policies scenario incorporates all stated plans or commitments, even where there are not specific policy actions to implement them as yet. It acts as a baseline or a business-as-usual scenario that incorporates anticipated changes. The generated emissions trajectory is consistent with long-term global warming of 3.5°C. As many stated plans extend only to 2020, extrapolation is made from 2020 to 2035 of emerging trends, such as declining global energy intensity. Given the uncertainty surrounding implementation, the new policies scenario is a conservative interpretation of stated plans, i.e., the lower end of the Copenhagen commitments is assumed to be met. The "450 scenario" (or 450 parts per million [ppm] in the current study) describes the least-cost pathway by which the world has a 50% chance of limiting greenhouse gas concentrations to 450 ppm carbon dioxide (CO_2) equivalent, analogous to 2°C of global warming above pre-industrial levels. The upper end of international pledges is assumed to be met. Potential mitigation measures are identified across countries and sectors and are implemented according to the greatest reductions per unit cost.

Other greenhouse gas emissions are included in the modeling, but are not the focus of policy constraints in the 450 scenario. Emissions from land use, land-use change, and forestry are assumed to decline at the same rate across all three scenarios.

Important policy assumptions for the different scenarios include the following:

- **Current policies:** Realization of the energy targets in the 12th Five Year Plan of the People's Republic of China (PRC); phasing out of fossil fuel subsidies in all non-Organisation of Economic Co-operation and Development (OECD) countries with current plans to do so.
- **New policies:** Carbon pricing in the PRC covering all sectors by 2020, starting at $10 and rising to $30 in 2035;a removal of fossil fuel subsidies in all non-OECD net energy importing countries by 2020, and all net exporters with current plans to do so; a shadow price of carbon of $15 in the United States (US) by 2015 affecting investment decisions; 70–80 gigawatts (GW) of nuclear power in the PRC by 2020; 20 GW of solar energy production capacity in India by 2022.
- **450 scenario:** Carbon pricing for power and industry in the US and Canada ($20 in 2020, $120 in 2035); Japan ($35 in 2020, $120 in 2035); the PRC, the Russian Federation, Brazil, and South Africa ($10 in 2020, $95 in 2035); all trading schemes are linked at a regional level and all have access to carbon offsets (leading to some convergence in carbon prices); international sectoral agreements; widespread deployment of carbon capture; and storage in power generation by 2020.

While the discussion in the present study largely focuses on the transition from the new policies to the 450 scenario, it should be noted that even fulfilling the assumptions of the new policies scenario may turn out to be ambitious. While the World Energy Outlook provides comprehensive results for some major countries, it does not provide them for all countries. Consequently, the presentation of IEA modeling for Indonesia, Thailand, and Viet Nam in the present study appears in a proxy referred to as other non-OECD Asia. This grouping describes data aggregated across all non-OECD Asian countries, except for the PRC and India, of which the three other study countries accounted for 46% of carbon emissions and 47% of energy demand in 2009 (IEA 2011).

Note: All quoted carbon prices are in 2010 US dollars per ton of CO_2.

Sources: IEA (2011a; 2011b).

Figure 3.3

Emission Profiles for the People's Republic of China and India

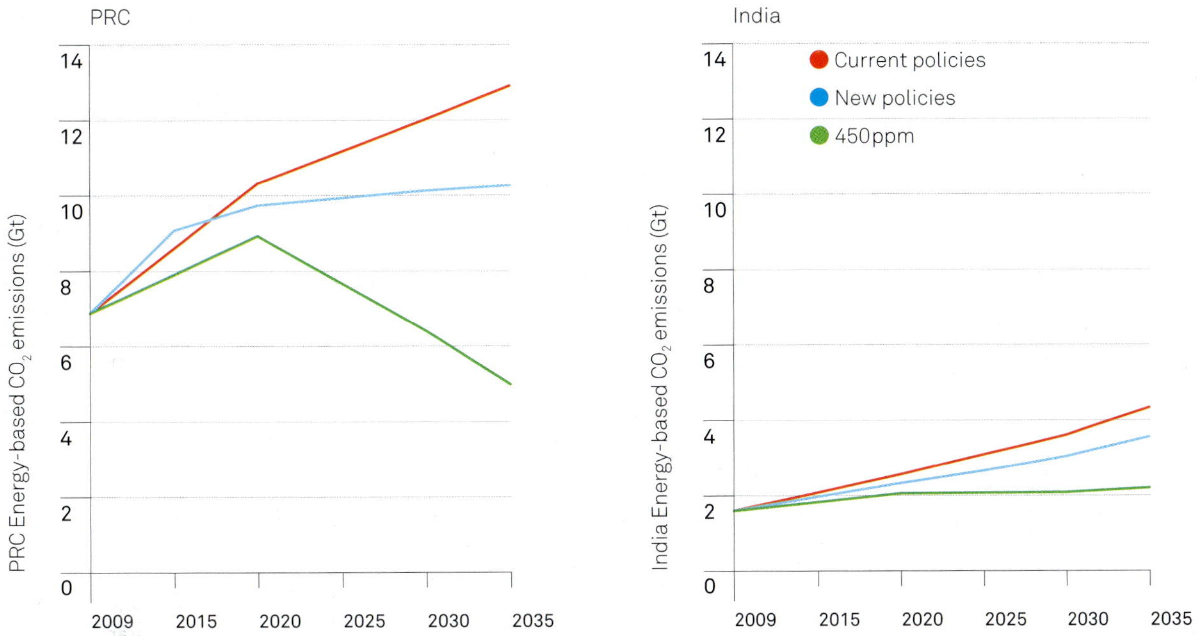

Source: IEA (2011a).

The IEA study estimates that the world has only until 2017 to shift to a 450 ppm trajectory before a lock-in effect of existing infrastructure requires that all investments made between 2020 and 2035 must be based on zero emission options (IEA 2011a). TERI modeling studies point out that, while it is important to take early actions to prevent lock-ins to high-carbon technologies and infrastructure, countries like the PRC and India do not have enough fuel technology choices to be able to change its energy development pathway significantly until 2016 (TERI 2008; 2010). All these studies, however, clearly indicate that future development paths need to see large-scale transformations, with opportunities for such transformation being made available as soon as possible (Howes and Wyrwoll 2012; TERI 2010).

Figure 3.4

Asia's Mitigation Efforts Need New Policies

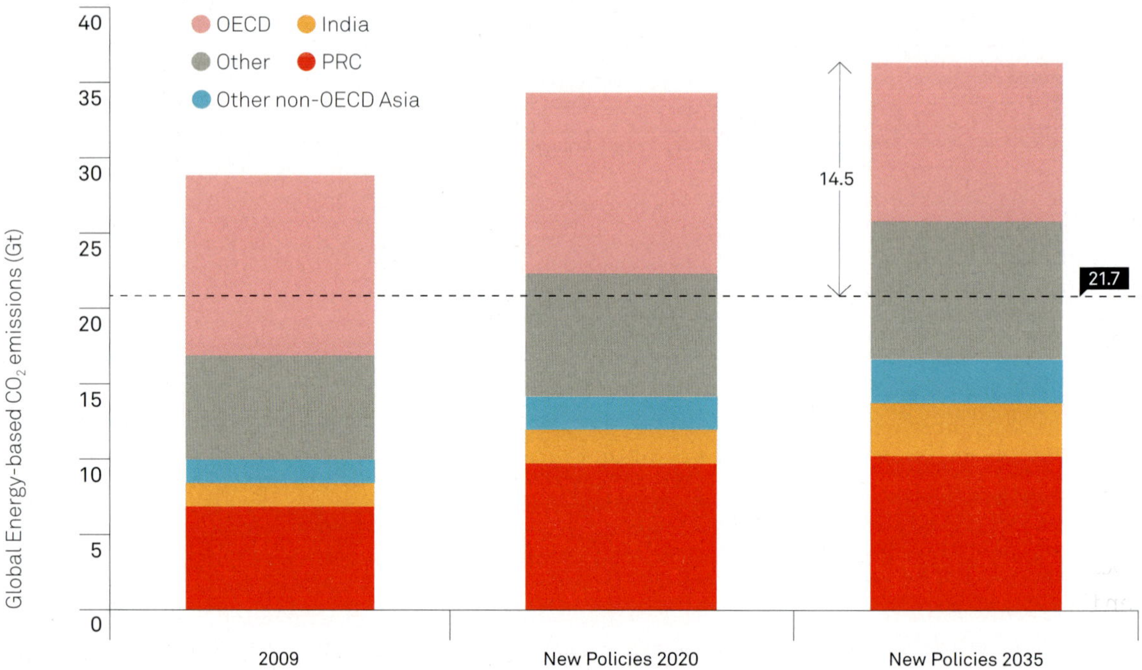

Note: Other Non-OECD Asia refers to developing Asia minus the PRC and India.
In 2009, Indonesia, Thailand, and Viet Nam jointly comprised 46% of emissions from this group.

Source: Howes and Wyroll (2012) based on data from IEA (2011a; 2011b).

3.5 Challenges for Developing Asia

Countries of developing Asia do not have easy solutions. Given the scale of transformational changes required and their capabilities and the availability of resources (natural and financial), the challenges are enormous. Despite the increasing willingness to move toward options that would reduce energy and emissions intensity, every country is not equally successful. While the PRC has moved ahead to achieve most of its planned targets, countries such as Thailand have faced several barriers in being able to achieve their planned targets. Even though Thailand's 15-year Renewable Energy Development Plan is formulated based on the country's renewable energy potential, Thailand has had limited success in being able to accelerate the implementation of wind, hydro, biomass, and waste-based generation. Finance is not the only problem: several other challenges include those of land acquisition for installing windmills (as most suitable areas are in conservation forest areas), hurdles in the construction of hydropower projects by government agencies and state-owned enterprises, implementation of suitable technologies for biomass use, and conflicts between locals and investors for utilization of municipality waste (Chotichanathawewong and Natapol 2012).

The challenges faced by developing Asia also need to be understood in terms of the availability of choices—Thailand, for instance, needs to increase its power generation capacity while decreasing its dependence on imported natural gas, for energy security. Given the challenges reflected in Table 3.7, renewable generation is likely to progress at slower rates than planned, making it necessary to continue looking at coal and nuclear as alternative choices to meet energy requirements. These are not easy choices, however. After the Fukushima incident in Japan, for instance, there has been strong resistance to nuclear plants, while coal power plants are also unwelcome because of air pollution. The challenges faced by Asia need to be understood not only as a matter of preferences, but of limitations in the availability of adequate and appropriate alternatives to meet increasing energy demands. While these countries should make every effort to improve governance and institutional capacities domestically, developed countries can also play an important role in facilitating technology transfer and know-how, investing in R&D, and providing financial support to make available cleaner and more efficient alternatives—thereby enabling countries to diversify toward green development.

Apart from energy related lock-in effects, countries such as Indonesia also face rigid labor markets with a large population of poor people stuck in the agriculture sector with little scope for movement across sectors, e.g., from agriculture to higher value-adding manufacturing. Therefore, policies need to focus on increasing agricultural productivity (in a more sustainable manner) and to improve farmers' access to wider opportunities like green manufacturing. This also applies to the peat and forestry sectors. In Indonesia, while Presidential Regulation Number 61 in 2011 laid out the policies and strategies for the key sectors, the policies and strategies do not match strongly and often have unnecessary overlaps (Patunru 2012). Much remains to be done in these countries to put together coherent and systematic approaches to meet emissions targets.

Budgetary constraints are another major challenge for developing Asian countries (Table 3.8).

Table 3.7

Challenges in Meeting Planned Targets in Thailand

Energy		Utilization in 2010	Target for 2010	Comparison	Key challenge
Wind	(MW)	5.61	45.00	(39.39)	Land acquisition for installing windmills (most suitable areas are in conservation forests)
Solar	Electricity (MW)	48.57	48.00	0.57	
	Heat (ktoe)	2.14	2.80	(0.66)	
Hydro	(MW)	58.85	142.00	(83.15)	Slow implementation for construction (by governmental agencies and state-owned enterprise)
Biomass	Electricity (MW)	1,650.00	2,454.00	(804.00)	Diversifying the biomass (suitable technologies for utilizing other agricultural residuals, beside rice husk and bagasse)
	Heat (ktoe)	3,136.00	3,130.00	(6.00)	
Biogas	Electricity (MW)	103.40	55.00	48.40	
	Heat (ktoe)	311.00	320.00	(9.00)	
Municipal waste	Electricity (MW)	13.13	58.00	(44.87)	Conflicts between locals and investors and lack of acceptance from local communities
	Heat (ktoe)	1.09	7.00	(5.91)	
Ethanol	(million liters/day)	1.23	2.11	(0.88)	
Biodiesel	(million liters/day)	1.72	1.35	0.37	

( ) = negative.

Source: Chotichanathawewong and Natapol (2012).

Table 3.8

Components of Government Spending, Emissions, and Public Debt

	GDP current ($ billion)	Public debt (% of GDP)	Population (million)	GDP per capita (current $)	CO_2 emissions (ton/capita)	Education (% of GDP)	Health (% of GDP)	R&D (% of GDP)	Military (% of GDP)	Debt service (% of GDP)	Tax revenue (% of GDP)
	2008	2008	2010	2008	2008	2000–07	2000–07	2000–07	2008	2008	2008
Australia	1,039.42	14.3	21.5	48,499	18.48	4.7	6.0	2.2	1.8	...	23.1
Bangladesh	79.55	39.4	164.4	497	0.29	2.4	1.1	...	1.0	1.2	8.8
Cambodia	10.34	...	15.1	710	0.31	1.6	1.7	0.0	1.1	0.4	8.2
PRC	4,532.79	15.6	1,354.1	3,422	4.92	1.9	1.9	1.5	2.0	0.8	9.4
India	1,214.21	54.9	1,214.5	1,065	1.25	3.2	1.1	0.8	2.6	2.7	12.9
Indonesia	510.50	28.3	232.5	2,246	1.69	3.5	1.2	0.0	1.0	4.8	12.3
Japan	4,886.97	172.1	127.0	38,268	9.02	3.4	6.5	3.4	0.9	...	...
Lao PDR	5.47	...	6.4	882	...	2.3	0.8	0.0	0.4	3.8	10.1
Malaysia	221.16	41.5	27.9	8,187	6.70	4.5	1.9	0.6	2.0	4.1	16.6
Mongolia	5.26	...	2.7	1,991	4.33	5.1	3.5	0.2	...	1.4	23.2
Myanmar	...	...	50.5	...	0.24	1.3	0.2	0.2	...	...	3.3
Nepal	12.61	...	29.9	438	0.12	3.8	2.0	...	2.0	1.3	10.4
New Zealand	115.45	17.4	4.3	27,045	7.74	6.2	7.1	1.3	1.1	...	31.7
Pakistan	165.18	51.0	184.8	994	0.81	2.9	0.8	0.7	2.6	1.8	9.8
Philippines	167.49	56.9	93.6	1,854	0.80	2.6	1.3	0.1	0.8	6.6	14.1
Singapore	193.33	95.9	4.8	39,950	9.16	2.8	1.0	2.6	4.1	...	14.6
Republic of Korea	931.40	24.4	48.5	19,162	10.31	4.2	3.5	3.5	2.8	...	16.6
Sri Lanka	40.72	81.1	20.4	2,020	0.61	7.1	2.0	0.2	3.6	3.1	14.2
Thailand	272.46	38.0	68.1	4,043	3.41	4.9	2.7	0.2	1.5	6.3	16.5
Viet Nam	90.64	48.8	89.0	1,051	1.19	5.3	2.8	0.2	2.4	1.5	...

CO_2=Carbon dioxide, GDP=gross domestic product, Lao PDR=Lao People's Democratic Republic, PRC=People's Republic of China, R&D=research and development.

Source: World Bank (2010); CIA (2010); IEA (2010); UNDP (2011); ADB–ADBI study team.

The fact that most developing countries have ambitious targets for renewable energy indicates that this is seen as an opportunity. Developing Asia has two-thirds of the world's poorest people—the most vulnerable in terms of the impacts of climate change not only on their livelihoods, but also on food and water security. Enhancing the capabilities of people through poverty reduction, equity and access to energy, ensuring stable and improved livelihood opportunities, and strengthening infrastructural capacities in developing regions are therefore center-stage and are key considerations in moving toward a Green Asia.

Access to sufficient and affordable energy is an overriding priority for these countries, and their inability to meet rising energy and infrastructure demands could seriously constrain economic growth and improvement in the well-being of the people in emerging Asia. The pressure on energy has been increasing rapidly with higher urbanization, and the need for the provision of infrastructure for delivering higher levels of energy and other basic services. As more people obtain access to modern energy, and shift away from traditional fuels, it is possible that energy intensity in some developing countries could increase, despite improvement in technological efficiency. For example, in Viet Nam, the commercial energy intensity increased from 387 kilograms of oil equivalent per thousand dollars (kgoe/'000 $1000)[1] in 2009 to 545 kgoe/'000 $ in 2009. The country continues to have about 30% of its energy consumption met by biomass in 2010, which is forecast to fall to 15.1% by 2020 and 7.5% by 2030 (Toan 2012).

In countries such as the PRC and India, while energy intensity has been decreasing, it is evident that energy demands and total emissions will continue to grow as more people seek to fulfill their aspirations and needs. Projections of motor vehicle ownership indicate that on current trends, in the PRC, the number of vehicles will increase from 130 million in 2008 to 413 million in 2035, while in India this may increase from 64 million to 372 million (ADB and the Department for International Development of the UK [DFID] 2006). Accordingly, unless efficiency improvements and the shift to renewables can outpace the increase from developmental transitions, energy requirements will rise.

While energy demands in most of the major countries in developing Asia have continued to increase, conventional domestic energy supplies have not kept pace. During 1992–2012, the PRC has joined India and Thailand in being a net importer of energy. Over time, Indonesia and Viet Nam are also expected to become net importers. It is expected that Viet Nam will shift from being a net energy exporter to one that imports energy to the extent of 53 Mtoe in 2020 and 143 Mtoe in 2030 under business as usual. So, energy security is a growing concern.

---

1 Year 2000 $.

Energy security considerations in Asia, which had thus far centered on oil, are now shifting toward coal. Domestic coal supplies in each of the five countries under study are limited and/or can be costly to access. India's extractable coal reserves have been significantly overestimated in the past, and recent estimates indicate that these are expected to last only 40–50 years with current trends of production and consumption (TERI 2011). High and rising energy import dependence in the major developing countries of Asia is likely to render these economies more vulnerable to energy price volatility, and larger risks and uncertainties associated with future supplies of imported fossil energy supplies. Accordingly, the adoption of energy efficiency and alternative fuel options in developing countries such as the PRC, India, and Thailand has not been driven primarily by climate change considerations so far, but mainly by considerations of energy security, industrial competitiveness, and sustainability in resource use. Further, with a rapid increase in fossil fuel consumption and growing congestion in urban centers, local environmental considerations in terms of air and water pollution as well as land degradation and biodiversity loss have become important domestic drivers toward energy saving and cleaner and renewable energy.

The challenge for these countries, therefore, is not only to provide much higher levels of energy, infrastructure, and services, but to manage this in a sustainable manner. Enabling transitions in energy intensity will also require significant efforts and technology to leapfrog to low-carbon fuels and efficient technologies, and in being able to finance such transitions, as well as building up capacity in terms of skills and policy and institutional frameworks.

Developing Asia is relatively well endowed with renewable energy resources and has a huge potential opportunity to adopt renewable energy and technologies. Both the PRC and India have large solar and wind resources, while Indonesia has the greatest potential for geothermal capacity, of which it has exploited only 3%. Many countries, including India, Thailand, and Viet Nam, also have significant untapped hydropower potential. Thailand has exploited less than 8% of its hydro potential, while India is estimated to have potential of about 150 GW of hydro against an installed capacity of only 38 GW in 2011.

Renewable energy options can (i) provide solutions to the problems of energy access in remote areas, where grid power is not available or is unreliable; (ii) reduce energy security concerns; and (iii) contribute to reducing environmental damage. They can also be a source of export revenue. The Government of the Republic of Korea sees the development of offshore wind as a huge opportunity for future exports of wind turbines. The PRC has emerged as a clear world leader with regard to renewable energy investment, accounting for half of the global manufacturing of solar modules and wind turbines, with most of its solar technology manufactured for export. India ranks 10th globally in clean energy investment, while Indonesia had the 4th highest growth rate in renewable energy investments between 2005 and 2010.

3.5.1
Challenges faced by Vulnerable Groups

While energy conservation measures and switching to renewable energy options may be economically and environmentally preferable in the long run, the transition toward these options is often difficult, especially for smaller industry units or the poorer sections of society, which are unable to bear the up-front cost of changeovers and have lower skills and capacities to take the lead on their own. This is also the case in small enterprises in most Asian developing countries. Instruments such as energy or carbon taxes could have undesirable implications for the poor and small businesses.

It is therefore important to ensure that, while steps are taken toward cleaner energy alternatives, equity and development considerations are given due consideration, and vulnerable groups are not marginalized.

There are several instances of innovative models and measures to address some of these concerns. For example, while large industries have adequate information about global markets and access to funds, micro, small, and medium-sized enterprises (MSMEs), which have limited information and access to funds, tend to minimize capital investments. This brings them to the lower end of the global value chain and hampers their competitiveness.

To support technology upgrades in small and medium-sized enterprises (SMEs), the Government of India has come up with innovative schemes that provide easy finance in the form of capital subsidies. The scheme focuses on enhancing the competitiveness of MSMEs through energy efficiency and product quality certification, and is one of the 10 components of the National Manufacturing Competitiveness Programme. The main objectives are to help the manufacturing MSME sector to use energy-efficient technologies and manufacturing processes to reduce the cost of production and emissions, and to introduce MSMEs to the benefits of the UN's Clean Development Mechanism. Another objective is to improve the product quality of MSMEs and encourage them to be globally competitive.

Similarly, the Government of the Republic of Korea has set up a capacity building program adapted to the needs of SMEs at different stages of their business development. The government created a Small and Medium Enterprises Green Management Support Group including both civilian and government experts to provide technical support to SMEs, and has created a Green Service Mall where SMEs can receive online training or consulting services for green management. Another innovative example is India's Lighting a Billion Lives initiative for rural lighting for poor households in remote rural areas. Under this scheme, solar lanterns not only provide a clean replacement for kerosene lanterns, but the government also ensures that households do not have to pay much more than they were paying for conventional fuel. On average, each household spent Rs100–Rs120 per month on kerosene. Solar lanterns disseminated under the Lighting a Billion Lives initiative have enabled communities to reduce this cost to Rs60–Rs90 per month. The initiative has provided additional productive hours to villagers who can now carry out income-generating activities such as basket-making, weaving, production of leaf plates, tuition, betel leaf farming, and selling vegetables at night. Income and savings have increased by an average of Rs500 per household per month.

While the challenges are huge, the implications of climate change across the globe and in particular for Asia are grave, and the situation can be viewed as a challenge and an opportunity for Asia. There are enough success stories and initiatives that offer opportunities for scale-ups and learning through regional cooperation, and developing Asia may be able to achieve larger and long-term benefits by pursuing a low-carbon development path, if facilitated by cooperative efforts and sharing of knowledge and experiences among the Asian countries.

3.6
Role of Low-Carbon Green Growth Strategies

3.6.1
Pace and Spread of Implementation

While many measures have already been undertaken, and efforts to enhance efficiencies and reduce emissions are being made across all the developing countries, these are often concentrated in a few sectors. The analysis of planned actions across countries, however, shows that much of the transition is expected to happen beyond 2020, under the assumption that the scope for immediate savings may be limited.

With climate negotiations failing to progress, reductions in emissions have remained limited. While domestic actions motivated by concerns other than climate change may help by encouraging higher levels of efficient technologies, as well as clean and renewable energy fuels and technologies, the scale and timing of changes vary significantly. A study of India that examines the energy and technology choices in an energy security scenario vis-à-vis successively more stringent climate scenarios shows a large difference in the pathways required to achieve these goals, which are not always aligned. One very difficult challenge will be retiring newly set up generation capacities before the end of their economic lifetime, to achieve the emissions reductions scientists say are needed. Therefore, building such capacity—including coal-fired power generation—now is likely to create problems for the future.

Failure to meet the rising demands for energy will constrain economic growth and dampen efforts to improve living standards. Low-carbon green growth, as defined in the earlier chapters, is essential to align the growth paths of countries in emerging Asia toward transformational and environmentally sustainable pathways. A holistic growth paradigm that brings together economic, environmental, and social co-benefits is necessary to break away from the traditional model of growth first, and thinking about the environment later.

Some of the potential challenges confronting developing Asia can be transformed into opportunities for regional cooperation. Lower carbon paths are possible, if countries move quickly to strengthen international cooperation, promote the efficient use of energy, and adjust policies in a low-carbon direction. Some of these areas are discussed below.

Need for extensive transfer of intellectual property rights for renewable technologies.
Extensive climate change mitigation in developing Asia will require extensive transfer of intellectual property rights for renewable technologies. If patent protection limits the ability of domestic manufacturers in Asia to adapt externally developed technologies, their dissemination is likely to be lower. To mitigate this obstacle, Mathur (2012) proposes that developing countries be involved in international collaborative partnerships from the R&D stage.

Effective technology transfer is conditional on capacity in developing countries.
Technology transfer is critical to the proliferation of renewable energy in developing Asia. Achieving widespread dissemination of renewable energy technology in developing countries requires the development of a local manufacturing base and

associated supply chains; systems for maintenance and marketing; a labor force that can build, use, and maintain the technology; and the adaptation of technology to local conditions. Ockwell et al. (2008) argue that domestic and international policy intervention must have a central role in building this capacity. More research, development, and demonstration spending is required globally, including in developing Asia. Globally, demand–pull policies have been heavily favored by governments rather than supply–push policies, but there is a strong case for a more balanced approach. To meet a 450 ppm target, the IEA (2010b) estimates that an extra \$40 billion–\$90 billion will have to be spent annually on clean energy research, development, and demonstration to 2050. Special local conditions, such as Indonesia's vast geothermal resources, justify targeted investments. Domestic investments will diminish some of the difficulties associated with transfer of intellectual property rights. Attaining commercial advantage provides another motive; despite being a leader in production volumes and investment, much of the PRC's wind turbine technology is well behind the technological frontier (UNDP 2009).

Public–private partnerships are an important mechanism for leveraging private investment.
Government finance and support provides greater assurance of private returns, while private companies can help to drive efficiency and cost reductions. Countries such as the Republic of Korea have demonstrated efficient role sharing and cooperation among public and private stakeholders. The experience of public–private partnerships for financing expensive public investments such as major infrastructure projects, and the familiarity of governments and industry with this mechanism can be used advantageously to further low-carbon green growth in developing Asia.

Policies need to be coherent and consistent across sectors, and harmonized with the country's overall development plans.
The analysis clearly indicates that it is not enough to simply design and implement low-carbon policies and strategies and expect them to be successful. Developing countries have many obstacles to policies and strategies: market failures, logistical costs and inefficiencies, the requirement for new and additional investments, poorly coordinated government departments, and weak institutional frameworks. Moreover, the environmental effectiveness and cost-efficiency of technology-based policies cannot always be guaranteed. Governments, therefore, need transparent, independent processes to assess the costs and benefits of policies before, during, and after their implementation. Post-implementation analysis will yield important lessons for future policy, domestically and in countries pursuing similar policies. Many different technology-based policies are available to governments, so picking the right ones, designing them well, and ensuring that they complement each other is critical.

3.7 Frameworks and Approaches to Delineate Road Maps to a Low-Carbon Asia

The scale of transformation required is huge and much more learning is required across countries, sectors, cities, and societies, to catalyze and enable much wider, deeper, and faster change across Asia. The use of appropriate frameworks for analyzing and delineating such road maps is therefore important. Scenario-based back-casting approaches to analyze the feasibility of meeting climate stabilization targets provide useful frameworks to delineate and prioritize the key sectors where changes can be brought about and to assess the extent of emission savings and overall co-benefits that can be attributed to various options and alternatives that countries may adopt. Several studies have analyzed alternative scenarios to meet climate stabilization targets (IEA 2011a; Kainuma and Ashina 2012). The Energy Revolution scenario and an Advanced Energy Revolution vision developed by Greenpeace (Krewitt et al. 2010) and the ECOFYS scenario by the World Wildlife Fund (Deng et al. 2011) explore the feasibility of achieving the global emissions reductions needed through greater use of renewable energy. The 2050 Pathways Calculator, developed by the Department of Energy and Climate Change in the UK, is a tool that helps delineate the implications of alternative development pathways for a country, and has been used in the UK to examine various trajectories for achieving a 80% emissions reduction target domestically by 2050.

TERI has similarly used back-casting to evaluate the changes that would be required by India under a carbon-budget approach and for pathways consistent with a 450 ppm scenario (TERI 2008; 2010). In the carbon budget approach, TERI has developed scenarios to assess the gap between what is expected to be achieved at the country level and what would be desired if emissions were to be equitably allocated and shared across countries, and to examine the extent of transformation required in the energy sector to meet the goal. The methodology provides a useful understanding of the scale of changes needed and allows for modeling an alternative pathway. The study pointed out that the scale of change required for India was not feasible only with using today's technologies and solutions. Some of the directions that the transformational scenario recommends include R&D as a key requirement for the rapid development of commercially viable new technologies, especially in the power and transport sectors; curtailing fresh investments in conventional fossil fuel generation; and maximizing energy conservation.

Although these studies have proposed stabilization pathways and feasible mitigation road maps that indicate what should be done over the next few decades at the global or national levels, achieving these will not be possible unless various stakeholders such as national and local governments, businesses, and citizens accept and work toward these. There is a need to use detailed back-casting approaches that identify leapfrog development pathways that can enable a shift to low-carbon emissions and low-resource consumption while improving daily life through economic growth.

3.8 Way Forward: Lessons for Scaling Up and Spreading Low-Carbon Transformation

The study of various countries, including both developed and developing countries across Asia, indicates that while the challenges are huge, numerous opportunities exist for Asia to bring about transformational changes in the coming decades. Developing Asia has strengths in its abundant human capital and enjoys the latecomer advantage of having a large window of opportunity to leapfrog to technologies, frameworks, and mechanisms that have been tried and tested in other countries. There is, however, a great sense of urgency for rapidly scaling up the efforts that countries in developing Asia are already making. While developed countries need to play a role in providing assistance for the development and uptake of appropriate technologies, adequate finance, assistance in human resource development, and institutional strengthening, developing countries should also attempt to align their growth paths toward transformational pathways that can prevent further lock-ins and promise a more sustainable growth path.

Box 3.5

Capacity Building to Perform Forest and Carbon Inventories through REDD+

In December 2009, at the United Nations (UN) climate summit in Copenhagen, nations decided to pay tropically forested countries for maintaining standing forests under a new process known as the UN Collaborative Programme on Reducing Emissions from Deforestation and Forest Degradation in Developing Countries (REDD+). Up to 20% of carbon emissions globally come from deforestation—more than from cars, trucks, planes, and ships combined. This process would reward countries for preserving and enhancing their forests, offering financial incentives in return for good stewardship. This could be a good source of income for developing countries with significant forest cover. By some estimates, for example, Indonesia could earn $1 billion a year if it manages to reduce its rate of deforestation by 1 million hectares annually, with revenues calculated on the basis of the price per ton on the carbon markets. If REDD+ is agreed as part of a post-2012 climate regime, this could also open the door to carbon storage payments for other kinds of nature-based management covering ecosystems such as grasslands, pasturelands, peatlands, and mangroves; and more environmentally-friendly kinds of agriculture from agroforestry to conservation farming, as they too can store large amounts of carbon in vegetation and soils.

REDD+ is being worked on under the auspices of the UN, and its final form is still uncertain. However, the underlying principle—that nations should be rewarded for conserving and enhancing these important carbon sinks—appears widely accepted.

Source: Forest Carbon Asia (2010).

3.8.1
Need for Cooperation—International and Regional

The need for cooperation in transitioning Asia toward a low-carbon green development path is clear. As illustrated by the difference in what developing Asia is capable of achieving on its own vis-à-vis the levels of transformation that may be required, it is imperative that developed countries step in to bridge the gap—in terms of financing needs, technology support, skill development, and research, development, and demonstration. Moreover, there is considerable scope for enhanced and rapid learning, even with regional cooperation and knowledge sharing mechanisms between developing countries in the region. There is a need for strengthening financial mechanisms, addressing the issue of global competition, technology transfer, and collaborative R&D.

Much larger and transformational financial support is needed from developed countries. The additional investment needs required for renewable energy, for example, are significantly high, albeit necessary, to prevent lock-ins with current technologies. In India, TERI indicated that the additional investment needs for the power sector alone are projected to be about $13 trillion from 2011 to 2051 in a carbon budget scenario (TERI 2010).

Viet Nam's national energy development strategy indicates a lack of access to financial resources for renewable energy as a major barrier. The allocation of official development assistance sources and loans from bilateral financial agreements for investing in the exploration and deployment of renewable energy is perceived to be an important priority (Toan 2012). While developing countries see the need to progress much faster in moving to renewable technologies, they face more immediate development priorities. So, developed countries need to play a key role in providing the additional finance needed. There are some good examples, such as Japan's Hatoyama initiative, which pledged to provide financial assistance to developing countries of about $15 billion including public and private finance up to 2012. Such initiatives need to be scaled up through effective international frameworks.

3.8.2
Leveraging Private Finance

It is estimated that the region will require over $6 trillion for new energy infrastructure by 2030. Private sector financing makes up the bulk of funding for low-carbon development at the global level. Some of the difficulties in pursuing low-carbon development and technological advancement in the developing countries in Asia include high up-front capital costs, limited availability of long-term financing, regulatory uncertainty, and technological risks, e.g., commercial banks financing clean energy projects in developing countries have relatively high transaction costs and lending premiums, and demand additional security and/or collateral requirements from project sponsors.

This discourages private sector investments because it imposes additional costs on business. In the absence of an efficient financial market, new approaches to low-carbon development financing (such as sharing risks and costs based on performance and other similar incentive schemes) are necessary to mitigate investment risks and foster the infant industry and market at a faster pace. It is therefore important to accelerate capacity development activities to create an enabling policy and regulatory environment in developing countries to attract private investments. There is an urgent need to deploy innovative financing mechanisms related to debt products, including mezzanine products such as convertible debt and guarantee products, to (i) buy down or otherwise reduce margins, base interest, guarantee fees, or other financing fees and costs and expenses; (ii) provide "first loss" protection; (iii) provide performance-based or other incentive financing; and (iv) support feed-in tariffs and other revenue streams. To facilitate this, development partners can collaborate to scale up the deployment of existing financial instruments such as guarantees, risk transfer products, and concessional loans focusing on leveraging private financing.

Some good examples of private sector investments are supported by ADB's private sector operations:

- Cleantech: Venture capital fund, two funds, $40 million, providing early stage support in the form of equity and knowledge advisory services to venture capital funds to invest in nascent companies with emissions-reducing and adaptation technology.
- India Solar Guarantee Facility: $150 million guarantees and $10 million UK grant. ADB will issue partial credit guarantees to international and local banks lending to early entrant solar power project developers. The guarantees cover nonpayment risk of up to 50% of the loan, which finance small solar projects from 2 MW to 25 MW. The Government of the UK is providing $10 million to buy down the guarantee fees, reducing the overall financing costs for the projects. ADB is providing technical assistance and training to banks on technology risks and technical due diligence.
- Thailand Solar PV output: the country's first large-scale PV farm, which benefit from a $2m grant from ADB, and reduces project costs and debt servicing.
- Bangladesh Industrial Energy Efficiency: $30 million credit line plus technical assistance to domestic private banks support the introduction of energy-saving technologies in the brick kiln and other targeted industries.
- Climate Public–Private Partnership (CP3): innovative investment vehicle that intends to catalyze large amounts from institutional investors, including large pension funds and sovereign wealth funds, into a $1 billion climate specific fund. These funds will be catalyzed by ADB and the DFID (about $200 million combined) as the anchor investors. By bringing in "patient capital" from pension funds, sovereign wealth funds, and other institutions, the fund can take the longer term investment horizon needed for mitigation and adaptation investments.

3.8.3
Shared Platforms for Learning

Platforms need to share learning and experiences across developed and developing countries. There are many similarities across developing countries in terms of the requirements, challenges, and possible solutions to pursue a green and low-carbon development path. Sharing of knowledge on the adoption of new technologies, ways of handling reform processes, and minimizing mitigation costs could bring about rapid scale-ups of successful models across the region. Moreover, there are several examples of traditional wisdom and knowledge that Asia can effectively harness to incorporate good practices in developing low-carbon societies. Japan's Mottainai concept, symbolizing the dislike of waste, resembles India's traditional system of reuse and recycling through the informal *kabadiwalas* (waste collectors). Innovative ways to formalize these systems and make them strongly embedded in societies can scale up benefits while providing new opportunities for businesses. Many opportunities such as one on REDD+ (Box 3.5) exist for strengthening learning and cooperation between countries across developing and developed Asia.

3.8.4
Avoid Lock-In (Energy Forms, Technologies, Activities)

Asia's aspiration for rapid growth and the greater well-being of its people implies the need for massive infrastructure development, which if done in the high-carbon manner of the past would result in the lock-in of investments, technologies, and infrastructure that would divert Asia from a low-carbon development path. For instance, fossil fuel power stations built today could still be operating in 30–50 years. So the years to 2020 need to be viewed as Asia's window of opportunity for enabling technology and investment choices that would help the region achieve a path of greater economic prosperity that is decoupled from high resource use and/or carbon intensity while reinforcing inclusive growth.

While pursuing rapid growth and development objectives, it is crucial that the major economies of developing Asia avoid locking in high-carbon infrastructure. Emerging Asia needs to seize this opportunity to gain competitive advantages, reap technological benefits by virtue of being latecomers, and show global leadership in taking up innovative measures and new technologies that can play a key role in preventing such damaging lock-in effects. Failing to seize this narrow window of opportunity could result in the region facing much higher costs for the required low-carbon transition in the future.

3.9
Reconciling the Needs with Regional Cooperation

The needs of developing countries in Asia are huge, but Asia also has countries such as Japan, the Republic of Korea, and Singapore that demonstrate the scope for seizing developmental opportunities and showcase excellent examples of creating low-carbon technologies. Greater cooperation between developed and developing countries will make transformational changes possible. Frameworks and mechanisms are needed to accelerate and scale up the possibilities for such large-scale changes. This calls for flexible and diverse frameworks that take into consideration the circumstances of each country, establish new international financial mechanisms to support developing countries, and initiate joint efforts across countries to enable innovations and scale-ups in technologies. Countries must also heed lessons from across the region and step up the involvement of societies, municipalities, and businesses; develop institutional capabilities and regulatory systems for improved and enhanced data and information setups; and introduce monitoring and reporting systems and sectoral coordination.

Chapter 4
Transition Lessons: Going Green as a Development Strategy

Chapter 4

Transition Lessons: Going Green as a Development Strategy

4.1 Opportunities in Green Growth

The transformation required if a low-carbon world is to be achieved entails many challenges to economic policy makers in Asia, as the previous chapters make clear, but it also opens up many opportunities to build more innovative, more sustainable, more resilient, and more socially inclusive economies. This potential means "going green" can propel economic development, if policies are well designed. This chapter reviews some of the major opportunities for enhancing development in key areas of social and economic policy. First, it considers the scope for low-carbon green growth to promote social inclusion and equity, which is of central importance if poverty is to be sharply reduced and development is to benefit all sectors of society. Then the chapter focuses on the possibilities for creating jobs and expanding aggregate demand. Job creation and full utilization of economies' resources are important in underpinning economic growth and providing opportunities to all sections of the population to share in its benefits. Neglecting low-carbon green growth risks missed opportunities for all economies. This chapter discusses the contribution that green growth policies could make to stimulate innovation across the whole economy, which is key to ensuring that growth continues in the long term. Finally, it draws attention to the potential role of low-carbon policies in improving energy security, from the perspectives of both energy-poor families and governments concerned to guarantee continuous access to energy supplies.

The framework for a low-carbon green growth development strategy is in Figure 4.1, which highlights how new growth implies action on social inclusion and equity, innovation, energy security and labor markets; without such action, there will be missed opportunities. The chapter elucidates this framework and provides examples of successes, identifies obstacles to be overcome, and discusses the implications for the design of policies.

Some low-carbon green growth opportunities are already being seized but the efforts began only in the past 5 years and progress varies across countries. There is much scope for policy makers to learn from each other, identify best practice, and adapt their strategies for growth and development to exploit synergies to halt human-induced climate change and enable more resilient and socially inclusive economies and societies. Without such adaptation, the prospects for poverty alleviation and a continuing convergence with living standards in developed countries will dim.

The transition to green growth requires nations to tackle environmental problems, especially human-induced climate change, which are threatening people's well-being and inhibiting the scope for sustained economic growth—particularly in some of the poorest countries, because of their vulnerability to climate change. Many of these environmental problems involve "externalities"—situations where those damaging the environment by their activities do not have to face the consequences of their actions, unless policy makers intervene. These externalities require policy interventions.

Figure 4.1

Low-Carbon Green Growth Development Strategy

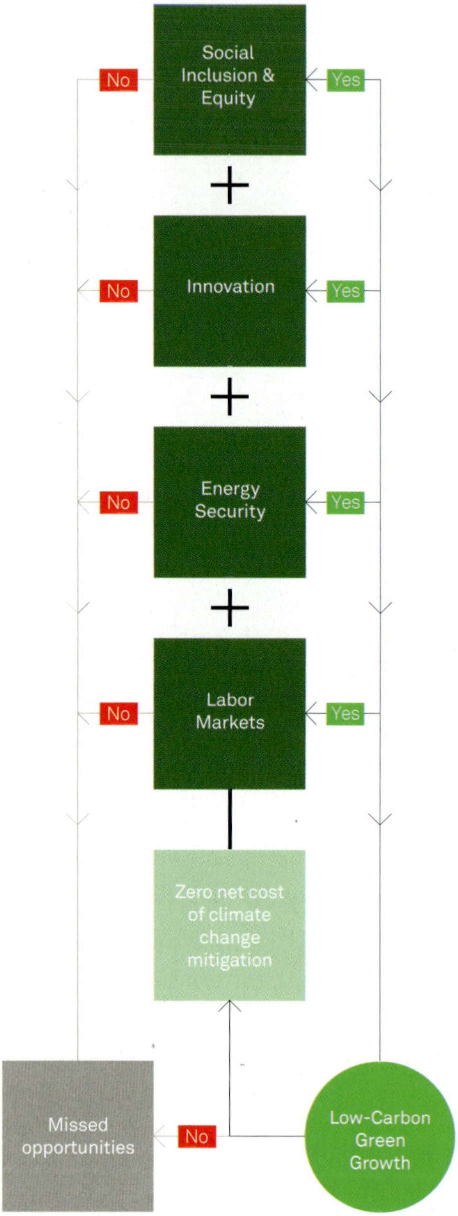

Source: ADB–ADBI study team.

Designing cost-effective policy interventions is not easy, even where the direct resource costs are low. In particular, policy makers have to identify market and policy failures and overcome opposition from groups with vested interests in the status quo. However, if policy makers take this challenge seriously, they can produce significant benefits, not only in the form of improved environmental outcomes but also in greater social inclusivity and fairness, higher economic growth, and better energy security. Just as climate change mitigation can generate so-called co-benefits from reduced local pollution, there are co-benefits for economic growth and well-being from tackling a broad range of environmental problems with the right tools and incentives. The key message is that a comprehensive set of policy instruments needs to be used if development prospects are to be enhanced and Asia's ambitious emission reduction and renewable energy targets are to be achieved. If countries grasp this opportunity, growth can be stronger, more sustainable, and more equitable.

[redacted]

4.2
Social Inclusion and Equity

4.2.1
Why Promoting Social Inclusion is Vital for Green Growth

Action on climate change that hinders development, discourages the inclusion of significant groups in economic and social activity, or is widely regarded as unfair can never build the global coalition on which effective, efficient, and equitable action depends (Stern, Kattumuri, and Rydge 2012). One issue of great importance to developing countries is to ensure a strategy whereby existing resources are used sustainably and in accordance with the needs of the local populace (Sathaye, Shukla, and Ravindranath 2006).

However, if climate change policies have regard for social inclusion, they can benefit development more broadly than just by reducing climate change risks. First, reductions in inequality tend to encourage conventionally measured economic growth, as argued by Duflo and Banerjee (2003) and illustrated by Wan, Lu, and Chen (2006) in the case of the People's Republic of China (PRC). Second, promoting social inclusion and reducing poverty are widely regarded as an integral part of development strategies and worthy ends in themselves. Third, empowering the poor will help the most vulnerable to develop the capacity to adapt to climate change that is now unavoidable.

Based on a case study in Bangladesh, Ayers and Huq (2008a) argue that combining mitigation and adaptation can contribute to the sustainable development goals of climate change. Goklany (2007) identifies that climate change could exacerbate existing climate-sensitive hurdles to sustainable development (hunger, malaria, water shortage, coastal flooding, and threats to biodiversity) faced by many developing countries.

Unmanaged climate change risks irretrievably damaging prospects for development and greater inclusion. About 1.29 billion people, 22% of the developing world's population, live on less than $1.25 a day (World Bank 2012d). A similar number have no access to electricity, while 3 billion lack adequate sanitation and 1 billion have no clean drinking water. For many of these marginalized communities, the daily struggle for survival will be made more difficult by the environmental shocks from climate change (Casillas and Kammen 2012). Even with a temperature rise of 1.0°C–2.5°C, the Intergovernmental Panel on Climate Change (IPCC 2007a) predicts serious effects, including reduced crop yields in tropical areas leading to increased hunger, the spread of climate-sensitive diseases such as malaria, and an increased risk of extinction of 20%–30% of all plant and animal species. Countries in Asia are among the most vulnerable to extreme weather (Table 4.1). Much adaptation to climate change will have to be undertaken at grassroots level, because climate change impacts across localities will be varied. Empowering vulnerable groups will enable them to mitigate their risks to climate change. Ensuring that climate change mitigation is socially inclusive thus promotes both mitigation and adaptation.

Table 4.1

Economies Most Vulnerable to Weather Impacts to 2015 (per 100,000 Population)

Economy	2008 Rank	2015 Rank	2008	2015 Climate only	2015 Climate & income	2015 Climate income, urbanization, & regulation
PRC	3	1	6,772	25,072	19,933	17,720
Djibouti	1	2	13,709	14,281	14,167	14,331
India	7	3	2,599	11,704	9,531	9,153
Kenya	2	4	6,807	7,752	7,620	7,617
Somalia	8	5	2,382	4,011	3,807	5,482
Mozambique	4	6	4,576	5,133	5,028	5,269
Philippines	10	7	2,134	5,161	4,607	5,102
Bangladesh	19	8	823	5,487	4,611	4,844
Sri Lanka	6	9	3,458	4,304	4,072	4,558
Ethiopia	5	10	3,791	4,892	4,747	4,540
Viet Nam	11	11	1,904	4,696	4,121	3,834
Bolivia	20	12	638	1,508	1,362	3,573
Hong Kong, China	17	13	1,251	3,877	3,147	2,413
Cuba	9	14	2,190	2,221	2,213	2,227
Madagascar	14	15	1,314	2,203	2,076	2,122
Honduras	18	16	1,237	2,303	2,148	2,104
Thailand	16	17	1,271	1,996	1,813	1,863
Zambia	12	18	1,718	1,877	1,847	1,853
Colombia	15	19	1,299	2,026	1,892	1,781
Zimbabwe	13	20	1,692	1,714	1,709	1,721

Source: Wheeler (2011).

Basu (2006; 2008) and Flipo and Schneider (2008) argue that the present triple threat of environmental, social, and economic crises offers the perfect opportunity to promote low-carbon green growth and the creation of opportunities leading to socially inclusive and equitable development.

Thus, there is a demand for a new development paradigm in which social transitions and sustainability go hand in hand with green growth initiatives. A low-carbon development path that is inclusive, equitable, and sustainable has the potential to create immense opportunities, empower communities, and protect the vulnerable.

There are many ways through which vulnerable communities can be strengthened while maintaining economic growth rates and mitigating greenhouse gas (GHG) emissions, including:

- Generating livelihoods and employment for the poor
- Empowering local institutions
- Generating environmental services
- Conserving natural resources
- Reducing vulnerability to climate risks.

These activities can be managed so that the poor are integrated into the green growth development path. Interventions ought to be cost-effective, leading to tangible economic benefits (such as increases in crop yield or water availability) and environmental benefits (such as reducing emissions or promoting biodiversity conservation).

Climate change exacerbates existing inequalities including wealth, access to energy, health, education, access to information, and access to resources (Masika 2002). Hence, low-carbon policies that are designed to promote social inclusion can have a doubly beneficial impact.

Figure 4.2

Distribution of Population without Electricity, 2008

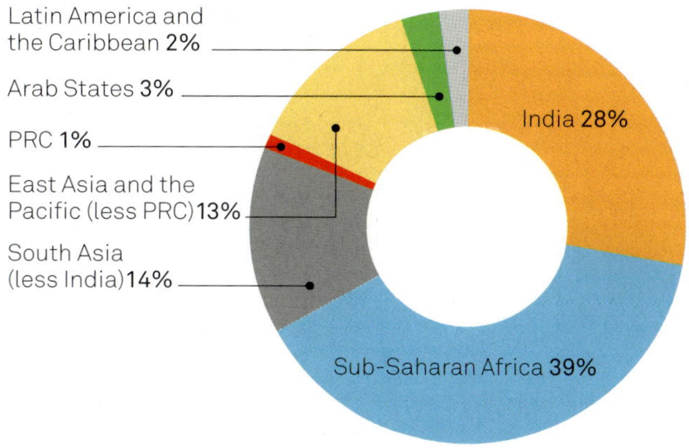

Sources: Derived from World Health Organization (WHO) and United Nations Development Programme (UNDP) 2009; ADB–ADBI study team.

About 28% of Indians and 14% in other South Asian countries lack access to electricity (Figure 4.2). Access to electricity is lowest in Bangladesh among the Asian countries for which data was available. Access to electricity is considerably lower in rural than in urban areas among the 10 Asian countries considered except in the PRC, Malaysia, and Thailand (Figure 4.3). Urban–rural inequality in access to electricity is severe in Bangladesh (76% of the urban population has access compared with 28% rural); India (93% of the urban population has access to electricity versus 53% rural); Indonesia (94% of the urban population has access compared with 32% rural); and Nepal (90% urban versus 34% rural).

Figure 4.3

Proportion of Rural and Urban Population with Electricity in Asia

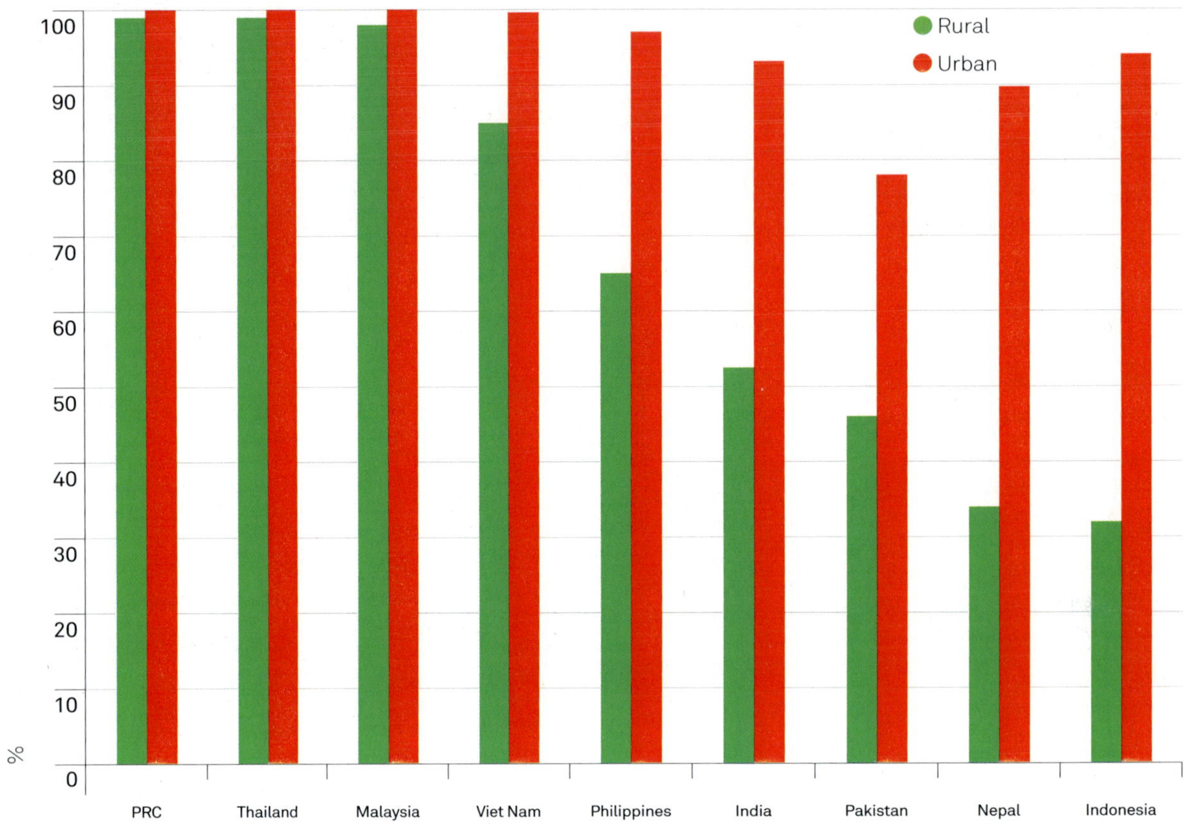

Source: Derived from data in WHO and UNDP (2009); ADB–ADBI study team.

Promoting low-carbon energy sources that are not dependent on costly infrastructure such as national electricity grids can be a cost-effective way of expanding energy access to the poor and marginalized groups.

Small communities in India have pioneered a wide range of innovative and "home-grown" technologies, activities, and approaches. The following are a few examples (UNDP-GEF 2003):

1 Smokeless stoves
2 Solar energy for drying herbs and pumping water
3 Biogas technology
4 Micro-hydropower plants that depend on sustainable watershed management
5 Developing the capacities of energy micro-enterprises
6 Improving decentralized power policy and legislation
7 Commercializing rural solar electrification; and inventing more efficient and nonpolluting brick kilns.

Box 4.1

Grameen Shakti, Bangladesh – Community Participation using a Market-Based Approach

In Bangladesh, it is impossible economically and logistically to reach the millions of off-grid rural people with electricity through conventional means. Grameen Shakti, set up in 1996 as a not-for-profit company, developed an integrated program—using markets and social networks—to popularize renewable energy technologies in the form of solar home systems to millions of rural villagers. This offers an excellent example of an inclusive strategy for low-carbon development.

Grameen Shakti has been very successful in promoting renewable energy technologies in Bangladesh because it has developed a unique approach involving soft credit for consumers, adaptive technology to reduce costs, the maximization of income generation, and effective after-sales service. Grameen Shakti had installed 100,000 Solar Home Systems by June 2007. Bangladesh now has one of the fastest-growing photovoltaic programs in the world.

Grameen Shakti has emphasized collective community participation and motivation. It has employed local youth as technicians, trained users on home-based troubleshooting, and provided scholarships for its clients' children. It has focused on ensuring the participation of women, training women from user families in repair and maintenance, and employing local women as technicians. Grameen Shakti has promoted the benefits of renewable energy to rural women through demonstrations and house-to-house contacts.

Source: Barua (2007).

The Asian experience: Women's Empowerment

Differential access to social and physical goods or resources is one of the key dimensions of gender inequality. A United Nations (UN) report on gender equality and climate change established that the links among energy supplies, gender roles, and climate change are strongest in countries with low availability of basic electricity and modern fuels, as well as high dependence on biomass for cooking, heating, and lighting (UN Women Watch 2009). Around 2 billion people in the developing world, many of them in Asia, use traditional biomass as their primary source of energy. The UN report showed that access to cleaner and affordable cooking energy reduces women's drudgery, the time they spend gathering fuel, and the health impacts of indoor air pollution. Furthermore, women's responsibilities in households and communities, as stewards of natural and household resources, position them well to contribute to livelihoods adapted to new climate change policies and changing environmental realities. Thus, it is very important to empower women in developing countries and engage them in decision making on climate change policies. Women should be given greater involvement so that dependence on biomass can be reduced, energy supplies can be decarbonized and managed more effectively, and communities can be raised out of extreme poverty (UN Women Watch 2009). Box 4.1 exemplifies such an approach in Bangladesh.

The Asian Experience: Sustaining Livelihoods Dependent on Natural Resources

Large populations within developing countries depend on climate-sensitive sectors such as agriculture, forestry, and animal husbandry. The natural resources that underpin these sectors, such as soil, water, grazing land, biodiversity, and forests, are subject to continued degradation as a result of changing climate and economic exploitation for short-run benefits. Several measures such as low-till agriculture, afforestation, and community forest management reduce resource degradation, sustain the livelihoods of the rural poor (including those without their own land), reduce GHG emissions from agriculture, and increase carbon sequestration by forests.

The poor are often highly dependent for their livelihoods on common property natural resources, such as fallow fields, forests, fishing grounds, pastureland, and wetlands. These are a source of food, fodder, building materials, fuel, and medicinal plants. The poorer the household, the more important the contribution from common property resources. Common property natural resources contribute to rural equity (Organisation for Economic Co-operation and Development [OECD] 2009b).

Depletion of natural resources resulting from global environmental change has led to faltering livelihoods for some communities. Forest improvement options should therefore be properly designed and implemented, taking into consideration the many livelihoods that depend on these resources. They should be designed to provide substantial co-benefits in terms of employment and income generation opportunities, biodiversity and watershed conservation, and provision of timber and fiber. Box 4.2 depicts such an effect in India.

Box 4.2

Himachal Pradesh Mid-Himalayan Watershed Development Project, India

The project is an integrated multi-sectoral watershed development project, being implemented in the Mid Hills and High Hill zone of Himachal Pradesh. The state of Himachal Pradesh is largely agrarian and people's livelihoods depend on rain-fed crops, horticulture, and livestock. Nine out of 10 households are rural, and most live in small settlements, often in remote valleys. The rural population is heavily dependent on forests and community land for fuelwood, fodder, and food. Their heavy dependence on natural resources has degraded the forests around them, reducing their contribution as carbon sinks. According to a government estimate, more than 15% of the natural water resources have dried up.

The project has three components: (i) institutional strengthening – building the capacity of communities and local governments to effectively manage watershed development in a participatory, transparent, and demand-driven manner; (ii) watershed development and management, including the financing of soil and water conservation, non-arable land treatments, crop and livestock production, and rural infrastructure; and (iii) enhancing mountain livelihoods – the promotion of value-added agriculture and income-generating activities. Through this project, sustainable agricultural practices are being adopted. Water harvesting structures, supported by communities, are helping to harness water that earlier flowed by unused, and irrigation channels are carrying this water to faraway fields. This has changed the way people farm. With water reaching their farmlands, the villagers are no longer dependent on traditional crops such as maize and wheat. They have begun to grow cash crops, such as vegetables. As incomes improve, families are beginning to spend more on livestock and better farming tools.

The 5,000 or so women's self-help groups have been one of the main driving forces behind the project. As the women undertake new income-generating activities, they are becoming more self-assured and assertive.

Source: World Bank (2012a).

Tropical forest peatlands are estimated to store at least 42,000 million tons of soil carbon in Southeast Asia. However, human activities such as deforestation, drainage, and fires have depleted these reserves and disturbed the carbon balance. Hooijer and colleagues (2010) estimated carbon dioxide emissions from draining lowland tropical peatlands for agricultural and forestry. They found that 12.9 million hectares (ha) of the 27.1 million ha of peatland in Southeast Asia had been deforested as a result of increased land development, and had been mostly drained by 2006. They suggest peatland drainage in Southeast Asia contributes 1.3%–3.1% of global carbon emissions. If current peatland development and management practices continue, Hooijer and colleagues predict these emissions will continue for decades. Hence, they recommend the inclusion of tropical peatlands in climate policies. The reduced emissions from the deforestation and forest degradation program (known as REDD+), which is supposed to generate carbon credits for forestry management projects, is therefore essential for sustainable forest management and climate change mitigation in Asia (World Bank 2007). Boxes 4.3 and 4.4 exemplify such an effect.

Box 4.3

Climate Partnership Program

This program is a global 5-year environmental research program among HSBC, The Climate Group, the Earthwatch Institute, the Smithsonian Tropical Research Institute, and the World Wildlife Fund aimed at reducing the impact of climate change on people, forests, fresh water, and cities; and accelerating the adoption of low-carbon policies. The partnership's key goals have been to:

- Carry out innovative scientific research
- Develop demonstration projects and test out new methodologies
- Create working models, showing how the new ideas work in practice
- Provide clear policy solutions for governments to enact legislation

The India Regional Climate Centre, which opened in 2009, is located in the Sirsi Forest Division, Karnataka State in South India. This ambitious five-year global research program is one of five similar climate research centers throughout the world operating under the umbrella of the HSBC Climate Partnership Program. The landscape in Sirsi is a combination of evergreen and deciduous forest, with a range of rainfall regimes. Some of the forest is protected as Forest Department reserves while some is community forestland; local communities have full access to forest resources and some areas are privately managed as plantations.

The center was set up to research the impacts of climate change on forests. Earthwatch is working with the Indian Institute of Science, which has been conducting ecological and socioeconomic studies in the reserve, and in community and private forests, for nearly 25 years. The research aim is to compare how different forest types respond to climate. Methods include monitoring tree growth, mortality, annual growth cycles, and regeneration in forests under different management regimes. These changes are related to variations in climatic conditions. The findings will help develop an understanding of how India's forests will respond to climate change. Earthwatch and its partner organizations will develop guidelines for government and community forest managers, helping them maximize the resilience of their forests, and hence the carbon sinks, to changing weather patterns.

Source: Earthwatch Institute. http://www.earthwatch.org

Box 4.4

Climate Partnership Program, People's Republic of China

In the People's Republic of China (PRC), the main goal of the HSBC Climate Partnership Program has been to improve water quality for 30 million people by restoring water sources and reconnecting rivers and lakes. As part of this goal, the following 10 actions enhance people's awareness of climate change, promote low-carbon development, and improve resilience to climate change by improving natural ecosystems, especially freshwater ecosystems.

- Develop a 2050 Energy Vision for the PRC
- Assess climate change vulnerability of the Yangtze River
- Restore the environmental quality of the Yangtze River
- Demonstrate water source protection in Shanghai
- Develop environment-friendly agriculture
- Establish the Yangtze wetland and dolphin conservation network
- Promote Estuary Partnership
- Initiate a low-carbon city in the PRC
- Promote Integrated River Basin Management
- Develop a "Save Energy, Save Water, Save Nature" Campaign

As a direct result of work on the Yangtze, the PRC Ministry of Water asked the World Wildlife Fund to advise on how international best practice should be incorporated into the PRC's next 25-year master plan for sustainable water management. This plan will require managers of the seven biggest rivers in the PRC to ensure proper functioning of the rivers and wetlands, benefiting hundreds of millions of people, as well as animal and plant species. The work is conducted at the Regional Climate Centre in the eastern PRC's Gutianshan Forest reserve.

Source: HSBC (2010).

Technologies, Resources Management, and Food Security

At least 3 billion people in developing countries rely on solid fuels (traditional biomass and coal) for cooking. About 2.6 billion rely on traditional biomass, while 400 million mostly use coal. Over 700 million people without access to modern fuels for cooking live in the least developed countries. Asia and the Pacific account for 75% of people in developing countries relying on solid fuels; India and the PRC alone account for 52% of the population in developing countries relying on solid fuels (Figure 4.4).

The majority of people in developing Asia use either wood or gas as their primary fuel for cooking. More than half of the people in South Asia use wood, straw, and agricultural residue, with dung a common fuel. Bioenergy is being developed to deal with rising fuel prices, increases in the demand for energy, and concerns about climate change and energy security (Escobar et al. 2009). Higher commodity prices from biomass and biofuels development will help farmers, and provide income to poor farmers and rural communities. This has the potential to create more jobs and employment. Developing Asian countries with tropical climates have an advantage in growing energy-rich biomass.

However, there are dangers. Higher commodity prices will mean price rises for consumers, even in countries in Asia without biofuel production (FAO 2008). International organizations have expressed concern about the impact of government policies to encourage increased biofuel production on food supplies and the incomes of the poor (OECD and IEA 2008). Studies show that rapid bioenergy expansion can cause some adverse impacts, such as upward pressure on international food prices, which cause staple crops to become less affordable for the poor (Msangi et al. 2007).

Figure 4.4

Population Relying on Solid Fuels for Cooking, 2007

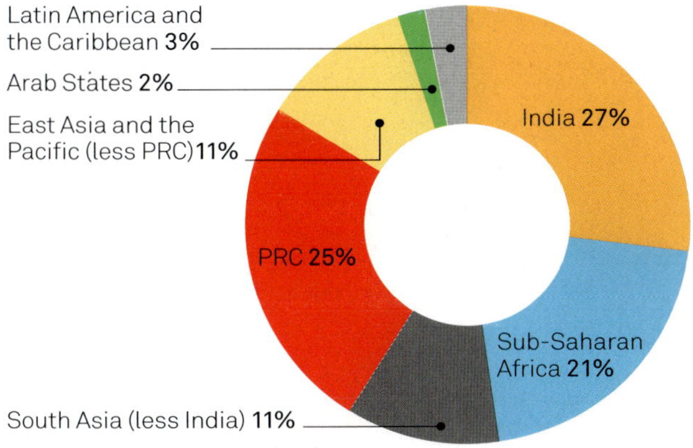

Source: Derived from WHO and UNDP 2009; ADB–ADBI study team.

Significant adverse impacts can occur to land (soil quality and fertility) and water resources; and biodiversity and ecosystems (Cui and Kattumuri 2010). The study by Msangi and colleagues (2007) showed a potential food and water-versus-fuel trade-off. Research suggests that it is possible to mitigate the adverse impacts resulting from increased biofuel production through improving technologies, innovation, increased investment in technologies for biofuel conversion, and crop productivity improvements (Msangi et al. 2007). Implementation and regulation of policies that encourage comprehensive, human-centered, and sustainable land and water governance are also essential (Cui and Kattumuri 2010).

Health

Many studies such as Bosello, Roson, and Tol (2006), McMichael et al. (2007), and Guttikunda (2010) indicate that the transition to low-carbon green growth could have tangible health benefits. Measures to reduce GHG emissions to 50% of 2005 levels, by 2050, could reduce the number of premature deaths from chronic exposure to air pollution by 20% to 40%, according to Bollen et al. (2009). The most important health benefit comes from improvements in local air quality and lower emissions of particulate matter, sulfur, and nitrogen pollutants.

Solid fuel stoves create indoor air pollution, leading to chronic respiratory illnesses (Table 4.2). A study by Massachusetts Institute of Technology (MIT) found a very high incidence of respiratory illness. About a third of adults and half of children among 2,400 households in Orissa, India, had experienced symptoms of respiratory illness in the 30 days preceding the survey, with 10% of adults and 20% of children experiencing a serious cough. The study found a high correlation between using a traditional stove and having symptoms of respiratory illness.

Furthermore, the World Health Organization (WHO 2006) identifies three diseases with evidence of a link with solid fuel use:

1. Child pneumonia (up to age 5 years): risk for exposed children increased 2.3 times.
2. Chronic obstructive pulmonary disease (30+ years): risk for exposed people increased 3.2 times for women and 1.8 times for men.
3. Lung cancer (30+ years: where coal is used (mainly PRC), risk for exposed people increased 1.9 times for women and 1.5 times for men.

Programs to introduce low-emission stoves could avert millions of premature deaths and reduce emissions. Decreasing the proportion of carbon-based electricity generation would provide health benefits worldwide, particularly in lower-middle-income countries.

Table 4.2

Deaths Attributable to Solid Fuel Use

Country	Pneumonia	Chronic Obstructive Pulmonary Disease	Lung cancer	All deaths
	Children <5 yrs	Adults 30> yrs	Adults >30 yrs	
Bangladesh	25,000	24,400	...	49,400
PRC	9,100	505,900	33,900	548,900
India	167,900	319,700	600	488,200
Indonesia	8,700	36,600	...	45,300
Nepal	5,100	3,600	...	8,700
Pakistan	29,800	26,300	<100	56,100
Thailand	1,000	9,500	...	10,500
Viet Nam	2,000	21,100	700	23,800

Source: UNDP (2009).

Another important advantage of reducing emissions is the health benefit from improved transport systems. The WHO (2011) indicates that cutting emissions through walking, cycling, and reducing use of motor vehicles, by providing better public transport, would bring health benefits from reduced exposure to outdoor air pollution.

A recent study on the estimated air pollution and health benefits of a metro system in Delhi found that increased use of metro-rail resulted in reductions of about 7% of particulate and CO_2 emissions from road transport. Health benefits were significant ($164 million–$469 million in value), including reduced mortality and morbidity rates in Delhi (Guttikunda 2010). A good public transport system reduces congestion, energy demand for transport, and outdoor air pollution.

4.2.2
Dealing with the Cost of Going Green

Although many opportunities exist in low-carbon green growth, the transition entails structural change, which is often accompanied by some costs. Climate-compatible development, for example, is more likely if there is widespread carbon pricing to reflect the damages associated with emitting GHGs and to provide a market incentive to switch to low-carbon goods and services. However, carbon pricing raises prices paid by the rich and poor alike, particularly for energy.

Unfortunately, the evidence from developed countries suggests that the impact of carbon pricing on real incomes via consumer prices is regressive—i.e., lower-income groups take a proportionately larger hit—unless offsetting measures are taken. This result emerges from studies based on input–output tables (Symons, Proops, and Gay 1994); econometric studies (Barker and Köhler 1998); and general equilibrium models (Hassett, Mathur, and Metcalf 2009). The picture is not quite the same in developing countries because the poorest people do not generally have access to commercial energy supply. Just as fuel subsidies disproportionately benefit the relatively wealthy in developing countries, with the poorest fifth of a country's population receiving on average only 10% of the benefits, the absolute loss of real income from carbon pricing would fall primarily on the well-off (Coady et al. 2010). However, the poor would still find it most difficult to cope, as they are so close to a subsistence standard of living already. In addition, poor people faced by energy price hikes often take drastic action to salvage their livelihoods, such as selling off their few assets such as livestock and foregoing educational opportunities (Anbumozhi and Kawai 2009).

There are, however, several ways for policy makers to soften the blow of carbon pricing for poor people. First, direct cash transfer programs can be introduced to offer financial recompense. This was the course taken by Indonesia in 2005, when the government doubled consumer prices for petrol and diesel, and tripled consumer prices for kerosene, but accompanied these increases with a targeted, means-tested program. Iran took similar action in 2010 when it reformed the regime for pricing petrol and diesel, using lump-sum transfers (Aldy and Stavins 2012).

Second, conditional cash transfer programs can be implemented which offer monetary transfers to socially vulnerable households in return for the fulfillment of development objectives, such as enrolling children in school or taking them for check-ups at health centers. Such programs are becoming more popular given the apparent success of several Latin American experiments (e.g., Progresa scheme in Mexico). There is scope for extending the range of activities rewarded by cash transfers to include environmental objectives such as more sustainable land management practices, developing synergies between the pursuit of social inclusivity via cash transfers and environmental goals (Rodríguez et al. 2011). Direct payments for environmental services should be part of the armory of policy tools to encourage the transition to green growth. Third, stronger environmental policies can be accompanied by establishing stronger property rights for poor people, at the individual or community level. For example, empowering local communities and letting them receive the revenues from the sustainable management of the eco-services provided by forests would support the preservation of forests.

Fourth, in the longer term, the evolution of more comprehensive social safety nets using progressive tax-benefit systems can provide an automatic offset to the impact of environmental pricing. This is illustrated by the example of the United States (US), where indexation of social security benefits means that the regressive impact of carbon pricing would be sharply reduced (Fullerton, Heutel, and Metcalf 2011).

Social safety nets have to be paid for, but one advantage of using environmental pricing and removing harmful fuel subsidies is that the approach provides the public authorities with revenue to finance them. Appropriate pricing is also important to discourage rebound effects—higher demand for environmentally damaging products as a result of cash transfers. International climate change finance, as agreed under the auspices of the UN Framework Convention on Climate Change (UNFCCC), and receipts from carbon markets and the Clean Development Mechanism, can also be used in part to support safety nets.

4.2.3 Policy Implications

The opportunities from the transition to low-carbon growth are multiple and varied and could bring several decades of more inclusive, equitable, and sustainable growth across the world, both for developing and developed countries. Such changes will not be easy and there are many barriers, including vested interests. But none is insurmountable (Stern, Kattumuri and Rydge 2012). Policies such as off-grid solar energy, better-managed forests, and more careful use of energy and water are likely to involve greater economic growth and social inclusion.

The PRC's 12th Five-Year Plan, 2011–2015, is designed to accelerate the transition to a low-carbon economy. This plan identifies two key objectives: (i) increasing the share of consumption, and (ii) moving to a low-carbon and less polluting economy. The Indian Planning Commission set up working groups; conducted consultations across the country by organizations representing various citizens' groups including women, historically and socioeconomically weaker communities, and youth; adopted a web-based inclusive, consultative, and participatory approach; and identified 12 strategic challenges for its 12th Five Year Plan, 2012–2017. Managing the environment and ecology are among the key strategic challenges for the 12th plan and comprises five components: mitigation and adaptation to climate change; land, mining, and forest rights; water management and pollution abatement; reducing the degradation of forests and loss of biodiversity; and managing environment sustainability. It aims to increase forest and tree cover by 5% during the period. The 12th five-year plans in the PRC and India, two countries with over 1 billion in population, provide an avenue for developing green growth and achieving their development strategies. The main challenge is implementation.

It is important not to overlook the varied social contexts and uneven social consequences of policy interventions on climate change. The following are some recommendations for enabling greater social inclusion and equity, achieving significant social co-benefits as well as increasing the likelihood of success:

1 Overcoming knowledge gaps. One of the reasons for the slow uptake of emissions-reduction measures and technologies within developing countries is the lack of awareness of social and economic benefits that low-carbon technologies can bring and inadequate knowledge of how to use them cost-effectively. This can be overcome through creating awareness, disseminating information, and educating people.

2 Collective action. The framework of governance around climate change policies needs to be inclusive for effective collective action. Community-based management of common resources has been gaining momentum in many developing countries because of their contributions to rural livelihoods and environmental conservation. There is still significant debate as to whether community-based approaches to the management of common property resources are equitable when significant socioeconomic differences exist within the community (Adhikari, Di Falco, and Lovett 2004). Thus, the challenge for governments is to empower the marginalized and poorer sections of society. Grassroots communities can be the most important participants in protecting the global environment. If the link between protecting the environment and generating local benefits is made clear and tangible, communities can be actively engaged to cope with the challenges of climate change.

3 Developing an enabling environment: Social inclusion can be achieved through capacity building and a strengthening of local policies and institutions. Developing an enabling environment should include bridging a supply-side deficit by building the skills of the workforce (through inclusive training and development programs); and ensuring the supply of complementary infrastructure to support the changes associated with green growth. These require some effort but will help eliminate barriers to planning and implementation.
4 Collaboration between the public sector, businesses, the academic community, the media, and members of the public is essential.
5 National, state level, and local development plans must be strongly linked. Mainstreaming mitigation and adaptation strategies within developmental frameworks is critical.
6 Research and demonstration projects are needed. Pilot projects allow for the practical demonstration of the benefits of low-carbon technologies to local communities, as well as to prospective developers, users, and investors. Demonstrations are likely to be more successful when conducted on a larger scale and through partnerships with local research institutions, non-governmental organizations, and private sector organizations. Successful pilot schemes must be followed up to ensure implementation and must also allow for community participation (Ravindranath and Rao 2011). The lack of data on this in Asia makes more research crucial.
7 Social safety nets must be strengthened to protect the poor against any adverse consequences from environmental pricing such as carbon taxes.

4.3 Green Jobs

4.3.1 Opportunities and Challenges in Labor Markets

The transition to a more sustainable, low-carbon economy requires structural change and the growth of industry sectors producing environmentally friendly products. Adopting green growth requires that more labor resources be devoted to low-carbon activities, particularly in the near to medium term when the capital stock for low-carbon production has to be put in place and the capital stock embodying environmentally destructive technologies replaced. That provides the opportunity to create new jobs and offer new skills to workers, both of which are central to the promotion of a socially inclusive economy. The United Nations Environment Programme (UNEP 2011: 16) has argued: "the greening of economies need not be a drag on growth. On the contrary, the greening of economies has the potential to be a new engine of growth, a net generator of decent jobs and a vital strategy to eliminate persistent poverty." The greening of economies is not generally a drag on growth but rather a new engine of growth; it is a net generator of decent jobs, and it is also a vital strategy for the elimination of persistent poverty." The recent global economic downturn triggered many proposals for green fiscal stimuli to promote growth and, in particular, jobs (see, for example, Barbier 2010). The OECD has also suggested that investing in green activities has significant job creation potential (OECD 2011).

Several sectors of the economy are likely to benefit. In all economies, the construction sector is likely to gain from efforts to improve the energy efficiency of factories, commercial buildings, and homes. As construction is relatively labor-intensive, the job potential is considerable, both in the new-build sector and in retrofitting insulation and more efficient heating and cooling technology. Similarly, forest management, afforestation, and reforestation are labor-intensive and offer the potential for more jobs across Asia, while helping to sequester carbon and exploiting the economic potential of well-managed forests. Some low-emissions agricultural practices are also more labor-intensive than conventional practices, requiring the substitution of labor for chemicals. In the emerging economies of Asia, there are significant opportunities for increased employment in the manufacture and export of low-carbon products such as low-emissions vehicles, photovoltaic cells, and wind turbines.

Just as with innovation, "going green" requires that market failures beyond those arising from the central environmental problems be tackled—in this case, market failures afflicting labor markets rather than innovation. If this is done, there are likely to be widespread benefits for the quality and quantity of employment and growth. This is a more subtle argument than the more common one that investing in projects to introduce and disseminate cleaner, more environmentally friendly technologies and products will create jobs. First, it implies that one should consider more than simply the jobs in occupations directly associated with providing environmental services—one common definition of "green jobs." One should go beyond considering employment created in a narrowly defined set of environmentally benign industries. Changing demands for different skills and new patterns of demand for labor across regions within countries should also be considered.

Second, policy makers should bear in mind the adverse consequences of environmental policies for employment and skills as well as the attractive consequences. Environmental policies are in part designed to bring about structural change in economies, and structural change usually results in job losses as well as job creation. For example, if low-carbon technologies replace fossil fuels in the energy sector, jobs may be created in the solar and wind power sectors but destroyed in coal mines. If forests are managed as carbon sinks and centers of biodiversity, jobs may be created in forest management but destroyed in the lumber industry.

Instead of focusing on the gross number of green jobs created, it would be more useful to consider the net labor market effects of introducing low-carbon growth policies. The sectoral and regional location and skill requirements of the new jobs created can be compared with the location and skill needs of the jobs destroyed to assess the extent of structural change required. Policy makers can then judge whether this is significantly more than the structural change the relevant economy is used to accommodating. As a result of unleashing market forces, many Asian economies have undergone faster structural change within the past 50 years than will be required by climate change mitigation, but the pattern of change will be different.

Three main factors are likely to determine the net labor market effects. First, are measures adopted to make labor markets work better in allocating workers and skills to the sectors where they are most needed—especially the expanding environmentally friendly ones? Promoting so-called active labor market policies to encourage the acquisition of skills and to make workers more mobile between industries and occupations would help the green transition while enhancing growth prospects more generally. In many Asian countries, this would include facilitating the movement of workers from low-productivity traditional agriculture to high-productivity manufacturing and services.

Second, to what extent is there involuntary unemployment and what is the reason for it? If unemployment arises from a deficiency of aggregate demand—in other words, a macroeconomic market failure—the transition to green growth is much more likely to lead to net job creation. In the wake of the most serious global economic and financial crisis since the Second World War, labor demand is still well below full employment levels in many Asian countries, even though Asia has not been as hard hit as Europe and North America. This was recognized early on by a number of Asian policy makers, who initiated green fiscal stimuli, notably in the Republic of Korea and the PRC (Barbier 2010). In circumstances of full employment, however, the net effect of the transition to green growth may be reduced overall labor supply, if real incomes are lower than they otherwise would be because of higher prices for carbon-intensive products (Goettle and Fawcett 2009). If involuntary unemployment results from labor market rigidities such as inflexible real wages or difficulties in moving workers from one sector to another, the transition may exacerbate the impact of these rigidities. The possible impact of constraints on real wage adjustment and on inter-sectoral flows of labor in different regions of the world have been analyzed by Babiker and Eckaus (2007), who found that the PRC and India are likely to be more adversely affected than the US and Europe by structural changes induced by carbon pricing, largely because the former need a larger reallocation of labor to implement low-carbon policy.

Third, are new green technologies more labor-intensive at prevailing wages, input costs, and interest rates than those they replace? An increase in renewable energy supply is a key component of global and local climate change policies. It appears that electricity generation from renewable energy is more labor-intensive than traditional fossil-fuel-based electricity supply, certainly per megawatt and probably per dollar, although there is uncertainty about how labor requirements are likely to evolve (Kammen, Kapadia, and Fripp 2004; Wei, Patadia, and Kammen 2010). Energy efficiency improvements also appear labor-intensive. Carbon pricing is likely to induce a substitution of labor for capital and energy more generally, although there is some debate about the impact on the demand for capital (see, for example, the discussion in Kemfert and Welsch 2000). Less is known about the labor market consequences of other environmental policies, such as support for biofuels and low-carbon land use. These are likely to be much more important in low-income countries than in high-income ones. In the longer run, there is also the question of how a shift toward technologies that are more labor-intensive might affect the returns on investment in capital and hence growth driven by capital accumulation.

The Asian Experience

There is considerable scope for creating new jobs in Asia's transition to green growth. Climate change mitigation offers opportunities for new employment in construction, manufacturing, transport, services, agriculture, and land management. Matta (2009) notes that, at a time when unemployment in several developing countries has been rising, there are greater benefits from moving toward a greener future by giving a major thrust to sectors that will generate employment, create durable assets, and help rebuild the livelihoods of the poor. Furthermore, since the advent of the world economic crisis, a greater focus has emerged on job creation in sectors with high labor–capital ratios. However, will a similar number of jobs be destroyed in existing industries, particularly in high-carbon sectors such as mining, by climate change mitigation efforts? Or, to put it another way, can policy makers ensure that green growth improves the quantity and quality of employment by improving the functioning of labor markets while putting in place stronger climate change and environmental policies? This section illustrates the potential for gross green job creation and the scope for net job benefits.

One problem in assessing the potential for gross green job creation is the paucity of quantitative information about green jobs around the world. This point is made forcefully by the Global Green Growth Institute (GGGI 2011: 141), which states: "It is impossible at this stage to get the current statistics for green jobs, as the concept of green jobs itself is yet to be clearly defined." Writing about the Republic of Korea, it goes on to note: "ROK has yet to come up with a report on green job statistics. Existing data does not provide adequate information to analyze the ever-expanding green job market in a comprehensive manner." (GGGI 2011: 142). In the absence of definitive data on existing green jobs in Asia, let alone forecasts of their future growth, one way to assess how much gross green job creation is possible is to note the extent of current and future employment in green industries where this has been estimated and then to gauge the current extent of environmental degradation and resource use in Asian countries compared with these benchmarks.

UNEP et al. (2008) suggests that, at a conservative estimate, there were more than 2.3 million jobs in the renewable energy sector around the world in 2006, and more in construction, providing improved energy efficiency in buildings, low-carbon transport, and other environmental activities. That compares with an employed labor force globally of about 1.8 billion. It seems unlikely that the share of green jobs according to the UNEP definition is much more than 0.25% of global employment (although it should be noted that it excludes employment in traditional agriculture and land management that could become greener). However, UNEP envisages an increase in employment in the renewable energy sector to 20 million by 2030 with appropriate policies—a 770% increase compared with expected world population growth of 20%.

The European Commission's Directorate-General for the Environment estimates the number of green jobs by using the OECD–Eurostat definition of the environmental goods and services industry (OECD and Eurostat 1999), which comprises "activities which produce goods and services to measure, prevent, limit, minimize or correct environmental damage to water, air and soil, as well as problems related to waste, noise and eco-systems. This includes technologies, products and services that reduce environmental risk and minimize pollution and resources."

On this basis, green jobs constitute about 1.7% of total paid employment in Europe (European Commission 2007). This is higher than the UNEP approach would suggest.

The Pew Center, using data about individual companies, estimated the clean energy economy of the US to account for about 0.5% of all US jobs (Pew 2009). Its definition of the clean energy economy covers five categories: clean energy, energy efficiency, environmentally friendly production, conservation and pollution mitigation, and training and support.

Although there is no generally accepted definition of green jobs in the Republic of Korea yet, the environment industry is thought to be responsible for about 1.6% of total employment, of which about 45% are directly employed in green jobs (GGGI 2011).

UNEP et al. (2008: 23) pointed out: "Green employment has gained an important foothold in the developed world, but with the major exception of PRC and Brazil, it is still quite exceptional in most developing countries." So for lower-income countries, there is likely to be at least the potential to increase employment in green jobs by at least 0.5% of their labor forces—and more if European levels of environmental goods and services production are reached. However, this is likely to be an underestimate, for two reasons. First, it does not take into account the need for countries, including those in Europe as well as Asia, to increase their efforts to mitigate and adapt to climate change. Second, it does not take into account the need for many Asian countries to bring about bigger structural change to achieve green growth because they start from a position where environmental needs are greater.

Studies have also illustrated the scope for green job creation in Asia. For example, the Global Climate Network sponsored case studies in a number of countries at different levels of development under the title Low Carbon Jobs in an Interconnected World (Global Carbon Network 2009). In the Indian study by Upadhyay and Pahuja (2010), the authors investigated the employment potential of the renewable energy industry, especially wind and solar power. The study focused on direct employment effects and did not consider second-round effects of expanding renewable energy supply through macroeconomic channels. The authors estimated the number of jobs that would be created per megawatt of energy generation capacity for a range of different technologies under various assumptions, drawing on India's National Action Plan on Climate Change. Such estimates are likely to show a bigger contrast between renewable and traditional energy than do estimates of jobs per dollar spent, because the cost of an extra megawatt of generating capacity is likely to be higher. There is a high degree of uncertainty about the employment needs of different renewable technologies, the authors acknowledged, but they concluded that extra employment would be a key co-benefit of a growing renewable sector in India – of the order of up to half a million jobs in wind and solar by 2020 and potentially up to 10 million jobs eventually in biofuels. Solar power looked more attractive than wind, because it is more labor-intensive and better able to meet India's requirements for small-scale, off-grid power; biomass, green transport, and public works in water and forest management also appeared to be effective ways of achieving both employment and environmental objectives.

This echoes Matta (2009), who argued that spending an additional $4 billion on forestry-related projects in India, through the mechanisms of the National Rural Employment Guarantee launched in 2005, could generate 1.5 billion person-days of employment, amounting to 8 million–10 million (part-year) jobs. Upadhyay and Pahuja (2010: 9) explicitly ruled out job losses in fossil-fuel power generation, believing that "investment in fossil fuels is going to be a mainstay" of the Indian economy, at least in the near term, given the need to expand the availability and reliability of electricity supplies. This, together with an implicit assumption of surplus labor, allows the authors to dismiss job displacement as an issue. However, the Global Climate Network study of the PRC, while noting the potential from increased employment in renewables, emphasized the potential employment losses from the planned sharp reduction in the energy intensity of PRC industry. The shift of the PRC economy toward services and away from heavy industry might generate more than enough jobs to compensate, however.

Carbon mitigation strategies can create employment through agriculture and forestry—afforestation, reforestation, improved management of natural forests, conservation, watershed protection, agroforestry, and urban forestry, among others. Deforestation rates are high in most of Asian countries (Figure 4.5). Nair and Rutt (2009) argue that providing employment in forestry activities would have the advantage of:

1 slowing down deforestation and degradation;
2 augmenting carbon sequestration through increased tree planting and improved management of forests; and
3 reducing the frequency and intensity of forest fires through better management.

Table 4.3 provides opportunities for job creation in key sectors. However, not all jobs created by the transition to green growth will be high-productivity: part of the benefit will be the creation of low-productivity jobs for those who would otherwise have no paid employment. As Upadhyay and Pahuja (2010: 19) write about India, "jobs like that of unskilled labor in biofuel and biomass production could be numerous but of low quality as they barely provide subsistence wages and have difficult work conditions." They suggest that environmental activities under India's National Rural Employment Guarantee Act, 2005, could be particularly beneficial in creating jobs for the unskilled, a point echoed by Matta (2009) (Box 4.5).

Box 4.5

Mahatma Gandhi National Rural Employment Guarantee Act, India

The National Rural Employment Guarantee Act is a rights-based parliamentary act of 2005 in India. It legally guarantees 100 days of employment to the poor in rural areas. It is the first nationwide employment scheme of this kind. The act is significant in three ways: it aims at eradicating acute poverty in villages by ensuring that the poorest of the poor are given sufficient employment; it aids in empowering local governments, as the act's implementation is vested with them; and it supports activities that create productive assets that could make villages self-sustaining. During 2006–2007, more than 100,000 villages implemented the scheme, each spending on average $20,000. Since April 2008, the act has been extended to all 596 districts in the country (Ministry of Finance 2009) and has an annual budget allocation of about $6 billion. As of April 2009, about 45 million workers, half of them women, were provided employment under the act (Ministry of Rural Development 2008).

Enhancing the natural resource base in rural areas is among the main activities of the act and it is regarded as the world's largest ecological restoration program. Many villages have already benefited from its support to water conservation programs—critical in rain-fed areas of India, which sustain 40% of the nation's population.

However, a key criticism facing the act is the insufficient attention given to the sustainability of the employment opportunities generated (Matta 2009). In view of the target-based approach, implementation of the act emphasizes easily implemented works such as road building. Currently, activities related to tree plantation and drought-proofing account for about 8% of the act's funding, but forestry could be included to a larger extent to help trigger broader economic growth. Indeed, the National Forest Commission has recommended a substantial increase in the allocation of funds to forestry and watershed operations, to reach 20% of Rural Development Program funding.

Source: Aidindia.com; The Hindu.com.

Figure 4.5

Average Annual Deforestation Rates, 1990–2000 and 2000–2010

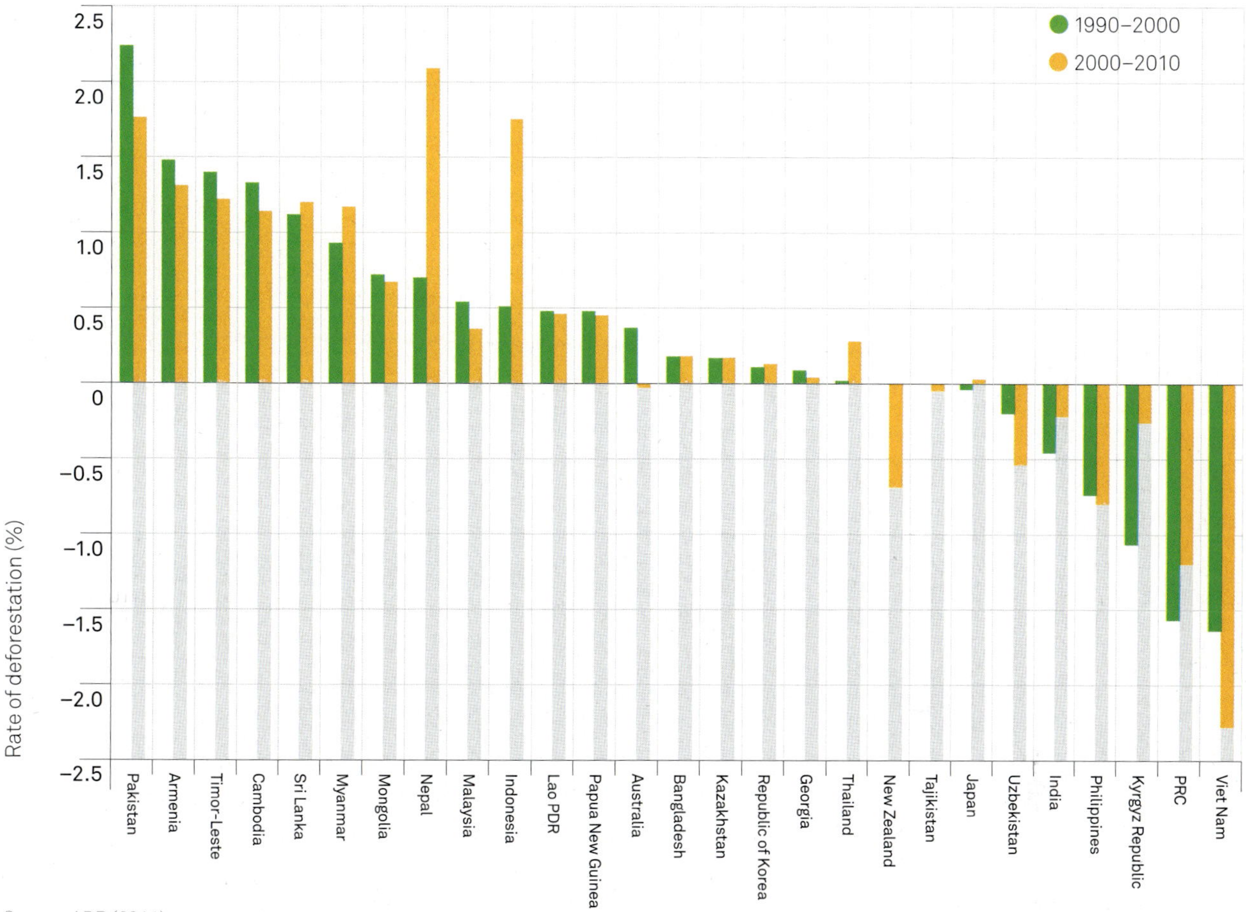

Source: ADB (2011).

Table 4.3

Opportunities for Job Creation from Green Policies

		Green potential	Green job progress to date	Long-term green job potential
Energy	Renewables	Excellent	Good	Excellent
	Carbon capture and storage	Fair	None	Unknown
Industry	Steel	Good	Fair	Fair
	Aluminum	Good	Fair	Fair
	Cement	Fair	Fair	Fair
	Pulp and paper	Good	Fair	Good
	Recycling	Excellent	Good	Excellent
Transportation	Fuel-efficient cars	Fair to Good	Limited	Good
	Mass transit	Excellent	Limited	Excellent
	Rail	Excellent	Negative	Excellent
	Aviation	Limited	Limited	Limited
Buildings	Green buildings	Excellent	Limited	Excellent
	Retrofitting	Excellent	Limited	Excellent
	Lighting	Excellent	Good	Excellent
	Efficient equipment and appliances	Excellent	Fair	Excellent
Agriculture	Small-scale sustainable farming	Excellent	Negative	Excellent
	Organic farming	Excellent	Limited	Good to Excellent
	Environmental services	Good	Limited	Unknown
Forestry	Reforestation/Afforestation	Good	Limited	Good
	Agroforestry	Good to Excellent	Limited	Good to Excellent
	Sustainable forestry management	Excellent	Good	Excellent

Source: ADB–ADBI study team based on UNEP (2008).

The Asia Business Council has drawn up a qualitative assessment of how well the countries in which it has members or activities are performing in establishing the conditions to create green jobs (Figure 4.6). It rates the PRC, Japan, and India as the countries where demand from firms to fill green jobs is highest (judging by "green job" postings on employment web sites and the extent of current employment in green sectors). Republic of Korea and Japan rank highest on policies to stimulate the transition to low-carbon green growth.

Figure 4.6

Preparing the Ground for the Creation of Green Jobs

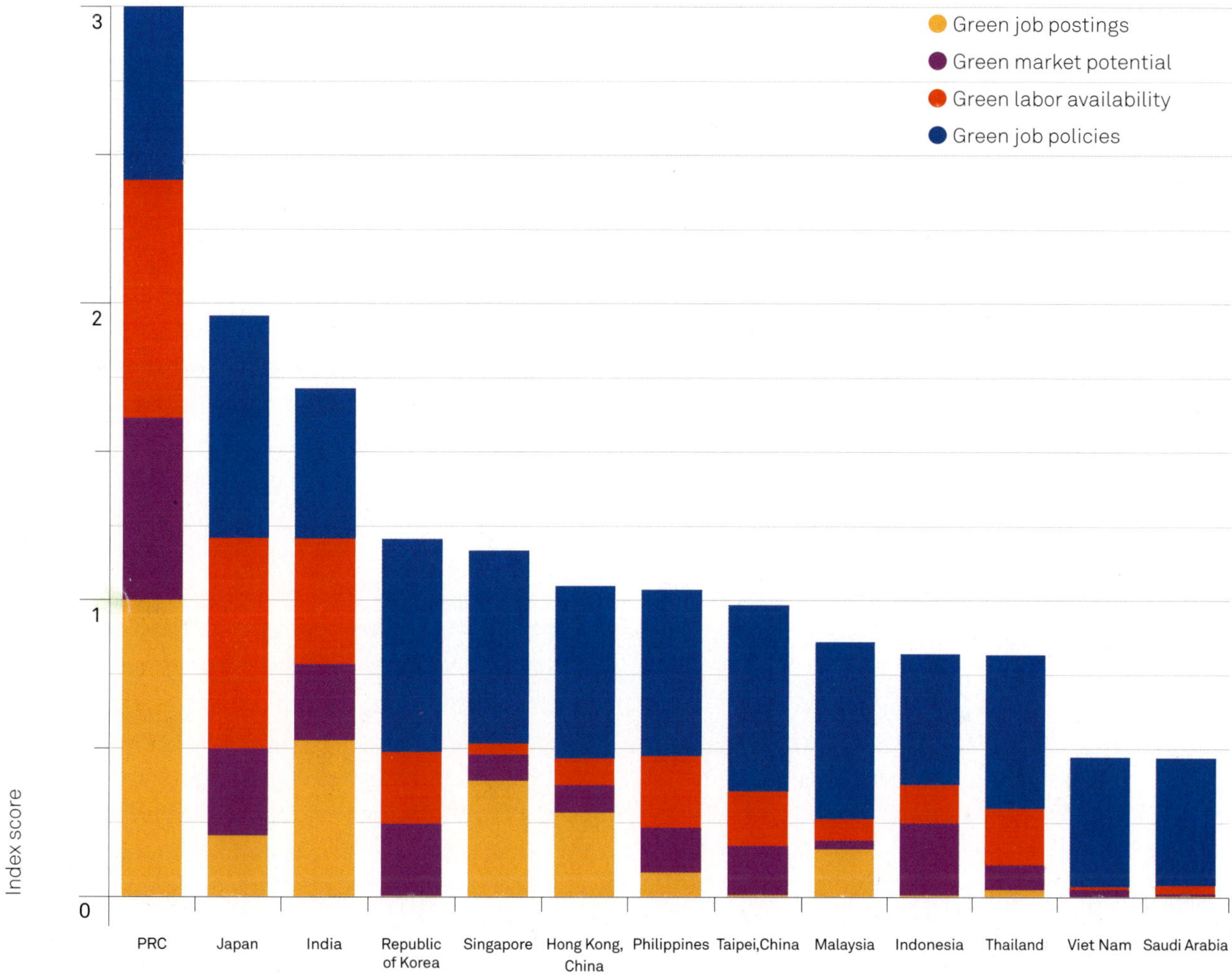

Note: Index scores range from 0 to 4; a higher score means more favorable conditions for green jobs.

Source: Asia Business Council (2009).

Figure 4.7

Relative Performance in Readiness for Green Job Creation: An Index of Green Job Enablers Plotted against an Index of Green Job Market Demand

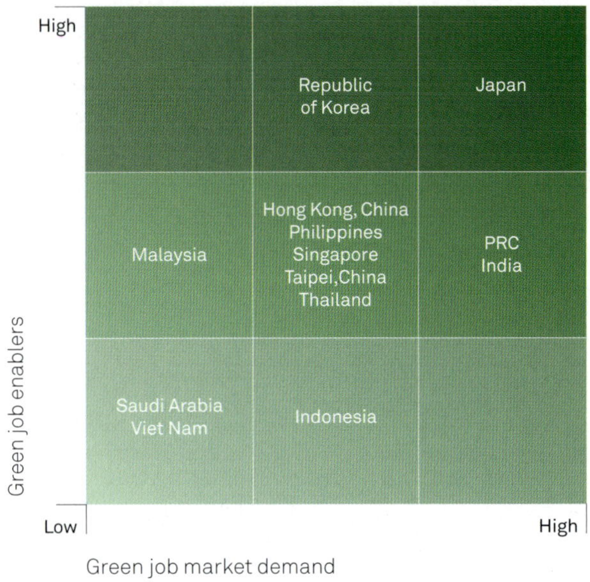

Source: Asia Business Council Analysis 2011.

One of the most thorough studies of green growth and skills so far is International Labour Organization and European Center for the Development of Vocational Training (2011), which attempted to synthesize lessons from the results of 21 country reviews (including the PRC, India, Indonesia, the Philippines, Republic of Korea, Thailand, and Bangladesh). This study argued that the demand for skills is being affected in three ways by the transition to green growth.

First, there is induced structural change across industries, increasing the demand for the skills specific to expanding industries such as renewable energy and reducing the demand for skills such as those associated with coal-mining. Many of the expanding industries are likely to be using new products and processes, reflecting the transition to low-carbon technologies, so the generic skill requirements of many of the jobs created are likely to be higher than average as they have to allow for assimilation of unfamiliar tasks and working methods and "learning by doing."

Second, some new occupations are emerging, such as photovoltaic panel fitters and carbon-footprint assessors. But there appear to be relatively few unique green skills.

Third, the content of many jobs in existing industries is changing to reflect the transition to green growth, such as increasing emphasis on energy efficiency, switching from fossil fuels to renewable energy, and producing capital equipment for expanding green industries. The ILO-CEDEFOP report argued that this third channel is likely to have the most pervasive effects on the labor market, particularly in developing countries.

Green jobs appear very diverse in their skill requirements, the sophistication of the skills required, and their degree of novelty. Already, skill shortages are being reported as a factor obstructing green growth. They appear to result from general failings in education and training systems and reflect long-standing issues such as the lack of incentives for employers to invest in developing the transferable skills of their workforces, the lack of access to time and finance for training on the part of the disadvantaged, and the stickiness of relative pay rates.

Overall, it appears the scope for gross green job creation in Asia is substantial—probably on average at least about 1%–2% of the labor force, which is enough to make a dent in unemployment rates but not likely to transform the overall balance of demand and supply in the labor market. It is larger in many of the poorer countries in the region, because of the greater need to improve environmental conditions and adopt more sustainable production patterns and because of the scope for increasing employment in sectors such as forestry and agriculture, which are more important in these countries and are often ignored in projections of green jobs. The opportunities for net job creation through the transition to green growth depend more on how labor markets work in individual countries. Some countries in Asia face the paradox that the opportunities are limited because their labor markets are already reasonably efficient in terms of achieving low and relatively stable unemployment.

According to the ILO's annual review of global trends in labor markets (ILO 2011), the labor market in East Asia has recovered relatively quickly from the global downturn, with unemployment rates low by international standards and falling, and high rates of labor force participation (Table 4.4). The picture in Southeast Asia and the Pacific is not quite as encouraging, because a strong rebound in output has not translated into strong employment growth and unemployment has eased down only a little.

However, in two other respects, several Asian labor markets, particularly in the lower-income economies, suffer disadvantages. First, the labor force is growing very rapidly in some countries, particularly India, Indonesia, and the Philippines (Figure 4.8) among the larger economies, and it is difficult to generate enough new jobs to employ all new labor market entrants. Second, underemployment and vulnerable employment—own-account workers and unpaid family workers—are at high levels in several of the poorer countries of Asia (Table 4.5), so the average incidence of vulnerable employment is high by world standards.

Together with the relatively high share of agriculture (Table 4.6) and traditional activities in these economies, this suggests scope for reallocating workers from low-productivity sectors to other sectors, including environmental services and climate change mitigation, which have higher private and social returns. The scope for improving the quality and productivity of jobs is illustrated by Asian Development Bank (ADB)(2011), which documents large differences across Asian economies. If policy makers in these countries work to remove the impediments to labor mobility, and barriers to entry to higher-productivity industries, that will facilitate the transition to green growth and reap substantial benefits in the form of new green jobs with higher productivity than those they replace.

Table 4.4

Regional Unemployment Rate Estimates

Region	2000	2005	2007	2009	Confidence Interval lower bound 2010	Preliminary estimate 2010	Confidence Interval upper bound 2010
World	6.3	6.2	5.6	6.3	5.9	6.2	6.5
Developed Economies and EU	6.7	6.9	5.8	8.4	8.5	8.8	9.1
Central and Southeast Europe (non-EU) and Commonwealth of Independent States	10.9	9.4	8.6	10.4	9.1	9.6	10.1
East Asia	4.5	4.1	3.8	4.4	3.9	4.1	4.3
Southeast Asia and the Pacific	4.9	6.3	5.4	5.2	4.8	5.1	5.4
South Asia	4.5	4.8	4.5	4.4	3.9	4.3	4.6
Latin America and the Caribbean	8.5	7.9	7.0	7.7	7.2	7.7	8.1
Middle East	10.6	11.2	10.5	10.3	9.6	10.3	10.9
North Africa	14.1	11.6	10.2	9.9	9.1	9.8	10.5
Sub-Saharan Africa	9.0	8.6	7.9	7.9	7.6	8.0	8.4

Source: International Labour Organization (2011).

Table 4.5

Share of Employment Deemed Vulnerable

Region	Agriculture		Industry		Services		Deemed vulnerable	
	1999	2009	1999	2009	1999	2009	1999	2009
World	40.2	35.0	20.6	21.8	39.1	43.2	53.5	50.1
Developed Economies and EU	5.6	3.7	27.6	23.4	66.9	72.8	11.1	9.7
Central and Southeast Europe (non-EU) and Commonwealth of Independent States	27.0	20.2	24.5	24.6	48.5	55.2	26.7	20.0
East Asia	47.9	36.9	23.8	27.8	28.3	35.3	60.2	50.8
Southeast Asia and the Pacific	49.3	44.3	15.9	17.8	34.8	38.0	66.2	61.8
South Asia	59.5	53.5	15.4	18.9	25.1	27.6	81.1	78.5
Latin America and the Caribbean	21.5	16.3	21.4	22.1	57.1	61.6	36.1	32.2
Middle East	22.1	19.1	25.9	26.1	52.1	54.8	36.0	32.7
North Africa	29.2	27.8	20.5	22.5	50.3	49.7	42.1	40.4
Sub-Saharan Africa	62.4	59.0	8.8	10.6	28.8	30.4	79.9	75.8

Sources: ADB (2011); ILO (2011).

Figure 4.8

**Projections of Labor Force Growth:
Change in Working Population Aged 15–64, 2010–2025**

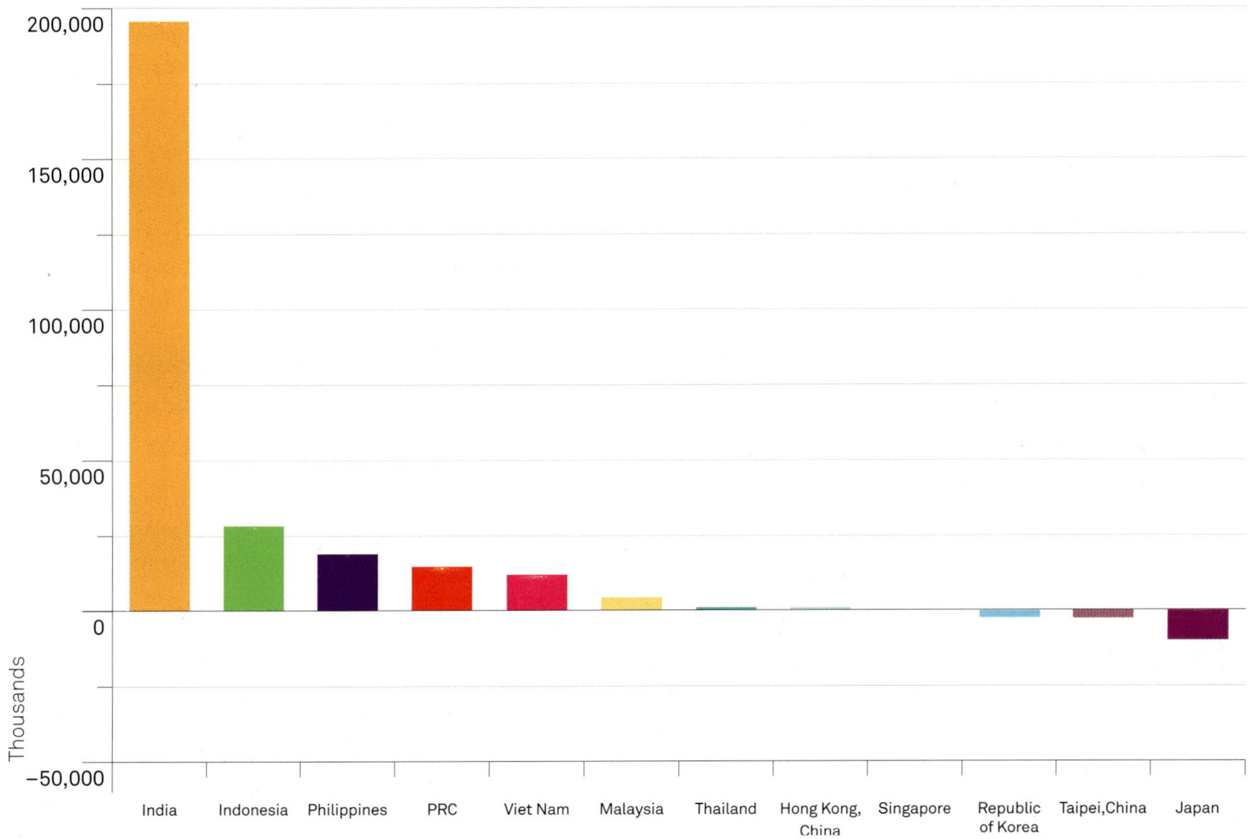

Source: World Population Prospects; United Nations Population Division; ABC analysis.

Table 4.6

Shares of Employment by Broad Sector

Economy	Sectoral labor productivity (2005 $ PPP per worker)		
	Agriculture	Industry	Services
Nepal	0.5	0.5	0.6
Bangladesh	0.6	1.7	1.1
Cambodia	0.3	1.3	13.4
Kyrgyz Republic	0.8	0.8	0.7
Pakistan	0.9	2.1	2.7
Viet Nam	0.5	2.4	1.8
India	0.5	2.2	4.0
Mongolia	0.9	1.2	1.5
Philippines	1.3	6.1	3.6
Indonesia	0.8	5.4	2.5
Samoa	1.4	4.1	21.1
Tonga	3.4	2.5	7.8
Sri Lanka	1.5	2.7	4.2
Georgia	0.6	5.9	4.4
Bhutan	1.2	5.2	2.4
Armenia	1.5	7.3	4.0
Maldives	4.1	4.8	8.9
PRC	0.9	6.9	4.7
Thailand	0.9	9.6	5.6
Azerbaijan	1.0	22.2	2.4
Kazakhstan	1.0	3.7	13.0
Malaysia	6.2	17.9	10.0
Republic of Korea	16.7	46.0	23.6
Hong Kong, China	13.4	36.4	60.3
Singapore	3.4	72.6	48.1

Source: ILO (2011).

4.3.2
Policy Implications

If governments can promulgate a coherent set of policies over the next 10 years to promote climate change mitigation, and convince the private sector these policies will remain in place over the long term, then the private sector will create new jobs across the economy wherever new low-carbon goods and services are produced. One challenge is to ensure the incentives are pervasive—across sectors and regions of the economy, types of enterprise, and varieties of occupation. Economy-wide carbon pricing is likely to be the most effective way of doing this. Policy makers also need to identify barriers to green employment creation and overcome them. These include insufficient innovation in low-carbon activities, slow adoption of new technologies from other countries, and insufficient attention to infrastructure needs, particularly in energy and transport. Some of these barriers will only be overcome by public intervention via regulation and consensus building about the future path of the economy.

Active labor market policies will be required. Otherwise, when jobs elsewhere in economies are destroyed, people will be left out of work. Several higher-income Asian countries have found ways of managing the labor market consequences of structural change effectively. In many countries, public employment programs are likely to be part of the solution (Lieuw-Kie-Song and Lal 2010). However, these require adequate public finance. Programs should be designed to encourage permanent employment increases in the longer term, and thus need to be underpinned by permanent price incentives to the private sector. Box 4.6 summarizes the policy conclusions of the ILO and CEDEFOP.

Box 4.6

Measures to Equip Developing Countries with the Skills for Green Growth

Developing countries need special measures to equip them with the skills for the transition to green growth:

- Capacity building for employers in the informal economy and micro and small enterprises to enter green markets in localities where they are most needed
- Entrepreneurship training and business coaching for young people and adults to start up green businesses in conjunction with microfinance projects
- Environmental awareness among decision-makers, business leaders, and administrators as well as formal and nonformal training institutions
- Capacity building to strengthen social dialogue and make training more accessible
- Increased capacity of formal education and training systems and institutions to provide basic skills for all and raise the skills base of the national workforce, including improving apprenticeship systems and building synergies with nongovernment organizations that provide education and training.

Source: ILO and European Centre for the Development of Vocational Training (2011).

Policy makers also need to dovetail green policies with macroeconomic demand management, taking advantage of periods of unexpectedly low aggregate demand to employ workers to reduce the backlog of socially beneficial environmental projects. The scope for job creation in rural areas should not be underestimated: managing common resources such as forests, water catchment areas, and biodiversity requires labor inputs. So does reducing pollution from current methods of farming, fishing, forestry management, water use, and natural resource extraction.

4.4 Expansion of Demand

4.4.1 Promoting Growth by Increasing Demand

Increased innovation and the removal of impediments to the efficient functioning of labor markets can increase the supply capacity of economies as well as tackling environmental problems. However, increased supply capacity has to be matched with increased demand if resources are not to remain idle and involuntary unemployment is not to rise. The ILO (2011: 2) found that, "In many developing economies, while growth has rebounded sharply, long-standing decent work deficits, including widespread vulnerable employment and working poverty continue to pose serious challenges, and the crisis has slowed progress on reducing these deficits."

Nations can also benefit from developing a comparative advantage in producing goods and services for which world demand is increasing rapidly. If labor markets are working effectively, this may not increase employment but will raise real incomes by improving countries' terms of trade. This is why well-designed macroeconomic policies in the short run and industrial policies in the longer term can generate growth that is both faster and greener.

Macroeconomic policies must stimulate demand while ensuring that debt-financed spending supports economic activities with high social returns, including environmental benefits (Bowen and Stern 2010). Given the degree of economic slack that still persists in several Asian nations, this provides an argument for increasing spending on green projects now, and being ready in future to respond to unexpected downturns by reducing the backlog of green investment projects that has arisen as more countries adopt more ambitious environmental targets.

4.4.2
The Asian Experience

Asia has several examples of countries using short-term macroeconomic policies and longer-term industrial policies sensibly to stimulate increases in employment and real incomes while speeding the transition to greener sustainable growth. However, the experience has not been uniform.

After the 2008 global slowdown, UNEP proposed a Global Green New Deal in March 2009, recommending the expenditure of 1% of global gross domestic product (GDP) on green initiatives, to be spent primarily by the Group of Twenty (G-20) countries, which account for two-thirds of the world's population, 90% of global economic activity, and at least three-quarters of global GHG emissions. Figure 4.9 shows fiscal stimulus spending of major economies in Asia. A year later, Barbier (2010: 155) concluded that "only a handful of economies devoted a substantial amount of their total fiscal spending to green investments." The PRC and the Republic of Korea stood out as notable exceptions. The Republic of Korea 'Green New Deal' accounted for nearly all of its fiscal response to the global recession. The PRC apportioned around a third of its total fiscal spending to green measures."

The Republic of Korea projected substantial short-run increases in employment from key green projects under its program—nearly 1 million extra jobs (Table 4.8) (about 4% of the workforce in an economy with a total labor force of about 24.37 million). Forestry restoration was projected to be particularly labor-intensive, with 76.6 jobs created for every million dollars of additional spending. The vehicles and clean energy sectors were projected to be at the other end of the spectrum, given their capital-intensive nature, with just 9.6 jobs being created per million dollars in extra spending.

The Republic of Korea announced its Low-Carbon Green Growth vision and strategy in 2008. It is designed to transform the economy over 2009–2050. Green technology is seen as a source of jobs and export revenues and the Republic of Korea plans to increase its share of this global market from 2% in 2009 to 10% by 2020, supported by increased innovation, technology transfer, and greater domestic spending on research and development (R&D).

The PRC's 12th Five Year Plan also projects a change in industrial structure to "green" the economy and allow the PRC to benefit from fast-growing international markets for more environmentally friendly goods and services. It envisages a shift generally to less carbon-intensive service industries but also clean-energy vehicles and inputs to renewable energy production. Already, the PRC has shown it is possible for Asian countries to exploit a comparative advantage in manufacturing to gain world leadership in clean technologies. On 16 December 2011, The *Washington Post* (citing Photon International, Earth Policy Institute, and Wiley Rein) reported that the PRC's share of global solar cell production climbed to almost 48% in 2010, up from about 38% in 2009. Its rise came largely at the expense of Japanese and German manufacturers (Japan still won a share of 8.5% and Taipei,China 12.7%). Two PRC companies, Sinovel Wind and GoldWind Science and Technology, accounted for over 20% of the global wind turbine market in 2010 (GlobalData.com, accessed 10 January 2012).

Table 4.7

Projections of the Employment Effects of the Republic of Korea's Green Fiscal Stimulus

Stimulus measure	Employment	$ (million)
Expanding mass transit and railroads	138,067	7,005
Energy conservation (villages & schools)	170,702	5,841
Fuel efficient vehicles and clean energy	14,348	1,489
Environmentally friendly living space	10,789	351
River restoration	199,960	10,505
Forest restoration	133,630	1,754
Water resource management[a]	16,132	684
Resource recycling (inc. fuel from waste)	16,196	675
National green information infrastructure	3,120	270
Total for the nine major projects	702,944	28,573
Total for the Green New Deal	960,000	36,280

[a] Small and midsize dams.

Source: Ministry of Strategy and Finance, Republic of Korea.

India is also preparing a 12th Five Year Plan with an emphasis on sustainable growth and improving energy supply, in part through clean energy sources (Government of India, Planning Commission 2011b). By contrast, there is less emphasis on winning a larger share of expanding global markets for low-carbon and other greener products. India has, however, already set up a variety of national missions to support its National Action Plan on Climate Change, such as the missions on solar energy and energy efficiency. Some successes are already evident, such as Suzlon, the fifth largest wind turbine group in the world with a global market share of about 8% (Suzlon 2012). Business leaders have acknowledged that "green industry could be a very useful tool to promote economic growth, stimulate job creation as well as support long-term environmental sustainability" (Federation of Indian Chambers of Commerce and Industry [FICCI] 2011: 1). Some commentators have expressed concern about the ability of policy makers to deliver fully on the National Action Plan, partly because of the split of responsibilities between the all-India and state-level governments, and partly because the capacity to support new industries and products is not always sufficiently developed (see, for example, Rai and Victor 2009; Ockwell et al. 2008).

Figure 4.9
Fiscal Stimulus Spending Plans (as of July 2009)

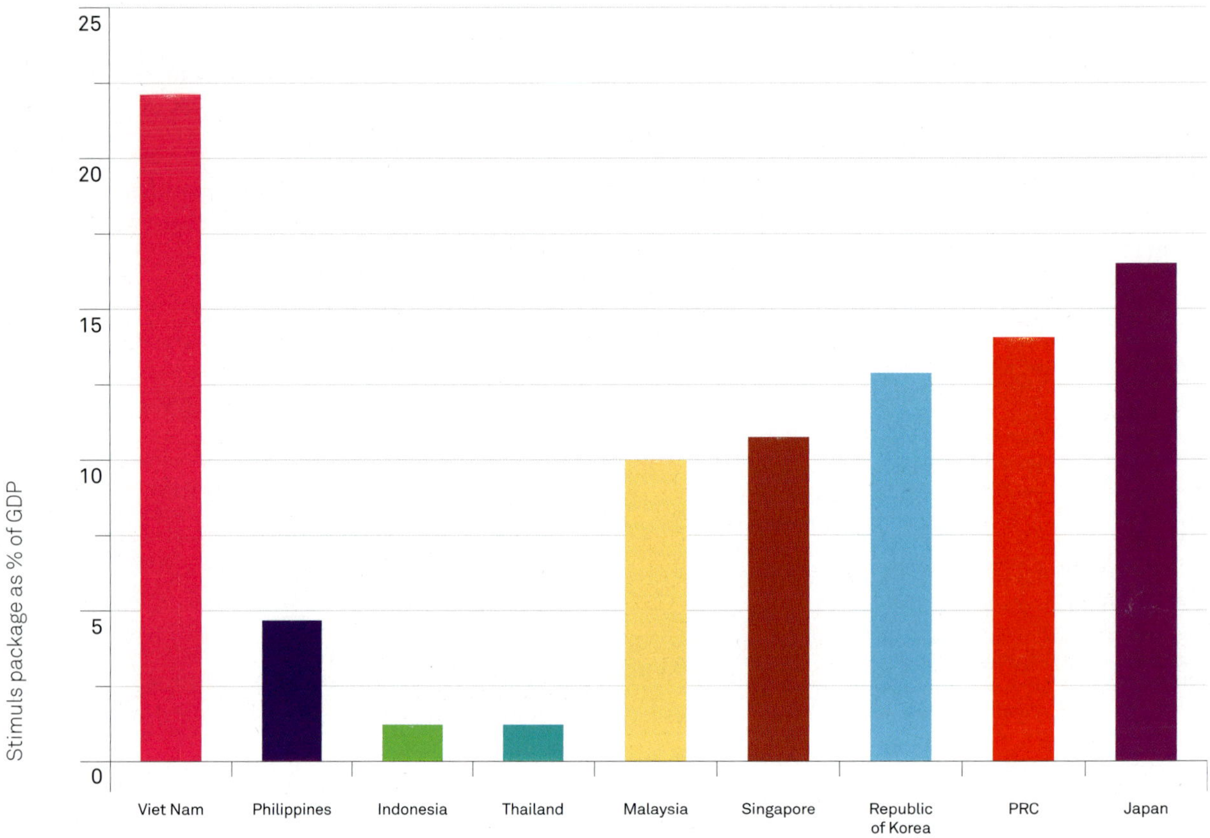

Source: Anbumozhi and Bauer (2009).

FICCI has listed a number of factors impeding structural change in a green direction, including inadequate infrastructure, lack of access to clean technologies and adequately skilled manpower, lack of funding, and lack of confidence in the sustainability of demand. This draws attention to the importance for all countries of well-articulated, long-term, and credible environmental policies, especially on climate change.

4.4.3 Policy Implications

As far as macroeconomic policy is concerned, the PRC and the Republic of Korea in particular have shown it is possible to fashion fiscal stimuli that accelerate the transition to green growth in a fiscally responsible way. Debt-financed fiscal stimuli must be implemented with due regard for the social returns from additional spending and should be designed with an exit strategy in mind. Many—but not all—green projects are particularly suitable (Bowen et al. 2009).

Project spending must either be temporary—e.g., catching up with any backlog of green projects that do not require long preparation, such as improving the insulation of public buildings and housing stock—or be underpinned by plans for financing future support from tax revenues.

It is too early to judge the success of the ambitious plans put forward by some countries, but the emphasis on drawing on existing comparative advantages in manufacturing gives grounds for optimism. It is always difficult to anticipate how countries' comparative advantages will evolve, so picking particular products or sectors as future winners worthy of government support is perilous. It is also impossible for all countries around the world to generate net exports in each expanding category.

Policy makers would be well advised to concentrate on correcting market and policy failures that could impede the growth of green sectors, in particular those affecting innovation and labor markets. Public authorities also need to stop well-established firms trying to discourage new entrants or new ideas that might challenge their traditional sources of revenue. Thus, competition policy is an important aspect of innovation policy.

Environmental pricing is a very efficient way of providing simple incentives to develop the new opportunities. This is central, for example, to recent recommendations (Box 4.7) addressed to the Republic of Korea by OECD researchers (Jones and Yoo 2011). They argue that the Republic of Korea's ambitious green growth program could be enhanced by more pervasive carbon pricing.

The unfamiliar nature of many of the products and industrial processes involved in low-carbon green growth is likely to inhibit private finance unless public agencies are able to reduce the risk facing private investments by providing expertise, seed capital, finance for demonstration projects, and innovative risk-sharing financial instruments. As one of the biggest risks involved is political risk—changes in governments' commitment to green policies, changes in regulatory regimes, and changes in international policy—some risk-sharing by the public sector, for example through public sector investment institutions, is desirable. International lending institutions such as ADB also have a key role to play.

Box 4.7

Recommendations for Mitigating Climate Change and Developing New Growth Engines in the Republic of Korea

Mitigating climate change

- Introduce market-based instruments as soon as possible to achieve the 2020 emission reduction target in a cost-effective way by ensuring abatement costs are equal at the margin across all options.
- Put a price on carbon emissions by creating a mandatory and comprehensive emissions trading system (ETS), thereby providing a clear price signal enabling appropriate investment decisions.
- Auction ETS permits and allow them to be banked for the future and, perhaps, borrowed.
- Introduce a carbon tax in areas not covered by the ETS and use the revenue, together with that from auctioning permits, to reduce other taxes.
- Accelerate the phasing out of environmentally-harmful energy subsidies and ensure that energy prices in each sector reflect the cost of production and distribution.
- Stop earmarking environmental taxes for transport construction, especially roads.

Creating new engines for growth

- Ensure good framework conditions, including openness to foreign investment and a strong competition framework, to facilitate the entry of new firms and the exit of firms in declining industries.
- Enhance flexibility in the labor market and ensure adequate training of workers.
- Ensure that the spending in the Five-Year Plan for Green Growth—2% of annual gross domestic product over 2009–2013—is implemented in a transparent and effective manner to address market failures.
- Promote innovation in green technologies by increasing their share of publicly funded research and development (R&D), focusing on basic research, particularly in areas related to large-scale projects by the private sector and in technologies too far from commercial viability to attract private investment.
- Improve the overall innovation framework by spending more on basic research; closely linking government research institutes, universities, and industry; and reducing the mismatch between human resources and research spending in universities.
- Encourage the development of renewable energy resources by removing noneconomic barriers and establishing a predictable and transparent support framework with incentives that decrease over time.
- Design the green certificate program and the green finance initiatives carefully to limit the risk of bubbles.

Improving the quality of life through a better environment

- Gradually reduce the level of emissions allowed under the cap-and-trade program covering air pollutants in the capital region to improve air quality to the level in advanced Organisation for Economic Co-operation and Development countries.
- Increase average fuel efficiency standards to reduce nitrogen oxide emissions.

Source: Jones and Yoo (2011).

4.5 Innovation

4.5.1 Why Innovation Matters

The transition to low-carbon green growth requires more innovation, particularly in low-carbon energy supply but also in the construction sector, transport, product and process design, urban planning, agricultural practices, and land management. New technologies need to be developed that are less dependent on fossil fuels, and existing technologies need to be made more efficient. Production processes need to be refined so that they are less polluting and resource-intensive.

However, innovation is inhibited by a range of market failures (Jaffe, Newell, and Stavins 2005), all capable of slowing the transition. For example, there are spillovers from new ideas because their use by those who first dream them up does not prevent their use by others. If someone thinks of a new way to reduce the use of water in an industrial process or a new product that is less carbon-intensive, many other people could use the new idea in principle. As a result, it is often difficult to appropriate all the returns on investment in generating knowledge, so people do not have the incentive to invest as much. Hence, the returns to R&D investment are often much greater than the private returns, perhaps on average by a factor of four (Jaffe 1986; Griliches 1992; Popp 2006). The returns to society as a whole from investing in environmental and energy technology R&D are likely to be comparable to those in other fields (Popp 2006). Some approaches to correcting this problem by creating legally recognized intellectual property rights (IPR) can give rise to monopoly power for the original innovators, which can be a market failure itself. New ideas may be inhibited from spreading.

Second, there can be a tendency to path dependence of the choice of technologies and lock-in of high-carbon plant and equipment, with well-established technologies benefiting from higher productivity because of the experience firms have had with them (Unruh 2000; Acemoglu et al. 2009). A switch to alternative technologies and the adoption of innovations may be desirable, but individual firms may not have sufficient incentive to undertake them unless confident that other firms will, too. Thus, policy makers have to set credible incentives over an extended period of time.

If Asian policy makers are to pursue green growth, they will have to tackle these market failures that hold back innovation. If they do so, they will be able reap benefits across the board from faster technological progress; more rapid adoption of ideas from other countries; and better adaptation of new ideas to local needs, endowments of raw materials, and preferences. As Crafts (2010: 1) notes: "Strong and sustained technological progress is the key characteristic of modern economic growth that distinguished the post-Industrial-Revolution world from earlier times and is the fundamental force which has raised living standards over the last 250 years." Yet, as Crafts points out, many economies relied more heavily on capital accumulation and the reallocation of workers from less to more productive sectors of the economy to fuel their growth in the past. The scope for Asian economies to continue along these lines will diminish as populations age, saving rates decline, and the movement of people out of rural agriculture into urban industry and services slows. This can already be observed in advanced Asian economies such as Japan and Hong Kong, China.

The transition to green growth can facilitate a broader transition to greater reliance on innovation as a source of sustainable economic growth.

4.5.2 The Asian Experience

The pattern and pace of innovation in Asia has been mixed, with some countries leading the world according to some measures while others have failed to benefit as much. The absolute level of annual investment in R&D in some countries such as the PRC, India, Japan, and the Republic of Korea is now substantial. However, R&D as a percentage of GDP varies considerably. The Republic of Korea and Japan have levels comparable to those of the US, while the PRC and India are some way behind. Similarly, the number of scientists and engineers as a proportion of the population is higher in some Asian countries (e.g., Japan; Singapore; the Republic of Korea; and Taipei,China). Among all countries spending more than $100 million per year on R&D, some Asian nations have very low R&D spending as a proportion of GDP: the figures for Indonesia, the Philippines, Thailand, and Viet Nam, are 0.25% or less (Figure 4.10).

In some cases, notably Japan, R&D effort has been high for many years. The Republic of Korea's spending has increased rapidly in the past decade, as has that of the PRC (Figure 4.11). Indian R&D spending has also been increasing significantly. According to the UN agency WIPO (2011), low- and middle-income economies increased their share of global R&D expenditure by 13% between 1993 and 2009, with the PRC accounting for most of this increase—more than 10 percentage points—propelling the PRC to be the world's second largest R&D spender in 2009.

Yet most R&D spending still takes place in high-income countries—about 70% of the world total. They spend about 2.5% of their GDP on R&D—more than double the rate of middle-income economies as a whole. This dominance is also true if one focuses more narrowly on environmental innovations, for example in pollution abatement technologies (Lanjouw and Mody 1996). R&D is only one aspect of innovation—product, process, and managerial innovations not captured in R&D and patent statistics are important, as is the ability to assimilate and adapt the fruits of R&D elsewhere. There is considerable scope for many Asian countries to increase their innovatory activities in these areas, and tailor the results of innovation elsewhere to their needs. Water pollution control technologies in developing countries have tended to rely more frequently than have air pollution control technologies on local innovation, because local conditions are more important in shaping what these technologies have to do; they are also less likely to have been patented elsewhere. Dechezleprêtre et al. (2011) found that the most common climate-friendly patented innovations in the PRC and the Republic of Korea included technologies designed primarily for local markets, such as geothermal and cement manufacture. Process innovation can be tailored to the mix of inputs available to the country concerned: many Asian countries have abundant supplies of unskilled labor but are less well-endowed with raw materials and energy resources.

Part of the impetus for increased innovation in several Asian countries has already come from efforts to start the transition to green growth. Table 4.9 shows how the PRC and the Republic of Korea, for example, have moved up the rankings for patenting green innovations.

Figure 4.10

World Research and Development Spending, 2010

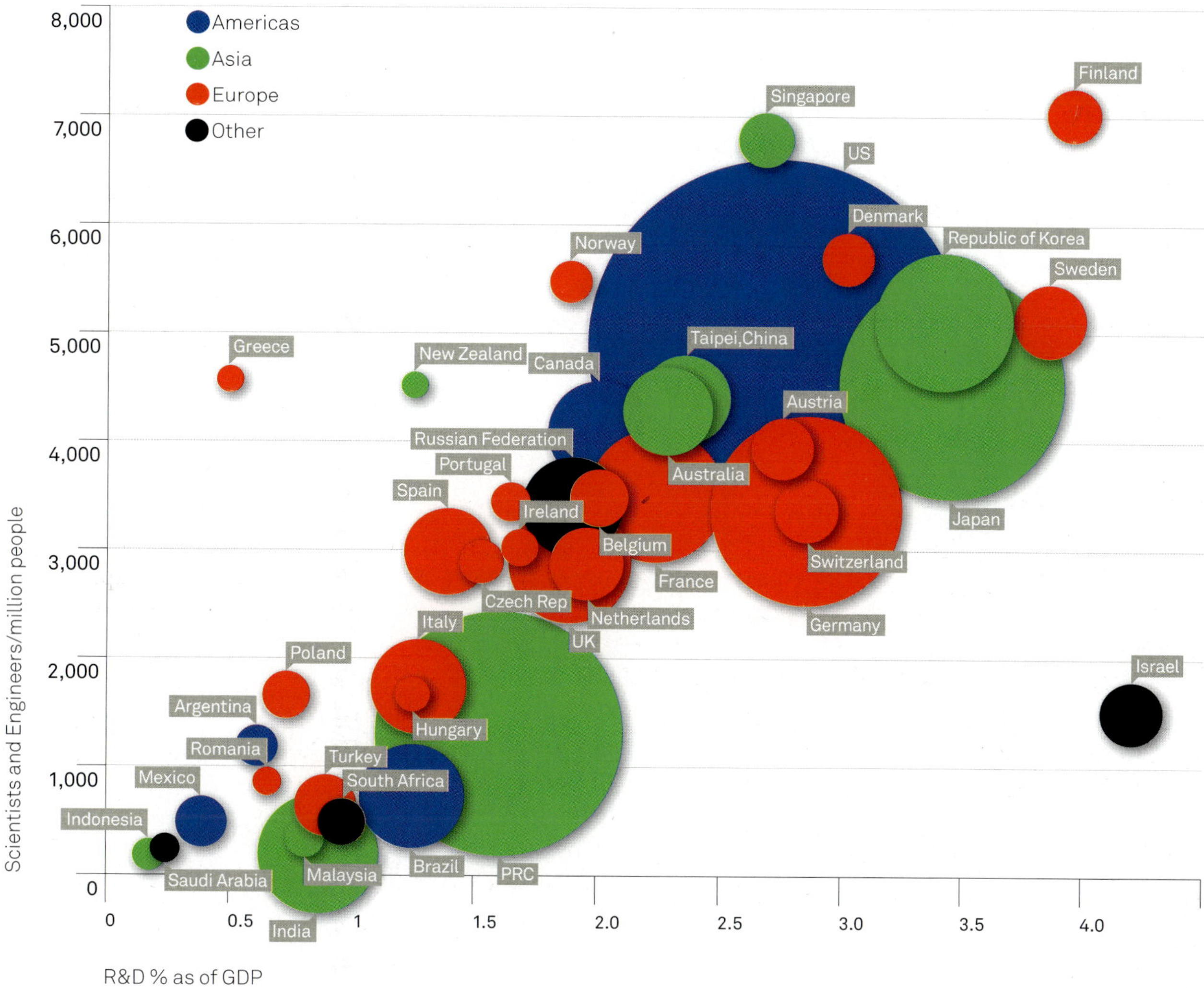

Source: R&D magazine (2010).

Figure 4.11

Total Research and Development Spending Relative to Gross Domestic Product among Major Global Economies—Public, Private, and Nonprofit

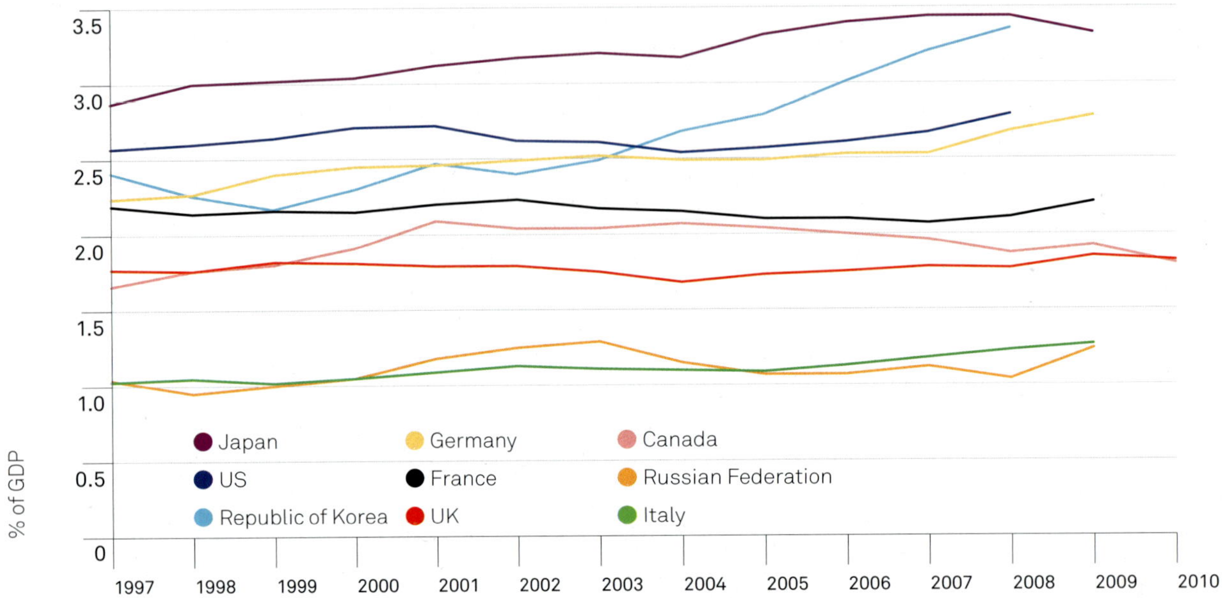

Source: OECD (2011).

Table 4.8

The Leading Countries for Green Inventions according to Patent Data

Country	1980–2007 Average % of world's inventions	1980–2007 Rank	2002–2007 Average % of world's inventions	2002–2007 Rank
Japan	20.2	1	20.8	1
Germany	19.8	2	17.8	2
US	15.4	3	14.1	3
France	5.1	4	4.4	5
UK	4.5	5	4.3	6
Australia	3.8	6	2.9	9
Sweden	3.3	7	1.7	13
Republic of Korea	3.1	8	5.6	4
Canada	2.2	9	3.0	8
Netherlands	2.1	10	1.8	12
Austria	2.0	11	2.1	11
Italy	1.9	12	2.3	10
Switzerland	1.9	13	1.3	15
PRC	1.9	14	3.9	7
Denmark	1.4	15	1.4	14
Total	88.6		87.4	

Source: Dechezleprêtre and Martin (2010).

The PRC's 12th Five Year Plan envisages increasing R&D expenditure to 2.5% of GDP by 2015 (broadly comparable to the current level in Germany), focusing on seven key strategic industries that are at the forefront of the transition to greener growth: environmental protection and energy efficiency, new types of energy supply, next generation information technology, biotechnology, high-end manufacturing, clean-energy vehicles, and high-technology materials.

Policy implications

In order for nations to stimulate green innovation in particular and innovation in general, they need to have effectively functioning national innovation systems, as stressed by two of the background papers to this report (Kumar 2012; Ramanathan 2012). Foxon and Pearson (2008) lay out five functions for which such systems are needed:

1. To create and diffuse knowledge
2. To guide and influence the direction of the search process among users and suppliers of technology
3. To facilitate the supply of required resources, including capital and competencies
4. To create positive external economies through the exchange of information, knowledge, and visions
5. To facilitate the formation of markets

The systems comprise institutions of government and the private sector, and also regulations and market-based incentives. They need to focus primarily on correcting the market failures in the innovation process. The key policy implication is that countries need to strengthen their national innovation systems. Policy interventions to promote eco-innovations need to ensure that the nation has the capacity not only to produce knowledge but also the ability to effectively deploy, internalize, and improve on it. That presents a particular challenge in poorer countries, in which small and medium-sized enterprises often have difficulty in assimilating innovations (Ramanathan 2012). However, some countries in Asia have much better developed national innovation systems (Kumar 2012); amongst them Japan, the Republic of Korea, the PRC, and Singapore. Even in these countries, there is scope for improving the pace and extent of innovation, as a recent OECD study of the Republic of Korea's innovation policy illustrates, emphasizing the desirability of green investments and services innovation.

Innovation in many Asian countries will rely to a large extent on adapting the outputs of basic R&D in high-income countries, so the IPR governing the international diffusion of innovation is important. At the moment, there are long lead times when developing-country firms try to acquire technology partners, finance, and skills (Ramanathan 2012). It is difficult to combine technologies derived from different sources subject to different IPR barriers, while potential partners are reluctant to transfer cutting-edge technologies. The United Nations Economic and Social Commission for Asia and the Pacific is tackling this issue with respect to energy through its Renewable Energy Cooperation Mechanism for Asia and the Pacific.

Policy makers have to make a sustained effort to redirect national innovation systems, because economies of scale and the higher returns to new ideas in larger, well-established industries tend to establish path dependence—firms will not be able to break out of their high-emissions paths without public assistance. This may entail support for infant green sectors, subsidies, and environmental pricing. Carbon pricing is an effective tool to direct innovation towards low-carbon techniques and products (Popp 2002), and its effects are non-discriminatory and pervasive.

4.6 Energy Security

4.6.1 The Two Dimensions of Energy Security

There are two distinct aspects to energy security. First, ensuring all who need energy have access to it. This is an element of ensuring social inclusion and fighting poverty. Second, the objective of maintaining an uninterrupted supply of energy in the short, medium, and long term. That requires a robust energy infrastructure, access to a variety of primary energy sources and diversification of sources of energy imports to reduce geopolitical risks. Coordination problems and economies of scale in the provision of networks such as electricity grids can impede purely private sector efforts to develop universal access to high-quality energy supplies. Government attempts to regulate the energy sector, maintain low energy prices, and control the rents from natural resource ownership can introduce inefficiency and even corruption. Energy resource endowments can therefore bring with them both market and government failures (Collier 2010).

This is another area where there are potential synergies between the pursuit of environmental objectives and other important development goals. For example, reducing dependence on traditional biomass can bring down particulate emissions. Asia has extensive renewable energy resources that could be further developed while extending access to energy. Greater use of electricity in the energy mix allows a variety of primary energy sources to be used while reducing the number of sites at which carbon is emitted.

Developing domestic renewable energy sources reduces dependence on foreign supplies of energy while mitigating climate change risks. This has been one of the major motivating factors, for example, of the European Unions (EU) ambitious efforts to increase the contribution of renewable energy from 11.6% in 2009 to 20% by 2020.

4.6.2 The Asian Experience

Both aspects of energy security are important for Asia. About 60% of the 1.6 billion people around the world who do not have access to electricity live in Asia (ADB 2009b). The electrification rate is only 20% in Cambodia and the Lao People's Democratic Republic (Lao PDR) and even lower, at 11%, in Myanmar. There is a high degree of reliance on traditional biofuels. In 2006, biomass and waste still accounted for 24% of energy for final use: 49% of the energy used in the residential sector in the PRC was derived from this source; in India, the figure was 68%.

Earlier in this chapter we discussed some of the successful initiatives in Asia to tackle this problem at the grassroots. More broadly, national energy policies have also facilitated a very rapid increase in energy supply. According to the US Energy Information Administration, electricity supply in Asia doubled between 1999 and 2006 and generation was growing at annual rates of 22.5% in Cambodia, 14.0% in the Maldives, 11.0% in Afghanistan, 9.5% in Bangladesh, 8.7% in Bhutan, and 7.9% in Nepal. Rural electrification has been very successful in several countries (e.g., Thailand).

However, energy demand has tended to outstrip domestic supply, notably but not only in the largest economies. The PRC switched from being a net coal exporter to be a major net importer in 2009 (Morse and He 2010). The PRC, India, and the Republic of Korea are among the world's top five oil importers.

Imported energy has become more important in the energy mix of most Asian countries and reliance on fossil fuels is greater than the global average. Import dependence will rise (Figure 4.12) unless there is a step change in the exploitation of domestic energy resources, including renewables.

Concerns about energy security have led the PRC and India to purchase foreign firms owning fossil-fuel resources in other countries. At the same time, significant inefficiencies remain in energy supply, notably electricity. Transmission and distribution losses have been high in Asia, amounting to 11% of the electricity consumed in 2006; transmission and distribution losses were as high as 37% of total consumption in India, 35% in Bhutan, 32% in Nepal, and 39% in Myanmar (ADB 2009c).

As the 2009 ADB study showed, one response has been to stimulate the production of renewables through various policy measures (Table 4.10). But so far, these have not made a major impact on countries' energy mixes. Of the countries reviewed in REN21 (2011), Thailand was the only country in Asia with more ambitious plans (in percentage points) than the EU to increase the share of energy from renewables. The pros and cons of nuclear power are discussed from this perspective in Box 4.8.

Figure 4.12

Energy Import Dependency in Emerging Asia

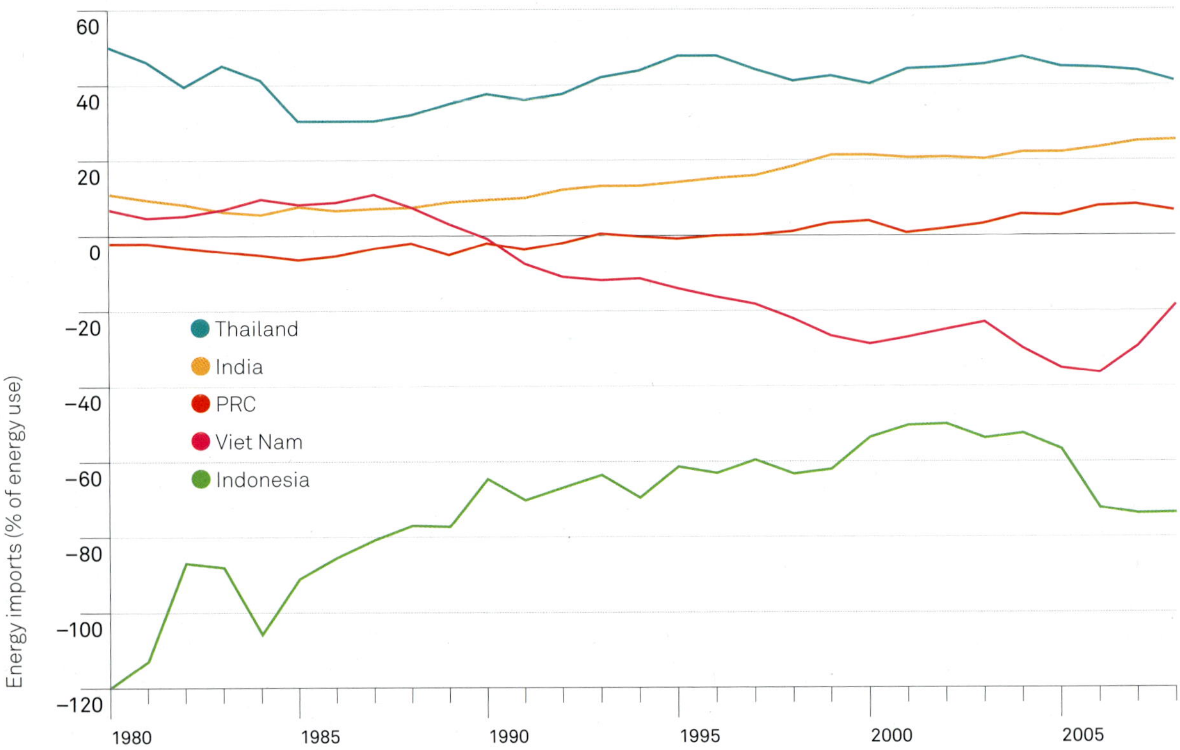

Source: Howes and Wyroll (2012), based on World Bank (2011).

Table 4.9

Low-Carbon Policies in Asia

Country	Feed-in Tariffs	Renewable Portfolio Standards	Capital Subsidies, Grants or Rebates	Investment or Other Tax Credits	Sales Tax, Energy Tax, Excise Tax, or Value-Added Tax Reduction	Energy Production Payments or Tax Credits	Net Metering	Public Investment Loans, or Financing	Public Competitive Bidding
Cambodia			●						
PRC	●		●	●	●			●	●
India	[a]	[a]	●	●	●	●	[a]	●	●
Indonesia	●								
Philippines			●	●	●			●	
Sri Lanka	●								
Thailand	●		●				●	●	

[a] Some states/provinces within these countries have state/province-level policies, but there is no national-level policy.
Only enacted policies are included in the table. However, for some policies shown, implementing regulations may not yet be developed or effective leading to lack of implementation or impacts.

Source: ADB (2009).

Box 4.8

Green Growth and Nuclear Power in Asia

The aspirations of Asian nations to maintain rapid economic growth, increase households' and firms' access to energy, and contain rises in the real price of energy raise the question of what role nuclear power might play. As with renewable energy sources such as wind, nuclear power is associated with much lower carbon emissions per unit of electricity than fossil fuel power generation, even taking into account the design and construction phases. Capital costs are also much higher than operating costs, for both renewable and nuclear power. However, unlike most forms of renewable power generation, nuclear power can generate electricity continuously (apart from interruptions for maintenance), thus promising a more reliable supply to satisfy base load requirements. Although nuclear power is not renewable, and depends on finite resources of fissile material for fuel, known reserves and technological alternatives (using breeder reactors and reprocessing) suggest supply constraints are unlikely to bind as soon as with oil and gas. For such reasons, the nuclear industry has been anticipating a nuclear renaissance.

That renaissance has been slow in materializing. Since the Chernobyl incident in 1987, installed nuclear power capacity has grown at an average rate of only 1.3% per year while average annual growth in electricity demand was around 3% per year. In the decade 1996–2006, while total global primary energy consumption increased by 26%, installed nuclear power increased by only 15%. Rising concerns about climate change brought an expansion of nuclear power back onto the agenda but the tsunami damage that destroyed the reactors at Fukushima, Japan, on 11 March 2011 led several countries to review their nuclear plans. Other problems over the years have included high construction costs, large cost overruns, concerns about the safe disposal of long-lived radioactive waste, worries about nuclear proliferation, and fears of catastrophic malfunctions.

Source: Herberg (2011); Pacific Energy Summit 2012 Summit Papers.

Figure 4.13

Nuclear Energy Consumption in Asia and the Pacific and the World

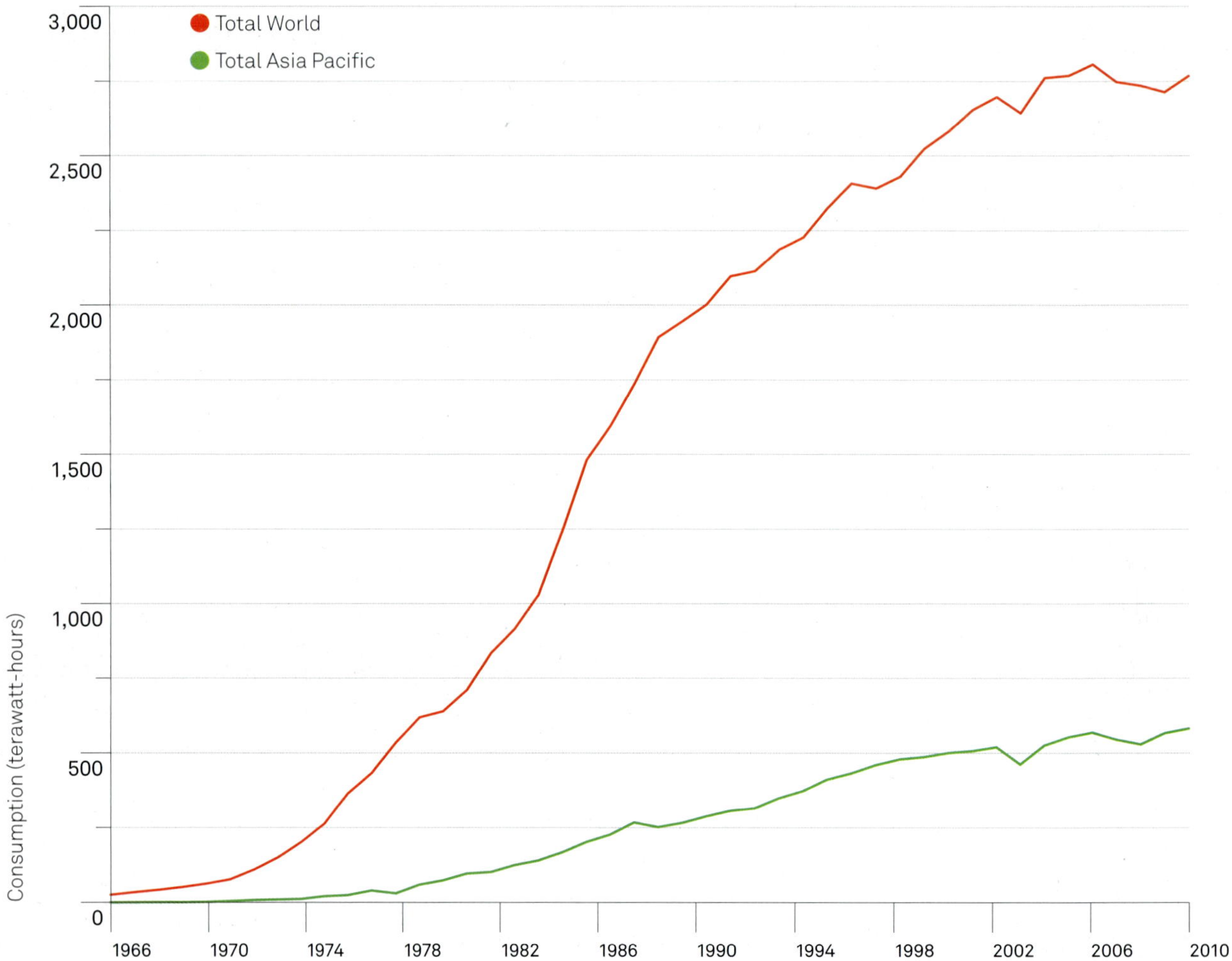

Source: BP. Statistical Review of World Energy June 2011.

Figure 4.14

Nuclear Energy Consumption in Asia and the Pacific

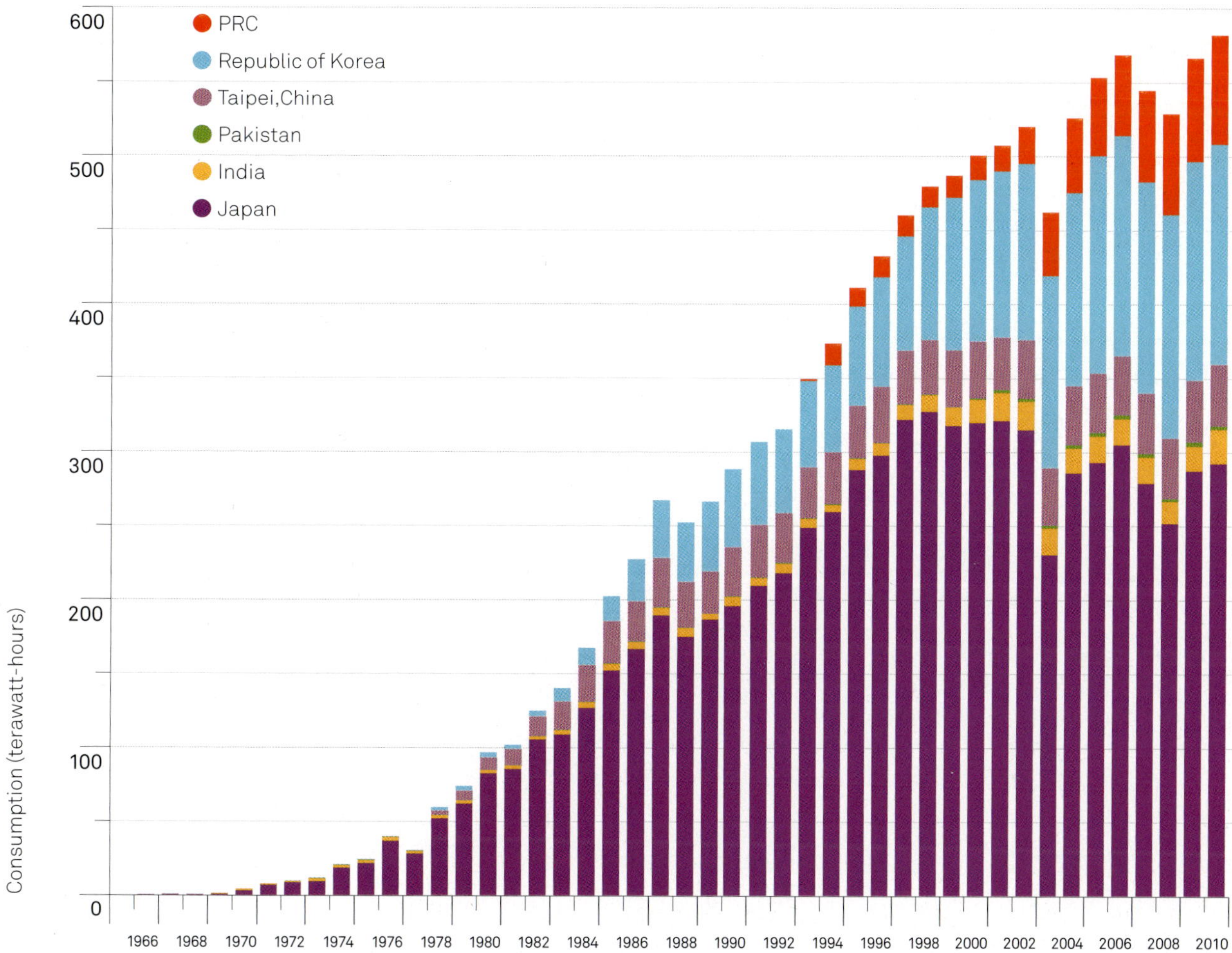

Notes: Based on gross generation and not accounting for cross-border electricity supply. Converted on the basis of thermal equivalence, assuming 38% conversion efficiency in a modern thermal power station. Nuclear energy data (expressed in terawatt-hours) are available at www.bp.com/statisticalreview.

Source: BP. Statistical Review of World Energy June 2011.

Table 4.10

Nuclear Electricity-Generating Capacity 2012

Country	Cumulative Installed Nuclear Capacity	Number of Reactors [a]	Share of Electricity from Nuclear in 2011	Reactors Under Construction*	Capacity Under Construction
	MW		%		MW
Japan	44,215	50	18	2	2,650
Republic of Korea	20,671	23	35	3	3,640
PRC	11,816	16	2	26	26,620
Taipei,China	5,018	6	19	2	2,600
India	4,391	20	4	7	4,824
Pakistan	725	3	4	2	630
Viet Nam [b]				4	4,000
Philippines [b]				4	2,400
Thailand [b]				2	2,000
Indonesia [b]				1	1,000
Bangladesh [b]				1	1,000
Asia Total	86,836	118		42	40,964

[a] Not all reactors are currently generating electricity; for example, as of 5 May 2012, all of Japan's "operational" reactors were offline with no set date for restart. [b] Source for each country from http://www-pub.iaea.org/MTCD/Publications/PDF/CNPP2011_CD/pages/countryprofiles.htm Accessed May 26th 2012.

Source: Compiled by Earth Policy Institute with capacity and number of reactors as of 13 May 2012 from International Atomic Energy Agency (IAEA), Power Reactor Information System (PRIS), "Operational & Long-Term Shutdown Reactors," www.pris.iaea.org updated 13 May 2012; nuclear share of electricity from IAEA, PRIS, "Nuclear Share of Electricity Generation in 2011," at www.pris.iaea.org updated 13 May 2012; UK and world totals adjusted to reflect closure of Wylfa 2 reactor, from "Wylfa 2 Bows Out," World Nuclear News, 26 April 2012; world share of electricity from nuclear in 2010 from IEA, IEA (2011b: 451).

Figure 4.13 shows the trends in nuclear energy consumption in Asia. More countries in the region plan to establish nuclear capacity (notably Viet Nam and the Philippines) and the PRC's expansion plans are particularly ambitious (Figure 4.14). The target announced by the PRC's National Energy Bureau for 2030 is a capacity of 160,000 MW, which would easily make the PRC the world's largest producer of nuclear power (Table 4.11). Sovacool and Valentine (2010) argue that seven key factors appear to underpin support for nuclear power development, especially in India, the Republic of Korea, and the PRC:

1. Strong state involvement in guiding economic development;
2. Centralization of national energy policy making and planning;
3. Campaigns to link technological progress with national revitalization;
4. The influence of technocratic ideology on policy decisions;
5. Subordination of challenges to political authority;
6. Low levels of civic activism;
7. The influence of climate policy.

The future role of nuclear power in Asia's green growth is uncertain. Public opinion appears to have turned against it in Japan, following Fukushima. But several other countries, particularly the PRC and India, are likely to press ahead. Countries must have a strong regulatory capacity if they are to take this route, given the sensitivity of investment, cost control, and safety practices to regulatory incentives. Nuclear power cannot replace fossil fuels by itself. A portfolio approach has attractions, increasing the resilience of national energy systems and promoting energy security.

4.6.3
Policy Implications

Energy supply and energy efficiency need major enhancements in Asia if the continent's rapid growth is to be sustainable and access to energy resources is to be made available to all households. These are necessary if rapid growth is to be green and low-carbon, so that it can both continue in the long term and avoid dangerously high emissions and climate risks.

The ADB (2009a) study on Improving Energy Security and Reducing Carbon Intensity in Asia and the Pacific identified policy initiatives which would reap benefits:

1 Reducing price distortions in energy markets, particularly by removing implicit and explicit subsidies on fossil-fuel production and consumption (while introducing more targeted support for poor households)
2 Scaling up successful pilot projects and local initiatives in renewable energy
3 Improving the governance of publicsector energy supply and regulation to improve its cost-effectiveness, including by increasing private sector involvement and competition
4 Improving regional collaboration on renewable energy R&D and the adaptation of energy technologies to Asian circumstances
5 Using new technology such as "smart" grids that can leapfrog older technologies used in Europe and North America, and improve energy efficiency by making it easier for demand to respond to prices and easier to integrate energy from renewable sources
6 Offering incentives to the private sector to invest in renewable energy and more energy efficient capital stock
7 Integrating energy efficiency projects more effectively in the UNs' Clean Development Mechanism.

4.7
Towards a New Policy Approach

Low-carbon green growth is an essential strategy for sustainable development in Asia, improving living standards, and saving resources. It requires policies across a wide range of areas to correct market and policy failures, particularly those arising from environmental externalities and inadequate incentives for innovation. Well-designed policies can improve the productivity of economies, stimulating growth rather than holding it back, and reducing the risk of environmental catastrophes. Action is required in five broad areas, as summarized in the matrix in Table 4.11.

Table 4.11

Key Policy Actions Required

Area of policy	Actions required	Reasons for these actions
Energy sector	Unwinding of energy subsidies; introduction of pervasive and broadly uniform carbon pricing.	To send a clear signal about the direction of energy policy; to improve energy efficiency and generate tax revenues to fund other national objectives.
Innovation	Stimulation of locally appropriate innovation in production technologies, products, and management. That needs sector-specific initiatives, including time-limited public support for low-carbon research, development, deployment, and diffusion; and more regional cooperation.	Innovation is a key driver, along with capital accumulation and skills acquisition, of economic growth. Asia will be able to rely less in future on very rapid capital widening, movement of workers from low-productivity to high-productivity sectors and "catch-up" with today's technological leaders.
Resource use	Improvement of incentives for efficiency, particularly in the use of natural resources and the services provided by the natural environment. The focus must be on what is appropriate for nations in the longer term, given the long lives of many investments, particularly in the energy sector.	Policy makers need to discourage private investors from locking in inefficient technologies when they invest, by offering clear signals about the potentially high returns from the transition to green growth.
Labor markets	The promotion of labor market mobility and the acquisition of new skills.	Active labor market policies are needed to facilitate rapid structural change, including the transition to a low-carbon economy; that also helps to share the benefits of green growth more equitably.
Social inclusivity	Integration of the social dimension of growth with the macroeconomic dimension; mitigating the adverse impacts on the poor of taking the low-emissions path; using local knowledge to stimulate appropriate innovation.	Green growth should be pro-poor and pro-job but will not be so automatically; enhancing communities' capacities for collective action should improve economic, social, and environmental outcomes across the board.

Source: ADB–ADBI study team.

In all five areas, no-regrets strategies are available where the resource costs of action are relatively small and the likely benefits significant, while dangerous risks are reduced or eliminated. Beyond those, many investments are likely to have a high social rate of return and a competitive private rate of return, especially if environmental pricing is implemented. The costs of climate change mitigation could be offset to a very large extent (and, in some countries, completely) by co-benefits such as faster technological progress, lower environmental pollution, improved health, better matching of potential workers with jobs, and enhanced energy security.

However, a number of obstacles need to be overcome, including the design of efficient policies, strengthening social safety nets, and the political challenge of improving governance and overcoming entrenched economic interests benefiting from the status quo. The danger is that such obstacles will lead to delay. Asia needs to take vigorous action now to be a low-carbon leader in the future.

Chapter 5
Regional Cooperation for Seizing the Opportunities

Chapter 5
Regional Cooperation for Seizing the Opportunities

5.1 Sharing and Learning from Each Other

Reducing greenhouse gas (GHG) emissions and tackling climate change are global public goods. Effective regional and international cooperation are central to achieving low-carbon societies. Countries in emerging Asia, some of which are among the biggest emitters, have an essential role to play in promoting the global move toward a green economy, and are well positioned to use regional cooperation to advance the uptake of low-carbon technologies, such as renewable energy and energy efficiency, in a cost-effective way. Effective cost reduction through economies of scale in some Asian countries would help others to overcome the cost barriers to widespread deployment if there was free trade in low-carbon technology goods and services. Countries will benefit from policies such as energy efficiency standards, labels, and certification for low-carbon goods only if non-tariff barriers in their trade regime are removed.

Adequate and affordable financing is also possible by mobilizing private capital to fund climate change mitigation projects. Unifying carbon markets and increasing the readiness of regional markets very much depends on establishing sectoral level GHG greenhouse gas inventories; strengthening capabilities for monitoring, reporting, and verifying these emissions at a national level; and establishing technology hubs at a regional level. In view of the scale, complexity, and range of challenges, there are increased roles for regional institutions such as the Asian Development Bank (ADB). Regional cooperation can be a win-win collaboration, as there is increasing recognition among countries in Asia that there are many areas where the experience and expertise of other countries, particularly those in East Asia, could be helpful in meeting their developmental challenges. Collaboration with neighbors will strengthen domestic energy reserves and improve energy security through diversification of resources.

Asian countries need a package of measures including public and private investments in technological innovations, technological diffusion, financing, regional cooperation through trade, investment, aid, and new institutions and governance systems. Specifically, this chapter focuses on seizing the market-based opportunities such as knowledge, trade and investment flows in low-carbon goods and services (LCGS); [1] non-market opportunities such as joint research and policy networking; and financing mobilization through regional cooperation. Following an evidence-based approach to transforming Asia into low-carbon green Asia, this chapter will also highlight a few good examples of policy initiatives taken across the region for other countries to emulate through knowledge sharing.

---

1 Low-carbon goods and services include a range of rapidly growing renewable energy technologies (such as hydro, wave and tidal power, geothermal, wind, and biomass), as well as a number of other emerging low-carbon activities (such as reduced emissions from within the transport, waste management and building sectors,energy management, carbon capture and storage, and carbon finance).

5.1.1
Regional Collaboration on Mitigation

As shown in Figure 5.1, developing Asia can reduce carbon emissions by 20% to 30% if commercially available "best practice" low-carbon technologies are disseminated and used across the region. For example, among the Asian emerging economies, the People's Republic of China (PRC) and India have been on a consistently high growth trajectory for years. The PRC has the potential to reduce carbon dioxide emission by 8.6 gigatons (Gt) by 2015, while India's reduction potential is about 1.8 Gt, if they adopted the 'best practice' of low-carbon technologies (IEA 2007).

It is well documented that, among the Asian countries, Japan has been in the forefront of controlling carbon emissions by instituting appropriate policy measures at the sectoral and national levels, which can be emulated by other Asian countries (Anbumozhi 2010; Kim 2011). Drawing on the experiences of Japan, Asia's big emerging economies, such as the PRC, India, and Indonesia, have begun taking actions in the form of voluntary targets and policy commitments to improve carbon efficiency (Howes and Wyrwoll 2012). However, the realization of these commitments in Asian emerging economies has varied and is constrained by barriers including a lack of technological innovation and dissemination, and a lack of finance for promoting innovation. Thus, international funding and technology innovation and transfer are essential for the success of mitigation actions in Asia. The region should enhance its capacity to make better use of existing institutions, human capital, and funding sources. The interesting question is what the emerging economies of Asia can demonstrate to other Asian economies in terms of instituting proper policy frameworks for low-carbon green growth, which is discussed briefly in the following sections.

Learning from Country Experiences

The similarities among some Asian countries enhance their opportunities to learn from each other. Among the common characteristics, factors such as urbanization measured by percentage change per annum in urban population and air pollution in cities are relevant. For example, the measure of urbanization between 2005 and 2010 for the PRC was 2.3, for India 2.4, and for the Association of Southeast Asian Nations (ASEAN) 2.2 (United Nations Economic and Social Commission for Asia and the Pacific [UNESCAP] 2011). Hence, discussion in this section is focused on what developing Asian countries can learn from the emerging Asian economies in sectors that have common characteristics. The creditable efforts of the PRC have included energy-saving laws and regulations, working out the implications of the National Energy Intensity Objective for sectors, and carrying out annual assessment evaluations, increased public budgets to encourage energy saving, adjustments in tax, price and financial policies, and eliminating outmoded, energy-inefficient production capacity. Policies towards strengthening forest and wetland restoration and afforestation have been implemented. Also, research on improving the carbon sink capacity of forests has been encouraged with financial support from government agencies.

The PRC's emission reduction methods seem to be cost-effective. In this context, it is worth noting the following statement: "What once seemed unattainable targets to Chinese economic authorities are now viewed with confidence. Officials have been pleasantly surprised at the rate of decrease in costs and are now talking confidently of reaching the high point of the emissions intensity reduction" (Garnaut 2011, p.11).

The PRC's afforestation program can be a good source of learning for Indonesia, which has serious problems with deforestation. Land use, land use change and forestry (LULUCF) are center

Figure 5.1

Potential to Reduce Emissions by Major Asian Countries, United States, and Russian Federation

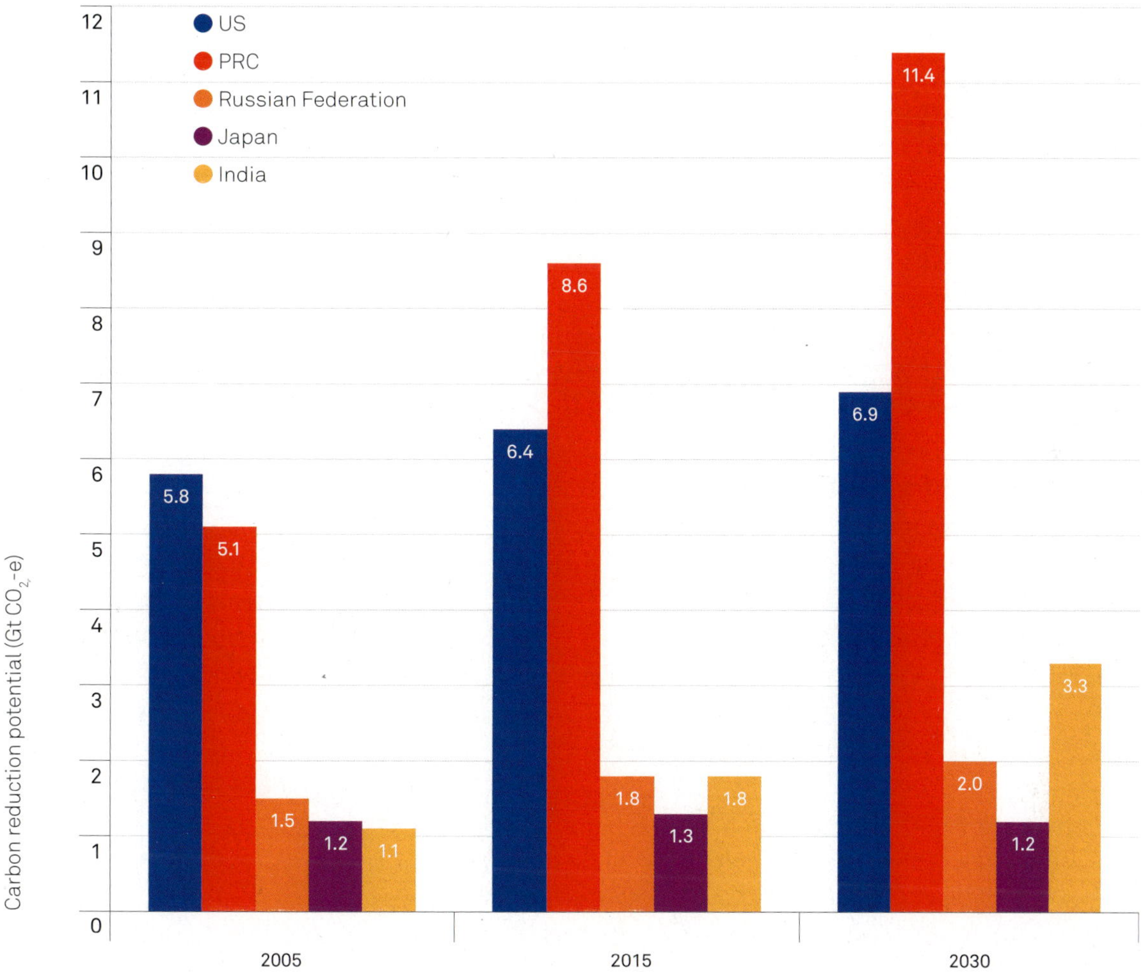

Source: Derived from IEA, World Energy Outlook (2010); ADB–ADBI study team.

stage for climate change discussions in Indonesia. Changes in these sectors have been strongly correlated with the country's emissions trajectory. It is important to note that over 80% of Indonesia's GHG emissions are LULUCF related. While the government has several plans to reduce GHG emissions, better forest management will be critical for reaping the highest social and environmental benefits from the reducing emissions from deforestation and forest degradation (REDD+) program. The potential for achieving such benefits is very high, if the management of forests is placed in the hands of those who would push for sustainable practices. In this context, it may be useful to observe India's forest management initiatives, which aim to strengthen the participation of communities for the sustainable use of forests. To achieve the active participation of communities, capacity building programs to increase the awareness of local communities in forest conservation have been implemented at the subnational level, which can be applied in Indonesia too.

Further, the Government of Indonesia's target of making its forests a major carbon sink by 2030 may be difficult to achieve so long as there are economic gains from carrying out unsustainable forestry practices, and government reforms such as land rights to constrain deforestation are weak. Howes and Wyrwoll (2012) argue that the effective reduction in the level of deforestation in the PRC and India, by use of appropriate blends of market-based and command-and-control instruments, could have been one of the reasons for the increased deforestation elsewhere in the region to meet demand in the region and beyond for forest products. Thus, the experiences of the PRC and India in controlling deforestation need to be studied closely by Indonesia through collaboration. For example, the PRC in 1978 launched a massive tree-planting scheme that is expected to cover about 400 million hectares, or 42% of the PRC's landmass, by 2050 and this would be the biggest human-made carbon sink in the world (Guardian 2009). Further, the State Forestry Administration says that in the past three decades, PRC volunteers planted about 58.9 billion trees across the country (China Daily 2011). These techniques could conceivably be applied in Indonesia to increase afforestation, provided Indonesia improves its capacity at local level to enforce such national policies.

Strict regulation is in place in the PRC for new vehicles to comply with airborne emission standards. Further, the PRC promotes the use of mixed-fuel motor vehicles and has popularized the use of gas-burning buses and taxis in cities. It has stepped up resources devoted to coal-liquefaction projects and encouraged research into alternative fuels.[2] India has concentrated its efforts on improving and promoting public transportation, with long-term plans to ensure the availability of efficient and convenient public transport for all. Like the PRC, India is supporting research and development (R&D) programs on the cellulosic extraction of ethanol and butanol from agricultural waste and crop residues.

Just like in the PRC, India has introduced compressed natural gas (CNG) operated public transport, including three-wheelers in big cities, which has significantly reduced air pollution. Government of India in 2004 made it mandatory for all city buses and auto rickshaws to run on CNG. In 2007, the California Energy Commission found that CNG reduces emissions by 30% in cars and 23% in buses compared to gasoline and diesel (Wang and Huang 2007).

According to a Channel News Asia report on 18 April 2008, CNG has been increasingly used by public transport vehicles such as buses and

---

2 Coal to liquids "results in a fuel with appreciably less (5%–12%) life cycle GHG emissions than the average US petroleum-derived diesel...Coal and Biomass to Liquids can produce fuels which are economically competitive when crude prices are equal to or above $93/bbl and which have 20% lower life cycle GHG emissions than petroleum-derived diesel" (National Energy Technology Laboratory 2009: vi).

taxis in Singapore. CNG use has proven to be cost-effective in the long run. The Ministry of Transport of Myanmar passed a law in 2005 which required that all public transport vehicles—buses, trucks, and taxis—be converted to run on CNG. The government permitted several private companies to handle the conversion of existing diesel and petrol cars, and to begin importing CNG buses and taxis (Linn 2010). Pakistan had the largest number of motor vehicles (2.74 million) using CNG within Asia in 2011, particularly in the public transport sector. In Malaysia, the use of CNG was originally introduced for taxicabs and airport limousines during the late 1990s, when new taxis were launched with CNG engines while taxicab operators were encouraged to send in existing taxis for full engine conversions (Zusman, Srinivasan, and Dhakal 2012). The practice of using CNG remained largely confined to taxicabs, predominantly in Kuala Lumpur and its suburbs, and Penang only (Bedi 2008).

Asian emerging economies like Indonesia and Malaysia suffer from heavy traffic congestion particularly during peak hours. For example, during 2008, the number of motor vehicles per kilometer of road was 40 in Indonesia and 83 in Malaysia; and the number of motor vehicles per thousand persons was 77 in Indonesia and 334 in Malaysia (World Bank 2010). Therefore, Indonesia and Malaysia can learn from the experiences of the PRC, Pakistan, Singapore, and India, and make public transportation cost-effective and efficient in reducing emissions.

Long-term energy policy (2010–2050) in Indonesia is focused on enhancing the use of domestic energy resources, minimizing fossil fuel use, and deploying energy sources such as nuclear power. In this context, Pakistan's experience is worth noting. The energy mix in Pakistan is the least polluting in the region, with a large share of hydro, nuclear, and gas. Another important factor that hinders the planning and implementation of energy efficiency improvements in industries in Indonesia is the lack of data and knowledge. Firms within same industries are reluctant to share data on energy use levels and patterns, making it difficult to examine patterns of consumption or assess precisely the level of savings possible. In order to support the government's commitment towards adopting new and renewable energy, Indonesia would need to be supported to enhance its knowledge base. There is an urgent need for Indonesia to benefit from strengthening regional cooperation in capacity building.

For Thailand, a key issue is the lack of knowledge of local governments about the Clean Development Mechanism (CDM). Thailand can learn from the experience of the PRC, which has a large number of CDM projects. The country also needs a road map toward emissions reduction from cities, and in this it can learn from Japan, which has used a back-casting modeling approach to develop its mid- and long-term road map. The city of Yokohama provides a good model of a low-carbon city (Nakada 2008). Just like Indonesia, Thailand also needs support from emerging economies in the region, such as the PRC and India, with respect to the collection of adequate data to establish baselines for emissions in different sectors and to allow estimates of possible savings at the subnational level to be calculated.

Although Viet Nam has initiated a National Target Programme for Climate Change in different sectors of the economy, its implementation has not been effective, mainly because of a lack of appropriate technology development and deployment, as well as a lack of appropriate pricing and finance policies. Also, institutions and regulatory mechanisms are not strong enough. Thus, unlike in the PRC and India, both market-based and command-and-control instruments appear to be ineffective in controlling emissions in Viet Nam. Another important issue concerns lack of data and information (Srinivasan, Ling, and Mori 2012). Capacity development is an issue, especially for small enterprises. Improvement in pricing policies, support for development of clean energy projects, and provision of incentives for renewables are required to boost the transition towards renewable energy use and energy efficiency in Viet Nam.

Malaysia has a national policy for promoting low-carbon green growth. However, the skills and technologies that are needed are not sufficiently abundant in Malaysia. Accordingly, capacity building and technical assistance are vital. Malaysia's 'Look East Policy' for accelerating and sustaining economic growth is expected to fill this gap. For example, cities like Kuala Lumpur and Penang in Malaysia, which have seen rapid population growth leading to the emergence of urban problems, can learn to tackle those problems effectively from the experience of Singapore (Box 5.1) and Yokohama in Japan. The city level emissions are mostly from households and transport. The Yokohama experience emphasizes the need to combine various aspects such as transport, waste management, water, where to live, and where to work to become a green city. New initiatives are still being taken in Yokohama to facilitate the transition to low-carbon development, and other cities can learn from these. One very successful example, in waste management, has been the Yokohama G30 Plan, which aimed at a 30% reduction of waste from the 2001 level of 1.61 million tons by 2010. The goal was achieved early and, as a co-benefit, CO_2 emissions were also reduced by significantly reducing the amount of garbage using a "3R" policy—reduce, recycle, and reuse. CO_2 emissions in 2006 were reduced by 780,000 tons compared with 2001 (Shimizu 2008). Based on this experience, the city administration and planners of Yokohama have been invited to undertake similar city-level development work in India.

Box 5.1

What Can Cities in Emerging Asian Economies Learn from Singapore on Mitigation?

The Energy Efficiency Singapore Program is a key market-based strategy in mitigating emissions and addressing climate change. It focuses on supporting research and development (R&D), raising awareness, promoting the adoption of energy-efficient technologies and measures, as well as building capabilities and expertise. For example, the Building and Construction Authority introduced Green Mark standards for both nonresidential and residential buildings in early 2008. Singapore has shifted toward the use of less carbon-intensive fuels, principally natural gas. Efforts are under way for Singapore's first liquid natural gas terminal to be ready by 2012. Efforts in promoting renewable energy such as biomass and solar energy are focused currently on R&D. Singapore is also one of the few countries in the world that incinerates almost all of its solid waste. The electricity from the incineration plants contributes 2%–3% of Singapore's energy supply. Moreover, Singapore is increasing the energy efficiency of its transport sector by improving and promoting the use of public transport; the government plans to achieve a target of 70% commuters using public transport during rush hours by 2020. A vehicle quota system and electronic road pricing are already used to reduce traffic congestion. A green vehicle incentive scheme to encourage the use of hybrid and compressed natural gas vehicles introduced a discount of 40% for purchase from their market value.

Source: Wyes and Lewandowski (2011).

Market-based instruments

Market-based instruments (MBIs) have the potential to become a major mechanism for managing a wide range of environmental concerns (Whitten, van Bueren, and Collins 2006). They require bringing market forces to bear on the issue, for instance by creating a market in externalities such as emissions. In some countries, a variety of MBIs are being tested and applied to environmental problems. As MBIs aim to achieve emissions reductions where the marginal reductions are cheapest, they have the potential to achieve efficiency gains compared with more traditional command and control (CAC) regulatory instruments. Thus, MBIs can be more pervasive than CAC instruments. Many countries in the region are considering introducing carbon pricing and trading schemes, which are MBIs designed to boost a low-carbon economy (ADB 2012a).

Cap-and-trade schemes can be used to raise revenue by auctioning the emissions permits and recycling the money to environmental projects or using it to cut income or corporate taxes. There has been a noticeable shift in favor of tradable permit programs in the Asia and the Pacific region in recent years. Asian countries are now at the forefront in proposing new tradable permit systems, whereas they lagged behind in the past (Kim 2012). For example, the Parliament of the Republic of Korea has voted through the proposal on carbon trading, but to start at a later date.[3] Though the New Zealand uncapped Emissions Trading Scheme covering all sectors and all GHGs was legislated in 2008, individual sectors of the economy have different entry dates. While emissions from stationary energy, industrial, and liquid fossil fuel sectors entered on 1 July 2010, agricultural emissions do not enter the scheme until 1 January 2015 (Government of New Zealand 2009). It is too early to say how well the scheme has worked. In 2011, the PRC approved a pilot emissions trading scheme in seven provincial regions with a view to a national scheme in 2015.

In 2011, as a market-based emissions reduction policy measure, India launched a scheme called Perform, Achieve, and Trade (PAT) to improve energy efficiency. In this scheme, India's largest energy users are set benchmark efficiency levels, with trade occurring between participants who exceed their targets and those who fail to meet them. The PAT instrument resembles a voluntary mechanism developed earlier in the PRC, known as Generation Rights Trading, in which coal-based electricity generators are assigned tradable quotas and the efficiency of electricity production is increased.

A carbon tax levied on fossil fuels has been advocated as a cost-effective instrument to boost energy security, stimulate economic growth, and tackle climate change (Howes and Wyrwoll 2012). Carbon taxes may generate indirect benefits, as the revenues can be used to reduce income or corporate taxes, or can be used to support environmental programs and provide finance for compensation measures to lower-income households affected by the tax. Asian countries have addressed these issues in their carbon tax strategies, and some have planned to recycle carbon tax fiscal revenue to support environmental and pro-poor projects.

The Australian Parliament passed the Carbon Pricing Bill in 2011, which has been effective from July 2012. Under the scheme, around 500 of the largest emitters in Australia will be expected to pay tax on each unit of carbon emitted to the atmosphere (Howes and Wyrwoll 2012). The Australian scheme covers a much wider spectrum of fossil fuel and industrial emissions than any existing scheme in the world. The carbon price is to be fixed at A$23 (approximately $24) for 3 years,

3 Source: http://www.bloomberg.com/news/2012-05-02/south-korean-parliament-approves-carbon-trading-system.html.

with an annual increase of 2.5% every year for the following 3 years. From 1 July 2015, the carbon tax will be converted into an emissions trading scheme. Thus, it acts like a tax in the first phase with an automatic transition into a market-based trading scheme. Thus, it is a middle ground and starting with a fixed price phase may be an attractive option for many other countries, which are planning to implement trading schemes for reducing emissions. Australia's carbon pricing scheme is the first of its kind in terms of reallocating a substantial percentage of the revenue back to households through income tax reductions for lower- and middle-income earners and increased pensions and welfare payments. Thus, there is an opportunity for tax reform in Australia's carbon pricing scheme. This can be emulated by developed and developing economies, which are concerned about the adverse impacts from carbon pricing on low-income earners.

In 2005, the Japanese Ministry of Environment proposed a tax of $28 for each ton of carbon that would result in tax revenues of $4.2 billion , which are to be used to support energy-efficient buildings, low-carbon technologies for automobiles, and forest programs. However, the government is facing pressure to delay, and the implementation of the taxes is not high on the political agenda (Shanahan 2012). Major opposition comes from other ministries and industrial stakeholders who fear negative effects on the economy.

India has become the first Asian country to lead the way to control emission with a domestic carbon tax, while other countries still debated the issue. As part of the tax, coal, which is used to generate more than half of India's electricity, will be taxed at Rs50 (approximately $1.05) a ton to help fund clean energy projects. The levy was proposed in the Federal Budget in February 2010, which became effective from 1 July 2010. The clean-energy levy would be applicable to imported coal too. Thus, the introduction of a carbon tax is a step toward helping India meet its voluntary target to reduce the amount of carbon dioxide released per unit of gross domestic product by 25% from 2005 levels by 2020 (Ministry of Environment and Forests 2010).

Command and control instruments

Command and control (CAC) instruments are the most common forms of environmental policies used in both developed and developing countries. The CAC approach consists of a "command", which sets a standard, and a "control", which monitors and enforces the compliance of the regulation. Those who do not meet the standard are penalized. Emissions standards can be either performance-based (specifying acceptable emissions limits) or technology-based (specifying emissions limits and the technology that must be used). The advantages of CAC approaches are that they are more widely understood and effective in emissions reductions because, unlike some trading schemes, they are enforceable. Noncompliance in a trading scheme is also enforceable. These approaches have disadvantages as well. It is not always possible to set optimum standards, especially with non-marketable goods (e.g., air); regulated agencies have no incentives to reduce pollution beyond the set standards; penalties for violating standards tend to be generally too low; and enforcement tends to be weak. For CAC approaches to be effective, standards need to be reviewed and revised frequently, but in practice these measures do not keep pace with changing market environments (Howes and Wyrwoll 2012).

Indonesia has implemented CAC instruments, such as "The blue sky program" and "Indonesia area traffic control system" to control the level of air pollutants in urban areas. It has introduced through Ministerial Decree No. 141/ Men-LH stricter regulations on energy efficiency and air pollutant emissions to motor vehicles to comply with Euro II standards (United States Agency for International Development [USAID] 2007). Nevertheless, peak hour traffic congestion in cities like Jakarta is very heavy, which emphasizes the need for further effective actions including MBIs toward reducing air pollution, such as emissions taxes, fees, and charges that place a per unit monetary charge on pollution emissions.

India has extensively used the CAC approach to bring in laws focusing on various aspects of corporate governance, including risk management and listing requirements (Indian Companies Act, 1956); pollution standards (Environment Protection Act, 1986); duty of care and the use of hazardous substances (Hazardous Waste (Management and Handling) Rules, 1989); waste management (Municipal Solid Waste (Management and Handling) Rules, 1999); workers' health and safety (Indian Factories Act, 1948); and collective bargaining rights (Indian Trade Unions Act, 1926). Over the years, India has particularly used the disclosure-based regulation to change corporate behavior and practices. For example, in 2009 it was made compulsory for companies selling packaged food to display nutritional information on the product. "Indian civil society thus has a strong tradition of working with disclosure; and as a policy approach, it has been tried and found to be reasonably successful" (Jairaj 2010: 3) Thus, these CAC instruments seem to be effective in India, and can easily be followed by other countries in the region.

As discussed in previous chapters, countries in the region are also learning from each other in bringing forward a green growth element to their green stimulus programs, such as encouraging investments in wind farms and installation of solar panels in households and other fiscal measures.

Environmental information disclosure

Environmental information disclosure in capital markets is important for promoting investment in green businesses and technologies. Capital markets may, in specific circumstances, provide appropriate financial incentives for investment. Information about the pollution efficiency of a firm, and its environmental performance, may act as a signal of its expected long-term profitability. A firm's performance information, if provided on a regular basis, is valuable for the market to evaluate the firm's worth. Therefore, governments can harness the forces of the capital markets by introducing structured programs requiring the regular release of information about environmental performance. The information will help reduce the risks of investments, protect the interests of investors, promote environmental transparency, encourage environmentally responsible investments, and enhance pollution control. Another example of a public disclosure mechanism is the Green Rating Initiative. This generic initiative invites voluntary participation by stakeholders, for example, private sector agencies and Non-governmental organizations (NGOs), to undertake independent evaluation of the environmental performance of a firm. Environmental performance ratings appear to have a positive impact on regulatory compliance in several Asian countries. This positive impact is demonstrated by increases in compliance rates of 24% in Indonesia, 50% in the Philippines, 14% in Viet Nam, 10% in Zhenjiang, the PRC, and 39% in Hohhot, the PRC (Hongo 2012).

Though countries can learn from each other in identifying appropriate institutions and policies to promote green growth, the pace of adoption depends on each country's resources, including human capital and political will. Developing countries have specific problems with infrastructure development, initiatives for poverty reduction and sustainable development, training, and capacity development. Given the diversity of countries in Asia and the Pacific, regional cooperation can be a powerful instrument by which the leading countries can lift the lagging countries toward greater technological innovation and diffusion, which depends on the supply of sufficient human and physical capital. In other words, by liberalizing the mobility of skilled personnel and investment across countries in the region and beyond, benefits from the innovation and transfer of environment-friendly technologies can be evenly spread across the region. Though it may be hard to conceive, official development assistance (ODA) can still be another important mechanism for international cooperation, especially where there is a shortage of private investment. Traditionally, ODA has been used by countries for socioeconomic development, but in recent times environmental protection has been included. Care needs to be taken that ODA funds being used for socioeconomic development are not shared with the funds going into environmental protection. ODA needs to be increased from its present level to accommodate developing countries' environmental protection strategies, though it looks difficult with the current global financial situation. Also, the large foreign reserves in Asia (Table 5.1) could be leveraged for green research and investment through regional cooperation (Kalirajan, Anbumozhi, and Singh 2010).

The diversity of the region does not appear to constrain regional cooperation as the region has several subregional cooperative agreements, largely covering financial and trade issues. These include, for example, ASEAN; the South Asian Association for Regional Cooperation (SAARC); Central Asia Regional Economic Cooperation (CAREC); Bangladesh, India, Myanmar, Sri Lanka and Thailand Economic Cooperation (BIMSTEC); Asia-Pacific Economic Cooperation (APEC); and the Greater Mekong Subregion (GMS).

Table 5.1

Foreign Reserves of Selected Countries

Rank	Country	Foreign Exchange Reserves ($ million)
1	PRC	3,254,674
2	Japan	1,295,839
3	Saudi Arabia	556,571
4	US	537,267
5	Russian Federation	497,410
6	Brazil	352,010
7	Switzerland	330,586
8	Republic of Korea	306,935
9	India	298,739
10	Singapore	234,104

Source: IMF Data and Statistics (2012). http://elibrary-data.imf.org/DataReport.aspx?c=1449311&d=33061&e=169393 (assessed December 2012).

Generally, subregional groupings such as the Southeast Asia Network of Climate Change, have committed to climate change and sustainable development, as demonstrated in the following example. At their 2008 SAARC meeting in Dhaka, the environment ministers adopted an action plan on climate change. It emphasized the need for regional cooperation on activities such as capacity building including the development of CDM projects and incentives for carbon sinks, exchange of information on best practices, and sharing the results of R&D for mitigating climate change. The action plan can be seen as South-South support for technology and knowledge transfer (Wyes and Lewandowski 2011). Also, the growing importance of South-South investments and aid is important in tackling the climate change issues, which can not be underestimated.

In 2010, the 16th SAARC Summit held in Thimphu, Bhutan, adopted a policy statement "Towards a green and happy south Asia" and an intergovernment expert group was established to develop policy direction and guidelines for regional cooperation on the issue. In this context, a study was commissioned to explore the feasibility of establishing a SAARC mechanism which would provide capital for projects that promote low-carbon technology and renewable energy. The study emphasized that 10 million trees should be planted in the region from 2010 to 2015, for instance. Another recommendation was the incorporation of materials in educational curricula to promote better understanding of the science and adverse effects of climate change. The SAARC Action Plan on Climate Change, 2009–2011 lists capacity building for CDM projects; exchange of information on disaster preparedness and extreme events; exchange of meteorological data; capacity building and exchange of information on climate change impacts (e.g., sea level rise, glacial melting, biodiversity, and forestry); and mutual consultation in international negotiations (SAARC Secretariat 2009).

5.1.2
Measurement, Reporting, and Verification

Carbon leakage can occur through the movement of carbon-intensive industries from one country to another and loss of competitive advantage as a result of differences in climate policies across countries. The European Union (EU) and the United States (US) have been considering the imposition of tariffs on goods imported from countries without similar carbon policies. The United Nations Conference on Trade and Development (UNCTAD 2010) states that carbon leakage has bearings on national and global emission reduction efforts and economic development. Though the extent of the phenomenon and its impacts are difficult to gauge, carbon leakage can be tackled through corporate governance mechanisms, such as improved environmental reporting and monitoring.

Developing countries are now urged by the United Nations Framework Convention on Climate Change (UNFCCC) to propose nationally appropriate mitigation actions (NAMAs) and make their emissions subject to measurement, reporting, and verification (MRV). The Cancun Agreements facilitated a framework for MRV of NAMAs. During the Copenhagen summit of 2009, many emerging Asian economies submitted NAMAs, which are subject to domestic MRV, reported through national communications with international consultation and analysis. The concept of NAMAs is still evolving: they can be a policy, a program, or a project proposed voluntarily by a developing country, but supported and enabled by technology, financing, and capacity building.

There are still many questions surrounding NAMAs and MRV. For example: how does one arrive at the baseline year? Should a system be established based on outcomes or on performance-related metrics? How can the international system support national measurement processes for emissions? What should be the frequency of reporting? Should domestically funded NAMAs be verified differently from internationally funded NAMAs?

To gain knowledge about how NAMAs and MRV systems operate in emerging Asian economies, more studies are needed. Wilkes et al. (2011), using a case study from the PRC, concluded that MRV systems would be credible when procedures are encoded in explicit rules for assuring quality control, with transparency in communication. The study suggested that to reduce costs and ease implementation, there should not be too many MRV systems. Countries such as Japan and the Republic of Korea, which have an excellent track record on MRV, can help more intensively other Asian countries to tailor country-specific MRVs (Box 5.2).

It is possible that some countries would consider any regional MRV organization a threat to their national sovereignty. Further, MRV systems involving a large number of countries could lead to delays in data collection and dissemination. Nevertheless, there are benefits of implementing regional MRV, which would facilitate maintaining a harmonized framework for measuring and verifying emissions regionally without any ambiguity.

Wyes and Lewandowski (2012: 29) argue: "The best platform for introducing a regional MRV system in Asia would certainly be ASEAN. The biggest advantage of ASEAN is that it has already established international structures and ongoing harmonization of policies. There is also broad understanding among the member states regarding climate change issues and related threats. Additionally, there is an opportunity for greater involvement of regional institutions like ADB and ESCAP in the establishment of regional MRV scheme among its members".

Box 5.2

Japan's Efforts to Establish Systems for Nationally Appropriate Mitigation Actions in Developing Countries

Japan launched feasibility studies in 2010 to provide proposals to establish measurement, reporting, and verification (MRV) criteria or standards and methods for nationally appropriate mitigation actions (NAMAs) in different sectors in developing countries. Three feasibility studies were conducted by Japanese private entities:

1 Feasibility Study for NAMA in Waste and Wastewater Management Sector in Thailand;
2 Feasibility Study on Transportation NAMA in Lao PDR;
3 Feasibility Study on NAMA for Sustainable Peatland Management in Indonesia.

Japan has proposed a bilateral mechanism that can promote the transfer and dissemination of low-carbon technologies, products, and services to developing countries, and can estimate the effectiveness of GHG reductions. It can also reflect national circumstances in both the technology transferring and technology receiving countries.

However, more case studies are needed. Therefore, the ministry decided to expand its feasibility study program. It is expected that nearly 30 studies will be implemented as case studies in various sectors or activities including NAMAs and REDD+. Japan hopes these will contribute to deepen understanding among developing countries and to lead concrete actions.

Source: Government of Japan, Ministry of the Environment (2011).

5.2 The Role of Free Trade in Low-Carbon Goods and Services

Exports of Low-Carbon Goods and Services

International trade facilitates the spreading of green economy gains across countries. Intra-Asian trade has been a major contributing factor to East Asian integration, which has also been boosted through foreign direct investment (FDI) (Kuroda, Kawai, and Nangia 2007). Trade and FDI can easily be identified as East Asia's twin-growth engines that have contributed to strengthening regional cooperation and a massive reduction in poverty. A key question is whether Asian countries collectively can contribute significantly to close the gap between the demand for and supply of LCGS in the region.

In spite of strong East Asian integration, unfortunately, trade and investment in LCGS are very low compared with trade and investment in pollution-intensive products (Mikic 2010). Generally, average tariff rates of LCGS are higher in developing countries than in developed countries. Figure 5.2 shows that among the developing countries, the average tariff is the highest in the least developed countries. Further, non-tariff barriers or "behind-the-border" constraints, such as lack of proper infrastructure and institutions, are very high in developing countries. What is important here is to provide quantitative measurements to demonstrate how much each country is losing potential export income due to the impact of the "behind-the-border" constraints.

Export potential is defined as the maximum amount that a country can export when there are no significant "behind-the-border" constraints such as institutional and infrastructural rigidities. The maximum possible output can be estimated from the actual data using the stochastic frontier gravity model framework, which facilitates incorporating the combined effect of the existing "behind-the-border" constraints in the gravity model framework discussed in Kalirajan (2012). The ratio of actual exports to the estimated maximum potential exports shows the loss of potential export income due to "behind-the-border" constraints.

To measure the impact of regional cooperation on export potential, the concept of cooperation has been classified into the following categories: (i) a grand regional coalition scenario (trade without any tariff and non-tariff barriers between countries within the region); (ii) limited cooperation scenario (trade without any tariff and non-tariff barriers at specified sectoral level, such as "management of waste and hazardous waste" rather than covering all LCGS exports within the region); and (iii) stand-alone scenario (business as usual, with the existing country-specific tariff and non-tariff barriers in the region). Next, the stochastic gravity model is used to obtain the potential exports for each of the above categories of cooperation. Differences in potential exports between categories show the impact of different levels of regional cooperation on potential exports.

Using data from the United Nations Commodity Trade Statistics, World Integrated Trade Solution, and World Investment Reports, covering 2000 to 2009 within a stochastic frontier gravity model framework, Kalirajan (2012) estimated potential exports of the World Trade Organization (WTO) 153 list of LCGS for eight Asian emerging economies—the PRC, India, Indonesia, Malaysia, the Philippines, Singapore, Thailand, and Viet Nam—under the three cooperation scenarios. [4] This analysis highlights the importance of regional cooperation for increasing the export potential of these emerging economies in LCGS. The results shown in Table 5.2 clearly indicate that

Figure 5.2

Average Tariff of Low-Carbon Goods and Services Categories

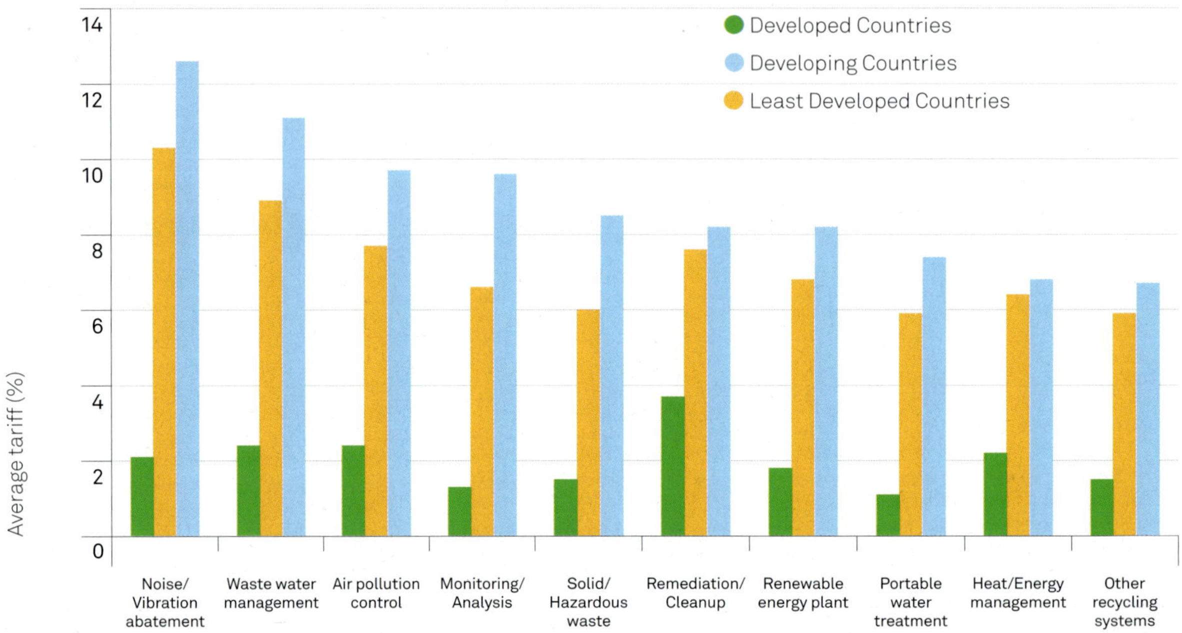

Source: Mikic (2010).

all the selected Asian emerging economies will enjoy increased export potential, more in the case of "grand coalition" than in the case of "limited coalition." The study also shows that "behind-the-border" constraints, such as poor infrastructure and inefficient institutions, have created a considerable gap between actual and potential exports in the selected economies and have stopped them seizing market-based opportunities. The gaps between actual and potential exports of low-carbon green growth under the grand coalition scenario are calculated for each year from 2000 to 2009 and the average export gap for the selected eight Asian emerging economies presented. The results indicate the PRC's gap between its actual and potential exports is the least, which means that on average the PRC is able to realize 80% of its potential exports. Nevertheless, 20% of potential export income was lost to the PRC due to its "behind-the-border" constraints during 2000–2009. Singapore is able to realize 73% of its potential exports, while the figure for India is 70%. Viet Nam appears to be realizing only about 62% of its export potential in LCGS. The implications are that countries like Viet Nam have lost about 40% of their potential exports revenue between 2000 and 2009 due to their existing infrastructure and institutional bottlenecks and that there is an urgent need to eliminate the "behind-the-border" constraints. What type of institutional framework can eliminate the "behind-the-border" constraints and thereby the export gaps across Asian emerging economies to help them seize market-based opportunities? The short and sharp answer is free trade in LCGS.

5.2.1
Asian Free Trade Agreement in Low-Carbon Goods and Services

Though Asia is a large market and has huge foreign reserves, the benefits for technological advancement in LCGS have not been reaped fully. East Asia has demonstrated it is possible to grow with each other's help, in spite of differences among governments on certain issues of national pride. It is high time for the rest of Asia, particularly the rest of the emerging Asian economies, to take cues from East Asia and form a grand Asian coalition with the help of neigbouring countries. The East Asian experience emphasizes that trade and investment in goods and services are two important instruments for regional and multinational cooperation. Other important factors are good transport and communication networks and institutional infrastructure.

The institutional infrastructure needed for grand cooperation is an Asian free trade agreement (AFTA) in goods and services that has the best chance of converging the member nations and ensuring stable economic growth under free trade. A political will also exists (Box 5.3). Such free trade agreements (FTAs) have worked well in other parts of the world. For example, the North American Free Trade Agreement (NAFTA) involving Canada, Mexico, and the United States has made North American businesses of all sizes more competitive by providing them with better access to intermediate inputs and capital sources from across the continent. The North American Agreement on Environmental Cooperation commits the NAFTA partners to work cooperatively to better understand and improve the protection of their environment. The agreement also requires that each NAFTA partner effectively enforce its environmental laws. [5] Additionally, the US and Mexico created two binational institutions. The Border Environment Cooperation Commission provides technical

---

4 "The WTO 153 list refers to the list of commodities specified in the Annex to WTO document JOB(07)/54 of 27 April 2007. This document concerns a non-paper by Canada, the European Communities, Japan, Korea, New Zealand, Norway, the Separate Customs Territory of Taipei,China, Penghu, Kinmen and Matsu, Switzerland and the US, presented pursuant to the continued work under paragraph 31 (III) of the Doha Ministerial Declaration (reduction of Customs tariff rates for environmental goods). The Annex to this WTO document tables descriptions of commodities as a basis for negotiations within the context of environmental protection" (Wind 2008)
5 Source: http://www.naftanow.org/myths/default_en.asp.

Table 5.2

Potential Exports of Low-Carbon Goods and Services under Different Scenarios: % increase

Regional cooperation scenario	Air pollution control		Clean or remediation of soil and waste		Cleaner and more efficient technology		Environmentally monitoring		Environmentally preferred products		Heat and energy management	
	2005	2009	2005	2009	2005	2009	2005	2009	2005	2009	2005	2009
PRC												
Stand-alone	20	22	30	28	28	30	40	35	35	33	38	35
Limited coalition	26	28	32	33	31	32	42	38	37	35	39	36
Grand coalition	32	33	35	36	33	34	44	41	38	36	40	37
India												
Stand-alone	30	32	31	32	32	33	40	42	37	38	38	37
Limited coalition	31	33	32	33	34	35	42	43	39	40	39	38
Grand coalition	32	34	34	35	35	36	44	44	40	42	40	40
Indonesia												
Stand-alone	44	42	33	30	35	36	40	40	35	33	38	35
Limited coalition	45	43	34	32	37	38	42	42	37	35	39	36
Grand coalition	46	44	35	34	38	39	43	43	38	36	40	37
Malaysia												
Stand-alone	34	35	35	36	35	36	33	34	40	41	30	32
Limited coalition	36	36	36	37	37	38	35	36	42	43	33	36
Grand coalition	38	38	38	38	38	39	37	38	44	45	35	37
Philippines												
Stand-alone	36	37	37	38	40	41	41	42	45	47	35	36
Limited coalition	38	39	39	40	42	43	43	44	47	48	36	37
Grand coalition	39	40	41	42	43	45	44	46	49	50	38	38
Singapore												
Stand-alone	23	24	30	31	28	29	27	29	28	29	31	32
Limited coalition	25	26	32	33	30	31	29	30	30	31	33	34
Grand coalition	27	29	34	35	33	34	31	32	32	33	36	35
Thailand												
Stand-alone	45	46	40	42	40	42	41	43	45	47	40	42
Limited coalition	47	48	41	43	43	44	43	44	47	49	42	44
Grand coalition	49	50	42	44	45	45	44	45	49	50	44	45
Viet Nam												
Stand-alone	46	47	38	40	40	42	42	43	40	41	38	39
Limited coalition	48	49	40	42	41	44	44	45	42	43	39	40
Grand coalition	49	50	42	44	43	45	46	48	44	45	40	41

Source: Kalirajan (2012).

Management of waste and hazardous waste		Natural resources protection		Natural risk management		Noise and vibration abatement		Renewable energy plant		Waste water management and potable water	
2005	2009	2005	2009	2005	2009	2005	2009	2005	2009	2005	2009
42	43	38	35	44	42	45	47	28	27	36	38
45	45	40	37	45	43	47	48	30	28	39	40
47	48	41	38	46	44	49	49	32	30	41	42
28	26	40	42	37	35	46	47	30	32	40	38
30	28	42	43	39	37	47	48	32	33	41	40
32	30	44	45	40	38	49	50	34	35	41	42
45	42	38	35	34	35	46	47	32	33	40	41
46	44	40	37	36	37	48	49	33	34	42	43
47	46	41	39	38	39	49	50	34	35	44	45
38	42	32	35	30	32	38	40	35	36	42	43
40	44	34	37	33	34	39	41	37	38	44	45
43	46	36	39	35	36	41	43	39	40	45	46
38	40	40	42	38	40	38	40	37	39	45	46
40	42	43	44	41	42	39	41	39	40	48	48
43	45	45	45	43	44	40	42	41	41	50	51
32	33	28	30	25	27	23	25	22	23	28	29
34	35	30	32	26	28	25	27	24	25	32	33
35	36	32	34	27	30	28	28	27	26	33	34
38	39	45	47	40	40	40	42	39	41	44	46
40	41	46	48	41	41	42	44	41	43	47	48
43	44	48	50	43	44	43	45	43	45	50	51
47	48	36	37	38	40	45	48	34	35	42	44
49	50	38	40	40	41	48	49	37	37	45	46
51	52	41	42	43	42	49	50	39	40	48	50

Box 5.3

Political Will for Establishing Asian Free Trade Area in Low-Carbon Goods and Services

Former Japanese Prime Minister Yukio Hatoyama was promoting the idea of an East Asian Community, while former Australian Prime Minister Kevin Rudd proposed an Asia-Pacific Community. Also, The Republic of Korea's President Lee Myung-bak has been mentioning a New Asia Initiative; and the PRC's President Hu Jintao convincingly argued that the PRC is promoting a Harmonious Asia, while India's Prime Minister Manmohan Singh has a vision of a future Asian Economic Community. Policy makers in Association of Southeast Asian Nations (ASEAN) have been in the forefront of transforming Asia into Green Asia by instituting a number of environment-related policies at the sectoral, subnational, national, and regional levels. Given the common objective of promoting green growth by improving carbon efficiency, cooperation in creating an Asian Free Trade Agreement (FTA) in low-carbon goods and services low-carbon goods and services (LCGS) seems likely to be achievable.

Source: ADB–ADBI study team.

support for the development of environmental infrastructure projects in the U.S.-Mexico border region.[6] The North American Development Bank finances these projects.[7]

A region-wide FTA in LCGS would generate much greater benefits than the existing Asian subregional FTAs by increasing market size and therefore specialization and economies of scale; facilitating investment and technology transfer; and simplifying tariff schedules, rules, and standards..

FTAs have the potential to push overall economic reforms, including trade policy and energy policy reforms, and they serve as a locking mechanism for sustaining reforms. Asian FTAs in LCGS, particularly concerning technology and intermediate inputs related to energy resources, could promote integration among countries, and be powerful instruments for creating and sustaining peaceful relations. Further, Asian equity markets have more investment links with the US and Europe than with Asian countries: this imbalance could be minimized through FTAs.

5.2.2 Seizing Market- and Nonmarket-Based Opportunities across Borders

Market-Based Opportunities

Besides the market-based opportunities that would arise from improved trade and investment through an AFTA, regional cooperation can bring other win-win opportunities. For example, regional energy collaboration, which provides great opportunities, is important for energy security. Consider India, which does not have the capacity to meet its burgeoning energy demand from domestic sources. By collaborating with Nepal on hydroelectricity; with Bangladesh and Myanmar on natural-gas-generated electricity; and with Iran and Turkmenistan (through Pakistan) on gas, a country like India may want to consider solving its energy shortage.

There are already a few energy collaboration programs in Asia that have been working reasonably well. For example, Japan has established energy collaborative projects such as the Energy Silk Road project involving the PRC, Turkmenistan, and the Trans-ASEAN gas pipeline network. The Trans-ASEAN gas pipeline and the ASEAN power grid projects have been set up to ensure regional access to gas reserves and greater stability and security of energy supply. That could also reduce emissions within ASEAN, if coal is substituted by gas. Developing a network connecting all ASEAN countries with high-voltage transmission lines could not only resolve energy shortages, but bring revenues from cross-border sales of electricity. For example, Lao People's Democratic Republic (PDR)

---

6 Source: www.cocef.org.
7 Source: www.nadbank.org.

has the potential to increase its renewable capacity, and export the excess power to its neighbors Cambodia and Thailand. Viet Nam's hydropower potential, which is huge, could also generate electricity for sale to neighboring countries (Thavasi and Ramakrishna 2009). Though power grid interconnection in ASEAN is technically possible, it is challenging. Nevertheless, such projects have the potential to integrate the energy markets of East Asia-ASEAN-South Asia.

Myanmar and Thailand have been cooperating on natural gas exports. There are other opportunities for the region in trading natural gas, as Asia is the centre of the global liquefied natural gas trade.

Japan and Malaysia have contributed $308 million on a biofuel joint venture with a target of producing about 0.2 million tons per year. Nepal enjoys huge hydropower potential and the excess hydropower can easily be exported to neighboring countries. Cross border opportunities for technological cooperation also exist in bio-energy sector (Box 5.4) and hydropower (Box. 5.5).

Box 5.4

Cross-Border Opportunities: Small-scale Biogas Plants under the CDM in Nepal

A registered Clean Development Mechanism (CDM) project in Nepal involves the placement of up to 1.9 million small anaerobic digesters to produce biogas in poor rural communities. The digesters capture biogas from toilets and animal waste that can be burned to generate thermal energy for cooking. The capacity of the installed biogas plants ranges from 1.16 to 2.32 kW. Emissions reductions result from the replacement of conventional fuel sources for cooking, such as fuel wood, thus easing the pressure on local ecosystems containing biomass. The project also mitigates nitrous oxide (N_2O) and methane emissions from waste, and the remaining bio-slurry in the digesters may be used instead of chemical fertilizers. So far, 150,000 biogas plants have been installed. The carbon revenue from the project goes into a fund used by microfinance institutions in rural areas. These organizations can provide microcredit to cover the up-front cost of biogas plant construction, enabling the poorest households to access the technology.

Nepal's biogas program is regarded as a model for the successful use of alternative energy for the rural sector in less developed countries. Nepal has overtaken the PRC and India in per capita use of biogas plants. The carbon credits generated for the emissions avoided are worth about $5 million, and can be bought by rich countries to offset their emissions. This money can be invested in clean energy, which would allow Nepal to trade more carbon credits even in the current climate of low CDM prices. The PRC and India have a comparative advantage in manufacturing digesters and countries like and Bangladesh, Nepal, and Sri Lanka, where the demand for biogas plants is increasing, provide a good opportunity for the PRC and India to reap the benefits from their comparative advantage.

Source: United Nations Convention to Combat Desertification (2008).

Box 5.5

Cross-Country Opportunities: Power Generation

Within Asia, some countries have further potential to increase energy exports. For example, the Lao People's Democratic Republic (Lao PDR) and Thailand have already implemented several cross-border hydropower trade projects. Among them, the most notable is the $1.2 billion Nam Theun 2, the biggest hydropower project in the Lao PDR. It is the result of a public-private and multilateral organization partnership. The project started full generation in early 2010, exporting 1,000 megawatt-hours (MWh) of electricity to Thailand. It is expected to bring the Lao PDR $80 million per year in the initial 25 years. In addition, Xekaman 3, commissioned in 2010, with 250 MW capacity, is exporting electricity to the Lao PDR and Viet Nam. The Theun-Hinboun expansion project with an installed capacity of 60 MW is expected to be commissioned in 2012 to supply electricity to the Lao PDR and Thailand. Nam Ngum 2 is another project with 615 MW capacity. It is expected to export electricity to Thailand in 2013.

Source: ADBI (2011).

Carbon Markets

Carbon markets provide one potential source of revenue to finance low-carbon technology transfer. In 2008, the global carbon market reached a value of $126 billion. Imposing a 3% tax on transactions in that market could mobilize $3.6 billion. If all developed countries adopted the more stringent cap-and-trade regimes required to stay within the 2°C target and auctioned the bulk of permits, the combination of a higher carbon price and increased trade could generate far larger revenues (World Bank 2009a; 2009c). A proposal from the Government of Norway estimates potential revenue of $20 billion–$30 billion. No doubt, much will depend on the degree to which the EU and the US lower the ceiling for emission quotas (or assigned amount units) and increase the share of quotas subject to auction. The strength of the Norwegian proposal is that it would create a mechanism that mobilizes finance for technology transfer independently of budget decisions in developed countries by directly tapping carbon mitigation markets (Government of Norway 2008). Though there is no universally acceptable formula for carbon pricing, it is imperative for countries to work together in a regional cooperation framework to make carbon markets work.

Non-Market Based Opportunities

There is a substantial technological and innovation gap for Asian economies in developing and adopting clean low-carbon technologies (Anbumozhi 2008). Many countries in Asia do not have enough resources to spend on R&D and have a chronic shortage of scientists, engineers, and managers with the skills needed. The shortage of R&D capacity and skilled workforces capable of low-carbon innovations in developing Asia emphasizes the importance of regional cooperation in pooling human capital resources through increasing the mobility of skilled personnel across countries. For example, the emerging Asian economies, through their experiences in promoting LCGS, can share knowledge of policies and practices with less developed Asian economies. In this context, it is worth noting the initiation of the Low-carbon Asia Research Network (LoCARNet) on 15 April 2012 by the Government of Japan, which was proposed by the Government of Japan and the International Research Network for Low-carbon Societies (LCS-RNet) in October 2011 in Cambodia at the ASEAN+3 Environment Ministers Meeting. The network, which is to be used as a platform for low-carbon growth in the East Asia Subregion, is composed of researchers who contribute directly to develop national low-carbon and green growth policy, and are involved in the policy-making process and contribute their knowledge to decision-making and policy planning. Through the network with government support, it is expected that knowledge and experience are shared, research cooperation related to low-carbon growth is promoted, and inputs to policy making are provided. This network should cover the entire Asian region rather than concentrating on just the East Asia Subregion. The private sector should be looked to for services such as training programs for technicians and training for government personnel (World Bank 2008).

India, Japan, the PRC, and the Republic of Korea, which have sufficient human capital to share with needy countries in the region, should do so for the development of NAMAs and MRV. Such a sharing of human capital can be formalized through LoCARNet. The role of institutions such as Asian Development Bank (ADB), Asian Development Bank Institute (ADBI), Climate and Development Knowledge Network (CDKN), and ESCAP is crucial to strengthen the activities of LoCARNet to achieve the common goal of low-carbon green growth in Asia.

The UN climate conference in Durban in 2011 committed countries to developing a legal framework for mitigation action. The framework is to be negotiated by 2015 and in force by 2020, and will require emissions curbs from major economies. Until the legal framework is negotiated and agreed, there should be a coordinated effort to have national legal frameworks prepared and implemented. The regional bodies need to take the initiative to maintain consistency across countries, though it is the task of the UNFCCC. The recently initiated LoCARNet would be of immense help.

5.3
International Cooperation on Innovation and Transfer in Low-Carbon Goods and Services

Developed countries such as the Group of Eight (G8) economies should take the leading role in urging other countries to agree a post-Kyoto deal by demonstrating their commitment to accelerating a low-carbon green growth society. At the Doha climate conference, countries made gradual progress toward a global framework of reducing GHG emissions. A global climate change agreement, to take effect from 2020, should be agreed by 2015. It is important that the major emerging economies such as Brazil, India, the PRC, and South Africa are given an equal seat at the negotiations, though they all take part in the UNFCCC. The demand for LCGS from the biggest markets, such as in India, Indonesia, and the PRC, will drive innovation for LCGS around the world with enthusiasm. The need to focus on growth and poverty reduction in the developing world means required cuts in emissions will be contingent on financial, technical, and institutional support from rich developed nations. Nevertheless, the contribution of the domestic private sector, which provides about 80% of low-carbon finance, can not be underestimated. So the importance of instituting a post-Kyoto regime based on common but differentiated responsibilities soon cannot be overemphasized. For example, it is important to engage countries like India, Indonesia, and the PRC in building consensus on their national targets in a progressive manner (Kawai 2008).

5.3.1
International Assistance for Developing Nationally Appropriate Innovation

Innovation in and dissemination of low-carbon technologies on a large scale are needed in Asia and globally. Large-scale investment in low-carbon systems is needed: the IEA (2007) estimated that a worldwide investment of $20 trillion is required by 2030. Of this, more than half will be required for developing Asia. As of April 2011, there have been 24 global funds operating with a total pledge of $30 billion, though the actual spending to that date was only about $2 billion. Such a big gap shows there is an urgent need to act. To fill this gap and generate additional funds, the financing has to come from a variety of sources, including public and private, bilateral and multilateral, external, and domestic sources. Bilateral and multilateral aid agencies, which possess sufficient resources and technical expertise for promoting green growth, are well placed to help countries with financial difficulties to develop low-carbon systems. For example, the Green Climate Fund can be of some help here, but only to the tune of $100 billion a year. Development partner countries, in conjunction with the private sector, need to invest in long-term carbon bonds issued by international financial institutions.

Facilitating collaborations between businesses, governments, and civil societies through the establishment of regional low-carbon innovation centers could be an effective way to raise awareness and encourage the behavioral changes needed for a green economy.

5.3.2
International Intellectual Property Rights Regime

The intellectual property rights (IPR) regime is important to helping technological innovation by developing countries from the basic R&D done in developed countries. At times, it may be necessary to combine technologies developed in different countries, which may pose problems due to the different IPR regimes in those countries. These problems may inhibit or slow down technological innovation and adaptation of green technology by developing countries. A possible solution is regional cooperation in harmonizing the IPR regimes across countries. UNESCAP through its Renewable Energy Cooperation Mechanism for Asia and the Pacific has been helping developing countries to overcome IPR issues in energy.

Concerning the smooth transfer of technology, an important factor is how closely the national IPR regime is integrated with the global IPR regime. The experiences of two major emerging economies in Asia, the PRC and India, are worth noting. The PRC has striven to conform to Trade-Related Aspects of Intellectual Property Rights (TRIPS) and has managed its enforcement issues with administrative and judicial policies to assure foreign investors and a growing number of local IPR holders of the security of their intellectual property How effectively the central government is in enforcing IPR policy at every level of government is an important benchmark for the PRC's success in integrating its national IPR regime with the global regime.

Signing the TRIPS Agreement in 1994 triggered significant changes in the IPR related legal framework in India. Since then, several legislative and institutional adjustments have been made to protect IPR.

Some of the key areas that need attention to facilitate the smooth transfer of technology are:

1. Strengthening institutional mechanisms—regulatory, legal, and administrative—for IPR, through assigning a high priority to legislative provisions to harmonize the IPR regime with international laws.
2. Strengthening the public–private R&D interface by adopting mechanisms such as an innovation bill to enhance the public R&D base wherein publicly funded researchers, organizations, and universities would be incentivized to commercialize their innovation.
3. Enhancing IPR literacy by disseminating information to stakeholders.

IPR has been often considered a constraint on international cooperation on green technology and a barrier to sharing technical know-how. Nevertheless, there have been success stories that suggest joint ventures between collaborators could provide a solution. A set of energy policy mechanisms are illustrated in Table 5.3.

Table 5.3

Intellectual Property Rights Regimes and Low-Carbon Industry Policies in Selected Asian Countries

Type of economy based on carbon-intensiveness	Trade in low-carbon goods and services	FDI	Trade in knowledge (licensing)	IPR	Low-carbon industrial policies
Domestic policies					
Low-carbon intensive: Lao PDR, Bangladesh, Nepal, Cambodia, and Sri Lanka	Liberal access	Non-discriminatory investment promotion	Improve information flows about public domain and mature technologies	Basic protection and minimum standards only	Basic education; reduce entry barriers, improve infrastructure
Medium-carbon intensive: Thailand, Indonesia, and Viet Nam	Liberal access	Non-discriminatory investment promotion	Improve information; limited incentives for licensing	Wider scope of IPR protection; employ flexibilities	R&D support policies, improve infrastructure, reduce entry barriers
High-carbon intensive: PRC and India	Liberal access	Upstream supplier support programs	Improve information; limited incentives for licensing	Apply full TRIPS	R&D support policies, improve infrastructure, reduce entry barriers
Developed-country policies towards emerging Asia					
Low-carbon intensive: Lao PDR, Bangladesh, Nepal, Cambodia, and Sri Lanka	Subsidize public good-type imports; free trade	Incentives for outward flows exceeding those for FDI	Subsidize transfer of public domain and mature technologies	Forbearance in disputes; differential pricing for exports of IPR products; competition policy assistance	Support for general low-carbon technology policies; public and public-private research facilities
Medium-carbon intensive: Thailand, Indonesia, and Viet Nam	Free trade; no controls	Incentives equal to those granted for own disadvantaged regions	Assistance in establishing joint venture partnerships; matching grants	Differential pricing of public-good type IPR protected goods; competition policy assistance	Support for general low-carbon technology policies; fiscal incentives for R&D performed in developed countries
High-carbon intensive: PRC and India	Free trade; no controls	Incentives equal to those granted for own disadvantaged regions	Assistance in establishing joint venture partnerships	Differential pricing of public-good type IPR protected goods; competition policy assistance	Support for general low-carbon technology policies; fiscal incentives for R&D performed in developed countries

Notes: FDI=foreign direct investment; IPR=intellectual property right; R&D=research and development; TRIPS=Trade Related Aspects of Intellectual Property Rights.

Source: ADB–ADBI study team.

5.4 Extent of Funding Needs for Low-Carbon Green Growth

One of the major constraints discouraging developing countries from reducing GHG emissions is the need to finance climate change policies, and this has a bearing on regional cooperation. IEA (2009) estimated that to achieve a 50% reduction in carbon emissions globally by 2030, an additional investment of $7,585 billion would be needed (Fig 5.3). Half of this funding is expected to come from industrialized countries.

Financial investment in clean energy in developing countries was estimated at $36.6 billion in 2008, representing an increase of 27% over the previous year with the PRC ($15.6 billion) and India ($3.7 billion) leading the way in Asia (UNEP 2009). Developing countries are unable to meet the large investment needs with their own resources. Generally, funding for climate change initiatives can be expected to come from developed countries, multilateral financial institutions, government funds, and private financial institutions. The multilateral funding agencies include The World Bank, regional development banks such as ADB and the UN agencies. However, the bulk of financing comes, and will continue to come, from the domestic private sector. Thus, it is necessary for the nations to work out ways to encourage private sector funding not only domestically, but also internationally through regional cooperation.

Figure 5.3

Additional Investment Needed for Emission Reduction by 2030 ($ billion)

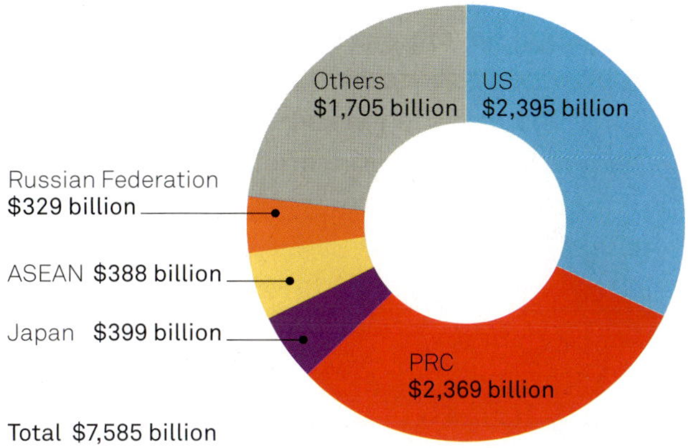

Notes: Sum of US, PRC, Japan, Association of Southeast Asian Nations (ASEAN) and Russian Federation accounts for 78% of world total. Additional investment required for achieving 450 ppm scenario (almost equal to 50% reduction by 2030).

Source: Derived from World Energy Outlook (IEA 2009); ADB–ADBI study team.

5.4.1
Major Sources of International Funding for Low-Carbon Green Growth

The first attempt to support developing countries to mitigate emissions was the CDM, which was defined in Article 12 of the Kyoto Protocol. It was designed to help developed countries meet a part of their emission reduction targets and to assist developing countries in achieving sustainable development. The projects of the CDM are awarded certified emission reduction (CER) credits, which can be sold, to industrialized countries that want to offset their own emissions. A review (UNFCCC 2011) on CDM projects showed they were making a contribution to sustainable development over and above the mitigation of emissions. The sustainable development benefits include increased employment rates, the reduction of pollution, and the protection of natural resources. The reviewers noted that investment flows under the CDM have been encouraging. However, the transfer of technologies between countries was found to be slow and modest. By mid-July 2011, there were over 3,200 projects under way worth $140 billion. About 75% of these projects were in India and the PRC. Small developing countries have been sidelined in the CDM so far at 1.5% of the projects and 0.4% of projected CER volume until 2012. Other problems with CDM projects include: high transaction costs, perceived lack of co-benefits, difficult determination of additionality, and lack of certainty about post-2012 CERs. So several reforms including (i) centralized database for baseline data, (ii) sectoral CDM approach, and (iii) crediting of CERs against domestic climate policy instruments are proposed.

The bilateral offset credit mechanism (BOCM) has the potential to supplement CDM and facilitate effective reductions in emissions, and encourage adaptation efforts of developing countries (Box 5.6). The key bilateral decisions that would be taken under the BOCM concern technology choice (technology neutral); the project registration and approval process; MRV methodologies; credit issuance; accreditation of verifiers; and the provision of funding either public or private. Japan emphasises that the BOCM is expected to deliver projects much faster and easier than in the CDM, which would reduce transaction costs and entice more private sector investment. It is also considered to better accommodate the specific and strategic needs of the parties than the CDM. In addition, bilateral cooperation would potentially pave the way for more engagements by developing countries in global emission reduction efforts in the future.

At the 2010 Cancun Climate Change Conference in Mexico, the establishment of a new Green Climate Fund (GCF) to support climate change action in developing countries was agreed. The Cancun Accord recognized the commitment undertaken by developed countries to provide new and additional resources for developing countries, of up to $30 billion for 2010–2012 (so-called "fast start" finance).[8]

An independent financial organization, the Global Environment Facility (GEF), is the largest funder of projects to developing countries and countries with economies in transition for projects related to biodiversity, climate change, international waters, land degradation, the ozone layer, and persistent organic pollutants. These projects benefit the global environment, linking local, national, and global environmental issues. The GEF has allocated $10.5 billion in grants and leverages $51 billion in co-financing for over 2,700 projects in over 165 countries until 2011. Through its Small

---

8 Fast-start finance refers to the collective commitment agreed by donor countries (in the Copenhagen Accord in 2009 and Cancún Agreements in 2010) to provide new and additional resources approaching US$30 billion over the period 2010–2012 to developing countries. This finance will support a range of actions to reduce carbon emissions (mitigation), enhance technology development and capacity building, and help developing countries adapt to the effects of climate change (adaptation). Developed countries contributing to fast-start finance include Australia, Canada, the countries of the European Union, Iceland, Japan, Liechtenstein, New Zealand, Norway, Switzerland and the United States. Source: http://www.climatechange.gov.au/government/international/finance.aspx.

Box 5.6

Bilateral Offset Credit Mechanism: An Overview

The objective of the Bilateral Offset Credit Mechanism (BOCM) are as follows: (i) to facilitate diffusion of leading low-carbon technologies, products, systems, services, and infrastructure as well as implementation of mitigation actions in developing countries; (ii) to appropriately evaluate contributions to greenhouse gas (GHG) emission reductions (in a much simpler way than Clean Development Mechanism (CDM) process) – in advanced countries through actions implemented in developing countries and use those emission reductions to achieve emission reduction targets of the developed countries; and (iii) to contribute to the ultimate objective of the United Nations Framework Convention on Climate Change (UNFCCC) process by facilitating global actions for emission reductions or removals.

While designing and implementing the BOCM, the following aspects need to be considered: (i) emphasizing environmental integrity and transparency; (ii) maintaining simplicity and practicality; (iii) promoting solid actions for global GHG emissions reductions; (iv) avoiding the use of the BOCM registered projects for the purpose of any other international climate mitigation mechanisms; and (v) assisting the adaptation efforts of developing countries with the conversion of the BOCM into the tradable credit mechanism.

A key feature of the BOCM is that, unlike the CDM, it is a decentralized structure with concerned governments and a joint committee; and provides a broader coverage. Another important difference in governance between the CDM and the BOCM is that credits are issued by governments under the BOCM, while they are issued by the executive board of the UNFCCC under the CDM.

Thus, international supervision under the BOCM is minimized to the bare minimum function of providing guidance for emissions measurement, reporting, and verification (MRV) and accounting rules only. A notable operational difference is that a third party entity, which does the validation, will do the verification of the same project under the BOCM, and this is not the case with the CDM. It is expected that the capacity building component of the BOCM will help the effective implementation of not only the BOCM projects, but also the CDM projects and developing nationally appropriate mitigation actions (NAMAs). For example, the Ministry of the Environment and the Ministry of Economy, Trade and Industry (METI) of Japan have been conducting various seminars, expert advice, and technical expert invitations to host countries through different organizations such as the Energy Conservation Center, Japan; International Center for Environmental Technology Transfer; and the Japan Coal Energy Center. Measurement, reporting, and verification (MRV) model and feasibility projects, and BOCM model and feasibility projects selected by METI involve such activities. The Ministry of Environment and METI of Japan have selected 36 BOCM feasibility study projects in 15 countries for the 2012 fiscal year. Of these, 30 projects are in the Association of Southeast Asian Nations (ASEAN) and South Asian Association for Regional Cooperation (SAARC) regions. Thus, the BOCM provides an excellent opportunity to strengthen the regional cooperation efforts in reducing emissions consistently and other capable countries in the region can emulate the Japanese proposal of the BOCM.

Sources: Ministry of the Environment, Japan (2012), and Ninomiya (2011).

Grants Programme, the GEF has also made more than 14,000 small grants directly to civil society and community-based organizations, totaling $634 million. During 2009–2010 alone, the GEF financed 202 projects for a total of $3.03 billion, investing $552.37 million in GEF resources and mobilizing an additional $2.479 million in co-financing from development partners. Of these 202 projects, climate change accounted for 93 projects. (GEF 2010).

The GEF partnership includes 10 agencies: the UN Development Programme, the UN Environment Programme, the World Bank, the UN Food and Agriculture Organization, the UN Industrial Development Organization, the African Development Bank, ADB, the European Bank for Reconstruction and Development, the Inter-American Development Bank, and the International Fund for Agricultural Development.

One way to tackle climate change is to protect forest cover. An estimated 13 million hectares are deforested per year, accounting for about 18% of global GHG emissions. The bulk of such deforestation is in developing countries. REDD+, which addresses this issue, is critically important as a source of international funding for green growth. Following the Copenhagen Climate Conference in December 2009, France took the initiative to host meetings on REDD+ in 2010, known as the Paris-Oslo Process. At the Oslo Climate and Forest Conference on 27 May 2010, the REDD+ Partnership was endorsed by 58 countries, and was endorsed by over 70 countries at the end of 2011. The REDD+ Partnership is a voluntary, non-legally binding agreement with the objective to provide a platform for countries to scale up REDD+ actions and finance, and improve the effectiveness, efficiency, transparency, and coordination of REDD+ initiatives.

Building on the $3.5 billion fast-start financing package for REDD+ announced in Copenhagen by Australia, France, Japan, Norway, the UK, and the US; six countries (Denmark, Finland, Germany, Slovenia, Spain, and Sweden) pledged an additional $500 million at the Oslo meeting, bringing the total package up to $4 billion. (Government of Australia 2012). In June 2010, Australia announced it would contribute A$599 million ($512.95 million) to fast-start financing for climate change, to be delivered using existing partnerships, mechanisms, and relationships. This fast start package includes A$146 million ($125.03 million) to the International Forest Carbon Initiative (IFCI), which was introduced by the Government of Australia in 2008, to assist developing countries with REDD+ activities. With respect to the results obtained, it may be noted that under the Kalimantan Forests and Climate Partnership (KFCP), local communities have started receiving incentive payments – approximately $450,000 so far until 2011, which are tied to the delivery of environmental projects. All seven villages in the project area signed village agreements that align development goals with emissions reductions and sustainable development objectives. Thirty-five community-based nurseries grew and planted more than 1.2 million seedlings in the KFCP area.[9]

Official Development Assistance

Developed countries, especially those in the Organisation for Economic Co-operation and Development (OECD), traditionally provide bilateral aid in the form of grants, loans, and technical cooperation for the promotion of economic development and welfare of developing countries (Hongo 2010). ODA financial flows comprise contributions of donor government agencies to developing countries and to multilateral

---

9 Source: http://www.ausaid.gov.au/aidissues/climatechange/Pages/initiative-international-forest-carbon.aspx.

10 Source: http://www.oecd.org/dac/aidstatistics/developmentaidreachesanhistorichighin2010.htm.

Table 5.4

Key ADB Funding Mechanisms for Environmental Projects

Fund	
Climate Change Fund (CCF)	The CCF was established in 2008 to provide grant funding for climate-related projects, research, and development, to assess causes and consequences. Funding is provided for projects that lead to the reduction of GHG emissions or adaptation to climate change.
Clean Energy Financing Partnership Facility (CEFPF)	The CEFPF was established in 2007 and provides grant funding to member countries in the region for improving energy security and transitioning to low-carbon economies, through cost-effective investments in technologies and practices. In addition to the funds allocated to CEFPF by ADB, the fund receives contributions from countries such as Australia, Japan, and Norway.
Asia Pacific Carbon Fund (APCF)	The APCF was established in 2007 as part of ADB's Carbon Market Initiative. The APCF provides financial assistance for clean energy projects. The APCF receives funding commitments from several European countries such as Belgium, Finland, Luxembourg, Portugal, Spain, Sweden, and Switzerland.
Future Carbon Fund (FCF)	The FCF was established in 2008 and provides funding for projects that will generate carbon credits for GHG reductions after 2012, to improve energy efficiency and renewable energy.
Water Financing Partnership Facility (WFPF)	The WFPF provides financial resources and technical support for water services and river basin water management.
Poverty and Environment Fund (PEF)	The PEF is a multi-donor trust fund, administered by ADB that promotes mainstreaming of environmental considerations into broader development strategies, programs, and projects.

Source: http://www.adb.org/themes/climate-change/financing.

institutions. In 2010, net ODA flows from members of the Development Assistance Committee (DAC) of the OECD reached $128.7 billion, representing an increase of 6.5 % over 2009.[10]

During just 1998–2000, ODA accounted for nearly 92% of financial flows to the less developed countries for development initiatives (van Aalst and Agrawala 2005). ODA is assisting developing countries to achieve their Millennium Development Goals through the commitment of the OECD countries to allocate 0.7% of their GDP by 2015. The funds addressing climate change are not part of this commitment. At Copenhagen, developed countries pledged that $100 billion a year would be available for developing countries for climate change by 2020; most of it is likely to come from the private sector.

Figure 5.4

ADB's Clean Energy Targets

Source: ADB (2009).

5.4.2 Major Sources of Regional Funding for Green Growth

ADB is a regional development bank that aims to assist member countries in Asia and the Pacific to reduce poverty and improve the quality of life for the people in the region. The Asia and Pacific region has one third of the world's poorest people, with 600 million people living on $1 a day or less. ADB's funding methods include loans, equity investments, guarantees, grants, and technical assistance. Funding for climate change is provided by ADB through different projects. A number of funding mechanisms have been devised as shown in Table 5.4.

In 2005, ADB launched its Energy Efficiency Initiative with the aim of expanding its clean energy program, enhancing the capacity for ADB's operations departments to develop clean energy projects, and establishing new and innovative financing instruments for clean energy investments (Figure 5.4). In 2011, ADB achieved clean energy investments of $2.1 billion, meeting its investment target of $2 billion annually by 2013, 2 years ahead of schedule (ADB 2012). ADB also provides support to low-carbon projects in a range of other sectors, including transport, waste management, and agriculture.

Private sector participation

The involvement of the private sector is crucial for energy-efficient technological innovation and transfer toward promoting green growth, as the magnitude of the investment necessary to manage climate change is huge, and the public-sector and international sources alone cannot meet the challenge. Particularly, "private finance plays an important role for mobilizing funds to developing countries and its share together with public finance is around 60% of total flows to developing countries from developed countries (2004–2008) (Figure 5.5). This is a much bigger share than Bilateral ODA (20.31%) and Multilateral (9.01%)" (Hongo 2010:7).

Regional institutions like ADB and bilateral institutions like Japan Bank for International Cooperation have been continuously innovating financial packages to encourage more private investment in the clean energy sector. ADB has developed more financial products to accelerate private capital flows into clean energy development. For example, ADB created a $150 million partial credit guarantee facility in India in April 2011 to support foreign and local commercial bank lending for solar power generation projects.

In 2011, ADB achieved more than its clean energy investment target of $2 billion per year. Of this, $895 million (42%) went to the private sector, whose investment increased by $300 million compared with 2010 investments. "ADB's efforts to intensify private sector involvement in clean energy development aim to help fill the gap in mitigation financing which, by 2030, can reach more than $100 billion a year in developing countries" (ADB 2011: 23).

Private sector participation in green growth investment can still be increased by reducing the financial risk that may be faced when the period of investment projects is longer. In this context, the public-private partnership is an important instrument, which has shown success in several cases (Box 5.7). ADB has been an important player in several public-private partnership programs in Asia. For example, in May 2011, it provided Bangladesh a grant of $3.3 million to set up a Public-Private Partnership Infrastructure Facility toward supporting the establishment of individual solar home systems and medium-scale renewable energy applications in rural areas with no access to grid electricity (ADB 2009b).

Figure 5.5

Clean Energy Investment Types and Flows, 2008 ($ billion)

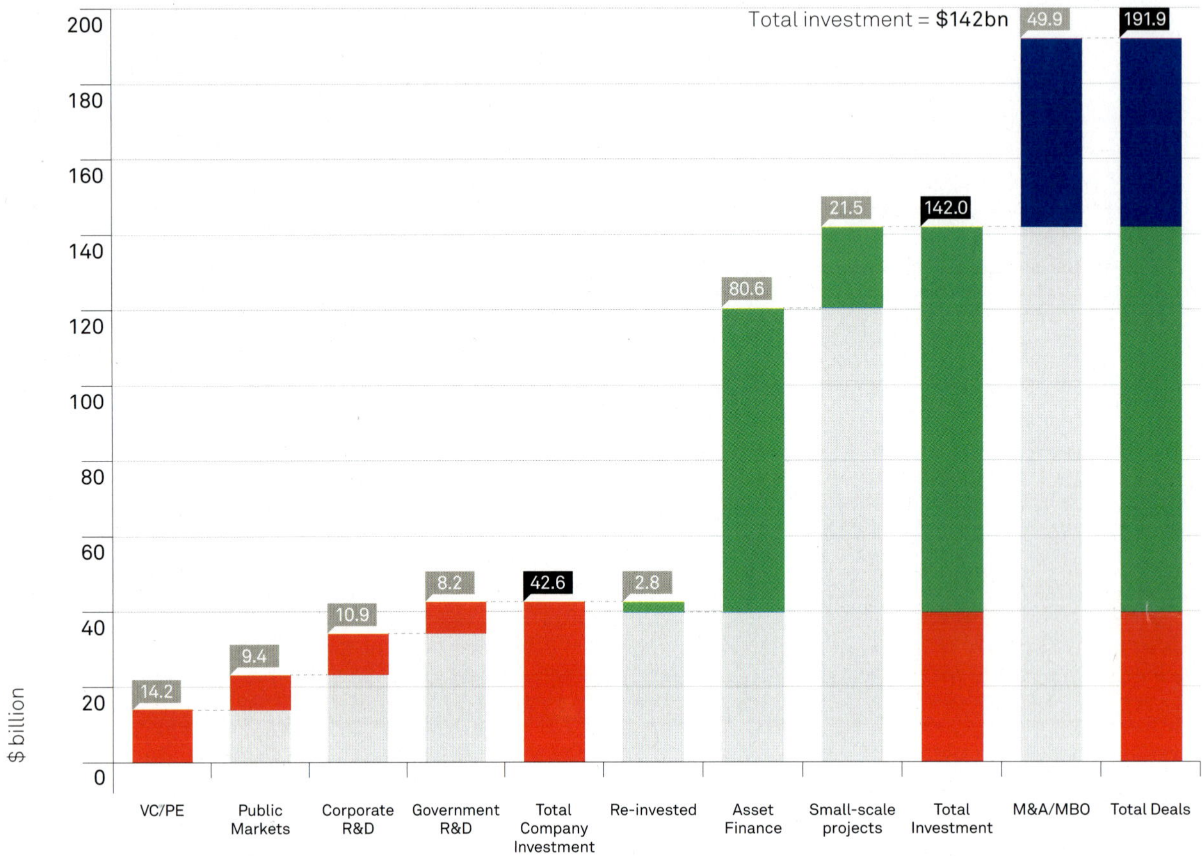

Note: VC=venture capital; PE=private equity; M&A=mergers and acquisitions; MBO=management buy-out.

Figures are adjusted to remove double counting. Investment categories used in this report are defined as follows: (i) Venture capital and private equity: all money invested by venture capital and private equity funds in the equity of companies developing renewable energy technology. Similar investment in companies setting up generating capacity through special purpose vehicles is counted in the asset financing figure. (ii) Public markets: all money invested in the equity of publicly quoted companies developing renewable energy technology and clean power generation. Investment in companies setting up generating capacity is included in the asset financing figure. (iii) Asset financing: all money invested in renewable energy generation projects, whether from internal company balance sheets, from debt finance, or from equity finance. Excludes refinancings and short-term construction loans. Mergers and acquisitions: the value of existing equity purchased by new corporate buyers in companies developing renewable technology or operating renewable energy projects.

Source: Derived from Hongo (2012). ADB–ADBI study team.

Box 5.7

A Successful Public–Private Partnership Project for Climate Change Mitigation

The Natural Energy Development Company (NED) is the private sector participant in a public-private partnership (PPP) solar power project that entails the construction of a 55 megawatt peak (MWp) solar generation plan in Central Thailand (73 MWp gross capacity). The project is Thailand's first large, utility-scale solar power generating facility.

The project's main objective is a demonstration effect of the feasibility and sustainability of a large-scale private sector solar farm—highlighting a model that can be replicated by other private sector investors in Thailand and other countries in the region. Of all renewable energy sources in Thailand, solar energy has the most potential, possibly offering more than 50,000 MW of installed capacity. The project is the first to demonstrate this unrealized potential. The project and its anticipated replication will diversify Thailand's energy mix by adding renewable energy capacity, helping the country to meet its target of obtaining 20.4% of its primary commercial energy from renewable energy by 2022.

Launched in December 2011, the NED solar plant in Lopburi was completed in just 18 months, helped by an ADB long-term loan of $70 million equivalent in Thai baht, representing 25% of the total loan financing. Other investors included KASIKORNBANK, Bangkok Bank, and Siam Commercial Bank, while Sharp supplied 540,000 solar panels to the plant.

NED is a joint venture between Hong Kong, China's CLP Renewables, Diamond Generating Asia, a wholly owned subsidiary of Mitsubishi and the Electricity Generating Public Company, Thailand's first and largest independent power producer. The plant has signed long-term power purchasing agreements to sell 55 megawatts to the Electricity Generating Authority of Thailand and 5 megawatts to the Provincial Electricity Authority at a fixed rate of B8 per kWh in addition to the wholesale tariff for the first 10 years of operations. The first electricity transmission was made in March 2012.

Source: ADB http://www.adb.org/features/solar-success.

Green finance as a facilitator

Green finance refers to the financial support for green growth, the advancement of the financial industry through the development of new financial products, and the improvement of risk management techniques. "ADB has developed more financial products to accelerate private capital flows into clean energy development. For example, ADB created a $150 million partial credit guarantee facility in India in April 2011 to support foreign and local commercial bank lending for solar power generation projects" (ADB 2011: 23). Among the financial intermediaries to promote green growth finance, ADB has created several private equity funds across Asia. For example, in 2003, it invested $10 million in the FE Global Asia Clean Energy Fund, which increased to $63.4 million in 2008. In terms of investments, 10 clean energy projects in India, the Philippines, the PRC, Singapore, and Thailand were undertaken. In 2008, it launched the following clean energy private equity funds with ADB equity of $20 million to each: the China Environment Fund III, the South Asia Clean Energy Fund, the MEACP Clean Energy Fund, and the Asia Clean Energy Fund. In 2009, with ADB equity of $15 million, The Mekong Brahmaputra Clean Development Fund was created. In 2010, it started the Clean Resources Asia Growth Fund and Renewable Energy Asia Fund with the total equity of $40 million to identify and invest in private companies to promote green growth technological innovation and dissemination across Asia.

Another example is the Republic of Korea's Low-Carbon Green Growth Basic Measure, which focuses on the: "formation of financial resources and capital support for a green economy and green industry; development of new financial products to support low-carbon green growth; revitalization of private investment to facilitate low-carbon green growth; strengthening of the public notice system on the green management information of companies; expansion of financial support for green companies; establishment of a carbon market, where the rights to emit GHG or results of GHG reduction and absorption are traded; and revitalization of business" (Kim 2011).

Various innovative financial products and services from private institutions that have been around the region already are useful in the development of capital markets for green growth. For example, concerning Bangladesh's industrial energy efficiency, ADB provided a $30 million credit line plus technical assistance to domestic private banks to support the introduction of energy saving technologies in the brick kiln and other targeted industries.

A strategy that needs to be considered by developing countries is to use, where feasible, their own resources to fund green growth, or to seek assistance from other countries within the region. Some Asian countries, such as the PRC and those of ASEAN, while spending large amounts of funds for green growth, have the capacity also to provide funding for the needy countries in the region. It is to be noted that the PRC and Japan are the second and third largest economies in the world and six out of the eight countries with the largest foreign currency reserves are in Asia.

Government's expanded role in green finance

Research has shown that public-private financial partnerships are crucial in financing green growth. Governments could act as facilitators and could monitor green growth and financing. Governments could also play a large part in creating an enabling environment, providing direction for low-carbon green growth, and improving the investment climate for the private sector.

Governments need to encourage private institutions, including the capital market, to participate in green finance. As most green industries are in the early stages of development and need long-term investments to achieve outcomes, many of these investments are considered to be of high risk. The sovereign wealth funds, owned by the governments, can play a major role in financing green growth. Efficient and consistent policies are necessary for banks to develop their capacity to provide green finance. There has been some increase in support for green industries in the capital market. Environmental information provided by firms will encourage investors in stock markets.

Countries in the Asian region have taken the necessary steps to encourage financial institutions to take active part in promoting green growth through their lending and investment activities. For example in July 2007, the Ministry of Environmental Protection of the PRC in association with the People's Bank of China and the China Banking Regulatory Commission introduced the "Green Credit Policy." The Green Credit Policy requires PRC financial institutions especially for banks at all levels to restrict providing loans to high energy consumption and high polluting companies and projects but to provide more support to those who favor energy efficiency and CO_2 reduction (Matisoff and Chan 2008).

Through the initiatives of the Ministry of Finance and Ministry of Environment and Forests, the banking sector in India has been active in enhancing the availability of green financing. For example, the Small Industries Development Bank of India (SIDBI) with the Japan International Cooperation Agency's (JICA) extended Line of Credit for financing energy saving projects in micro, small, and medium-sized enterprises (MSMEs) provides financial assistance to MSMEs (SIDBI 2011).

The Netherlands Green Fund Scheme

Banks need incentives from governments to participate in green finance. The Netherlands Green Fund Scheme is an example of government support for bank financing to green growth. Green banks are certified by the government, and the majority of major Netherlands banks are designated as green banks. Projects that are assessed to be sufficiently "green" are awarded a green certificate, which qualify for low-interest loans.

Green banks can issue bonds or accept deposits at rates below the market rate to finance green projects. Investors and depositors are compensated with tax breaks.

Green Bank in the United Kingdom

The UK is setting up a Green Investment Bank with £1 billion from taxpayers and up to £2 billion from sales of government assets, with the objective of investing in green projects such as the development of LCGS. The initial funding is expected to encourage private sector money into the green sector: the chancellor is confident the bank can generate £15 billion of green investment from the private sector. (Harvey 2011).

Green bank proposal in the United States

A green bank proposal with initial capital of $10 billion through the issuance of green bonds by the US Department of Treasury, with a maximum authorized limit of $50 billion in green bonds outstanding at any one time was put forward in 2009. Unfortunately, the proposal did not materialize due to the controversial nature of the proposed energy legislation. Nevertheless, recently, the Green Bank proposal and a competing form of financing institution, the Clean Energy Development Authority is being put forward by both the Republicans and Democrats as a source for employment generation (Thurston 2011).

5.5 An Outlook on Cooperation Pathways

Low-Carbon Green growth cannot be handled by any single country effectively, but requires considerable cooperation across countries in the region and beyond. Given the strong regional blocks such as ASEAN, SAARC, CAREC, and APEC, Asia is in an excellent position to work under a regional cooperation framework to maximize the market-based and non-market-based opportunities. Market-based trade and investment are pivotal to boost and strengthen regional cooperation. The analysis in this chapter clearly indicates that all the selected Asian emerging economies will enjoy increased export potential in LCGS, more in the case of "grand regional coalition" than in the case of either "limited regional coalition" or "stand-alone business-as-usual" scenario. It is imperative to implement the regional institutional framework of an AFTA to help Asian emerging economies to realize their market-based potential opportunities in the green economy. An FTA can contribute to technological innovation in LCGS through sufficient financing for R&D and dissemination.

Capacity building is needed to contribute to R&D in LCGS, to improve the attitudes of consumers, producers, and policy makers toward low-carbon green growth. In this context, established regional institutions like LoCARNet, ESCAP, and ADB need to play the coordinating role, in sharing knowledge, technology, and finance.

It is necessary to support the establishment of new and innovative regional private financing mechanisms, especially for risk transfer and insurance instruments.

For this to occur, regional R&D efforts are necessary and these require regional funding with liberal assistance from countries enjoying large foreign reserves within Asia. The carbon market in Asia is fragmented and unification of the market under a grand regional coalition scenario can improve regional financing for green growth.

In order to establish a green economy based on low carbon emissions and increased human welfare, it is necessary to have a core set of indicators that can be used to MRV the progress of a country moving to a low-carbon economy. These indicators should capture green growth and poverty reduction initiatives, beyond the traditional indicators such as GDP per capita. International collaboration in this regard will help in disseminating cost effective low carbon technologies, develop green industries, and create jobs. Such actions can also support the proactive participation of Asian countries in global negotiations such as those over the Green Climate Fund.

Chapter 6

Conclusions and Recommendations: Policy Innovations for a Low-Carbon Green Asia

Chapter 6
Conclusions and Recommendations:
Policy Innovations for a Low-Carbon Green Asia

6.1 Changing Policy Perspectives and Strategic Priorities for Climate Change Mitigation

The emerging economies of Asia have enjoyed remarkable growth since the 1980s despite two financial crises. If growth follows its recent trajectory, this will be the Asian century, wherein Asian gross domestic product (GDP) per capita income will rise significantly, from $6,700 in purchasing power parity (PPP) terms in 2011 to $40,800 in 2050. The Asian share of global output will increase from 27.7% in 2010 to 52.3% in 2050. Asia will become the major force of global growth. To accomplish this growth, Asia has to overcome serious challenges such as poverty eradication and the reduction of social inequality as well as the need to halt environmental degradation, such as that caused by greenhouse gas (GHG) emissions. This has raised the need to abandon the conventional economic model of development, to be replaced by a low-carbon green growth model wherein the Asian values of enhancing social cohesion, preserving ecological equilibrium, and creating material wealth become key components. This transition has started in Asia. Spurred by rising expectations, a number of emerging economies have grasped the challenges and opportunities of moving to low-carbon green growth. This book analyzes the critical policies and recommends practical and concrete actions that can help countries do more and do better.

6.1.1 Motivations for Low-Carbon Green Growth

The convergence of climate change and economic and social challenges is the result of the scale and patterns of economic growth. The policy-making landscape in Asia has therefore changed. Policy actions to mitigate climate change and accelerate green growth have gained particular momentum since 1997, when the Kyoto Protocol was signed. The 2012 Doha Climate Gateway, agreed at the United Nations climate talks, demonstrated emerging Asia's resolve to move forward to limit GHG emissions and conceded the need for a legally binding framework. Two of the key elements of the 2011 Durban platform were to quantify emissions reduction targets and implement actions by a target year, but actionable policy measures are already being developed and will advance further before and after specific target dates. Nationally appropriate mitigation actions (NAMAs), as reported in national communications, at the end of 2012, amounted to some 400 policy announcements that vary widely in stringency, scope, and mix (Figure 6.1). In most of emerging Asia, there are regulations on renewable energy supply and energy efficiency. However, where regulatory frameworks exist, they often do not target emissions directly but achieve emissions reductions as co-benefits of economic, environmental, and social policies that emphasize inclusive and sustainable development (e.g., policies that encourage renewable energy uptake in off-grid areas, energy savings by low-income households, and investment in air quality improvement).

Figure 6.1

Number of Key Policy Initiatives and Low-Carbon Actions Taken by Selected Asian Countries

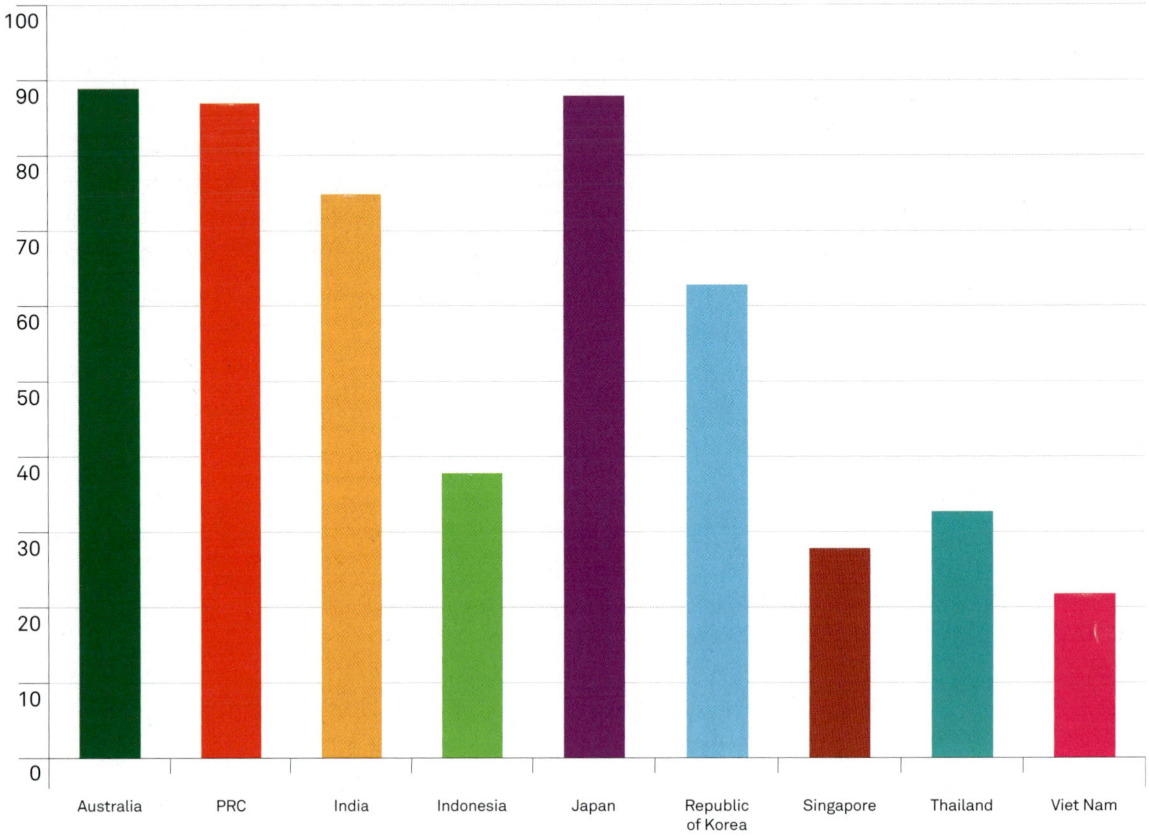

Source: ADB–ADBI study team.

For an increasing number of Asian countries, decoupling emissions from economic growth is becoming part of the national developmental framework. For example, the National Climate Change Program of the People's Republic of China (PRC), announced in 2007, aims to reduce energy consumption per unit of GDP by 20% from its 2005 level. The 12th Five-Year Plan for National Economic and Social Development considers it a major strategic objective to build an energy-conserving and environment-friendly society. India released its first National Action Plan on Climate Change in 2008, because of concerns over energy security and scarcity. It has led to the launch of national missions, including a solar mission that aims to create an enabling policy framework for the deployment of 20,000 megawatts (MW) of solar power by 2022 to off-grid consumers and enhance energy efficiency that is expected to help save about 5% of annual energy consumption. Other countries such as Indonesia, Malaysia, and Thailand target contributions to national energy supply from low- or zero-carbon resources, measures and incentives for energy efficiency, the preservation of natural resources, and promoting growth across all sectors of their economies. These strategies are based wholly on the idea of mitigation through economic development. Economic growth and climate change mitigation are not seen as mutually exclusive but as a way to promote sustainable and socially inclusive development.

6.1.2 Emerging Asia's Policy Innovations for Low-Carbon Green Growth

Based on past economic performance, the region's economies can be classified into three groups: (i) high-income developed economies such as Japan, the Republic of Korea, and Singapore; (ii) fast-growing economies such as the PRC, India, Indonesia, Thailand, and Viet Nam, in which per capita income is catching up with that of developed economies; and (iii) countries such as the Philippines and Sri Lanka and that are currently aspiring to achieve more modest growth. From these groups, the fast growing economies produce 52% of Asian GDP and 67% of emissions while comprising 77% of the population. However, they are responding to the calls for decoupling with a growing body of policy instruments that are significant in their impact, replicable, and may be scaled up. Those policies can be categorized as regulations, market-based instruments, and voluntary schemes. Future policy developments are expected in this area. Chapters 2 and 3 tackled the questions of why and how Asian policy makers embraced the key aspects of emission reduction that are needed to pave the way for low-carbon green growth, by taking a closer look at policy initiatives at the national and subnational levels. Asian policy initiatives clearly incorporate the main ingredients for a successful transition toward a low-carbon green future. Their content can be summarized as follows:

1 Emerging Asian economies acknowledge the need to approach low-carbon green growth from a broader perspective, as is shown through the emphasis on a wide set of pledges, policies, and programs, which are integrated in developmental plans. Although exact arrangements vary from country to country, standards and regulations are being continuously updated, while further measures are being developed.

2 Emerging Asia also pays attention to the integration of low-carbon green growth in a broader context, acknowledging the strong links between climate-friendly policies and other environmental, economic, and social issues. Aligning climate policies with the three pillars of broader development strategies (economic growth, co-benefits, and social inclusion), while maintaining the overall objective of emission reductions, is a promising way of improving the long-term performance of each sector as well as the sustainability of development.

3 Asian policy makers acknowledge the broader challenge of implementing low-carbon resource-efficient development, aiming for actions that affect not only the macroeconomic and technological realms but also the everyday decisions of individuals. Behavioral changes and lifestyle choices are therefore a major issue, and awareness and communication strategies to mobilize actors at national and local levels are envisaged.

4 Given the difficult changes needed to bring down emissions, Asian policy initiatives have recognized the need to grasp the "low-hanging fruits" – opportunities with low up-front costs – such as energy efficiency. The implementation of low-carbon development policies is easier if policies have multiple benefits.

5 Asian experiences across different sectors of the economy have revealed that technological change is a catalyst for transition. To encourage this, governments work to reduce the cost of technologies, developing technology, research and development (R&D), education, and training to bring about green growth. To conquer the cost barrier of new technologies, some Asian governments and industries have cooperated successfully in generating a mutually reinforcing cycle of market expansion and cost reduction. This has contributed to the large-scale development of new technologies and provides a means for other countries to overcome the cost barriers of new technologies.

6 Finally, a strong partnership of public authorities with the private sector to ensure an effective flow of financial resources to companies reinforces the long-term implementation of programs organized around market-based initiatives. The private sector can ensure appropriate monitoring and follow-up activities. Various funding channels and economic instruments are also being tested.

6.1.3 Key Enablers of Low-Carbon Green Growth

The challenge of decoupling carbon emissions from economic growth is confronting the traditional development strategies of Asia with new risks and opportunities. A number of countries have turned the risks into opportunities through early and effective action and innovation. For some, there has been a direct upside to climate change mitigation, because new standards and consumer demand are creating new needs and new markets, such as renewable energy technologies, insulation for buildings, mass transport for cities, energy-efficient appliances, electric cars, specialized businesses such as Energy Service Companies, and financial advisory services for users of the United Nations Clean Development Mechanism.

The sheer volume of activities precludes a complete detailing of all relevant policies in each country. Table 6.1 illustrates the policy landscape.

Table 6.1

Classification of Climate Change Mitigation Instruments

Technology-based		Carbon pricing
Fiscal	Regulatory	Fiscal
Investment subsidies	Technology performance standards	Emission trading
Preferential tax treatment	Renewable fuel/energy standards	Carbon tax
Government investment in venture capital	Building regulations	Hybrid trading-tax schemes
Public investment vehicles	Automobile regulations	
Demonstration grants	Information standards	
Public R&D		
Feed-in tariffs		
Tax credits		
Public procurement		
Renewable energy certificate trading		
Subsidies for energy-efficiency purchases		

Source: Howes and Dobes (2012).

Tax Incentives and Credit Lending for Deployment of Low-Carbon Technology

A variety of subsidies and incentives are used to reduce the costs of investing in technology demonstration and deployment. Examples include reduced taxes on inputs, tax holidays, accelerated depreciation, matched investment funding, and import duty exemptions. Governments offer concessional loans to reduce up-front costs, or loan guarantees to reduce financiers' risks. For example, Thailand's Revolving Fund provides capital to banks that is made available to borrowers at concessional rates, with the repayments from existing borrowers financing new projects.

Other measures include government rebates to purchasers of energy-efficient devices or solar panels, and low-interest green loans on retro-fitting projects. These interventions, in partnership with private financial institutions, have brought prices down for users of low-carbon products, which can assist economies of scale by producers and cut prices, further stimulating demand for low-carbon goods and services.

Regulations and Standards

The governments of emerging Asia have introduced many different regulations and standards that cut emissions across sectors. Examples include ethanol blending in fuel; emissions and fuel economy standards for cars; minimum efficiency standards and compulsory labeling of energy appliances; and compulsory replacement of small, inefficient fossil fuel based power plants with large highly efficient ones. In the PRC, the Energy Saving Power Dispatch mechanism prioritizes dispatch to the energy grid based on their efficiency and emissions. Priority is given to nonadjustable sources of renewable energy (such as solar and wind), then adjustable renewable sources (such as hydropower), nuclear, with coal and oil lowest in the ranking. This has helped to raise thermal power energy efficiency from 32.86% in 2005 to 37.24% in 2010 by decommissioning more than 70 gigawatts (GW) of inefficient power plans.In India, government regulations have converted many of Delhi's three-wheeler taxis to natural gas, reducing urban air pollution.

Green Certificates or Renewable Energy Portfolios and Other Market-Based Mechanisms
Renewable energy certificates create a market mechanism for utility companies to meet mandated targets for renewable portfolio standards. Renewable energy operators are issued with credits for each unit of electricity they produce, and these credits can then be purchased and/or traded by utilities in fulfillment of their portfolio obligations. This provides incentives for renewable energy operators to compete in lowering their costs. However, when multiple forms of energy are covered by the same scheme, the lowest-cost technology is favored, often wind power. In 2011, India was the first of the countries to launch a Renewable Energy Certificate (REC) scheme, providing a means for states and utilities to meet portfolio standards. The implementation of RECs accompanies the Perform, Achieve and Trade (PAT) mechanism, whereby India's largest energy users are set benchmark efficiency levels, with trade between participants who exceed their targets and those who fail to meet them. The PAT instrument echoes a voluntary mechanism developed in the PRC, known as Generation Rights Trading (GRT), in which coal-based electricity operators are assigned tradable quotas, with the objective to expand the share of supply provided by high-efficiency operators and reduce the share of low-efficiency operators. In 2007, the use of GRT across 23 PRC provinces was estimated to involve a total transaction quantity of 54 terawatt-hours (TWh), saving 6.2 million tons of coal equivalent.

Feed-in Tariffs
Feed-in tariffs are commonly used policy instruments that ensure renewable energy operators receive favorable terms. Although the exact arrangements vary from country to country, generally they share three standard characteristics: guaranteed access to the electricity grid; long-term contracts; and generated power purchased by grid companies at higher prices than that from fossil fuel sources, reflecting the currently higher generation costs of renewables. These instruments have played an important role in the rapid development of the PRC's wind power industry. The effectiveness of feed-in tariffs, however, can be limited by inappropriate design. For example, the feed-in tariff may be too low to stimulate investment, as in the case of India, or, as in the case of Indonesia, grid companies may be insufficiently compensated by government to incur the higher costs of a feed-in tariff and be unwilling to participate in the arrangement.

Public Finance for Research, Development, and Deployment
The public good characteristics of low-carbon R&D represent an attractive use of public finance. Various policy instruments as shown in Table 6.2 serve this purpose, such as specialized national research institutes, direct government grants to firms, matched investment funding, student scholarships, and tax subsidies. All the study countries have some form of R&D funding, most of it in the PRC and India.

Targeted Planning by Local Governments
Local governments are also key. In the PRC, promotion for senior government officials has long been dependent on achieving centrally determined targets. Until the 11th Five Year Plan, 2006–2010, such targets almost exclusively focused on macroeconomic measures, such as GDP growth. Today, promotion requires the achievement of environmental targets, thus building strong incentives for provincial officials to set and meet targets or follow through on central government initiatives.

Table 6.2

Public Policy Mechanisms for Supporting Low-Carbon Innovations

Stage	1 Early research	2 Demonstration and commercialization	3 Market update
Key policy challenges	Increase the volume of early-stage research Improve the flow of funding to promising research Transfer academic research into commercial environment Do not write off promising technologies too early	Identify scalable, lab-proven technologies Provide soft credit where it is required to achieve target returns Establish clear performance standards Do not try to pick winners, but cull losers aggressively Develop a replicable blueprint for large-volume rollout Provide support to close cost gap with mature technologies Ensure availability of credit despite market and policy risk Ensure economic system can absorb new technologies and remain stable Support/create lead customers	Ensure energy diversity, if necessary provide long-term support for higher-cost technologies Protect public budgets Avoid locking in uncompetitive market structures Shift emphasis to "polluter pays" rather than maintaining subsidies indefinitely
Enabling policies			
Regulation		National/state/local procurement targets Feed-in tariffs Reverse auctions/requests for contract Renewable portfolio standards/green certificates/PET Renewable fuel standards	Top-runner requirements utility regulation
Finance Mechanisms for Innovation	Incubators National laboratories Prizes National/state-funded venture capital National/state-run venture capital R&D grants	Project grants	Technology transfer funds National/State/Local infrastructure funds
Credit Mechanisms		Venture loan guarantees Green bonds Loan guarantees Debt funds	Export trade credit Microfinance Sovereign/policy risk insurance National/state/local Energy Service Co. (ESCO) funds
Tax-based Policies	Capital gains tax waivers R&D tax credits	Innovation clusters Accelerated depreciation Investment tax credits Production tax credits	Carbon tax
Carbon Market Mechanisms		Monitoring, Reporting and Verifying (MRV)	Domestic carbon cap and trade Project-based carbon credits National/Multilateral carbon funds

Source: ADB/I Study Team.

Regional planning—through which urban and rural planners develop land-use, forest-use, and traffic and transport programs—offers powerful instruments to reduce the carbon footprints of the rapidly urbanizing and industrializing areas of Asia. Housing construction, road networks, and the spatial structure of an urban area "lock in" carbon footprints for the indefinite future. Cities such as Yokohama in Japan, Tianjin in the PRC, and Ho Chi Minh in Viet Nam are planned as compact communities, so they require less energy for moving residents from their homes to workplaces, conveying water, and managing wastes.

6.1.4
Policy Support Mechanisms and their Selection

As illustrated by Table 6.1, it is clear that a portfolio of policies in each region, country, and sector is needed to drive the transformation to low-carbon green growth, but how should the right policy portfolio be assembled? The already extensive deployment of technology policies in emerging Asia reflects a range of factors. Any policy mechanism needs to reflect the stage of development of the low-carbon technologies that are to be deployed. This should influence the type of regulation and standards deployed and the financing that the private sector should be encouraged to commit.

6.2
Paths for Raising the Pace of Low-Carbon Green Growth

As discussed in Chapters 4 and 5, there is significant potential to reduce GHG emissions and emerging Asia can do much more to accelerate the transition to pro-poor, pro-environment, pro-job growth. The three levels of interventions shown in Figure 6.2 could be considered a nested hierarchy for policy intervention for maximizing co-benefits, with an increased degree of integrated structuralization from the local, sectoral, and regional level. Regional cooperation is key. At that level, windows of opportunity open through inter-linkages and interaction between economies to scale up the markets. There is an urgent need to develop clearly articulated strategies at the national and regional level. In many emerging economies, the institutional framework is underdeveloped.

6.2.1
Greater Use of Market-Based Instruments

Market-based instruments are at an early stage of development in the emerging economies of Asia. This is partly because of limited development of institutions and research. High levels of fossil fuel subsidies, which are often a considerable part of the national budget, further hinder the pace of low-carbon green growth. Concerns over the burden of market-based instruments on poor households and their impact on competitiveness may also discourage their use. Both theory and evolving experiences in Japan, the Republic of Korea, Australia, and Singapore suggest that greater use of market-based instruments could raise low-carbon green growth rates.

The burden of carbon taxes on poor households and small and medium-sized enterprises (SMEs) could be mitigated by reducing other taxes or through distributive policies. More use could also be made of market-based instruments in urban waste management. The development of carbon taxes is likely to be most effective if done in consultation, and where appropriate, with cooperation among the region's economies to share experiences and best practice, to avoid distortions in competitiveness and deal with trans-border issues.

The use of other market-based instruments will not be easy, at least in the short run when the

Figure 6.2

Dynamic Multilevel Cooperation Framework for Accelerating Low-Carbon Green Growth

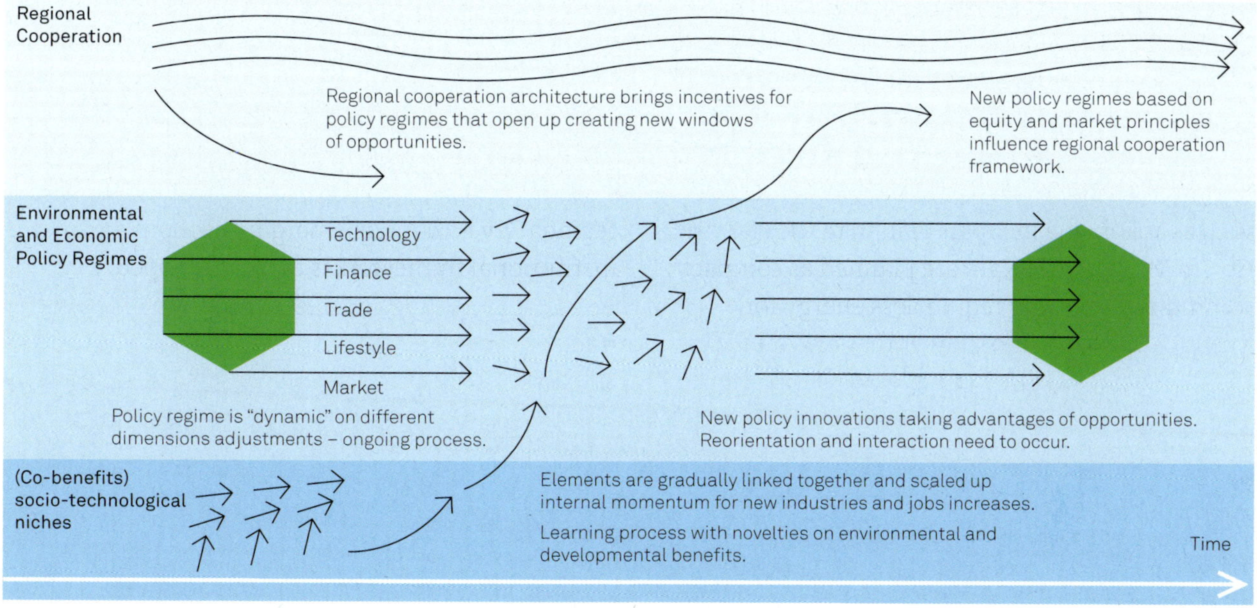

Source: ADB–ADBI study team.

institutional and economic capacity is limited. Carbon pricing will raise the cost of electricity and fossil fuels, a politically dangerous proposition. Energy is still a luxury good in much of developing Asia: wealthier households are more likely to own cars and household electrical appliances. Wealthier households, which are more politically powerful, may be opposed to rising prices.

Unless significant progress is made on carbon pricing in other parts of the world, the introduction of carbon prices in emerging Asia is likely to be slow, rendering them less effective, if they are introduced at all. Developing regional carbon markets by linking existing markets could be a priority action.

Though current actions on fuel pricing based on the carbon content is limited, the emerging Asian countries are likely to introduce carbon prices as climate change becomes more evident and they ramp up their mitigation activities to meet their NAMA goals; upon committing to substantial mitigation, they will seek the most efficient means. Domestic political constraints may be more difficult to overcome. From the perspective of poor households, welfare concerns may diminish as living standards continue to rise, but perhaps not if energy consumption continues to rise. For both poor and wealthier households, political support for carbon pricing may be contingent on the development of compensation instruments such as conditional cash transfer programs.

6.2.2
Public–Private Partnerships for Low-Carbon Technological Innovations

Technological progress is a key driver of low-carbon green growth and energy, infrastructure, and transportation; and plays an important role in the decoupling of economic growth from emissions. A huge gap remains, though, between the innovations and technologies that are needed and those available. Innovation goes beyond the development of new technologies, products, and operation methods; and includes finding new ways of doing business by integrating products and services. However, they are not being developed at the rate required because of technological, skills, financial, commercial, and regulatory barriers. Globally, demand–pull policies have been favored by governments over supply–push policies; there is a strong case for a more balanced approach. While developed countries will probably account for the bulk of future expansion, R&D in developing Asia must also be increased. For example, special local conditions, such as Indonesia's vast geothermal resources, justify targeted investments. Domestic investments will diminish some of the difficulties associated with intellectual property regimes.

Experiences from Japan, the Republic of Korea, and Singapore indicate that effective innovation needs to encompass commercial, institutional, and financial structures as well as the technology itself. Establishing low-carbon innovation and diffusion centers in emerging Asian countries could enhance local and regional engagement with global technology developments and catalyze their domestic capacity to develop, adapt, and diffuse beneficial innovations. Public–private partnerships are an attractive option for leveraging private investment. Government finance and support provide greater assurance of private returns. Private companies have an advantage in driving efficiency and cost reductions, increasing the prospects of commercialization compared with a solely public financed and operated project. Public–private partnerships have been extensively used in the past to finance expensive public investments in developing Asia, such as major infrastructure projects.

6.2.3
Harnessing Regional Cooperation Opportunities

In addition to domestic technology policies, an important issue for emerging Asia is access to low-carbon technologies available elsewhere. There are a wide range of technologies at various stages of development that could contribute to low-carbon green growth goals. Liberalization of trade and reduced tariff rates for low-carbon green products and services would accelerate technology transfer. Table 6.4 presents a framework of policies to do this. New opportunities, all of which have the potential to generate job growth and provide competitive advantage, include (i) production and export of solar and wind technology; (ii) trade in ethanol fuel and technology and flex-fuel vehicles technology; and (iii) new high-tech energy industries and the green services sector. In the context of global mitigation, an outstanding and significant issue is the prospect of extensive transfer of IPR. If patent protection limits the ability of domestic manufacturers in Asia to adapt externally developed technologies, then, of course, their dissemination is likely to be lower. In order to mitigate this obstacle, large, emerging economies could be involved in international collaborative partnerships from the R&D stage. Achieving extensive technology and financial transfer from advanced economies will also require new arrangements and, perhaps, willingness on the part of developed countries to forgo some commercial advantage for their own industries.

The integration of regional carbon markets is also a prerequisite for reducing emissions cost-effectively but there may be problems with this. For example, mandatory emissions targets in advanced economies could create incentives for polluting and high-carbon industries to move to developing Asian countries without emissions caps. This represents an opportunity for increased foreign direct investment in emerging Asia, but border tax adjustments are being considered by some developed countries, in part to prevent this carbon leakage, which could have consequences for access to other export markets that were previously open to developing Asian countries. The introduction of

Table 6.3

Intellectual Property Rights Regimes and Low-Carbon Industry Policies in Selected Asian Countries

Type of economy based on carbon-intensiveness	Trade in low-carbon goods and services	FDI	Trade in knowledge (licensing)	IPR	Low-carbon industrial policies
Domestic policies					
Low-carbon intensive: Lao PDR, Bangladesh, Nepal, Cambodia, and Sri Lanka	Liberal access	Non-discriminatory investment promotion	Improve information flows about public domain and mature technologies	Basic protection and minimum standards only	Basic education; reduce entry barriers, improve infrastructure
Medium-carbon intensive: Thailand, Indonesia, and Viet Nam	Liberal access	Non-discriminatory investment promotion	Improve information limited incentives for licensing	Wider scope of IPR protection; employ flexibilities	R&D support policies, improve infrastructure, reduce entry barriers
High-carbon intensive: PRC and India	Liberal access	Upstream supplier support programs	Improve information limited incentives for licensing	Apply full TRIPS	R&D support policies, improve infrastructure, reduce entry barriers
Developed-country policies towards emerging Asia					
Low-carbon intensive: Lao PDR, Bangladesh, Nepal, Cambodia, and Sri Lanka	Subsidize public good-type imports; free trade	Incentives for outward flows exceeding those for FDI	Subsidize transfer of public domain and mature technologies	Forbearance in disputes; differential pricing for exports of IPR products; competition policy assistance	Support for general low-carbon techn'gy policies; public and public-private research facilities
Medium-carbon intensive: Thailand, Indonesia, and Viet Nam	Free trade; no controls	Incentives equal to those granted for own disadvantaged regions	Assistance in establishing joint venture partnerships; matching grants	Differential pricing of public-good type IPR protected goods; competition policy assistance	Support for general low-carbon techn'gy policies; fiscal incentives for R&D performed in developed countries
High-carbon intensive: PRC and India	Free trade; no controls	Incentives equal to those granted for own disadvantaged regions	Assistance in establishing joint venture partnerships	Differential pricing of public-good type IPR protected goods; competition policy assistance	Support for general low-carbon techn'gy policies; fiscal incentives for R&D performed in developed countries

Source: ADB–ADBI study team.

carbon labeling and associated regulations could shift this to emerging Asia's comparative advantage.

Emerging Asia would benefit greatly from the replicable experiences and practices in technology development, energy efficiency, and resource management of advanced economies such as Japan, the Republic of Korea, and Singapore. They have had energy conservation laws for a long time and are reducing emissions through market-based approaches and regulatory reforms to develop green technologies and products.

Strengthening IPR regimes and liberalization of trade will accelerate diffusion of low carbon technologies (Table 6.3). Regional cooperation extends beyond developed countries. The major economies of developing Asia share two important characteristics: high rates of growth and the need to alter their development trajectories. Achieving further decoupling of emissions from economic growth will throw up many policy challenges. The exchange of knowledge about how to overcome these will be mutually beneficial, particularly with regard to least-cost technology innovation and adoption, reform processes, and the minimization of mitigation costs. Coordination of national policies may reduce the prospect of intra-regional carbon leakage. If and when national carbon prices arise, regional links could reduce mitigation costs by exploiting areas of comparative advantage in reducing emissions, such as deforestation in Indonesia, agriculture in Viet Nam, or improving the efficiency of coal-fired power plants in India.

6.2.4
Galvanizing International Support for Financing Green Growth

Financing is a major obstacle to low-carbon green growth. Private sector participation is critical. However, many low-carbon projects have a long payback time. Governments can play a catalytic role by setting up low-carbon funds and changing tax policies and subsidies to cushion private investment risks.

From the perspective of equity and historical responsibility, it is in the developed world's interests for developing Asia to cut emissions, so developed countries should help to finance the significant gap between the up-front benefits and costs of mitigation. The domestic motivations, such as energy security, employment generation, and improved local environmental conditions, involve substantial benefits over time, but may not be enough to drive the transformations required. Substantial additional investments in, for example, renewable energy need to occur soon to avoid locking in future emissions. While some countries, such as the PRC, may be able to access the large investment necessary independently, developing Asian economies have other development priorities. It is important that developed countries fulfill their climate finance commitments; the major economies of developing Asia cannot be expected to carry the full burden of their mitigation costs alone.

6.2.5
Strengthening Inter-Sectoral Synergy for Low-Carbon Green Growth

Governments will need to develop institutions to drive low-carbon green growth. Creating the institutions is hard enough; doing so in developing countries where institutional capacity may already be lacking even harder still. A large body of skilled professionals in planning agencies will be required. In some cases, where government is based on a federalist system, fundamental changes may be necessary in the location of taxation agreements and other domains of economic and social governance.

6.3 Net Costs and Social Embeddings of Low-Carbon Green Growth

6.3.1 Net Benefits of Moving to a Low-Carbon Economy

A transition to a low-carbon economy can benefit emerging Asia in at least four ways:

1. Many low-carbon interventions have important co-benefits for Asia, including enhanced energy security from energy efficiency and renewable energy projects; human health benefits from reducing air pollutants; and environmental benefits from forestry and agricultural management, waste reduction, and employment programs.
2. Numerous "low hanging–no-regret" low-carbon interventions, which have positive rates of return and short payback times and should be undertaken irrespective of climate change considerations, can contribute substantially to economic development.
3. Asian countries that pursue low-carbon development, including the transfer of financial resources through the carbon market and new public programs that support climate change mitigation are likely to reap strategic and competitive advantage at the regional and international level.
4. Because the emerging countries of Asia are likely to suffer disproportionately from the impacts of climate change (drought, increased severity of tropical storms, sea level rises, etc.), Asia has a strong interest in being a leading participant in global efforts on both mitigation and adaptation.

Almost all the interventions have been implemented in Asia to some extent as commercial-scale investment projects or pilot programs, demonstrating the feasibility of implementing them in the medium term. Scaling up these initiatives will require new policies and the financing of incremental investments, as well as other institutional and behavioral changes. Many high-priority mitigation interventions in the energy, transport, forestry, and urban sectors have net costs that are low or negative.

6.3.2 Net Costs of Climate Change Mitigation on Economic Growth

Previous Asian Development Bank (ADB) studies, reports of the Intergovernmental Panel on Climate Change, and the Stern Review described a range of costs for the mitigation of climate change. They estimated that to deploy low-carbon technologies on the scale required to stabilize the atmospheric concentration carbon dioxide (CO_2) equivalent at 450–550 parts per million would cost 1.0%–3.5% of world GDP a year. This wide range reflects the uncertainties about the future costs of alternatives to fossil fuels and low-carbon technologies. The range is large in absolute terms (1% of global GDP is projected to exceed $1 trillion per year by 2050), but small in relation to the expected growth over the next 40–50 years. Emerging Asia's GDP is $12 trillion in 2012 and expanding at 4%–9% per year, so it is likely to exceed $78,417 billion by 2030. Therefore, the cost of mitigation need not disrupt the prospects of economic prosperity in emerging Asia, even if costs rose to the upper end of range.

Chapter 1 suggested that climate change is the greatest market failure of all time and recognizes that policies taken to reduce climate change also affect other externalities (such as health, social, and environmental damages).

Therefore, the net cost of mitigation would be lower than it appears at first. For example, studies in the PRC show the benefits of reducing health-damaging air pollution more than offset the cost of CO_2 reduction, by up to 10%–20%. There are other benefits, such as energy security, employment generation, and air quality improvement. The benefits of those services are underestimated or neglected in many conventional economic cost–benefit analyses.

The growth stimulus from policies to promote low-carbon technological progress could outweigh the growth-reducing effect associated with a higher cost of carbon, especially if there is rapid growth in the demand for low-carbon goods and services. In addition, efforts to restore forests or avoid deforestation or land degradation in some countries may also have beneficial economic effects, for example, if they help improve flood controls in watersheds. Some mitigation policies generate revenues (e.g., carbon taxes, carbon trading systems) and thus provide opportunities to stimulate growth through the judicious use of the revenues raised. If revenues from a carbon tax are spent on innovation, health, and education, the overall impact of mitigation could be positive.

6.3.3
Making Low-Carbon Green Growth Pro-Poor

To date, low-carbon green growth research and policy actions have been mainly taken in high- and middle-income countries. However, low-carbon green growth can be an opportunity for low-income countries to pursue pro-poor development in a carbon-constrained world. Development paths that aim to tackle climate change, while seeking social and economic development and achieving the millennium development goals, are needed.

Growth in lower-income countries is often heavily agriculture-based initially, and can be made strongly pro-poor and low-carbon. Forestry has been a major source of income for some low-income countries, and, given the great importance of forests as a carbon sink, the potential value of avoided deforestation and reforestation could be a significant source of finance for those countries through mechanisms such as the Clean Development Mechanism and the United Nations Programme on Reducing Emissions from Deforestation and Forest Degradation (REDD), although considerable progress still needs to be made in developing these mechanisms. The complexity of rules makes it more difficult for forest countries like Indonesia, Thailand, and Viet Nam to harness the potential of these mechanisms.

Countries with heavy dependence on agriculture are targeting a variety of agricultural activities, from improved soil management and improved agronomic practices through management of fertilizers and afforestation. They need greater understanding and awareness of the impact of climate change to take advantage of possible new growth opportunities. Educating the population and giving them the skills and knowledge to understand the changing global policy environment and hence the potential impact on their livelihoods, and to capitalize on any new opportunities, will help to improve growth prospects.

In middle-income economies, policies for pro-poor green growth can be devised. Government revenues from low-carbon green industries could be distributed to pro-poor sectors such as agriculture, health, and education and to support skill development in specific sectors that are crucial for the poor such as agriculture and forestry. This will also provide opportunities to involve isolated communities in decision making and share profits on a local level, such as through rural electrification with renewable energy.

6.4
Conclusions

The analysis throughout this book makes a strong case that developing Asia must be at the center of the global agenda on low-carbon and green growth. Asia has much at stake in the global fight against climate change—the region being the most populous, having had high economic growth and a rising share of global emissions, and being the most vulnerable to looming climate risks.

Developing Asia has been taking action. Increasingly, the region's policy makers and other stakeholders see the new economic opportunities that low-carbon green growth offers for inclusive and sustainable growth. This is evident from the great weight that energy efficiency and renewable energy receive in policy discussions in Asia and from the many initiatives that Asian countries have started to implement in recent years. It is certainly the case that recent policy announcements and targets have transformed emissions trajectories, and developing Asia is making a major contribution to collective global efforts to tackle climate change.

This book has focused on the importance of a broad approach to addressing climate mitigation that extends across all sectors of the economy and involves the private sector and all levels of government. While it is too early to judge the efficacy of many of the policies that have been set out, a focused assessment of policy actions is critical to distill lessons for timely feedback and to speed up further actions to ensure an effective response. What emerges from the cross-country review is that isolated or sector-focused policies will not be sufficient for the switch to a low-carbon, environmentally sustainable trajectory.

The current level of effort remains insufficient and Asia can do much more. The countries considered in this report are some of the principal sources of current and future emissions, especially in the case of the PRC and India. Further action is needed, and quickly, to avoid locking in emissions-intensive infrastructure as Asia's energy demand surges, and to reduce the costs of mitigation. While the transition to a low-carbon economy offers fertile ground for innovation, governments must establish the regulatory certainty and incentives needed to make the required, often long-term and risky, investments. Analysis elsewhere shows that even if the world's developed countries reduced their emissions to zero, the developing countries of Asia would still need to make substantial cuts in emissions to achieve the global emissions levels scientists say are needed to avoid dangerous climate change.

The book's analysis concludes that for developing Asia, resource-efficient, low-carbon green growth is not only imperative, but also feasible and attractive. This is elaborated in the following 10 key messages:

1. **Current patterns of economic growth in Asia are unsustainable and have to change.** By any standard, Asia's economic performance over the past three decades has been impressive. GDP growth averaged 5%–10% a year and millions of people were lifted out of poverty. Further improvement in Asia faces a physical constraint: the environmental carrying capacity of the planet, including the carrying capacity of the atmosphere for carbon. Over the past two centuries, rapid industrialization and high fossil fuel based growth has enabled Europe and the Americas to escape a life of hunger and poverty. Asia contains most of the world's population, industrial production, and energy

consumption. If Asia follows the patterns of western industrialization and urbanization, such capacities would be depleted to an irreversible level even if developed countries cut their emissions to zero. Furthermore, millions of people in Asia do not have access to cooking fuel or electricity. New development paths are therefore needed. Low-carbon green growth can achieve economic and social development while tackling climate change.

2 **Convergence in perspective and diversity in practice characterize developing Asia's approaches to low-carbon green growth.** Asian countries are increasingly adopting national climate change strategies. The policies being implemented are designed to fit well with other national development goals. They include (i) improving energy security, (ii) tackling local environmental problems, and (iii) seeking low-carbon technological advance as a growth opportunity. Co-benefits, such as improved air or water quality, are increasingly a key policy motivation for introducing climate mitigation policies. For example, some Asian countries overcome the high cost of renewable energy by spreading the costs to a larger pool of consumers through mandated renewable energy portfolios and feed-in tariffs. This has mobilized strong interest from the private sector and the resulting expanded deployment has accelerated cost reductions through economies of scale, creating green jobs, and enhanced competitiveness in green technology industries.

3 **The keys to effective action include clearly set long-term targets and plans, policy interventions, and proper signals to business.** The common drivers and causes for the shift to low-carbon green growth in Asia can be summarized as (i) using less energy, improving the efficiency with which energy is used, and moving to low-carbon energy resources such as solar and wind; (ii) protecting and promoting natural resources, such as forests and peatlands that store carbon; (iii) designing, disseminating, and deploying low-carbon technologies and business models that bring co-benefits; and (iv) policies and incentives that discourage carbon-intensive practices and behaviors. Through a mix of regulations, public investments, energy and industrial polices, and specialized institutions, many low-cost opportunities can be seized. Setting emission reduction targets and ambitious standards for low pollution and energy- and resource- efficient industries spurs private investments. Hence, robust institutional mechanisms are especially important to catalyze the transition to low-carbon green growth.

4 **Actions taken so far are remarkable, but implementation efforts must be strengthened and the low-carbon agenda needs to cover all sectors, not just energy.** The analysis in the book has shown that several countries have moved in this direction. For example, the PRC, India, and Indonesia have established a low-carbon agenda at provincial and state level. The current energy system, heavily dependent on fossil fuels, has received most policy attention, though other sectors such as transport, the built environment, manufacturing industry, agriculture, and forestry are showing great progress. Better land-use planning and efficient mass transit systems in megacities have reduced urban congestion, urban sprawl, and local air pollution.

5 **The window of opportunity for accelerated low-carbon actions on all fronts is narrowing.** Emerging Asia's numerically dominant young generations aspire to greater prosperity. Asia's requirement for massive infrastructure

investments implies the risk of a significant degree of high-carbon investment lock-in. These factors, combined with the likely impacts of global climate change, suggest strongly that Asia must act aggressively and swiftly, to decouple economic prosperity from high resource and carbon intensity, and seek inclusive growth for all its people. There is mounting evidence that economic growth and carbon emissions have already begun to decouple. The carbon intensity of the PRC has dropped 23% since 1990. Economic growth has also increased faster than carbon emissions in India since that time. Although the transition to low-carbon green growth is a long-term process, the coming years are crucial for emerging Asia to seize the opportunity, gain competitive advantages, and show global leadership. It could catch up with and even surpass other regions and countries like Japan, because of the advantage of being a latecomer. Emerging Asia can meet additional demands by building new low-carbon productive capacity and infrastructure without eliminating existing capital. Emerging Asia's present level of economic development is only one-tenth of the level of developed countries, measured in terms of per-capita energy use, car ownership, and other indicators such as ecological footprints. If the emerging economies of Asia do not seize the opportunity, their economies will lock into a high-emission structure, lose competitiveness, and face much higher costs for the low-carbon transition in the future.

6 **Asia's ambitious low-carbon agenda will only be achieved by harnessing the full range of available policy instruments.** This will require (i) internalizing external costs, such as the appropriate pricing of carbon sources—as a no-regret strategy to improve energy efficiency and raise considerable revenue; (ii) sectoral reforms, with a focus on pervasive subsidy removal from fossil fuels, and incentives for green industries; and (iii) inter-sectoral synergies to avoid excessive investment and lock-in effects. By relying too much on inflexible regulatory measures, resources for reducing carbon emissions have not been optimally allocated and compliance has been uneven. Although targets for reducing energy intensity and carbon intensity are the result of negotiated political processes, they are rigid. This also increases compliance costs. There are some short-term measures worth taking. First, convert the current intensity targets into total emission reduction targets, to create the conditions for introducing more flexible market mechanisms. Then, distribute emission caps in accordance with advanced industrial emission standards and other criteria. Finally, introduce flexible and diverse mechanisms such as emission trading, a carbon tax on fuels, and regional cooperation mechanisms. The above approach internalizes the externalities by putting a price on carbon. Unsustainable growth that is promoted by environmentally damaging subsidies in areas such as energy, transport, and agriculture, should be eliminated; external environmental and social costs should be internalized. Governance failure also happens because low-carbon development decisions are being made in sectoral compartments, with environmental, social, and economic dimensions addressed by separate, competing structures. Better communication and coordination from the design stage to implementation will unlock synergies.

7 **Economy-wide low-carbon innovation holds the key for developing Asia to decouple future economic growth from its resource and carbon intensity, and reinforces the inclusive growth agenda.** Incremental improvement is not enough

for Asia. Existing and breakthrough technologies must be innovatively applied to realize the full potential of low-carbon green growth. Asia needs to invest more in innovation now, if it is to be a low-carbon leader in the future. Education and training are as essential as R&D. Low-carbon innovations must support and reinforce the inclusive growth imperative. The analysis presented in this book points out that this can be achieved. Moving toward interdependent low-carbon green growth policies will bring higher costs to some sectors, isolated regions, and weaker groups. Policy reforms, technological or fiscal, should ensure compensation for the vulnerable. Fiscal transfers, sector-specific approaches, and job training should be part of the policy package.

8 **Regional cooperation will make it easier to pursue low-carbon green growth.** Regional actions cannot merely be seen as complementing national efforts and global initiatives. Asia's leaders have already reached a high level of consensus on the importance of tackling climate change and promotion of free trade. This can be done either through market-based mechanisms to encourage low-carbon trade and investment flows between countries, or through nonmarket mechanisms such as joint region-wide initiatives. The PRC and India have vast domestic markets that provide excellent conditions for the formation of green supply chains and new green industries. Effective cost reductions through economies of scale in some Asian countries would help others to overcome the cost barriers for large-scale deployment if free trade in low-carbon technology goods and services is realized. Countries will benefit from policies such as energy efficiency standards, labels, and certification for low-carbon goods only if non-tariff barriers in their trade regimes are removed. Scale, combined with high investment levels and the ability to implement decisions quickly based on the best available knowledge, means many opportunities can be exploited ahead of competitors. Stronger incentives and price signals are needed to unlock the potential for emissions reductions by industries and households. Given the advantage of its large market, ability to attract foreign investments, and abundant human capital, this region could quickly acquire, adapt, and master new technologies when regional level low-carbon innovation centers are established.

9 **Leveraging and catalyzing low-carbon financing, especially raising private capital, requires special policy attention.** Unifying the carbon markets and increasing the readiness of regional markets very much depends on establishing sectoral level GHG inventories; strengthened monitoring, reporting, and verification capabilities at the national level; and establishing technology hubs at the regional level. In view of the scale, complexity, and range of challenges, there is an increased role for regional institutions like ADB. Considerable international support is also required for developing Asia to reach a low-carbon trajectory. There are substantial domestic benefits to mitigation, but probably not enough to drive all the large, up-front investments that, in the global interest, are needed in developing Asia's energy infrastructure. Given the necessity of meeting short-term social priorities, such as raising living standards, governments in developing Asia cannot bridge the gap between costs and benefits alone. If it is in the interests of developed countries to see extensive climate change mitigation in emerging Asia, then it is in their interests to provide substantial assistance, financial or otherwise.

10 **Tackling the remaining challenges on the road towards low-carbon green growth calls for an institutionalized mechanisms at regional level.** With the rich diversity of country experiences comes the opportunity for continued sharing of and learning about policy insights and good practices. Now is the time for Asia to move beyond independent energy transition policies to interdependent regional low-carbon green-growth policies for the benefit of all. Although many national and subregional initiatives are in place and being contemplated, it is useful to summarize these, as shown in Table 6.4. Successful implementation needs effective knowledge-sharing programs covering good policy practices, to multiply the number of competent decision makers in government, business, and civil society.

This book analyzed policy contributions and recommended shifts in public policy choices that will be required to avoid dangerous climate change. Based on current trends, national policies and new measures need to be much more ambitious to provoke a major economic transition. Taking collective actions at regional level would be in the political interest of all governments for these reasons:

1 A more direct region-wide push on energy efficiency, technology, investment, and deforestation is essential to add credibility to the NAMA pledges and national targets without losing economic competiveness.
2 Given the scale of investment required and the recent deterioration of public finances in many countries, only coordinated policies and regional mechanisms could leverage private sector capital.
3 Since it will take time to agree on the details of a global climate deal, it is important to press ahead with concrete actions so that the strong regional force generated by collective action can provide the international community with an insurance policy.

Near-Term Recommendations for Asian Countries to Pursue Collectively

Developing Asia must be at the center of the global agenda on low-carbon green growth. Asia has much at stake in the fight against climate change as the region is the world's most populous, and has had high economic growth with a rising share of global GHG emissions, and certain subregions areas are among the most vulnerable to looming climate risks. Nowhere are production, resource consumption, and emissions growing faster than in developing Asia. High-priority actions have already been proven effective in some parts of Asia and could be scaled up at a regional level.

A decision to act together immediately on the 10 common key issues highlighted in box 6.1 would transform Asia into a test bed and role model for the world.

Table 6.4

Sector-Specific Policy Actions for Achieving Low-Carbon Green Growth in Emerging Asian Economies

	Near-term policies	Medium- to long-term targets
Energy	**Seek cost-effective, market-based solutions for the uptake of existing technologies** • Invest in reducing the cost of existing low-carbon energy-efficient technologies such as solar, wind, and bioenergy. • Continue to focus on lowering energy intensity and improving carbon productivity by changing the energy mix • Gradually remove energy sector (fuel) subsidies and introduce appropriate energy pricing through mechanisms such as feed-in tariffs (FITs) and renewable portfolio standards (RPS) • Progressively amend laws in order to scale up renewable energy in a competitive market dominated by fossil fuels	**Develop an efficient and competitive energy sector with innovative technologies** • Deploy new technologies such as carbon capture and storage (CCS) and geothermal, using sector-wide approaches • An energy mix in which renewable energy meets nearly one-third of primary energy demand • Emerging Asia becomes global showcase and leader in renewable energy, with more of the population having access to clean and green energy • Implement cap-and-trade systems for utilities sectors
Energy Efficiency	**Using a combination of regulations and market-based policy instruments to improve energy efficiency** • Launch top-runner programs for industrial technologies and electrical appliances • Expand carbon reduction labeling programs for high-impact sectors • Develop a focused and well-packaged regulatory system for small and medium-sized enterprises (SMEs) that integrates efficiency standards and targets by assisting with compliance mechanisms, including providing funds and matching grants with goals • Develop sectoral guidelines and training to achieve energy efficiency standards	**Deepen sector-wide reforms to achieve efficient use of energy derived from nonrenewable energy resources** • Two-thirds of the nation to meet and use the top runner standards • Strengthen the instruments of an integrated economic and environmental assessment program by drawing on international practices adjusted to the context of emerging Asia • Providing training and capacity building to SMEs on new business opportunities • Evaluate, expand, and strengthen bank guarantee system
Transport	**Develop new regulations, policies, and financing mechanisms to alter current fleet growth patterns** • Introduce new performance-based targets and incentive systems such as tax exemption for low-carbon vehicles for the transport sector • Progressively improve the fuel efficiency and pollution standards for passenger cars and light duty vehicles • Introduce retail sales of biofuels such as ethanol • Develop a consistent framework for integrating externalities such as local air pollution and use that to promote efficient and seamless multimodal transport systems	**Remove market distortions** • Provide subsidies to increase investments and reduce the production cost in manufacturing hybrid vehicles • The entire vehicle fleet must meet standards set at a regional level • Increase the number of retail service stations that sell hybrid fuels to 100% at a national capacity • Socioeconomic objectives achieved through connectivity, strategic development of transport corridors, and green transport options

Source: ADB–ADBI study team.

	Near-term policies	Medium- to long-term targets
Agriculture & Forestry	**Identify and implement the immediate actions needed to restore carbon sink** • Introduce new market-based incentives to restore degraded forests and provide rural job • Increase inspection capacity and higher penalties for illegal logging • Scale up pilot schemes for enhancing carbon sink such as carbon sequestration and reduction of water and fertilizer use • Extend awareness of market-based instruments to isolated communities and poor farmers	**Bring all major ecosystems under sound management to significantly reduce the cost of climate change mitigation** • Fully functioning REDD+ systems • Deforestation and land degradation is halted 100% • Ensuring sectoral mitigation opportunities are used to their full potential • Fully functioning carbon markets
City-level Measures	**Scale up coordinated policies for land use planning, urban finance, and city governance** • Change regulations and standards in building that lead to inefficient use of energy materials • Pilot market-based mechanisms such as carbon pricing and cap-and-trade to encourage the efficient use of public resources • Encourage and provide advice on low-carbon lifestyle choices and mentoring programs for neighborhoods • Remove barriers to mass transit networks, improving transport inter-modality of urban freight solutions, etc.	**Create carbon-efficient, and more habitable smart cities** • Low-carbon status achieved through improving overall resource use efficiency, benchmarked internationally • Fully functioning carbon markets in all megacities and municipalities • Integration of technologies and business models for local wealth creation • Roll out performance indicators for all regional governments
Industry & Trade	**Scale up and accelerate innovation** • Integrate low-carbon targets and objectives into central and local level state industrial policy • Link industrial promotion incentives and innovations to carbon performance • Reduce the tariff rate for low-carbon environmental goods and services and strengthen intellectual property regimes • Provide information and training on existing and emerging technologies, management practices, and related business opportunities	**Create competitive markets focused on high value added, low-carbon products and services** • Industrial competiveness reaches that of current advanced economies • Global economic growth is driven by innovations implemented in Asia • Asian economies employ world-class technologies and business practices in an open competitive market • Social capital for eco-restructuring of Asian industries
Fiscal	**Identify and implement immediate actions needed to introduce market-based instruments** • Pilot budgetary reforms with gradual increase in energy taxes and elimination of fuel subsidies • Introduce performance-based tax incentive systems for achieving sectoral emission targets • Explore innovative financing instruments and accelerate support for future industries • Improve efficiency, transparency, and accountability in the financial sector, by including rating programs and measurement, reporting, and verification systems linked to credit lines	**Revenue-neutral budgets for carbon-neutral economy** • Reduction in social security contributions and corporate income tax to compensate in part for raising more energy tax/carbon tax/quota auction receipts revenue • Budgetary reforms to mobilize private capital • Integration of capital, technology, goods, and labor markets • Main stream carbon taxes or auction emission quotas in a broad-based uniform cap-and-trade system

Box 6.1

Regional Level Actions for Accelerating Low-Carbon Green Growth in Asia

Regional Carbon Market

- Promote the linkage of national carbon trade schemes, which will require the setting up of a regional public–private policy dialogue and framework to prepare the ground for the linkage of carbon trade schemes including transparent agreements/rules (for instance, measurement, reporting, and verification systems) and institutional arrangement.
- Encourage investment in cross-border, low-carbon energy infrastructure and transport projects.

Regional Energy Partnership

- Promote a regional partnership on renewable energy, setting national renewable energy targets and favorable feed-in tariffs and renewable energy portfolio standards.
- Promote the partnership to work toward a set of applicable national efficiency standards developed and applied to a limited but critical range of energy-intensive industrial and consumer goods, and buildings. Governments may also develop energy efficiency labeling for electrical appliances, consumer products, and industrial manufacturing processes, building on work currently under way according to mutually agreed timetable.

Private Sector Participation

- Implement effective capacity development program at a regional or subregional level to help create an enabling policy and legal environment to attract private sector participation. International development institutions, national governments, and financial institutions should use risk-mitigating products (e.g., political risk guarantees, credit risk guarantees, etc.) to encourage private sector investment in low-carbon infrastructure development.
- Promote a regional public–private portfolio of several large-scale integrated smart city and smart grid demonstration projects across different regulatory regimes.

Technology Transfer

- Establish a network of regional low-carbon innovation centers modeled on the Consultative Group on International Agricultural Research, to help developing countries accelerate the uptake of low-carbon technology. Regional development institutions such as ADB may play leading role for promoting climate technology transfer and diffusion, helping countries learn from each other.
- Forge a free-trade agreement within Asia for high-impact green and low-carbon technologies and services.

Finance

- Encourage the phasing out of pervasive fossil fuel subsidies, using a regionally coordinated approach. This should be done as a prelude to introducing fiscal reforms that encompass a range of pricing and taxation instruments, including taxes on fossil fuels and other resources.
- Set up a regional platform to encourage REDD+ (reduced emissions from deforestation and degradation) projects. This platform should be hosted by key forest nations of the region and involve the international community, regional financial institutions, civil society, and the private sector.

Source: ADB–ADBI study team.

References and Bibliography

2050 Japan Low-Carbon Society Scenario Team. 2009. Japan Roadmaps towards Low-Carbon Societies (LCSs). Tokyo: National Institute for Environmental Studies and Mizuho Informational and Research Institute.

Aalst, M. van, and S. Agrawala. 2005. Analysis of Donor-Supported Activities and National Plans. In *Bridge Over Troubled Waters: Linking Climate Change and Development,* edited by S. Agrawala. Paris: Organisation for Economic Co-operation and Development (OECD).

Acemoglu, D. et al. 2009. The Environment and Directed Technical Change. National Bureau of Economic Research (NBER) Working Paper 15451. Cambridge, MA: NBER.

Adhikari, B., S. Di Falco, and J.C. Lovett. 2004. Household characteristics and forest dependency: evidence from common property forest management in Nepal. *Ecological Economics* 48(2): 245–257.

Agrawala, S. 2005. *Bridge Over Troubled Waters—Linking Climate Change and Development.* Paris: OECD.

Aldy, J.E., and R.N. Stavins. 2012. The Promise and Problems of Pricing Carbon: Theory and Experience. *The Journal of Environment & Development* 21(2): 152–180.

Anbumozhi, V. 2008. Responsible Business – Energy Efficiency Solutions. In Climate Change Policies in the Asia-Pacific: Reuniting Climate Changes and Sustainable Development. Institute for Global Environmental Strategies (IGES) white paper.

———. 2010. Financing Green Growth through Fiscal Policy Reforms. Asia-Pacific Economic Cooperation (APEC) Study on Green Finance. Draft final report (mimeo).

Anbumozhi, V., and A. Bauer. 2009. Impact of the Global Recession on Sustainable Development and Poverty Linkages. Paper presented at the 3rd China–Association of Southeast Asian Nations (ASEAN) Forum on Social Development and Poverty Reduction, 4th ASEAN+3 High-Level Seminar on Poverty Reduction, and Asia-wide Regional High-level Meeting on The Impact of the Global Economic Slowdown on Poverty and Sustainable Development in Asia and the Pacific.

Anbumozhi, V., and M. Kawai. 2009. Towards a Low Carbon Asia: Challenges of Economic Development. Paper presented at the OECD and Kyoto University conference on Measuring and Fostering Progress of Societies: Key Issues for the Asia and Pacific Countries. Kyoto. 23–24 March.

Andersen, M., and P. Ekins. 2009. *Carbon Energy Taxation: Lessons from Europe.* New York: Oxford University Press.

Arts, K. 2009. A Youth Perspective on Climate Change Opportunities and Challenges for Climate Change Resilient Development. New Challenges for Poverty Reduction. Cheltenham, United Kingdom (UK): Edward Elgar Publishing.

Ashina, S., and J. Fujino. 2012. Methodology for Designing Quantitative Roadmap towards Low Carbon Societies by Backcasting Approach. Tsukuba: National Institute for Environmental Studies.

Asia Business Council. 2009. Addressing Asia's New Green Jobs Challenges. Hong Kong, China: Asia Business Council.

Asian Development Bank (ADB). 2009a. *The Economics of Climate Change in Southeast Asia: A Regional Review.* Manila: ADB.

———. 2009b. *Improving Energy Security and Reducing Carbon Intensity in Asia and the Pacific.* Manila: ADB.

———. 2009c. Rethinking Transport and Climate Change. Manila: ADB.

———. 2011a. *Asian Development Outlook 2011: South–South Economic Links.* Manila: ADB.

———. 2011b. *Key Indicators for Asia and the Pacific 2011.* Manila: ADB.

———. 2012a. *Asian Development Outlook 2012.* Manila: ADB.

———. 2012b. Addressing Climate Change and Migration in Asia and the Pacific. Manila: ADB.

Asian Development Bank (ADB) and Department for International Development of the United Kingdom (DFID). 2006. Energy Efficiency and Climate Change Considerations for On-road Transport in Asia. Manila: ADB.

Asian Development Bank (ADB) and Institute for Global Environmental Strategies (IGES). 2008. Toward Resource-Efficient Economies in Asia and the Pacific: Reduce, Reuse and Recycle. Manila: ADB.

Asian Development Bank (ADB), United Nations Economic and Social Commission for Asia and the Pacific (ESCAP), and United Nations Environment Programme (UNEP). 2010. *Green Growth, Resources, and Resilience.* Bangkok: UNEP. http://www.unescap.org/esd/environment/flagpubs/GGRAP/ (accessed31 December, 2012).

Asian Development Bank Institute (ADBI). 2011. Kazakhstan's Green Growth Strategy – Astana "Green Bridge" Initiative. Inception Workshop for the ADB-ADBI study on Climate and Green Asia, Tokyo. 31 January–1 February.

Asian Productivity Organization. 2009. Greenhouse Gas Emissions: Estimation and Reduction. Tokyo.

Asuka, J. 2012. Regional Cooperation: Climate Regime. Background paper prepared for the ADB–ADBI Study for Climate Change and Green Asia.

Ayers, J.M., and S. Huq. 2008a. The value of linking adaptation and mitigation: a case study of Bangladesh. *Environmental Management* 43(5): 753–764.

———. 2008b. Supporting Adaptation to Climate Change: What role for Official Development Assistance? Paper presented at Development Studies Association (DSA) Annual Conference 2008: Development's Invisible Hands: Development Futures in a Changing Climate. London. 8 November.

Azis, I. 2001. Intergovernmental Transfers and Decentralisation in Indonesia, *Bulletin of Indonesian Economic Studies* 37(3): 345–362.

Babiker, M.H., and R.S. Eckaus. 2007. Unemployment effects of climate policy. *Environmental Science and Policy* 10: 600–609.

Banse, M., and H. Grethe. 2008. Effects of a Potential New Biofuel Directive on EU Land Use and Agricultural Markets. Paper presented at the 107th Seminar of the European Association of Agricultural Economists. Seville. 30 January–1 February.

Barbier, E. 2010a. *A Global Green New Deal: Rethinking the Economic Recovery.* Cambridge, UK: UNEP and Cambridge University Press.

———. 2010b. Green Stimulus, Green Recovery and Global Imbalances. *World Economics*. 11(2): 149–177.

Barker, T., and J. Köhler. 1998. Equity and ecotax reform in the EU: achieving a 10 per cent reduction in CO_2 emissions using excise duties. *Fiscal Studies* 19 (4): 375–402.

Basu, K. 2006. Globalization, Poverty, and Inequality: What is the Relationship? What can be Done? *World Development* 34(8): 1361–1373.

———. 2008. The Enigma of India's Arrival: A Review of Arvind Virmani's *Propelling India: From Socialist Stagnation to Global Power. Journal of Economic Literature* 46(2): 396–406.

Baruna, D. 2007. Greening the Business and Making Environment a Business Opportunity. Dhaka: Grameen Shakt.

Barton, J. 2007. Intellectual Property and Access to Clean Energy Technologies in Developing Countries: An Analysis of Solar Photovoltaic, Biofuel and Wind Technologies. Issue Paper 2. International Centre for Trade and Sustainable Development (ICTSD) Trade and Sustainable Energie Series Issue Paper 2. Geneva: ICTSD.

Bedi, R. 2008. Motorists rush to check out NGV system. *The Star Online.* 8 June.

Bergh, J., and F. Bruinsma. 2008. *Managing the Transition to Renewable Energy: Theory and Practice from Local, Regional and Macro Perspectives.* Cheltenham, UK: Edward Elgar Publishing.

Bernanke, B.S. 2011. Promoting Research and Development: The Government's Role. Speech at the New Building Blocks for Jobs and Economic Growth Conference. Washington, DC. 16 May.

Bollen, J., B. Guay, S. Jamet, and J. Morlot. 2009. Co-Benefits of Climate Change Mitigation Policies: Literature Review and New Results. OECD Economics Department Working Paper 693. Paris: OECD.

Bosetti, V., R. Gerlagh, and S. Schleicher. 2009. *Modelling Sustainable Development: Transitions to a Sustainable Future.* Cheltenham, UK: Edward Elgar Publishing.

Bosello, F., R. Roson, and R.S. Tol. 2006. Economy-wide estimates of the implications of climate change: Human health. *Ecological Economics* 58(3): 579–591.

Bowen, A., S. Fankhauser, N. Stern, and D. Zenghelis. 2009. An outline of the case for a 'green' stimulus. London: The Grantham Institute on Climate Change and the Environment.

Bowen, A., and N. Ranger. 2009. Mitigating climate change through reductions in greenhouse gas emissions: the science and economics of future path for global annual emissions. London: Grantham Research Institute on Climate Change and the Environment and the Centre for Climate Change Economics and Policy. http://www.cccep.ac.uk/Publications/Policy/Policy-docs/bowen-Ranger_MitigatingClimateChange_Dec09.pdf (accessed 31 December, 2012).

Bowen, A., and N. Stern. 2010. Environmental Policy and the Economic Downturn. *Oxford Review of Economic Policy* 26(2): 137–163.

Bowen, A., and R. Kattumuri. 2012. The Transition to Green Growth – Opportunities and Missed Chances. Background paper presented to the ADB–ADBI Study on Climate Change and Green Asia.

Bratasida, L. 2011. Low carbon green growth and development policies in Indonesia; REDD+ data based on the United Nations Framework Convention on Climate Change (UNFCCC) Bali Action Plan. http://unfccc.int/files/meetings/cop_13/application/pdf/cp_bali_action.pdf (accessed 31 December, 2012).

Brown, L., J. Larsen., J., Dorn, and F., Moore. 2008. Time for Plan B: Cutting Carbon Emissions 80% by 2020. Washington, DC: Earth Policy Institute.

BTM Consult. 2009. World Market Update 2009 (Forecast 2010–2014). Copenhagen.

Carbon Market Institute. 2012. Evolution of the Australian Carbon Market: Lessons from Commodity and Financial Markets. Melbourne: Carbon Market Institute.

Carbon Mitigation Initiative. 2011. http://www.cmi.princeton.edu. (accessed 31 December, 2012).

Casillas, C.E., and D.M. Kammen. 2012. Quantifying the social equity of carbon mitigation strategies, *Climate Policy* 12(6): 690–703.

Central Intelligence Agency (CIA). 2010. http://www.cia.gov/ (accessed 11 January 2013).

China Daily. 2011. Chinese leaders join in tree planting campaign. 2 April. (accessed 31 December, 2012).

Chotichanathawewong, Q., and T. Natapol. 2012. Development Trajectories, Emission Profile, and Policy Actions: Thailand. ADBI Working Paper 352. Tokyo: ADBI.

Choudhury, R. 2012. Engaging the Private Sector. Background paper prepared for the ADB–ADBI Study on Climate Change and Green Asia.

Climate Analysis Indicators Tool (CAIT) Version 9.0. 2012. Washington, DC: World Resources Institute.

Cline, W. 1992. The Economics of Global Warming. Washington, DC: Peterson Institute for International Economics.

Coady, D., M. El-Said, R. Gillingham, K. Kpodar, P, Medas, and D. Newhouse. 2006. The Magnitude and Distribution of Fuel Subsidies: Evidence from Bolivia, Ghana, Jordan, Mali, and Sri Lanka. International Monetary Fund (IMF) Working Paper 247. Washington, DC: IMF.

Coady, D., R. Gillingham, R. Ossowski, J. Pietrowski, S. Tareq, and J. Tyson. 2010. Petroleum Product Subsidies: Costly, Inequitable, and Rising. IMF Staff Position Note SPN/10/05. Washington, DC: IMF.

Coelli, T.J. 1996. A Guide to FRONTIER Version 4.1: A Computer Program for Stochastic Frontier Production and Cost Function Estimation. Centre for Efficiency and Productivity Analysis Working Paper 78/96. Department of Econometrics. Armidale: University of New England.

Collier, P. 2010. *The Plundered Planet: Why We Must—and How We Can—Manage Nature for Global Prosperity.* Oxford: Oxford University Press.

Conference of the Parties. 2009. Report of the Conference of the Parties on its fifteenth session. Part Two: Action taken by the Conference of the Parties at its fifteenth session. Copenhagen. 7–19 December. http://unfccc.int/resource/docs/2009/cop15/eng/11a01.pdf#page=4 (accessed 31 December, 2012).

———. 2010. Outcome of the work of the Ad Hoc Working Group on Long-term Cooperative Action under the Convention. Draft decision – /CP.16. Cancun. 11 December. http://unfccc.int/files/meetings/cop_16/application/pdf/cop16_lca.pdf (accessed 31 December, 2012).

Cosbey, A. 2010. Competitiveness Impacts of Climate Change on LDCs' Export Trade. Commonwealth. Trade Hot Topics Issue 79. London: Commonwealth Secretariat. http://www.thecommonwealth.org/files/232780/FileName/TradeHotTopics79FINAL.pdf (accessed 31 December, 2012).

Crafts, N. 2010. The contribution of new technology to economic growth: lessons from economic history. Centre for Competitive Advantage in the Global Economy Working Paper No. 1. Coventry: University of Warwick.

CSIRO Marine and Atmospheric Research. 2006. Climate Change in the Asia/Pacific Region. Aspendale: CSIRO Marine & Atmospheric Research.

Cui, S., and R. Kattumuri. 2010. Cultivated Land Conversion in China and the Potential for Food Security and Sustainability. London School of Economics and Political Science (LSE) Asia Research Centre Working Paper 35. London: LSE.

Dechezleprêtre, A., M. Glachant, I. Hašcic, N. Johnstone, and Y. Ménière. 2011. Invention and Transfer of Climate Change – Mitigation Technologies: *A Global Analysis. Review of Environmental Economics and Policy* 5(1): 109–130.

Dechezleprêtre, A., and R. Martin. 2010. Low carbon innovation in the UK: Evidence from patent data. Report for the UK Committee on Climate Change. London: Centre for Climate Change Economics and Policy and the Grantham Research Institute on Climate Change and the Environment.

Deng, Y., S. Cornelissen, S. Klaus, K. Blok, and C.J. van der Leun. 2011. *The Energy Report*, WWF International, Gland, Switzerland/Ecofys, Utrecht, The Netherlands, OMA, Rotterdam/The Netherlands.

Dervis, K., and A. Jones. 2009. Climate Change Policy: Recommendations to Reach Consensus. 2009 Brookings Bulm Roundtable "Climate Crisis, Credit Crisis." Washington, DC: Brookings Institution.

Dittrich, M., S. Giljum, S. Lutter, and C. Polzin. 2010. Green economies around the world: Implications of resource use for development and the environment. Vienna: Sustainable Europe Research Institute.

Doshi, T. 2012. Development Trajectories, Emission Profile and Policy Actions: Singapore. Background paper prepared for the ADB–ADBI Study on Climate Change and Green Asia.

Drysdale, P. 2005. Regional Cooperation in East Asia and FTA Strategies. Pacific Economic Papers 344. Canberra: Australia-Japan Research Centre and Asia Pacific School of Economics and Government.

Duflo, E., and A. Banerjee. 2003. Inequality and Growth: What Can the Data Say? *Journal of Economic Growth* 8(3): 267–299.

Duflo, E., M. Greenstone, and R. Hanna. 2008. Cooking Stoves, Indoor Air Pollution and Respiratory Health in Rural Orissa. *Economic & Political Weekly* 43(32): 71–76.

Duscha, V. et al. 2010. Post-2012 climate regime: How industrial and developing nations can help to reduce emissions – assessing emission trends, reduction potentials, incentive systems and negotiation options. The German Federal Environment Agency. http://www.umweltbundesamt.de/uba-info-medien/mysql_medien.php?anfrage=Kennummer&Suchwort=3954 (accessed 31 December, 2012).

Eco Canada. 2010. Canadian Environmental Sector Trends: Labour Market Research Study. Calgary: Eco Canada.

Edenhofer, O., N. Bauer, and E. Kriegler. 2005. The impact of technological change on climate protection and welfare: Insights from the model MIND. *Ecological Economics* 54(2): 277–292.

Enkvist, P., T. Nauclér, and J. Rosander. 2007. A cost curve for greenhouse gas reduction. *The McKinsey Quarterly* 1: 35–45.

Environmental Systems Research Institute (ESRI). 2009. Masdar City: The World's First Carbon-Neutral City: Masdar City. Aylesbury: ESRI (UK).

Escobar, J., E. Lora, O. Venturini, E. Yáñez, E. Castillo, and O. Almazan. 2009. Biofuels: Environment, technology and food security. *Renewable and Sustainable Energy Reviews* 13(6–7): 1275–1287.

European Commission. 2007. Facts and Figures: Links Between EU's Economy and Environment. Luxembourg: Office for Official Publications of the European Communities.

———. 2008. Directive 2009/28/EC of the European Parliament and the Council on the Promotion of the Use of Energy from Renewable Sources and Amending and Subsequently Repealing Directives 2001/77/EC and 2003/30/EC. Luxembourg: *Official Journal of the European Union.*

Fan, Y. 2011. ASEAN, the PRC and India: the Great Transformation?. Background paper prepared for the ADBI/ADI Study on Energy Security Outlook for a Green and Sustainable Asia.

Faure, M., and M. Peeters. 2008. *Climate Change and European Emissions Trading: Lessons for Theory and Practice.* Cheltenham, UK: Edward Elgar Publishing.

Federation of Indian Chambers of Commerce and Industry (FICCI). 2011. Low Carbon Green Growth in Asian Emerging Markets. New Delhi: FICCI.

Flipo, F., and F. Schneider. 2008. Proceedings of the First International Conference on Economic De-Growth for Ecological Sustainability and Social Equity. Paris. 18–19 April.

Food and Agriculture Organization (FAO). 2008. The State of Food and Agriculture 2008 – BIOFUELS: prospects, risks and opportunities. Rome: FAO.

———. 2009. How to Mainstream Climate Change Adaptation and Mitigation into Agriculture Policies. Rome: FAO.

———. 2010. Information systems for monitoring, assessment and reporting on forest resources – a case study in Cambodia and Lao PDR. http://www.fao.org/forestry/22673-0255399057f5a47a799a6280d7a47a581.pdf (accessed 31 December, 2012).

———. 2012. Asia-Pacific Forests and Forestry to 2020: Forests for a greener future. Forest Policy Brief 01. Rome: FAO.

Forest Carbon Asia. 2012. Forest Carbon Projects. http://www.forestcarbonasia.org/activities/forest-carbon-projects/ (accessed 31 December, 2012).

Forest Climate Centre. 2010. Forest Sector Plans. http://forestclimatecentre.org/guidance.php (accessed 31 December, 2012).

Foxon, T., and P. Pearson. 2008. Overcoming barriers to innovation and diffusion of cleaner technologies: some features of a sustainable innovation policy regime. *Journal of Cleaner Production* 16(1): S148–S161.

Frankel, J. 2009. An Elaborated Global Climate Policy Architecture: Specific Formulas and Emission Targets for All Countries in All Decades. NBER Working Paper 14876. Cambridge, MA: NBER.

Friel, S., A.D. Dangour, T. Garnett, K. Lock, Z. Chalabi, I. Roberts, A. Butler, C.D. Butler, J. Waage, A.J. McMichael, A. Haines. 2009. Public health benefits of strategies to reduce greenhouse-gas emissions: food and agriculture. *The Lancet* 374(9706): 2016–2025.

Fujino, J., T. Ehara, Y. Matsuoka, T. Masui, and M. Kainuma. 2008. Backcasting analysis for 70% emission reduction in Japan by 2050. *Climate Policy* 8 (Supplement): 108–124.

Fullerton, D., G. Heutel, and G.E. Metcalf. 2011. Does the Indexing of Government Transfers Make Carbon Pricing Progressive? *American Journal of Agricultural Economics* 94(2): 347–353.

Gagnon-Lebrun, F., and S. Agrawala. 2006. Progress on adaption to climate change in developing countries: an analysis of broad trends. Paris: OECD.

Garnaut, R. 2011a. Garnaut Climate Change Review Update 2011: Progress towards effective global action on climate change. Canberra: Commonwealth of Australia.

———. 2011b. The Garnaut Review 2011: Australia in the Global Response to Climate Change. New York: Cambridge University Press.

Geng, Y., J. Fu, J. Sarkis, and B. Xue. 2011. Towards a national circular economy indicator system in China: an evaluation and critical analysis. *Journal of Cleaner Production* 23 (1): 216–224.

German Institute for Economic Research (DIW Berlin). 2009. Global Demand for Environmental Goods and Services on the Rise: Good Growth Opportunities for German Suppliers. *Weekly Report* 20(5). Berlin: DIW Berlin.

Ghosh, J. 2010. Poverty Reduction in China and India: Policy implications of recent trends. United Nations (UN) Department of Economic and Social Affairs (DESA) Working Paper 92. New York: DESA.

Giljum, S., S. Lutter, C. Polzin, M. Dittrich, and S. Bringezu. 2010. Resource use and resource efficiency in Asia – Trends over the past 25 years. SERI Working Paper 11. Vienna: Sustainable Europe Research Institute. http://seri.at/wp-content/uploads/2010/05/SERI-Working-Paper-11.pdf (accessed 31 December, 2012).

Gill, I., and H. Kharas. 2007. An East Asian Renaissance: Ideas for Economic Growth. Washington, DC: World Bank.

Global Access Partners. 2009. Low Carbon Economy: Business Opportunities for Australia. Chippendale, New South Wales: Low Carbon Economy Task Force.

Global Carbon Network. 2009. Low-Carbon Jobs in an Inter-Connected World. Washington, DC: Center for American Progress and Global Climate Network.

Global Green Growth Institute. 2011. Green Growth in Motion: Sharing Korea's Experience. Seoul: Global Green Growth Institute.

Goettle, R.J., and A.A. Fawcett. 2009. The structural effects of cap and trade climate policy. *Energy Economics* 31(2): S244–S253.

Goklany, I.M. 2007. Integrated strategies to reduce vulnerability and advance adaptation, mitigation, and sustainable development. *Mitigation and Adaptation Strategies for Global Change* 12(5): 755–786.

Golub, S.S., C. Kaufmann, and P. Yeres. 2011. Defining and Measuring Green FDI: An Exploratory Review of Existing Work and Evidence. OECD Working Papers on International Investment 2011/2. Paris: OECD Investment Division.

Government of Abu Dhabi. 2009. *The Abu Dhabi Economic Vision 2030*. Abu Dhabi.

Government of Australia, Department of Climate Change and Energy Efficiency. 2012. Reducing emissions from deforestation and forest degradation in developing countries. Canberra. http://www.climatechange.gov.au/government/international/redd.aspx. (accessed 31 December, 2012).

Government of Cambodia, Ministry of Environment and UNESCAP. 2009. The National Green Growth Road Map. Phnom Penh.

Government of India (GOI). (Page 1) http://www.mnre.gov.in/file-manager/UserFiles/mission_document_JNNSM.pdf. (accessed 4 January, 2012).

Government of India, Ministry of Rural Development. 2008. Poverty Eradication in India by 2015: Rural Household Centered Strategy Paper. New Delhi.

Government of India, Planning Commission. 2008. Eleventh Five Year Plan, Planning Commission. New Delhi.

———. 2011a. Low Carbon Strategies for Inclusive Growth: An Interim Report. New Delhi: Government of India.

———. 2011b. Faster, Sustainable and More Inclusive Growth: An Approach to the Twelfth Five Year Plan. New Delhi.

———. 2011c. Interim Report of the Expert Group on Low Carbon Strategies for Inclusive Growth. New Delhi.

Government of Indonesia, Ministry of Environment. 2010. Indonesia Second National Communication under the United Nations Framework Convention on Climate Change. Jakarta.

Government of Indonesia, Ministry of Finance. 2009. Ministry of Finance Green Paper: Economic and Fiscal Policy Strategies for Climate Change Mitigation in Indonesia. Jakarta: Ministry of Finance and Australia Indonesia Partnership.

Government of Japan, Ministry of Foreign Affairs. 2009. Japan-U.S. Joint Message on Climate Change Negotiations. http://www.mofa.go.jp/region/n-america/us/pv0911/climate.pdf (accessed 31 December, 2012).

Government of Japan, Ministry of the Environment. 2007. Building a Low Carbon Society. Presentation by the Office of Market Mechanism, Climate Change Policy Division, Ministry of the Environment. Tokyo.

———. 2011. Japan's Initiative Toward Establishment of New Mechanisms – Lessons Learnt from Case Studies 2010. Tokyo.

———. 2012. Annual Report on the Environment: the Sound Material-Cycle Society, and the Biodiversity in Japan 2011. Tokyo.

Government of Kazakhstan. Concept of the Partnership Prgramme Framework on Implementation of the Astana Green Bridge.

Government of New Zealand. 2009. Summary of the Proposed Changes to NZ ETS. Emissions trading bulletin 11. Wellington.

Government of Norway. 2008. Towards Greener Development: on a coherent environmental and development policy. White Paper. Ministry of Foreign Affairs.

Government of Pakistan. 2011. Pakistan Economic Survey 2010–11. Economic Advisor's Wing. Finance Division. Islamabad.

Government of Singapore, National Environment Agency. 2010. Singapore's Second National Communication under the United Nations Framework Convention on Climate Change. Singapore.

Government of Thailand, Ministry of Energy. 2011. Thailand 20-Year Energy Efficiency Development Plan (2011–2030). Bangkok.

Government of Viet Nam, Ministry of Natural Resources and Environment. 2010. Viet Nam's Second National Communication to the United Nations Framework Convention on Climate Change. Hanoi.

Griliches, Z. 1992. The Search for R&D Spillovers. NBER Working Paper No. 3768. Cambridge, MA: NBER.

Guardian, The. 2009. China's loggers down chainsaws in attempt to regrow forests. 11 March.

Guttikunda, S.K. 2010. Estimated Air Pollution and Health Benefits of Metro System in Delhi. SIM-air Working Paper 32. New Delhi: www.urbanemissons.info (accessed 31 December, 2012).

Harvey, F. 2011. Budget 2011: Osborne's green bank attacked from all sides. The Guardian. 23 March. http://www.guardian.co.uk/environment/2011/mar/23/budget-2011-george-osborne-green-bank (accessed 31 December, 2012).

Hashimoto, T. 2012. Cities and Local Carbon Green Growth Strategies. Background paper prepared for the ADB–ADBI Study for Climate Change and Green Asia.

Henry, C., and J. Stiglitz. 2010. Intellectual Property, Dissemination of Innovation and Sustainable Development. *Global Policy* 1(3): 237–251.

Herberg, M. 2011. Natural Gas in Asia: History and Prospects. Paper presented at the 2011 Pacific Energy Summit. Jakarta. 21–23 February.

Herold, A. et al. 2011. Review of Decision No 280/2004/EC (Monitoring Mechanism Decision) in view of the agreed Climate Change and Energy package. Berlin: Directorate General for Climate Action (DG CLIMA).

Hirano, T. et al. 2007. Carbon dioxide balance of a tropical peat swamp forest in Kalimantan, Indonesia. *Global Change Biology* 13 (2): 412–425.

Hongo, T. 2010. Green Finance for Green Growth. Paper presented at the Green Finance Experts Panel. Seoul.

———. 2012. Private Capital and Carbon Markets. Background paper prepared for the ADB–ADBI Study on Climate Change and Green Asia.

Hooijer, A. et al. 2010. Current and future CO_2 emissions from drained peatlands in Southeast Asia. *Biogeosciences* 7: 1505–1514.

Howes, S. and L. Dobes. 2012. Climate Change and Fiscal Policy: A Report for APEC. World Bank: Office of the Chief Economist, East Asia and Pacific Region.

Howes, S., and P. Wyrwoll. 2012. Climate Change Mitigation and Green Growth in Developing Asia. ADBI Working Paper 369. Tokyo: ADBI.

HSBC. 2010. HSBC Climate Partnership Review 2010. http://www.hsbc.com/1/PA_esf-ca-app-content/content/assets/sustainability/110208_hcp_review_en.pdf (accessed 31 December, 2012).

ICLEI World Secretariat. 2010. Green Urban Economy. ICLEI Briefing sheet. United Nations Development Programme–UNEP.

Institute for Global Environmental Strategies (IGES). 2004 Urban Energy Use and Greenhouse Gas Emissions in Asian Mega-Cities: Policies for Sustainable Future. Tokyo: IGES.

———. 2009. Stakeholder Dialogue on Low Carbon Societies – LCS-RNet – International Research Network for Low Carbon Societies. Report based on the International Forum for Sustainable Asia and the Pacific Expert workshop and opening session. Hayama, Japan. 26–27 June.

———. 2011. Negotiating a Low Carbon Transition Asia: NAMAs and MRV. Kanagawa: IGES.

———. 2012. Greening Governance in Asia-Pacific. IGES White Paper IV 2012. Kanagawa: IGES.

Institute for Integrated Economic Research. 2011. Low Carbon and Economic Growth – Key Challenges. Meilen: Institute for Integrated Economic Research.

Institute of Energy Economics, Japan. 2011. Hand Book of Energy and Economic Statistics in Japan.

Intergovernmental Panel on Climate Change (IPCC). 1990. The IPCC First Assessment. Geneva: World Meteorological Organization and UNEP.

———. 1995. IPCC Second Assessment. Climate Change 1995. Geneva: World Meteorological Organization and UNEP.

———. 2000a. *IPCC Special Report: Emissions Scenarios.* Cambridge, UK: Cambridge University Press.

———. 2000b. *IPCC Special Report: Methodological and Technological Issues in Technology Transfer.* Cambridge, UK: Cambridge University Press.

———. 2007a. Climate Change 2007: Impacts, Adaptation and Vulnerability – Contribution of Working Group II to the Fourth Assessment Report of the Intergovernmental Panel on Climate Change. Geneva: IPCC.

———. 2007b. Climate Change 2007: Mitigation of Climate Change – Contribution of Working Group III to the Fourth Assessment Report of the Intergovernmental Panel on Climate Change. Geneva: IPCC.

———. 2007c. Climate Change 2007: *Mitigation of Climate Change.* Working Group III Contribution to the Fourth Assessment Report of the Intergovernmental Panel on Climate Change. UK: Cambridge University Press.

———. 2007d. Climate Change 2007: Synthesis Report – Contribution of Working Groups I, II and III to the Fourth Assessment Report of the Intergovernmental Panel on Climate Change. Geneva: IPCC.

———. 2007e. Climate Change 2007: Synthesis Report – Contribution of Working Groups I, II and III to the Fourth Assessment Report of the Intergovernmental Panel on Climate Change. Geneva: IPCC.

———. 2011. Renewable Energy Sources and Climate Change Mitigation. Geneva: IPCC.

International Energy Agency (IEA). 2006. *World Energy Outlook.* Paris: OECD Publishing.

———. 2009. *World Energy Outlook 2010.* Paris: IEA.

———. 2010a. *Key World Energy Statistics 2010.* Paris: IEA.

———. 2010b. Global Gaps in Clean Energy RD&D: Update and Recommendations for International Collaboration. IEA Report for the Clean Energy Ministerial. Paris: IEA.

———. 2010c. *World Energy Outlook*. Paris: OECD Publishing.

———. 2011a. *World Energy Outlook 2011.* Paris: OECD and IEA.

———. 2011b. *Key World Energy Statistics 2011.* Paris: IEA.

———. 2012a. *Renewables Information 2012.* Paris: OECD Publishing.

———. 2012b. *World Energy Outlook 2012*. Paris: OECD Publishing.

International Energy Agency (IEA), Organization of the Petroleum Exporting Countries (OPEC), OECD, World Bank. 2010. Analysis of the Scope of Energy Subsidies and Suggestions for the G-20 Initiative. Paper submitted to the G-20 Summit Meeting. Toronto, Canada. 26–27 June.

International Labour Organization (ILO). 2009. *World of Work Report: The Global Jobs Crisis and Beyond.* Geneva: ILO.

———. 2011. Global Employment Trends 2011: The challenge of a jobs recovery. Geneva: ILO.

International Labour Organization (ILO) and European Centre for the Development of Vocational Training (CEDEFOP). 2011. Skills for Green Jobs: A Global View. Geneva: ILO.

Jackson, T. 2009. *Prosperity without Growth? The transition to a sustainable economy.* London: Sustainable Development Commission.

Jaffe, A.B. 1986. Technological Opportunity and Spillovers of R&D: Evidence from Firms' Patents, Profits, and Market Value. NBER Working Paper 1815. Cambridge, MA: NBER.

Jaffe, A.B., R.G. Newell, and R.N. Stavins. 2003. Technological Change and the Environment. *Handbook of Environmental Economics* 1: 461–516.

———. 2005. A tale of two market failures: Technology and environmental policy. *Ecological Economics* 54(2–3): 164–174.

Jairaj, B. 2010. A Disclosure-based Approach to Climate Change in India? Early Lessons from Business Regulation. Centre for Policy Research Climate Initiative Working Paper 2010/2. New Delhi: Centre for Policy Research.

Japan Bank for International Cooperation. 2012. Guidelines for Measurement, Reporting and Verification of GHG Emission Reductions in JBIC GREEN Operation. Tokyo: JBIC. http://www.jbic.go.jp/en/about/environment/j-mrv/pdf/jmrv-guideline-en.pdf (accessed 31 December, 2012).

Jha, V. 2009. Climate Change, Trade and Production of Energy Supply Goods: the need for leveraging the playing field. Presentations at OECD Seminar on Trade and Environment. May 10, 2008. Paris.

Jiang, K. 2011. Potential Secure, Low Carbon Growth Pathways for the Chinese Economy. Working paper. Washington, DC: Center for Strategic and International Studies.

Johnstone, N. 2007. *Environmental Policy and Corporate Behaviour.* Cheltenham, UK: Edward Elgar Publishing.

Jones, R.S., and B. Yoo. 2011. Korea's Green Growth Strategy: Mitigating Climate Change and Developing New Growth Engines. OECD Economics Department Working Paper 54. Paris: OECD Publishing.

Jotzo, F. 2010. Comparing the Copenhagen Emissions Targets. Crawford School Centre for Climate Economics and Policy Paper 1.10. Canberra: Australian National University.

Jupesta, J., R. Boer, G. Parayil, Y. Harayama, M. Yarime, Jose O. Puppim, Suneetha M. Subramanian. 2011. Managing the Transition to Sustainability in an Emerging Economy: Evaluating Green Growth Policies in Indonesia. *Environmental Innovation and Societal Transition* 1 (2): 187–191.

Kainuma, M. and S. Ashina. 2012. Development Trajectories, Emission Profile, and Policy Actions: Japan. Background paper prepared for the ADB–ADBI Study for Climate Change and Green Asia.

Kalirajan, K. 2007. Regional Cooperation and Bilateral Trade Flows: An Empirical Measurement of Resistance. *The International Trade Journal* 21(2): 85–107.

———. 2012. Regional Cooperation towards Green Asia: Trade and Investment. ADBI Working Paper 350. Tokyo: ADBI.

Kalirajan, K., V. Anbumozhi, and K. Singh. 2010. Measuring the Environmental Impacts of Changing Trade Patterns on the Poor. ADBI Working Paper 239. Tokyo: ADBI.

Kalirajan, K., K. Singh, S. Thangavelu, V. Anbumozhi, and K. Perera. 2011. Climate Change and Poverty Reduction: Where Does Official Development Assistance Go? ADBI Working Paper 318. Tokyo: ADBI.

Kameyama, Y., A. Sari, M. Soejachmoen, and N. Kanie. 2008. *Climate Change in Asia: Perspectives on the Future Climate Regime.* Tokyo: United Nations University Press. http://unu.edu/publications/books/climate-change-in-asia-perspectives-on-the-future-climate-regime.html#overview (accessed 31 December, 2012).

Kammen, D.M., K. Kapadia, and M. Fripp. 2004: Putting renewables to work: how many jobs can the clean energy industry generate? Report of the Renewable and Appropriate Energy Laboratory. Berkeley: University of California.

Kang, S. 2012. Development Trajectories, Emission Profile, and Policy Actions: Republic of Korea. Background paper prepared for the ADB–ADBI Study for Climate Change and Green Asia.

Kang, S.J., and S.I. Kang, eds. 2011. Green Growth: Global Cooperation. Green Forum 2010 Volume 2. Seoul: National Research Council for Economics, Humanities and Social Sciences and Random House Korea.

Kawai, M. 2008. Japan–China Cooperation for Achieving Carbon Neutral Society. Tokyo: Economists for Peace and Security.

Kawai, M., and G. Wignaraja. 2011. Asian FTAs: Trends, Prospects and Challenges. *Journal of Asian Economics* 22(1):1–23.

Kawai, M., and J. Lee. 2010. Rebalancing for Sustainable Growth: Asia's Postcrisis Challenge. Highlights of a joint study of the Asian Development Bank and the Asian Development Bank Institute. Tokyo. 26 April.

Kawase, R., and Y. Matsuoka. 2012. 2 Degree Targets towards Asian Low Carbon Society and their Feasibility. Kyoto: Global Environmental Research.

Kaya, Y., and K. Yokobori. 1993. *Environment, Energy, and Economy: Strategies for Sustainability.* Tokyo: United Nations University Press.

Kemfert, C., and H. Welsch. 2000. Energy-Capital-Labor Substitution and the Economic Effects of CO_2 Abatement: Evidence for Germany. *Journal of Policy Modeling* 22(6): 641–660.

Kim, C. 2008. The Impacts of Climate Change on the Agricultural Sector: Implications of the Agro-Industry for Low Carbon, Green Growth Strategy and Roadmap for the East Asian Region. Background policy paper for the Low Carbon Green Growth Roadmap for Asia and the Pacific. http://www.unescap.org/esd/environment/lcgg/documents/roadmap/Policy-Papers/The-Impact-of-Climate-Change-on-the-Agricultural-Sector.pdf (accessed 31 December, 2012).

Kim, J. 2012. Public role in financing a low-carbon economy in Asia. Background paper prepared for the ADB–ADBI Study for Climate Change and Green Asia.

Kohli, H., A. Sharma, and A. Sood. 2011. *Asia 2050: Realizing the Asian Century.* Manila: ADB.

Krewitt et al. 2010. Energy [r] evolution – A sustainable world energy outlook, 3rd edition, Greenpeace. http://www.greenpeace.org/international/Global/international/publications/climate/2010/fullreport.pdf

Kumar, S. 2012. Co-benefit Technologies, Green Jobs, and National Innovation Systems. Background paper prepared for the ADB-ADBI Study for Climate Change and Green Asia.

Kumar, S., N. Goteti, and P. Savargaonkar. 2012. Indicators for Low Carbon Green Growth in the Asia-Pacific. Background paper prepared for the ADB-ADBI Study for Climate Change and Green Asia.

Kuroda, H., M. Kawai, and R. Nangia. 2007. Infrastructure and Regional Cooperation. ADBI Discussion Paper 76. Tokyo: ADBI.

Lanjouw, J.O., and A. Mody. 1996. Innovation and the international diffusion of environmentally responsive technology. *Research Policy* 25(4): 549–571.

Lee, B., I. Iliev, and P. Felix. 2009. Who Owns Our Low Carbon Future? Intellectual Property and Energy Technologies. London: Royal Institute for International Affairs, Chatham House.

Lieuw-Kie-Song, M., and R. Lal. 2010. Green Jobs for the Poor: Why a Public Employment Approach is Needed Now. Brasilia: UNDP – International Policy Centre for Inclusive Growth.

Linn, H. 2010. Rangoon's Road Worriers. *The Irrawady* 18(8): 1–2.

Lobell, D.B., M.B. Burke, C. Tebaldi, M.D. Mastrandrea, W.P. Falcon, and R.L. Naylor. 2008. Prioritizing Climate Change Adaption Needs for Food Security in 2030. *Science* 319(5863): 607–610.

Lockhart, R. 2011. Low-carbon technology and finance. Paper prepared for the ADBI Climate Change and Green Asia Workshop. Tokyo. 28 February –1 March.

Lohani, B. 2008. Energy and Climate Change: What Should the Policy Makers in Asia Do? Asia Policy Briefs, Maxwell School of Syracuse University.

Loulou, R., M. Labriet, and A. Kanudia. 2009. Deterministic and stochastic analysis of alternative climate targets under differentiated cooperation regimes. *Energy Economics* 31: S131–S143.

MacDonald, M. 2010. Developing countries, monitoring and reporting on greenhouse gas emissions, policies and measures – Country report Indonesia. Arnhem: Euroconsult Mott MacDonald.

Managi, S., and S. Kaneko. 2009. *Chinese Economic Development and the Environment.* Cheltenham, UK: Edward Elgar Publishing.

Masika, R., ed. 2002. *Gender, Development, and Climate Change: Focus on Gender.* Oxford: Oxfam.

Masripatin, N. 2010. Progress of REDD+ Readiness in Indonesia. C3S-WHRC Workshop. Samarinda. 8 November. http://www.whrc.org/education/indonesia/pdf/Indonesia_Nur_Masripatin.pdf (accessed 31 December, 2012).

Mathur, R. 2012. Development Trajectories, Emission Profile, and Policy Actions: India. Background paper prepared for the ADB–ADBI Study for Climate Change and Green Asia.

Matrinot, E., and L. Junfeng. 2007. Powering China's Development: The Role of Renewable Energy. Washington, DC: Worldwatch Institute.

Matsuoka, Y., J. Fujino, and M. Kainuma. 2008. National Implications of a 50% Global Reduction of Greenhouse Gases, and its Feasibility in Japan. *Sustain Sci.* 3:135–143.

Matsuoka, Y., M. Kainuma, J. Fujino, and T. Ehara. 2012. How to Approach Asian Low Carbon Societies. Tsukuba: National Institute for Environmental Studies.

Matta, J.R. 2009. Rebuilding rural India: potential for further investments in forestry and green jobs. *Unasylva* 60(233): 36–41.

Ma, Q., J. Liu, and W. Du. 2009. How Chinese Forestry is coping with the challenges of global economic downturn. *Unasylva* 60(233): 43–48.

McKibbin, W., A. Morris, and P. Wilcoxen. 2011. Comparing Climate Commitments: A Model-Based Analysis of the Copenhagen Accord. *Climate Change Economics* 2(2): 79–103.

McMichael, A., J. Powles, C. Butler, and R. Uauy. 2007. Food, livestock production, energy, climate change, and health. *The Lancet* 370 (9594): 1253–1263.

Mikic, M. 2010. Trade in Climate Smart Goods: Trends and Opportunities in Asia and the Pacific. Paper presented at the United Nations Economic and Social Commission for Asia and the Pacific (ESCAP) Regional Symposium on Low Carbon Economy. Bali.13–14 October.

Ministry of Energy. 2009. 15-Year Renewable Energy Development Plan. http://www.dede.go.th/dede/fileadmin/upload/nov50/mar52/REDP_present.pdf (access on 9 June 2011).

Ministry of Environment. 2012. Annual Report on the Environment, the Sound Material-Cycle Society, and the Biodiversity in Japan.

Ministry of Strategy and Finance, Republic of Korea. 2009. Office of Management and Budget, Cost Estimates.

Mohanty, B. 2012. Lifestyle Choices and Societal Behavior Changes as Local Climate Strategy ADBI Working Paper 398. Tokyo: ADBI

Morse, R., and G. He. 2010. The World's Greatest Coal Arbitrage: China's Coal Import Behavior and Implications for the Global Coal Market. Program on Energy and Sustainable Development Working Paper 94. Palo Alto: Stanford University.

Msangi, S., T. Sulser, M. Rosegrant, and R. Valmonte-Santos. 2007. Global Scenarios for Biofuels: Impacts And Implications For Food Security And Water Use. Paper presented at the 10th Annual Conference on Global Economic Analysis. Indiana: Purdue University.

Murphy, D., C. De Vit, J. Drexhage, and J. Nolet. 2009. Expanding Agriculture's Role in a Post 2012 Climate Change Regime. Winnipeg: International Institute for Sustainable Development.

Murshed, M. 2009. Humans are the measure of all things: Resource conflicts versus cooperation. In *Climate Change and Sustainable Development: New Challenges for Poverty Reduction,* edited by M. Salih. Cheltenham, UK: Edward Elgar.

Nair, C.T.S., and R. Rutt. 2009. Creating forestry jobs to boost the economy and build a green future. *Unasylva* 60(233): 3–10.

Nakada, H. 2008. Yokohoma, an environmentally friendly city. Our World 2.0. Tokyo: United Nations University. http://ourworld.unu.edu/en/yokohama-an-environmentally-friendly-city/ (accessed 31 December, 2012)

National Development and Reform Commission. 2007. China's National Climate Change Programme. Beijing.

———. 2011. People's Republic of China's 12th Five Year Plan (2011–2015). English translation by the Delegation of the European Union in People's Republic of China.

National Energy Technology Laboratory. 2009. Affordable, Low-Carbon Diesel Fuel from Domestic Coal and Biomass. DOE/NETL-2009/1349. Washington, DC: United States Department of Energy.

National Sample Survey Organisation. 2008. Household Consumer Expenditure in India, 2007–08. NSS 64th Round. National Sample Survey Organisation. New Delhi.

Ninomiya, Y. 2011. New Market Mechanisms in a post-2012 regime: what are the issues and possible structure? Presented at Panama Climate Conference.

Nippon Keidanren. 2010. Achieving Growth through Green Innovation – Proposals for Japan's New Growth Strategy and Other Initiatives in the Environmental Sector. Tokyo: Nippon Keidanren. http://www.keidanren.or.jp/english/policy/2010/019.html (accessed 31 December, 2012).

Ocampo, J. 2005. The Quest for Dynamic Efficiency: Structural Dynamics and Economic Growth in Developing Countries. In *Beyond Reform: Structural Dynamics & Macroeconomic Vulnerability,* edited by J. Ocampo. Palo Alto and Washington, DC: Stanford University Press and the World Bank.

Ockwell, D.G., J. Watson, G. MacKerron, P. Pal, and F. Yamin. 2008. Key Policy Considerations for Facilitating Low Carbon Technology Transfer to Developing Countries. *Energy Policy* 36(11): 4104–4115.

Oppenheim, J., and E. Beinhocker. 2009. Climate Change and the Economy: Myths versus Realities. McKinsey & Company.

Organisation for Economic Co-operation and Development (OECD). 2005. Environmental Fiscal Policy Reform for Poverty Reduction. Development Assistance Committee (DAC) Reference Document. Paris: OECD.

———. 2009a. Financing Climate Change Action, Supporting Technology Transfer and Development: Key messages and recommendations from recent OECD work. Paris: OECD.

———. 2009b. Main Science and Technology Indicators. http://www.oecd.org/sti/msti (accessed 31 December, 2012).

———. 2009c. *Natural Resources and Pro-Poor Growth: The Economics and Politics.* Paris: OECD.

———. 2009d. *OECD Reviews of Innovation Policy: Korea.* Paris: OECD.

———. 2009e. *The Economics of Climate Change Mitigation: Policies and Options for Global Action Beyond 2012.* Paris: OECD.

———. 2010. Transition to a Low-Carbon Economy: Public Goals and Corporate Practices. Paris: OECD.

———. 2011. *Towards Green Growth: A summary for policy makers.* Paris: OECD.

———. 2012a. *Southeast Asian Economic Outlook 2011/12.* Paris: OECD.

———. 2012b . *Towards Green Growth: Monitoring Progress.* Paris: OECD.

———. World Indicator Total Primary Energy Supply (TPES). (accessed 31 December, 2012).

Organisation for Economic Co-operation and Development (OECD) and Eurostat. 1999. *The Environmental Goods & Service Industry: Manual for Data Collection and Analysis.* Paris: OECD.

Organisation for Economic Co-operation and Development (OECD) and International Energy Agency (IEA). 2008. *Biofuel Support Policies: An Economic Assessment.* Paris: OECD.

Paciornik, N. 2008. Capacity-Building in Brazil. Presentation made at the Meeting on Experiences with Performance Indicators for Monitoring and Evaluation of Capacity-Building in Developing Countries. Rio de Janeiro. 6–7 November.

Parajuli, R. 2011. Access to Energy in Mid/Far West Region-Nepal from the Perspective of Energy Poverty. *Renewable Energy* 36(9): 2299–2304.

Patunru, A. 2012. Development Trajectories, Emission Profile, and Policy Actions: Indonesia. Background paper prepared for the ADB–ADBI Study for Climate Change and Green Asia.

Peters, G.P., G. Marland, C. Le Quéré, T. Boden, J.G. Canadell, and M.R. Raupach. 2011. Rapid growth in CO_2 emissions after the 2008–2009 global financial crisis. *Nature Climate Change* 2:2–4.

Pew Charitable Trusts. 2009. The Clean Energy Economy: Repowering Jobs, Businesses and Investments in America. Washington, DC: Pew Charitable Trusts.

Popkin, B., S. Horton, and S. Kim. 2001. The Nutrition Transition and Prevention of Diet-related Diseases in Asia and the Pacific. *Food and Nutrition Bulletin* 22(4): 3–58.

Popp, D. 2002. Induced Innovation and Energy Prices. *The American Economic Review* 92(1): 160–180.

———. 2006. Innovation in climate policy models: Implementing lessons from the economics of R&D. *Energy Economics* 28(5–6): 596–609.

Presidential Committee on Green Growth (PCGG). 2009. Comprehensive Strategy for Development and Commercialization of Core Green Technologies. Seoul: PCGG.

———. 2010. Road to Our Future: Green Growth – National Strategy and the Five-Year Plan (2009–2013). Seoul: PCGG.

PricewaterhouseCoopers. 2008. The World in 2050: Can rapid global growth be reconciled with moving to a low carbon economy? Pricewaterhouse Coopers. http://www.pwc.com/world2050. (accessed 31 December, 2012).

Productivity Commission. 2011. Carbon Emission Policies in Key Economies. Canberra.

Rai, V., and D.G. Victor. 2009. Climate Change and the Energy Challenge: a Pragmatic Approach for India. *Economic and Political Weekly* 44(31): 78–85.

Ramanathan, K. 2012. Eco-Innovation and International Technology Transfer. Background paper prepared for the ADB–ADBI Study for Climate Change and Green Asia.

Ravindranath, D., and S.S. Rao. 2011. Bioenergy in India: Barriers and policy options. Technology Transfer Perspectives Series, Risø Centre, Denmark: UNEP.

REN21. 2011. Renewables 2011: Global Status Report. Paris: REN21 secretariat.

R&D Magazine. 2010. 2011 Global R&D Funding Forecast. December. Advantage Business Media in association with Batelle.

Research and Information System for Developing Countries (RIS). 2008. Towards a Global Compact for Managing Climate Change. RIS Policy Briefs 34. New Delhi: RIS.

Richardson, B., Y. Le Bouthillier, H. McLeod-Kilmurray, and S. Wood, eds. 2009. *Climate Law and Developing Countries: Legal and Policy Challenges for the World Economy.* MA, US: Edward Elgar Publishing.

Robinson, J.B. 1991. Futures under glass: a recipe for people who hate to predict. *Futures* 22(8): 820–842.

Robbins, N., R. Clover, and D. Saravanan. 2010. Delivering the green stimulus. London: HSBC Global Research.

Rodríguez, L.C., U. Pascual, R. Muradian, N. Pazmino, and S. Whitten. 2011. Towards a unified scheme for environmental and social protection: Learning from PES and CCT experiences in developing countries. *Ecological Economics* 70(11): 2163–2174.

Rogelj, J. et al. 2011. Emission pathways consistent with a 2°C global temperature limit. Nature Climate Change 1: 413–418.

Rose, A. 2009. *The Economics of Climate Change Policy: International, National and Regional Mitigation Strategies.* Cheltenham, UK: Edward Elgar Publishing.

Sachs, J. 2011. *The Price of Civilization: Reawakening American Virtue and Prosperity.* New York: Random House.

Sachs, J., and S. Someshwar. 2012. Green Growth and Equity in the Context of Climate Change: Some Considerations ADBI Working Paper 371. Tokyo: ADBI. Salih, M., ed. 2009. *Climate Change and Sustainable Development: New Challenges for Poverty Reduction.* Cheltenham, UK: Edward Elgar Publishing.

Salim, E. 2012. Pro-growth, pro-poor, Pro-Job, Pro-environment. Keynote address at the ADB–ADBI workshop on Climate Change and Green Asia Book Discussion Forum. Jakarta 19–20 Januray.

Sathaye, J., P.R. Shukla, and N.H. Ravindranath. 2006. Climate change, sustainable development and India: Global and national concerns. *Current Science* 90(3): 314–325.

Schipper, L., H. Fabian, and J. Leather. 2009. Transport and Carbon Dioxide Emissions: Forecasts, Option Analysis and Evaluation. Sustainable Development Working Paper 9. Manila: ADB.

Schneider, F., G. Kallis, and J. Martinez-Alier. 2010. Crisis or opportunity? Economic degrowth for social equity and ecological sustainability. Introduction to this special issue. *Journal of Cleaner Production* 18(6): 511–518.

Schumpeter, J. 1962. *Capitalism, Socialism and Democracy: Third Edition.* New York: Harper Torchbooks.

Shanahan, L. 2012. Japan's Energy Crisis puts ETS Launch on Ice. *The Australian.* 29 February.

Sharan, D. 2008. Financing Climate Change Mitigation and Adaptation Role of Regional Financing Arrangements. ADB Sustainable Development Working Paper Series. Tokyo: ADBI.

Sharp, J. 2009. Low Carbon and Environmental Goods and Services: an industry analysis. London: Department for Business Enterprise and Regulatory Reform.

Shimizu, S. 2008. Tackling for G30. Resources & Wastes Recycling Bureau. City of Yokohama (mimeo).

Shrestha, M., S. Pradhan, and M. Liyanage. 2008. Effects of carbon tax on greenhouse gas mitigation in Thailand. *Climate Policy* 8(1): S140–S155(16).

Skea, J., and S. Nishioka. 2008. Policies and practices for a low-carbon society. *Climate Policy* 8 (Supplement): S5–S16.

Small Industry Development Bank of India (SIDBI). 2011. JICA-SIDBI Financing Scheme for Energy Saving Projects in MSME Sector (Phase II). http://www.sidbi.com/sites/default/files/JICA%20-SIDBI%20financing%20scheme%20for%20MSME%20projects%20Phase%20II.pdf. (assessed 31 December, 2012).

Socolow, R., and S. Pacala. 2004. Stabilization Wedges: Solving the Climate Problem for the Next 50 Years with Current Technologies. *Environment* 46(10): 8–19.

South Asian Association for Regional Cooperation (SAARC) Secretariat. 2009. Area of Cooperation: Environment. http://www.saarc-sec.org/areaofcooperation/cat-detail.php?cat_id=54. (accessed 31 December, 2012)

Sovacool, B.K., and S.V. Valentine. 2010. The socio-political economy of nuclear energy in China and India, *Energy* 35: 3803–3813.

Srinvasan, A., F.H. Ling, H. Mori. 2012. Climate Smart Development in Asia. London: Earthscan.

Srinivasan, T. 2000. The Gains from Trade Liberalization. Working Paper 101. New Haven: Yale University.

Srivastava, L. et al. 2010. National and International Policy Responses to the Carbon Budget Approach: An Indian perspective. The Energy and Resources Institute (TERI) Discussion Paper Prepared for the 16th Conference of the Parties (COP) to the United Nations Framework Convention on Climate Change.

Stavins, N.R. 1998. Market-Based Environmental Policies. Resources for the Future (RFF) Discussion Paper 98–26. Washington, DC: RFF.

———. 2001. Experience with Market-Based Environmental Policy Instruments. RFF Discussion Paper 01–58. Washington, DC: RFF.

Steenblik, R. 2006. Liberalisation of Trade in Renewable Energy and Associated Technologies: Biodiesel, Solar Thermal and Geothermal Energy. OECD Trade and Environment Working Paper 01. Paris: OECD.

Stern, N. 2007. *The Economics of Climate Change: The Stern Review.* Cambridge: Cambridge University Press.

———. 2009. Deciding our future in cooperation: will the world rise to the challenge of climate change? Policy Briefs. London: Grantham Research Institute on Climate Change and the Environment and the Centre for Climate Change Economics and Policy. http://www2.lse.ac.uk/publicEvents/ppt/20091201%20Lord%20Stern.pdf (accessed 31 December, 2012).

———. 2011. Raising Consumption, Maintaining Growth and Reducing Emissions. *World Economics* 12(4): 13–34.

Stern, N., R. Kattumuri, and J. Rydge. 2012. Low-Carbon Growth, Development and Inclusion. In *The New Oxford Companion to Economics in India,* edited by K. Basu and A. Maertens. Oxford: Oxford University Press.

Stiglitz, J. 2010. *Freefall: America, Free Markets, and the Sinking of the World Economy.* New York: W.W. Norton & Company.

Stillwell, T. 2007. The Tradable Permit Approach to Protecting Commands: Lessons for climate change. Ecology Law Quarterly. 36: 189.

Sudomori, T. 2012. Climate Finance and International Financial Institutes. Background paper prepared for the ADB–ADBI Study for Climate Change and Green Asia.

Sustainable Europe Research Institute. Database. Vienna: SERI.

Suzlon. 2012. About Suzlon: Genesis & Growth. http://www.suzlon.com/about_suzlon/l3.aspx?l1=1&l2=1&l3=11 (accessed 30 December 2012 January 2012).

Symons, E., J. Proops, and P. Gay. 1994. Carbon taxes, consumer demand and carbon dioxide emissions: a simulation analysis for the UK. *Fiscal Studies* 15 (2): 19–43.

Tata Institute of Social Sciences. 2010. Global Carbon Budgets and Equity in Climate Change. Discussion Paper, Supplementary Notes and Summary Report of the Conference on Global Carbon Budgets and Equity in Climate Change. Mumbai. 28–29 June. (accessed 31 December, 2012).

Thavasi, V., and S. Ramakrishna. 2009. Asia Energy Mixes from Socio-Economic and Environmental Perspectives. *Energy Policy* 37(11): 4240–4250.

The Energy Resources Institute (TERI). 2008. Mitigation Options for India – The Role of the International Community. TERI paper presented at COP 14. Poznan.

———. 2010. National and International Policy Responses to the Carbon Budget Approach. TERI Paper presented at COP 16. Cancun.

———. 2011. India's Coal Reserves are Vastly Overstated: Is Anyone Listening? Policy Brief. March.

———. 2012. India's Green Economy: Road map to an inclusive and equitable growth. Background paper. http://www.teriin.org/events/rio_20_paper.pdf (accessed 31 December, 2012).

Thurston, C.W. 2011. Time for a Green Bank? *PV Magazine* 10. http://www.pv-magazine.com/archive/articles/beitrag/time-for-a-greenbank_100004498/86/?tx_ttnews%5BbackCat%5D=176&cHash=eddcdddc5708efeaffcaa6ef5686ebce#axzz1sS3R9EDl (accessed 31 December, 2012).

Tiwari, R. et al. 2011. MGNREGA for Environmental Service Enhancement and Vulnerability Reduction: Rapid Appraisal in Chitradurga District, Karnataka. *Economic & Political Weekly* 46(20): 39–47.

Toan, P. 2012. Development Trajectories, Emission Profile, and Policy Actions: Viet Nam. Background paper prepared for the ADB–ADBI Study for Climate Change and Green Asia.

Touffut, J-P., ed. 2009. *Changing Climate, Changing Economy.* Cheltenham, UK: Edward Elgar Publishing.

Tsosie, R. 2007. Indigenous People and Environmental Justice: the Impact of Climate Change. *University of Colorado Law Review* 78: 1625–1677.

Turner, A. 2010. *What do banks do?* Why do credit booms and busts occur and what can public policy do about it? The Future of Finance. The LSE Report. http://harr123et.files.wordpress.com/2010/07/futureoffinance5.pdf (accessed 31 December, 2012).

UKaid. 2010. The future climate for development: scenarios for low-income countries in a climate-changing world. London: forum for the future – action for a sustainable world.

United Nations (UN). 1987. *Report of the World Commission on Environment and Development: Our Common Future.* New York: UN.

———. 2009. *World Economic Situation and Prospects 2009.* New York: UN.

———. 2010. Report of the Secretary-General's High-Level Advisory Group on Climate Change Financing. New York: UN.

———. 2011. World Population Prospects: the 2010 Revision. New York: UN.

United Nations Commodity Trade Statistics Database. http://comtrade.un.org/db/ (accessed 31 December, 2012).

United Nations Conference on Trade and Development (UNCTAD). 2010. World Investment Report 2010: Investing in a Low Carbon Economy. New York: UNCTAD.

United Nations Convention to Combat Desertification (UNCCD). 2008. The Climate Change Mitigation and Adaptation Information Kit: Linkages between the United Nations Framework Convention on Climate Change (UNFCCC) and UNCCD. Prepared for the Seventh Session of the Committee for the Review of the Implementation of the Convention. New York: UN.

United Nations Department of Economic and Social Affairs. 2009. World Economic and Social Survey 2009: Promoting Development, Saving the Planet. Geneva: UN.

United Nations Development Programme (UNDP). 2011a. *Human Development Index.* New York: UNDP.

———. 2011b. MDG Acceleration Framework: Operational Note. New York: UNDP.

United Nations Development Programme (UNDP) and the Global Environment Facility (GEF). 2003. Responding to Climate Change, Generating Community Benefits – A Review of Community Initiatives supported by the Global Environmental Facility's Small Grants Programme 1992–2003. New York: UNDP.

United Nations Economic and Social Commission for Asia and the Pacific (UNESCAP). 2011. Conceptual Framework of Green Economy and Green Growth. Bangkok: UNESCAP.

———. 2011. *Statistical Yearbook for Asia and the Pacific 2011.* Bangkok: UNESCAP.

UNESCAP, ADB, and UNDP. 2012. Accelerating Equitable Achievement of the MDGs: Closing the Gaps in Health and Nutrition Outcomes. Asia-Pacific Regional MDG Report 2011/12. Bangkok.

United Nations Environment Programme (UNEP). 2007. *Green Financial Products and Services: Current Trends and Future Opportunities in North America.* A report of the North American Task Force (NATF) of the United Nations Environment Programme Finance Initiative. Nairobi: UNEP.

———. 2008. *Reforming Energy Subsidies.* Paris: UNEP and OECD/IEA.

———. 2009. Global Trends in Sustainable Energy Investment 2009 Report: Analysis of Trends and Issues in the Financing of Renewable Energy and Energy Efficiency. Nairobi: UNEP.

———. 2010. Overview of the Republic of Korea's National Strategy for Green Growth. Nairobi: UNEP.

———. 2011. Towards a Green Economy: Pathways to Sustainable Development and Poverty Eradication – a Synthesis for Policy Makers. Nairobi: UNEP.

———. 2012. Green Economy: Measuring Progress Towards a Green Economy. Nairobi: UNEP.

UNEP, ILO, International Organisation of Employers, and International Trade Union Confederation. 2008. Green Jobs: Towards Decent Work in a Sustainable, Low-Carbon World. Nairobi: UNEP.

United Nations Framework Convention on Climate Change (UNFCCC). 2007. Investment and Financial Flows to Address Climate Change. http://unfccc.int/resource/docs/publications/financial_flows.pdf (accessed 31 December, 2012).

———. 2008. Investment and Financial Flows: To Tackle Climate Change. Bonn: UNFCCC.

———. 2009a. Appendix I – Quantified economy-wide emissions targets for 2020. http://unfccc.int/meetings/copenhagen_dec_2009/items/5264.php (accessed 31 December, 2012).

———. 2009b. Appendix II – Nationally appropriate mitigation actions of developing country parties. http://unfccc.int/meetings/cop_15/copenhagen_accord/items/5265.php (accessed 31 December, 2012).

———. 2009c. Ideas and Proposals on Paragraph 1 of the Bali Action Plan. Ad Hoc Working Group On Long-Term Cooperative Action Under The Convention. Fourth session. Poznan. 1–10 December 2008. http://unfccc.int/resource/docs/2008/awglca4/eng/16r01.pdf (accessed 31 December, 2012).

———. 2010. Nationally Appropriate Mitigation Actions. Bonn: UNFCCC.

———. 2011. Benefits of the Clean Development Mechanism. Bonn: UNFCCC.

United Nations Industrial Development Organization. 2010. Green Industry for a Low-Carbon Future. Vienna: United Nations Industrial Development Organization.

United Nations Population Fund (UNPF). 2007. *State of World Population 2007: Unleashing the Potential of Urban Growth.* New York: UNPF.

United Nations Secretary-General's High-Level Panel on Global Sustainability. 2012. Resilient People, Resilient Planet: A Future Worth Choosing. New York: UN.

United Nations Women Watch. 2009. Women, Gender Equality and Climate Change. New York: UN.

United States Agency for International Development (USAID). 2007. From Ideas to Actions: Clean Energy Solutions for Asia to Address Climate Change. Bangkok: USAID.

Unruh, G.C. 2000. Understanding Carbon Lock-in. *Energy Policy* 28(12): 817–830.

Upadhyay, H., and N. Pahuja. 2010. Low-Carbon Employment Potential in India: A Climate of Opportunities. New Delhi: Centre for Global Environment Research, TERI, and Global Climate Network.

Wan, G., M. Lu, and Z. Chen. 2006. The inequality–growth nexus in the short and long run: Empirical evidence from China. *Journal of Comparative Economics* 34(4): 654–667.

Wang, M.Q., and H-S. Huang. 2007. A Full Fuel-Cycle Analysis of Energy and Emissions Impacts of Transportation Fuels Produced from Natural Gas. Research Report No. ANL/ESD-40, Centre for Transportation Research, Energy Systems Division, Argonne National Laboratory. Illinois: University of Illinois.

Ward, M. 2008. The Role of Sectoral No-Lose Targets in Scaling Up Finance for Climate Change Mitigation in Developing Countries. Prepared for the International Climate Division, Department for Environment, Food and Rural Affairs of the UK.

Wei, M., S. Patadia, and D.M. Kammen. 2010. Putting renewables and energy efficiency to work: How many jobs can the clean energy industry generate in the US? *Energy Policy* 38(2): 919–931.

Weisz, H. et al. 2006. The physical economy of the European Union: Cross-country comparison and determinants of material consumption. *Ecological Economics* 58(4): 676–698.

Weizsäcker, E., A. Lovins, and L. Lovins. 1998. Factor Four: Doubling Wealth, Halving Resource Use. London: Earthscan.

Wheeler, D. 2011. Quantifying Vulnerability to Climate Change: Implications for Adaptation Assistance. Center for Global Development Working Paper 240. Washington, DC: Center for Global Development.

Whitten, S., M. van Bueren, and D. Collins. 2006. An Overview of Market-Based Instruments and Environmental Policy in Australia. 6th Annual National AARES Symposium, Canberra.

Wind, I. 2008. HS Codes and the Residential and Commercial Buildings Sector. ICTSD Programme on Trade and Environment. Geneva: ICTSD.

Wilkes, A., S. Wang, T. Tennigkeit, and J. Feng. 2011. Agricultural Monitoring and Evaluation Systems: What can we learn for the MRV of agricultural NAMAs? International Center for Research in Agroforestry (ICRAF) Working Paper 126. Beijing: World Agroforestry Centre.

Women's Environment and Development Organization. 2008. Gender and Climate Change Finance – A Case Study from The Philippines. New York: Women's Environment & Development Organization.

World Bank. 2005. Environmental fiscal reform: What Should Be Done and How To Achieve it. Washington DC: World Bank.

———. 2005. World Bank President to G8: World Energy Scenario 2000. Washington, DC: World Bank.

———. 2006. *Clean Energy and Development: Towards an Investment Framework.* Washington, DC: World Bank.

———. 2007. An Innovative Forest Project in Indonesia Creates Alternatives for Illegal Loggers. Washington, DC: World Bank.

———. 2008. Trade and Investment Policies to Promote Climate Friendly Technologies in APEC Economies: East Asia and Pacific Region. Washington DC: World Bank.

———. 2009a. *Global Economic Prospects: Commodities at the Crossroads.* Washington, DC: World Bank.

———. 2009b. India: Options for Low-Carbon Development. Synopsis of a study by the World Bank for Government of India. Washington, DC: World Bank.

———. 2009c. *Low Carbon Growth: Country Studies Program: Mitigating Climate Change through Development. South Asia Region.* Washington, DC: World Bank Institute.

———. 2010a. *World Development Report 2010: Development and Climate Change.* Washington, DC: World Bank.

———. 2010b. The Poverty Reduction and Equity: Poverty and Inequality Analysis. http://web.worldbank.org/WBSITE/EXTERNAL/TOPICS/EXTPOVERTY/0,,contentMDK:22569747~pagePK:148956~piPK:216618~theSitePK:336992,00.html (accessed 12 December 2010).

———. 2011. *World Development Indicators DataBank.* Washington, DC: World Bank.

———. 2012a. China 2030: Building a Modern, Harmonious, and Creative High-Income Society. Development Research Center of the State Council, the People's Republic of China. Washington, DC: World Bank.

———. 2012b. Green Infrastructure Finance: Framework Report. Washington, DC: World Bank.

———. 2012c. *Inclusive Green Growth: The Pathway to Sustainable Development.* Washington, DC: World Bank.

———. 2012d. World Bank Sees Progress Against Extreme Poverty, But Flags Vulnerabilities. Press release No:2012/297/DEC. Washington, DC: World Bank.

———. 2012e. Himachal Pradesh Mid-Himalayan Watershed Development Project (online) http://www.worldbank.org/projects/P093720/himachal-pradesh-mid-himalayan-watershed-development-project?lang=en. (accessed 12 December 2010).

World Business Council for Sustainable Development. 2005. The Climate, Trade and Technology Linkage. Geneva: World Business Council for Sustainable Development.

World Health Organization (WHO). 2006. Fuel for Life – Household energy and Health, National burden of disease estimates, Geneva: WHO Publications.

———. 2011. Health in the green economy: Health co-benefits of climate change mitigation – Transport sector. Geneva: World Health Organization.

World Health Organization (WHO) and United Nations Development Programme (UNDP). 2009. The Energy Access Situation in Developing Countries; A Review Focusing on the Least Developed Countries and Sub-Saharan Africa. New York: UNDP Publication.

World Intellectual Property Organization. 2011. World Intellectual Property Report 2011: The Changing Face of Innovation. Geneva: World Intellectual Property Organization.

World Trade Organization (WTO). 2001. Ministerial Declaration. Ministerial Conference. Fourth Session. Doha. 9–14 November.

Wyden, R. 2010. U.S. Trade in Environmental Goods: Follow-Up Report to Major Opportunities and Challenges to U.S. Exports of Environmental Goods. Washington, DC: United States Senate.

Wyes, H., and M. Lewandowski. 2011. Narrowing the Gaps through Regional Cooperation Institutions and Governance Systems. Paper presented at the ICLEI World Secretariat Green Urban Economy. ICLEI Briefing sheet. United Nations Development Programme–UNEP Poverty-Environment Initiative.

Wyes, H and M. Lewandowski. 2012. Narrowing the Gaps through Regional Cooperation Institutions and Governance Systems. ADBI Working Paper 359. Tokyo: ADBI

Yangyang, L., and W. Zheng. 2011. China's Pilot Transaction on Forestry Carbon Sequestration Officially Kicked Off. *Forest Carbon Portal*. 1 November.

Yergin, D. 2006. Ensuring Energy Security. *Foreign Affairs* 85(2): 69–82.

Yuezhong, Z. 2012. Development Trajectories, Emission Profile, and Policy Actions: People's Republic of China. Background paper prepared for the ADB–ADBI Study for Climate Change and Green Asia.

Zhai, F., and Z. Zhuang. 2012. Agricultural Impact of Climate Change: A General Equilibrium Analysis with Special Reference to Southeast Asia. In *Climate Change in Asia and the Pacific: How can countries adapt?*, edited by V. Anbumozhi, M. Breiling, S. Pathmarajah, and V. Reddy. Sage Publications and ADBI.

Zhang, Z. 2010. Copenhagen and Beyond: Reflections on China's Stance and Responses. *Fondazione Eni Enrico Mattei (FEEM) Sustainable Development Nota di Lavoro* (Working Paper) 91. Honolulu, US: FEEM.

Zhu, Y. 2012. Development Trajectories, Emission Profile and Policy Actions: People's Republic of China. Background paper prepared for the ADB–ADBI Study for Climate Change and Green Asia.

Zhuang, J. 2011. ACI Growth Projections 2010–2030. Prepared for ADB–ADBI Technical Workshop on the Role of Key Emerging Economies – ASEAN, PRC, and India – for a Balanced, Sustainable and Resilient Asia. 30 May–1 June.

Zhuang, J., and Y. Niimi. 2011. Measuring Quality of Life in Asia. Prepared for the ADB–ADBI Seminar on Quality of Life Indicators. 5 October.

Zusman, E., A. Srinivasan, and S. Dhakal. 2012. Low Carbon Transport in Asia. London: Earthscan.